# Economic Development in Modern China Before 1949

As the first volume of a two-volume set on Chinese economic history, this book investigates Chinese economic development between 1912 and 1949 and unravels the overall level during that time.

From the perspective of development economics, the two-volume set studies the economic history and development of China since 1912, with a focus on the quantitative analysis of economic activities. Comprised of two core parts, this first volume, centering on the period of the Republic of China, first describes the historical process and characteristics of the economy at different stages and then looks into the momentum and inner logic that underpin the economic development. The former part covers issues of agriculture, industry, population, and labor force, urbanization, price changes, people's consumption and living standard, regional differences, etc. The latter part includes discussions on natural and human resources, capital formation and technological progress, the role of government and finance, international trade, and foreign capital.

This title will be an interesting read for scholars and students working on Chinese economic history, the Chinese economy, and modern Chinese society.

**Guan Quan** is Professor at the School of Economics of Renmin University of China. His research interests include development economics, international economics, Chinese economy, and Japanese economy. His recent publications with Routledge include the two-volume *Industrial Development in Modern China: Comparisons with Japan.*

# China Perspectives

The *China Perspectives* series focuses on translating and publishing works by leading Chinese scholars, writing about both global topics and China-related themes. It covers Humanities & Social Sciences, Education, Media and Psychology, as well as many interdisciplinary themes.

This is the first time any of these books have been published in English for international readers. The series aims to put forward a Chinese perspective, give insights into cutting-edge academic thinking in China, and inspire researchers globally.

To submit a book proposal, please contact the Taylor & Francis Publisher for the China Publishing Programme, Lian Sun (Lian.Sun@informa.com)

Titles in economics include:

**The Emission Reduction Effects of Spatial Agglomeration**
*Zhang Ke*

**China's Economic Development**
Implications for the World
*Cai Fang*

**State-Owned Enterprise's Ownership Reform**
A Chinese Modernization Approach
*Zhigang Zheng*

**Comprehensive Land Consolidation in China**
*Yan Jinming, Xia Fangzhou*

**Economic Development in Modern China Before 1949**
*Guan Quan*

**Economic Development in Modern China Since 1949**
*Guan Quan*

For more information, please visit www.routledge.com/China-Perspectives/book-series/CPH

# Economic Development in Modern China Before 1949

Guan Quan

LONDON AND NEW YORK

First published in English 2024
by Routledge
4 Park Square, Milton Park, Abingdon, Oxon OX14 4RN

and by Routledge
605 Third Avenue, New York, NY 10158

*Routledge is an imprint of the Taylor & Francis Group, an informa business*

© 2024 Guan Quan

The right of Guan Quan to be identified as author of this work has been asserted in accordance with sections 77 and 78 of the Copyright, Designs and Patents Act 1988.

All rights reserved. No part of this book may be reprinted or reproduced or utilised in any form or by any electronic, mechanical, or other means, now known or hereafter invented, including photocopying and recording, or in any information storage or retrieval system, without permission in writing from the publishers.

Trademark notice: Product or corporate names may be trademarks or registered trademarks, and are used only for identification and explanation without intent to infringe.

English Version by permission of China Renmin University Press.

*British Library Cataloguing-in-Publication Data*
A catalogue record for this book is available from the British Library

ISBN: 978-1-032-53117-5 (hbk)
ISBN: 978-1-032-53120-5 (pbk)
ISBN: 978-1-003-41038-6 (ebk)

DOI: 10.4324/9781003410386

Typeset in Times New Roman
by Apex CoVantage, LLC

# Contents

| | |
|---|---|
| *List of figures* | *vii* |
| *List of tables* | *ix* |
| *Preface to the Chinese edition* | *xii* |

**PART I**
**Preparatory investigation**                                          1

  1  Overview of modern economic development                  3

**PART II**
**Processes and characteristics**                                     21

  2  Changes in agriculture                                  23

  3  Development of industry: part 1                          46

  4  Development of industry: part 2                          89

  5  Population, labor force, and urbanization               119

  6  Changes in consumer prices and living standards         137

  7  Imbalance in regional development                       150

**PART III**
**Conditions and causes**                                            171

  8  Natural resources and human resources                  173

  9  Capital formation and technological progress           192

10  Role of government and finance                                   209

11  International trade and foreign capital                          229

vi   *Contents*

**PART IV**
**Comparison and revelation**                                           243

12   Summary and outlook                                                245

   *References*                                                         *257*
   *Index*                                                              *263*

# Figures

| | | |
|---|---|---:|
| 2.1 | Growth rate of actual value added and intermediate inputs in agriculture (%) | 34 |
| 2.2 | Relationship between large livestock per 100 people and per capita value added in agriculture in mainland China | 42 |
| 2.3 | Dual structure of agriculture in Northeast China in the 1930s | 43 |
| 3.1 | Relationship between the number of spindles per capita and per capita production value from 1916 to 1920 | 51 |
| 3.2 | Relationship between the horsepower per 100 people and the per capita production value in factories nationwide in 1933 | 59 |
| 3.3 | Actual production value and actual value added by Chinese factories and Japanese factories | 65 |
| 3.4 | Production index by Chinese and Japanese factories (1937 = 100) | 66 |
| 3.5 | Relationship between horsepower per 100 people and per capita value added (1934, 1939) | 70 |
| 3.6 | Annual growth rates for years from 1934 to 1941 | 72 |
| 3.7 | Size of Chinese factories (1936) | 73 |
| 3.8 | Size of Japanese factories (1936) | 74 |
| 3.9 | Development of industry in the northeast in the 1930s | 75 |
| 3.10 | Relationship between horsepower per 100 people and per capita value added in factories in North China in 1942 | 79 |
| 3.11 | Size distribution of factories in North China in 1942 (Japan) | 80 |
| 3.12 | Size distribution of factories in North China in 1942 (China) | 81 |
| 3.13 | Changes in industry in the rear area | 86 |
| 4.1 | Relationship between the amount of capital per capita and the per capita net production value of industry 12 cities in 1933 | 93 |
| 4.2 | Industrial and mining production index from 1912 to 1949 | 101 |
| 4.3 | Number of newly established and actual number of flour mills invested by national capital | 106 |
| 4.4 | Number of cotton mills by country from 1890 to 1936 | 109 |
| 5.1 | Age structure of the population during the Republic of China period | 125 |
| 6.1 | Consumer price index in rural areas (1926 = 100) | 138 |
| 6.2 | Wholesale consumer prices index for cities (1933 = 100) | 139 |
| 6.3 | Retail price index for cities (1926 = 100) | 140 |

viii  *Figures*

| | | |
|---|---|---|
| 6.4 | Monthly wages in some industries | 144 |
| 7.1 | Relationship between per capita capital amount and per capita production value | 160 |
| 7.2 | Relationship between per capita capital amount and per capita production value (provinces and cities) | 160 |
| 7.3 | Relationship between per capita capital amount and per capita production value (industries in provinces and cities) | 161 |
| 7.4 | Binary structure of China's industry in 1933 | 165 |
| 8.1 | Actual production value and value added of the mining industry | 178 |
| 8.2 | Mining production index | 178 |
| 8.3 | Changes in some industrial and mineral products as well as infrastructure in modern Japan | 181 |
| 8.4 | Changes in some industrial and mineral products as well as infrastructure in modern China | 182 |
| 9.1 | Number of spindles, looms, and reeling machines | 194 |
| 9.2 | Proportion of mechanized coal and iron production (1912–1937) | 200 |
| 9.3 | Labor and capital input of the Yamei Silk Factory | 202 |
| 9.4 | Capital and labor input in the flour industry | 204 |
| 9.5 | Imports of various machinery and equipment nationwide | 205 |
| 10.1 | Changes in the actual number of new-style banks and Shanghai old-style Chinese private banks | 224 |
| 10.2 | Proportion of various types of currency in circulation | 226 |
| 11.1 | China's foreign trade in modern times | 230 |
| 11.2 | Various indexes of China's foreign trade as well as terms of trade in modern times | 231 |
| 11.3 | Proportion of foreign investment in coal mining | 238 |
| 12.1 | (a) Pattern of industrial development in modern Japan. (b) Pattern of industrial development in modern China | 247 |
| 12.2 | Production function of development in China and Japan in modern times | 249 |
| 12.3 | Patterns of economic development in modern China and Japan | 250 |
| 12.4 | Factors influencing economic development | 251 |

# Tables

| | | |
|---|---|---:|
| 1.1 | China's position in the world | 7 |
| 1.2 | Industrial structure in modern China | 11 |
| 1.3 | GDP structure of modern China | 12 |
| 1.4 | Changes in GDP structure | 13 |
| 1.5 | Structure of national income | 14 |
| 1.6 | Number and proportion of employed persons | 16 |
| 1.7 | Actual output per capita in the 1930s | 17 |
| 2.1 | Various estimates of population, cultivated land, and cultivated land per capita in modern times | 25 |
| 2.2 | Agricultural production, average and marginal productivities in modern times | 26 |
| 2.3 | Basic state of agricultural production | 28 |
| 2.4 | Yield and yield per *mu* of major crops | 29 |
| 2.5 | Livestock yield | 31 |
| 2.6 | Growth rate of actual value added in agriculture | 32 |
| 2.7 | Production volume, input, and value added of the primary sector in China's hinterland | 33 |
| 2.8 | Yield of major agricultural products and per unit yield in the hinterland | 35 |
| 2.9 | Quantity of livestock and poultry in China's hinterland | 36 |
| 2.10 | Actual production volume and value added of the primary sector in Northeast China | 37 |
| 2.11 | Yield and per unit yield of major agricultural products in Northeast China | 39 |
| 2.12 | Actual capital stock for agriculture in Northeast China | 40 |
| 2.13 | Agricultural per capita capital stock, per capita production value, and per capita value added | 41 |
| 3.1 | Overview of industry from 1912 to 1921 | 47 |
| 3.2 | Overview of factories from 1912 to 1915 | 48 |
| 3.3 | Number of factories and number of employees by industry | 50 |
| 3.4 | Production index of various manufacturing sectors in the hinterland in the 1930s (1933 = 100) | 53 |

x  *Tables*

| | | |
|---|---|---|
| 3.5 | Proportion of production value and value added of the manufacturing industry in the hinterland in the 1930s | 54 |
| 3.6 | Basic situation of factories | 55 |
| 3.7 | Characteristics of factories | 57 |
| 3.8 | Number of factories | 61 |
| 3.9 | Number of employees | 63 |
| 3.10 | Average number of factory employees | 67 |
| 3.11 | Actual per capita value added (at 1937 price, yuan per person) | 68 |
| 3.12 | Horsepower per 100 people | 69 |
| 3.13 | Growth rate (average, 1934–1941) | 71 |
| 3.14 | Overview of factories in North China in 1942 by industry | 77 |
| 3.15 | Characteristics of factories in North China in 1942 by industry | 78 |
| 3.16 | Industry distribution of factories in the rear area in 1942 | 82 |
| 3.17 | Industry characteristics of factories in the rear area in 1942 | 84 |
| 4.1 | Overview of industry in 12 cities (1933, 1947) | 92 |
| 4.2 | Overview of industry in major cities in 1947 (1) (industry) | 94 |
| 4.3 | Overview of industry in major cities in 1947 (2) (industry) | 97 |
| 4.4 | National capital in coal mines in modern times | 104 |
| 5.1 | Population during the Republic of China period | 122 |
| 5.2 | Proportion of the rural population by occupation from 1929 to 1933 | 128 |
| 5.3 | Proportion of occupations in the census in the first half of the 20th century | 129 |
| 5.4 | Migration of people from regions inside Shanhaiguan Pass to three northeastern provinces from 1917 to 1944 | 131 |
| 5.5 | Cities with a population of more than 100,000 in 1918 | 133 |
| 6.1 | Composition of living expenses of workers' households in 30 cities in 1930 | 143 |
| 6.2 | Composition of national income in 1933 | 148 |
| 7.1 | Changes in population in provinces during the Republic of China period | 152 |
| 7.2 | Rural population and cultivated land area index in modern China (1873 = 100) | 153 |
| 7.3 | Distribution of shops by province in 1933 | 154 |
| 7.4 | Situations of factories in various regions in 1912 and 1915 | 156 |
| 7.5 | Overview of factories by province and city | 158 |
| 7.6 | Overview of factories in the rear in 1942 | 168 |
| 8.1 | Output and net exports of major metal ores | 174 |
| 8.2 | National steel output and import volume from 1896 to 1937 | 175 |
| 8.3 | Real production value, value added, and production index of the mining industry | 176 |
| 8.4 | World mining production index | 179 |
| 8.5 | Comparison of some industrial and mineral products as well as infrastructure between China and Japan | 180 |

| | | |
|---|---|---|
| 8.6 | Schooling and literacy level of rural population in China from 1929 to 1933 | 183 |
| 8.7 | Proportions of people with various levels of education in the census in the first half of the 20th century | 184 |
| 8.8 | Proportion of the population with various education levels to the total population in some areas in 1947 | 185 |
| 8.9 | Total daily consumption of calories and protein by adult males as well as the proportion of calories supplied by various types of food from 1929 to 1933 | 189 |
| 9.1 | Estimated capital in modern times | 195 |
| 9.2 | Railway construction | 197 |
| 9.3 | Number of railway cars owned, carrying capacity, and capacity of transport | 197 |
| 9.4 | Classification of tonnage of ships in modern times | 198 |
| 9.5 | Gaps between foreign products and domestic manufactured products | 206 |
| 10.1 | Factories established by national capital in late Qing Dynasty | 212 |
| 10.2 | Output of heavy industrial products operated by the Resource Committee | 215 |
| 10.3 | Industrial production index in the rear area from 1938 to 1945 | 216 |
| 10.4 | Fiscal revenue and expenditure of the Beiyang government | 218 |
| 10.5 | Actual fiscal revenue and expenditure from 1946 to 1948 | 221 |
| 10.6 | Deposits and loans of banks of various types from 1937 to 1945 | 224 |
| 10.7 | Money in circulation | 225 |
| 11.1 | Proportion of imports and exports of various goods in modern China | 232 |
| 11.2 | Trade structure during the Republic of China period | 234 |
| 11.3 | Output and proportion of foreign-invested coal mines from 1913 to 1942 | 237 |
| 11.4 | Monopoly power of foreign capital in iron ore and pig iron production in modern China | 239 |
| 11.5 | Comparison of spindles, wire bars, and looms in Chinese and foreign cotton mills | 239 |
| 11.6 | Foreign investment in China during wartime | 240 |
| 12.1 | Changes in per capita GDP in China and Japan | 246 |

# Preface to the Chinese edition

## Purpose and significance

As a result of rapid growth since the reform and opening up, China, which was a poor country with a low per capita GDP ranking in the world, has become the world's second largest economy, despite its medium-level per capita GDP in the world. This achievement is hard-won because we have wasted much effort and failed to make full use of opportunities in the planned economy and in the modern and the Republic of China periods.

Reform and opening up are vital for China's economic development. We explain the achievements made today in terms of two areas. As a result of reform, the people were no longer tied to collective units as they had been during the planned economy, and they could bring their energy and abilities into play. For example, in the era of people's communes, commune members could only earn a few workpoints a day and could receive cash only when the production team made settlement at the end of the year. Moreover, the income was meager. Work was treated equally, regardless of the quantity and quality, which dealt a serious blow to the enthusiasm of the capable. In addition to expanding the market and stimulating competition, opening up has also introduced foreign investment, improved technical and management levels, and broadened the people's horizons. During the planned economy period, inefficiency and waste of resources caused by the rigid system, coupled with the rapid increase in population, aggravated the shortage of resources and materials. The planned economy, which excludes the market from economic activities and operates in a way set by the planning department, is too idealistic, mechanized, and unimaginative.

In modern times, due to the long-term domestic turmoil and foreign aggression, coupled with incompetent government, China failed to stimulate the initiative of the people and as a result lost many precious opportunities, including the opportunity for an economic take-off. Before the Xinhai Revolution, China found it impossible to truly develop its economy under the rule of imperial power. Even the people of insight such as those who launched the Self-Strengthening Movement found it hard to change the essence of imperial rule despite their active efforts. After the founding of the Republic of China in the wake of the Xinhai Revolution, China began to develop a market economy with some results, introducing many emerging industries and technologies and producing a number of entrepreneurs. However,

*Preface to the Chinese edition* xiii

due to the sustained oppression by foreign powers, the government was unable to accelerate economic development. Eventually, the sound economic achievements made during the Republic of China came to nothing due to full-scale Japanese Aggression and the subsequent civil war. As a result, the precious economic growth during this period became a "failed take-off".

We believe that China's economic development since modern times can be generally divided into two periods: before 1949 and after 1949. The period before 1949 can also be divided into two periods: before the Xinhai Revolution and during the Republic of China period. The period after 1949 can also be divided into two periods: the planned economy period and the reform and opening up period. In this chronological order, China's economic development will be explained as follows. The period before the Xinhai Revolution was only a preparation or background, and there was no economic development in the modern sense, no matter whether it developed or not. The Republic of China period saw the emergence of a market economy in the modern sense, and there was actually a good momentum of development, although the economic take-off failed. Nevertheless, it can be seen as a good foundation and a meaningful attempt for subsequent (after 1949) genuine take-off. Despite inefficiencies during the planned economy period, a certain industrial (especially heavy industry) foundation was laid, thanks to the practice of "bringing together the resources needed to accomplish great tasks", paving the way for the rapid development after reform and opening up. We believe that this is the period when China's economy moved from take-off to "self-sustaining growth". The previous preparations and foundation made possible the rapid economic growth after reform and opening up.

Because of these chronological order and the role of each period, we believe that it is necessary to study the economic development in modern China, especially during the Republic of China period. The focus of this book is on the Republic of China period for two reasons. First, China was under imperial rule before the Republic of China, and it was not a modern society, and therefore truly developing the economy was impossible. During the Republic of China period, China adopted a modern political system, and it was basically a market economy and was capable of initiating modern economic growth. Second, in terms of development economics, the premodern period and even the pre–Xinhai Revolution did not belong to the research scope of this discipline. China differed from Japan in modern times because Japan quickly became a modern society (Meiji Restoration in 1868) after meeting the Western challenge (the American Perry Fleet in 1853), while the period from the Opium War (1840) to the Xinhai Revolution (1911) in China lasted 70 years. This period of history is very special and is not easily positioned. Historians and economists hold different positions and views in this regard, and we follow the views of development economics.

**Features of this book**

The rapid growth and development of China's economy has drawn great attention from many researchers, at home and abroad, who have published numerous

xiv  *Preface to the Chinese edition*

research findings. Such research primarily studies China's economic development since the reform and opening up as well as relevant areas, such as the transformation of government functions, the reform of state-owned enterprises, "issues relating to agriculture, rural areas, and rural people", income distribution, and development strategies. These are all hot issues of general concern. A few studies have focused on the period of planned economy, covering the system and institutional arrangements at that time, such as the people's commune system and the efficiency of economic planning. These mainly study economic history, except for some monographic studies.

This book studies economic development in modern China, primarily during the Republic of China period, for two reasons. First, we believe that China's modern history should begin with the Xinhai Revolution or the Republic of China because the Xinhai Revolution overthrew the Qing Dynasty government to end China's imperial rule that had lasted more than 2,000 years, and gave rise to the Republic system. It was a revolutionary change of epoch-making significance. Second, as a result of this change, a market economy featuring the private sector of the economy emerged during the Republic of China period, and a large number of emerging industries were introduced, which promoted urban development and exhibited signs of modern economic growth and economic take-off.

Many studies focus on the economic history of this period, but there is a lack of research from the economics perspective, especially from the perspective of development economics. This book belongs to this kind of research, with its general idea and details covering the theories and methods of development economics. This book is not arranged chronologically but rather focuses on discussions on economic activities. The main content is divided into two parts. One is the process and characteristics of development, including changes in agriculture, industrial development, population and labor mobility, price changes and the life of the people, and regional development. The other is the conditions and causes of development, including natural and human resources, capital formation and technological advancement, the role of government as well as fiscal and finance issues, international trade and development strategies.

Another feature of this book is quantitative analysis. We have collected data on all aspects of economic activities, some of which are valuable data and some not widely recognized. One of the strengths of quantitative analysis is objective results that avoid arbitrary judgments or inferences. Despite the fact that modern China was weak in terms of its statistical system and statistical surveys, and there is a lack of data in many fields that can be used for economic analysis, we can gain a rough idea of the basic situation of economic development at that time by simply processing these data.

Furthermore, Japan is involved in many parts of the book, although it is not a comprehensive one-on-one comparison. This is highly associated with our view that China's economic development 150 years ago should be compared with that of Japan and 70 years ago with that of India. The gap between China and Japan began to widen around 150 years ago, when Japan embarked on the path to modernization through the Meiji Restoration, while China was still under imperial rule. After

*Preface to the Chinese edition* xv

the Opium War in 1840, China began to introduce Western European technology in the late 19th century, such as launching the Self-Strengthening Movement, and some government-run enterprises were established. Nevertheless, it was impossible to develop the economy during this period due to the severe constraints and flaws of the system. China could only wait until after the founding of the Republic of China through the Xinhai Revolution. In the contemporary era, India gained independence in 1947 and the People's Republic of China was founded in 1949. Both countries began to develop their economies from this time. Moreover, the foundation at the beginning of economic development in both countries was almost the same. As populous countries with a long history, China and India share a high degree of similarity.

Finally, it is difficult to include both the research achievements of many scholars and some scholars' individual opinions and research findings. It is impossible for a scholar to conduct unique research on every section of a book that comprehensively introduces China's economic development, let alone to accomplish anything in all areas. This is a significant challenge because this book is not devoted to the study of specific aeras. A book is merely introductory reading material if the author does not provide individual and independent opinions and viewpoints. It is not easy for the author to present independent opinions and viewpoints in a book that discusses China's economic development comprehensively because it is impossible for a single person to perform in-depth research on all issues. We have done our best in this regard.

## Structure of the book

The book is divided into four parts. Part I, "Preparatory Investigation", deals with the general situation of China's economic development and changes in modern times. It includes one chapter, Chapter 1 "Overview of Modern Economic Development", which introduces the basic situation of China's economic development in modern times. With a focus on the Republic of China period from 1912 to 1949, it studies the economic and social foundation in the preparatory stage for China's modern economic growth.

Part II examines the process and characteristics of economic development and consists of six chapters. Chapter 2, "Changes in Agriculture", focuses on the evolution of agriculture during the Republic of China period. China is an ancient agricultural country. There was no obvious progress in agriculture since the beginning of modern times due to a lack of modern economic growth, but some changes took place in the area of cropland, input and output of agricultural production, agricultural productivity, etc. Therefore, there was no development but only some changes in agriculture in this period.

Chapter 3, "Development of Industry: Part 1", and Chapter 4, "Development of Industry: Part 2", examine the issues of industrialization. The two chapters are added because this issue is important, and we also have research experience to share. Usually, for a large country, industrialization lies at the center of economic development, and there is basically no economic development without industry

xvi  *Preface to the Chinese edition*

development. In modern times, China has shown some signs of industry development. Particularly in the Republic of China period, some cities showed a good momentum of development, and many emerging industries and technologies were introduced. Unfortunately, modern economic growth did not take place due to negative internal and external factors.

Chapter 5, "Population, Labor Force, and Urbanization", examines population increase and structural changes, as well as labor mobility and urbanization. In modern times, China's population increased without initiating modern economic growth, but there was no "explosive" growth. Labor mobility saw people flowing from rural to urban areas (modern type) and from rural to rural areas (traditional type) because urbanization progressed slowly during this period. As society opened up and the number of emerging industries increased, urbanization picked up speed, but there was no large-scale urbanization. These indicate that during the Republic of China period, China was in a period of transition from a traditional society to a modern society.

Chapter 6, "Changes in Consumer Prices and Living Standards", examines the issues of prices, living standards, and income distribution. The overall price change was small because China did not achieve modern economic growth in modern times, but, due to reasons such as wars, serious inflation occurred in some years, especially during the civil war period from 1945 to 1948. People had low living standards for a long time, without obvious improvement, except some slight improvement in the living standards of some urban residents. Therefore, there was uneven income distribution to some extent, but the issue was not very serious.

Chapter 7, "Imbalance of Regional Development", studies the distribution of economic resources in various regions in China, examining regional differences in China in modern times in terms of population, agriculture, service sector, industry, etc. There was little difference in population, agriculture, and service sector, while there were obvious regional differences in terms of industry. On the one hand, cities developed unevenly, and the pace of development varied from region to region. On the other hand, due to the influence of factors such as wars, there were obvious differences in industry at different times in different places. For example, the Northeast China region saw rapid development in the 1930s due to the Japanese occupation. Many enterprises moved inland due to the War of Resistance against Japanese Aggression, and Southwest China saw rapid development for some time.

Part III, which consists of four chapters, examines the conditions and causes of economic development. Chapter 8, "Natural Resources and Human Resources", discusses resource exploitation, education, and health issues. The resource exploration in modern times in China was obviously passive. In other words, mineral resources must be exploited due to the invasion of foreign powers. Of course, with the exploitation of resources, transport developed to a certain extent, which objectively speaking has positive significance. Education saw new changes, and a modern education system was gradually established. Although it was flawed and not universally available, it is of great significance. In terms of health, due to a lack of economic development, the people had a very low level of health, with an average life expectancy of only 35–40 years.

*Preface to the Chinese edition*  xvii

Chapter 9, "Capital Formation and Technological Progress", examines investment and production equipment in the course of economic development, as well as the associated technologies. As we know, investment is the primary driver of economic growth, and it is supported by savings. Because of a low level of economic development in modern times in China, there were little savings, and the level of investment was low. Therefore, it was difficult to drive economic growth. Capital equipment is highly correlated with technological level. In modern times, China imported new technologies from the West and could only imitate relatively simple machinery and equipment almost without the ability to carry out independent research and development.

Chapter 10, "Role of Government and Finance", discusses an old topic. While this topic is important for developed countries, it is even more important for developing countries with imperfect market and inexperienced governments. The role of the Chinese government in modern times is discussed based on two periods: before the Xinhai Revolution and after the founding of the Republic of China. The latter is mainly studied here and is also further subdivided into two periods: the period of the Beijing Government (Beiyang Government) and the period of the Nanjing Government (Nationalist Government). Neither of the two governments during the Republic of China period was competent enough to unite all parties to achieve economic growth, despite the influence of a host of objective factors. In terms of fiscal and finance affairs, a modern fiscal and financial system was put in place during the Republic of China period. However, due to stagnant economic development, a large shortage of funds, and an underdeveloped market, it failed to play a significant role.

Chapter 11, "International Trade and Foreign Capital", examines changes in international trade as well as foreign investment in China. When China was forced to open to the world in the second half of the 19th century, China passively participated in international trade and passively accepted foreign investment. Due to the limited economic development, China could only export primary products and import manufactured goods. Therefore, international trade at that time belonged to typical vertical division of labor, and it could even be said that China fell into the "comparative advantage trap". Foreign investment in China was of a distinct predatory nature, and foreign investors held an absolute advantage, suppressing the growth of China's local capital. This situation is a typical manifestation of the basic conditions of the semicolony at that time.

Part IV, "Summary and Outlook", contains one chapter – Chapter 12. First, it identifies the gap between China in modern times and Japan, a neighboring country, through their comparison. Japan was the first non-European and non-American country in modern times to move toward modernization and achieve success. China lagged behind Japan because of late institutional reform and setbacks. This chapter also studies the conditions and influencing factors of economic development, primarily in terms of the market and the government. It studies the specific factors contained in the two. We conclude that China possessed certain market conditions in modern times, but due to the system and the government's limited competence, the market mechanism was not brought into play. Despite some achievements

xviii  *Preface to the Chinese edition*

made during the Republic of China period, China did not achieve economic take-off and start modern economic growth on the whole, or it was a "failed take-off".

**Feelings and acknowledgments**

In 1988, I was sent by the Chinese government to study in Japan. I was admitted to Hitotsubashi University in Japan to study Japan's economy under the tutelage of Ryoshin Minami and other teachers. Under the master's program, I studied the tutor's book *The Economic Development of Japan*. This book has been translated into English, Chinese, Korean, and other languages. From the standpoint of development economics, the tutor conducted an in-depth analysis of Japan's long-term economic development and presented opinions from diverse sources as well as his unique insights. The book contains theoretical explanations and empirical analysis, with a focus on the latter. He also pointed out the general and unique nature of Japan's economic development through comparison with other developed countries. I was involved in the translation of the second edition of the book into Chinese [Ryoshin Minami. *The Economic Development of Japan*, 2nd ed, trans. Bi Zhiheng and Guan Quan (Beijing: Economy & Management Publishing House, 1992)]. As a result, I gained a deepened understanding of the tutor's intention and methods and was also impressed by his profound research competence. Thereafter, I nurtured an idea of writing a similar book on China's economic development. However, due to a hectic schedule of my master's and doctoral studies and research (the main focus of research at that time was Japan's economy) and my limited knowledge of the Chinese economy, this idea was mothballed for more than 20 years.

At the end of the 20th century, the Institute of Economic Research of Hitotsubashi University launched a major program, "Asian Long-term Economic Statistics", which covered more than a dozen Asian countries. I was honored to participate in the writing of the Chinese volume, mainly responsible for the collection of and research on industry in modern times. During this period, I completed several discussion papers: (1) Guan Quan, "Estimation of China's Industrial Production Volume in the 1910s: Evaluation and Revision of the *Agricultural and Commercial Statistics Table*", Discussion Paper No. D97–16, Institute of Economic Research of Hitotsubashi University, January 1998; (2) Guan Quan and Makino Fumio, "Estimation of China's Mining Production Volume: 1912–1949", Discussion Paper No. D99–7, Institute of Economic Research of Hitotsubashi University, December 1999; (3) Toru Kubo, Guan Quan, Fumio Makino, "Industrial Output Estimates in Republican China", Discussion Paper No. D99–14, Institute of Economic Research of Hitotsubashi University, February 2000; and officially published papers: (1) Guan Quan, "Industrial Production in Puppet Manchukuo: Estimation of *Factory Statistics*", *Tokyo Keizai University Journal*, No. 245, March 2005; (2) Makino Fumio and Guan Quan, "The Development of Mining Production in Pre-War China", Minutes of Tokyo Gakugei University: Department of Humanities and Social Sciences 2, Episode 58), January 2007. By participating in this work, I gained knowledge of the Chinese economy since modern times and collected data. The research I conducted in Japan was on technological innovation in Japan in modern times, and

*Preface to the Chinese edition*    xix

my doctoral dissertation was published in Japan: Guan Quan, *Technological Innovation in Modern Japan: Patents and Economic Development* (Fukosha, 2003). This boosted my interest in the Chinese economy in modern times. It can be said to be the basic starting point of this book. After returning to China, I collected materials while working, and I kept studying and working out the idea of a book. I first completed *Industrial Development in Modern China: Comparison with Japan* (China Renmin University Press, 2018). I then published *China's Economic Development: Centennial Course* (China Renmin University Press, 2019). This book is equivalent to the part of that book on modern times.

While I was writing *China's Economic Development: Centennial Course*, graduate students Zhang Mingxia, Du Yuming, Peng Yutao, Wang Li, Yin Sisi, etc. provided a wealth of references, and Zhang Mingxia also conducted much quantitative analysis work. Professor Wang Zhigang from Renmin University of China, his doctoral student Zhou Haiwen, and Meng Haoqi from the Guizhou Insurance Society read the whole book and gave valuable comments. My thanks go to all of them.

Finally, I would like to thank the editors of China Renmin University Press. The publication of this book would be impossible without their recommendation and careful review.

Guan Quan
June 2020

# Part I
# Preparatory investigation

# 1 Overview of modern economic development

## 1.1 Introduction

The theme of this book is China's economic development in modern times. By definition, economic development in a narrow sense usually encompasses growth in aggregate economic output and structural changes. In a broad sense, it even includes political change and social progress. It is similar to the idea of modernization in this sense.[1] Of course, economic development is generally centered on economic growth and structural changes. Specifically, it is long-term development but not short-term growth. It is comprehensive development but not one-sided improvement. It is sustainable development but not quick results. It is the overall economic development of a country promoted by the extensive application of scientific and technological achievements after the Industrial Revolution rather than the growth of individual regions and areas in the traditional sense. In this sense, the development process and results of the United Kingdom, followed by other Western European countries, as well as Japan, and other countries and regions in North America and Oceania, confirm this definition. In these countries and regions, the per capita income has increased significantly, and the majority of the people have moved from rural to urban areas and have shifted from agricultural to nonagricultural areas in terms of occupation. All of them have received a high level of modern formal education, there is a higher level of democracy, and society is more equitable. These are the connotations of economic development. Economic development is driven by natural resources, a higher level of capital stock, an abundant high-quality labor force, developed science and technology, sound and fair markets, flexible and efficient government, and peaceful and just international relations.

While the real process of economic development is not necessarily consistent with what was just described, at least most of the conditions should be met. It is difficult to achieve normal economic development if there are serious flaws. For example, economic development is usually built on modern politics. At least none of the successful countries have achieved it under feudal autocracy or slavery, let alone in primitive tribal societies. If there is a lack of a modern education system, the quality of the labor force will be low, and they will be unable to perform complex jobs, which will severely hamper economic development. Furthermore, if an inappropriate development strategy is adopted, development potential will not be

DOI: 10.4324/9781003410386-2

## 4 *Preparatory investigation*

brought into play, and the comparative advantages will be wasted. There is even the risk of falling into the "comparative advantage trap".

According to this simple explanation, China's economic development began after – not before – 1949, whether judging from a strict definition or a loose definition. Sustained economic development usually calls for a process of start-up, which Simon Smith Kuznets calls "modern economic growth" and Walt Whitman Rostow calls "economic take-off". The connotations of the two are highly similar. Details about these two concepts and the specific time for China's economic development are not discussed here[2] because China did not initiate modern economic growth or achieve economic take-off before 1949.

Of course, this does not mean that there is no need to pay attention to China's economic development before 1949, especially during the Republic of China period, because although China's economy as a whole stagnated during this period, it was of great significance to subsequent economic development. To begin with, China made some progress in modern industries, including textiles, silk reeling, flour, mining, railways, communications, customs, and trade, which laid the groundwork to some extent for subsequent economic development. The rapid growth of economy in Northeast China in the 1930s also provided conditions for subsequent development. Second, if economic development during this period was unsatisfactory, some lessons can be learned to provide reference for the subsequent formulation of development strategies, such as regarding unreasonable land rules and corruption among officials. Finally, although the socialist China founded after 1949 is different from that the Republic of China in terms of institutions, its population and labor, natural resources, capital stock, and other social resources are continuous and available. In particular, those factories and mines built (although they were severely damaged in the wars), as well as experienced technicians and workers, can play a role.

Based on these reasons, this chapter focuses on the economic development of the Republic of China rather than on the situation before that period because the Xinhai Revolution that began in 1911, regardless of its political nature, was significant for overthrowing the imperial rule that lasted for over 2,000 years. This is an epoch-making change and also the political basis for realizing economic development. Economically, although China's economy developed somewhat at the end of the 19th century, such as with the introduction of military factories, the establishment of mines, and the construction of railways through the Self-Strengthening Movement, there were generally government-run factories, and the role of the market did not come into play. Another situation is also very important. In the subsequent Republic of China period, relatively abundant statistics could be used for economic analysis, which reflected economic and social progress. The more traditional the society is, the scarcer the statistics are, because the significance of statistics is not known. Moreover, if the economy and society remain stagnant for a long time, statistics are of little significance. Although the statistics during the Republic of China period were scarce and of low quality, progress was significant compared with the time before. In a sense, the history of statistics is also the history of social progress.

## 1.2 Background of economic development

This section is added to the book primarily because of the peculiarity of China. Some people may not agree that China is unique, but we have the following basis. First, China was once a strong power rather than a weak country, at least before the Industrial Revolution in Western Europe.[3] This shows that China changed from a strong country to a weak country and was not a country that had been always weak. This point is highly important. Unlike China, many other countries had persistently been backward, and it is only due to invasion by colonialism by Western powers in modern times that they had the opportunity to develop. There is almost no country in the world that is the same as or similar to China. The four ancient civilizations except for China have changed beyond recognition, and even the new civilization has little to do with civilizations at that time.

Second, many countries became colonies after being controlled by Western powers in the colonial era. Although they achieved development somewhat under colonial rule, they had no sovereignty or decision-making power, and there was no independent economic development to speak of. A case in point is India. Due to the long-term colonial rule under Britain, India lost the possibility of achieving independent economic development. It was not until the end of World War II that it gained freedom through the independence movement and gradually became eligible to kickstart modern economic growth. The same goes for many other countries in Southeast Asia, Africa, and Latin America, with the only difference that Latin American countries gained independence earlier. China has always been independent. Although China nearly became a colony or some areas became colonies,[4] China has not only maintained sovereignty but also achieved independent development to some extent.

Third, relevant to the first point, what exactly was the situation of China in the pre-modern era. There is controversy over this issue. Several views are put forward: the first view is that China was highly developed under the reign of Kangxi, Yongzheng, and Qianlong emperors during the Qing Dynasty, but only gradually declined in the 19th century. The second view holds that China gradually declined from the beginning of the Ming Dynasty, and the so-called "prosperous era under Kangxi, Yongzheng, and Qianlong emperors" in the Qing Dynasty was only a momentary successful period. The third view even holds that China was on the wane after the Song Dynasty, at least in terms of Chinese culture. The fourth view is that China, despite its slow development, never declined before the Opium War and that it was the invasion of Western powers that upset the course of China's development.[5]

In any case, to study China's economic development, it is necessary to introduce earlier circumstances because they reflect the basic or initial state of economic development and are largely necessary and meaningful. However, we shall not simply introduce China's own development but need to discuss it with reference to the development of other countries. The author first introduces some main links in China's history, with a focus on the years after 1500, because most Western historians regard the year 1500 as a dividing line to examine the modern history of

## 6 Preparatory investigation

the world, as distinct from the historical stages in China. The West regards the year 1500 as a watershed mainly because of the key influence of enhanced navigation and great geographical discovery. It linked the world as a whole, and, although this link was a disaster for the regions and the peoples it linked, colonialism began to prevail, and the world was carved up by the great powers.[6] In 1500, it was the middle period of the Ming Dynasty in China, but the world underwent major changes, and China fell behind unwittingly. More interestingly, Zheng He's seven voyages to western oceans (1405–1433) in China were actually the precursor to the great navigation period, but China voluntarily withdrew from it thereafter.

The position of the Chinese economy in the world from 1500 to 1950 can be observed through data. Table 1.1 shows the status of China's population and gross domestic product (GDP) in the world, as well as the per capita GDP of major countries and regions. In terms of the proportion of China's population in the world, the population rose from 23.5 percent in 1500 to 36.6 percent in 1820 and then began to decline, falling to 21.7 percent in 1950. It showed an "inverted U" shape. That is to say, China's population increased faster than the world population before 1820, but the opposite has been true afterward. Other countries and regions exhibited different tendencies of change. The proportion of the Western Europe's population to the world population remained at around 13 percent before 1820 and then rose to nearly 15 percent from 1870 to 1913. It then began to decline, and in 1950, it fell below the historical norm, at just 12.1 percent.[7] The proportion of the population in Russia (including the Soviet Union for some time), the United States, Latin America, etc. to the world population increased significantly, especially after 1820. Only Japan's population did not increase after hitting a high in 1700 and maintained relatively stable. India is similar to China, except that its population increase peaked in 1700 instead of 1820 and has been declining thereafter. The population of Africa as a whole did not change much but declined between 1820 and 1913 and gradually increased after 1950.[8]

In terms of GDP, China's GDP as a percentage in the world changed basically in line with its population, but there are numerical differences, particularly after 1820. From 1500 to 1820, the proportion of China's GDP was almost the same as the proportion of its population, indicating that the rest of the world did not initiate modern economic growth during this period and that their economic development was not much faster than China's. At least China did not lag far behind.[9] After 1820, there were significant changes. The proportion of China's GDP declined much faster than that of its population, from 32.9 to 17.1 percent in 1870, to 8.8 percent in 1913, and then to 4.5 percent in 1950.[10] With consideration given to the proportion of China's population, China's economic development after 1820 lagged far behind that of the world as a whole.[11] Although it is somewhat arbitrary, these data may show that China began to see a backward economy around 1820 and that the level of economic development declined much faster compared to its population. In other words, other countries started modern economic growth while China stagnated, and it was no surprise that China was overtaken. It is impossible to judge whether China developed better than other countries before 1820 because the world as a whole (the vast majority of regions) did not enter a stage of modern

*Overview of modern economic development* 7

*Table 1.1* China's position in the world

| Item | 1500 | 1600 | 1700 | 1820 | 1870 | 1913 | 1950 |
|---|---|---|---|---|---|---|---|
| **Population proportion (%)** | | | | | | | |
| Western Europe | 13.1 | 13.3 | 13.5 | 12.8 | 14.7 | 14.6 | 12.1 |
| Russia (including the Soviet Union for some time) | 3.9 | 3.7 | 4.4 | 5.3 | 7.0 | 8.7 | 7.1 |
| United States | 0.5 | 0.3 | 0.2 | 1.0 | 3.2 | 5.4 | 6.0 |
| Latin America | 4.0 | 1.5 | 2.0 | 2.1 | 3.2 | 4.5 | 6.6 |
| Japan | 3.5 | 3.3 | 4.5 | 3.0 | 2.7 | 2.9 | 3.3 |
| China | 23.5 | 28.8 | 22.9 | 36.6 | 28.1 | 24.4 | 21.7 |
| India | 25.1 | 24.3 | 27.3 | 20.1 | 19.9 | 17.0 | 14.2 |
| Africa | 10.6 | 9.9 | 10.1 | 7.1 | 7.1 | 7.0 | 9.0 |
| World | 100.0 | 100.0 | 100.0 | 100.0 | 100.0 | 100.0 | 100.0 |
| **GDP as a percentage (%)** | | | | | | | |
| Western Europe | 17.8 | 19.8 | 21.9 | 23.0 | 33.0 | 33.0 | 26.2 |
| Russia (including the Soviet Union for some time) | 3.4 | 3.5 | 4.4 | 5.4 | 7.5 | 8.5 | 9.6 |
| United States | 0.3 | 0.2 | 0.1 | 1.8 | 8.8 | 18.9 | 27.3 |
| Latin America | 2.9 | 1.1 | 1.7 | 2.2 | 2.5 | 4.4 | 7.8 |
| Japan | 3.1 | 2.9 | 4.1 | 3.0 | 2.3 | 2.6 | 3.0 |
| China | 24.9 | 29.0 | 22.3 | 32.9 | 17.1 | 8.8 | 4.5 |
| India | 24.4 | 22.4 | 24.4 | 16.0 | 12.1 | 7.5 | 4.2 |
| Africa | 7.8 | 7.1 | 6.9 | 4.5 | 4.1 | 2.9 | 3.8 |
| World | 100.0 | 100.0 | 100.0 | 100.0 | 100.0 | 100.0 | 100.0 |
| **GDP per capita (international dollar)** | | | | | | | |
| Western Europe | 771 | 890 | 998 | 1204 | 1960 | 3,458 | 4,579 |
| Russia (including the Soviet Union for some time) | 499 | 552 | 610 | 688 | 943 | 1,488 | 2,841 |
| United States | 400 | 400 | 527 | 1,257 | 2,445 | 5,301 | 9,561 |
| Latin America | 416 | 438 | 527 | 692 | 681 | 1,481 | 2,506 |
| Japan | 500 | 520 | 570 | 669 | 737 | 1,387 | 1,921 |
| China | 600 | 600 | 600 | 600 | 530 | 552 | 439 |
| India | 550 | 600 | 550 | 533 | 533 | 673 | 619 |
| Africa | 414 | 422 | 421 | 420 | 500 | 637 | 894 |
| World | 566 | 595 | 615 | 667 | 875 | 1,525 | 2,111 |

*Note:* GDP per capita is measured using 1990 international dollar, which is a theoretical value calculated in multilateral purchasing power parity. See Maddison (2003).

*Data source:* Maddison (2008) pp. 265–271.

economic growth at that time. However, it can be seen that economic development was also not fast in major Western countries from 1500 to 1600, only that Western Europe's per capita GDP exceeded that of China. To put it another way, in terms of modern economic growth, the world except for Western Europe should have been in a state of economic stagnation before 1820, particularly before 1700. The level of development varied from country to country, but not significantly, because they

# 8 *Preparatory investigation*

were all agricultural or traditional societies, where science and technology were not widely applied, governments were not transformed, and little social progress was made. China was also at a standstill. Observing the changes in other countries and regions affords food for thought. The development of Western Europe began to pick up speed very early, and it maintained a high proportion even in 1913 but then declined somewhat.[12] It shows the rise of Western Europe's status as the birthplace of the Industrial Revolution and the subsequent relative decline. Russia, the United States, and Latin America exhibited an upward tendency to varying degrees economically.[13] Similar to China, India and Africa showed a downward trend, with India beginning to decline after 1700 and Africa earlier.[14]

In terms of the changes in per capita GDP, only Western Europe (771 international dollars) exceeded China (600 international dollars) in 1500. It can be considered that China and Western Europe were the two poles of the world at that time, although they were not related. China did not lag behind other countries during this period. Thereafter, Western Europe surged forward as a result of its great geographical discovery and great navigation, as well as the subsequent Industrial Revolution. China's economy stagnated for a long time, beginning to decline after 1820 and even falling behind India in 1950. According to these observations of population and GDP, with 1820 as the dividing line, many countries had surpassed China, with only India and Africa behind China. There are two situations. One is that before 1820, these countries, mainly in Western Europe, had a higher growth rate than China. The other is that these countries were originally behind China but later grew faster than China, such as Russia (including the Soviet Union for some time), the United States, Latin America, and Japan. During the Republic of China period, only China and India saw a decline from 1913 to 1950. Even from 1870 to 1913, China only saw slight growth, not as much as India and Africa.

These data are not very accurate and can only serve as reference because it is difficult to obtain data on the GDP of many countries at that time, especially in underdeveloped countries. Only the data on Western Europe, North America, and Japan are relatively accurate.[15] Through the observation of historical data and the course of development, we have a rough idea of the basic economic situation of the various countries during this period. It can be believed that China's economy was stagnant, or at least it should not be said that China's economy developed substantially at the end of the Qing Dynasty or before the Republic of China period. As will be discussed later, China's economic development during the Republic of China period was generally stagnant.

## 1.3 Overview of economic development

### 1.3.1 Economic growth rate

Has China's economy developed or not in modern times? If it developed, what is the growth rate? There are quite a few studies on this issue by both domestic and foreign scholars. Some put forward the "stagnation theory", and others raise the "theory of rapid growth". There are several noteworthy issues. First is the issue of

*Overview of modern economic development*  9

time or time span. The research results differ depending on whether the study of China's economic development in modern times includes the entire modern period, only the Republic of China period, or only the 1930s.[16] Second, there is the issue of information. Generally speaking, the statistics on modern China are too incomplete to calculate the long-term aggregate economic output. Therefore, the research findings are not accurate enough. Third, there is the issue of methods. Due to scarce data for some periods, many scholars use certain methods to supplement the data, including complement and estimation. The results calculated vary depending on the different bases. Fourth, the issue of scope. If only modern industries such as mining, textiles, flour, military, and railways are included, the growth rate is relatively high, but if it includes all economic sectors, there is little growth.

The findings of the study on economic growth in modern China can be divided into two types. One is the "theory of rapid growth", represented by Thomas G. Rawski. The estimated growth rates in 1914–1918 and 1931–1936 were 1.4 percent and 1.9 percent, respectively.[17] The studies conducted by Ye Kongjia, Dwight H. Perkins, and Liu Foding fall into this category, and the economic growth rates in modern China they calculated are 1.1 percent, 1.4 percent, and 1.45 percent, respectively.[18] The other is the "stagnation theory", such as by Maddison, Ryoshin Minami, and Makino Fumio. Although their estimates involve different periods, the economic growth rate does not exceed 1 percent, or there is even no growth at all.[19] Ryoshin Minami, Makino Fumio, and others estimated that China's real GDP amounts in 1932 and 1940 (at 1933 prices) were 22.2 billion yuan and 21.6 billion yuan, respectively, which clearly declined, although it reached 24.2 billion yuan in 1936.[20]

Given this situation, our view is as follows. First, if it is calculated from the end of the Qing Dynasty or the middle and late 19th century, China's economy had grown. Because the low starting point, there was naturally some progress. If it was calculated for the period from 1912 to 1936, the growth rate is also relatively high. However, there is a lack of conclusive evidence for calculating aggregate economic output during these periods, and the data are mostly crude, such as the calculation of national income in 1850, 1887, and 1914.[21] If only the growth rate for the 1930s was calculated based on comprehensive data, the growth rate was less than 1 percent. Second, if only modern industries are counted, the growth rate is relatively high because these industries have high productivity and high profit margin. Coupled with a gradually expanding market, the growth is significant.[22] If China's economic growth across the board is calculated, there may not be significant growth because modern industries accounted for a small proportion, and the vast majority of people lived in rural areas and engaged in traditional agricultural production, which belongs to natural economy. Third, in the period from 1937 to 1949, China's economic growth was basically zero or negative. In fact, it is not easy to see the overall situation of this period, but it can be glimpsed from the data for the years around 1937.[23] For example, Maddison (2009) calculated that China's GDP based on purchasing power parity (PPP) in 1990 was 239.903 billion yuan in 1950, 288.549 billion yuan in 1938, and up to 303.324 billion yuan in 1936.[24] It declined in 1950, no matter which year it is compared with. It indicates the seriously negative impact of the war.

## 10   Preparatory investigation

### 1.3.2   Changes in industrial structure

As mentioned, in addition to economic growth, the study of economic development also focuses on changes in the industrial structure. According to the "Petty–Clark Theorem", the result of economic development is that the proportion of the primary industry in the total economic output continuously declines, while the proportion of the secondary and tertiary industries continuously rises. Judging from the development experience of various countries, the proportion of the primary industry fell from 70 to 80 percent to less than 10 percent; the proportion of the secondary industry rose from less than 10 percent to 30–40 percent, and then fell to 20–30 percent; the proportion of the tertiary industry gradually rose from about 20 to more than 70 percent. The same trend applies to the proportion of labor force, except that the absolute value of the proportion is different from GDP. The proportion of the primary industry is higher than that of GDP, and the proportion of the secondary industry is lower than the proportion of GDP, because the primary industry has low labor productivity, and the secondary industry has high labor productivity. The proportion of the primary industry to GDP fell from 26 percent in 1820 to 5 percent in 1944 in Britain and from 43 to 20 percent in France, and it fell to 8 percent in the United States and to 20 percent in Japan. In terms of the proportion of the labor force, it fell to 8 percent in Britain, 32 percent in France, 22 percent in the United States, and 36 percent in Japan.[25]

What was China's economy like before 1949? It depends on the specific periods. Describing it is difficult even in 1840, which is usually believed to be the beginning of modern society, the late 19th century, or the early 20th century, because there are no complete data, that is, no data on output for the three industries. In terms of demand, there is also no complete data on consumption, investment, as well as total volume of imports and exports. Therefore, only a brief description can be given here.

Table 1.2 shows the industrial structure of modern China, from which we can roughly observe the basic proportions of the three industries. Several discontinuous time points show differences, but there are no major changes on the whole, especially before 1940. The share of agriculture was 50 to 71 percent, industry was 9 to 16 percent, and the proportion of the service sector, which is calculated according to the surplus of agriculture and industry sectors, was 19 to 36 percent. Importantly, the industrial structure had not changed significantly in more than 100 years, or at least there were no obvious – or there were only very weak – signs of industrialization. It must have occurred after 1910, which is reasonable to some extent.

Of course, it cannot be concluded from this indicator that China's economy did not develop before 1949. In fact, there was a certain degree of development and progress. According to some studies, the average annual growth rate of China's economy from 1840 to 1949 was 0.4 percent. It was 0.6 percent from 1840 to 1911 (0.3 percent from 1840 to 1894), 1.4 percent from 1911 to 1936, and −2.1 percent from 1936 to 1949. Another estimate is similar: it was −0.64 percent (−0.38 percent) from 1850 to 1887, 1.0 percent (0.3 percent) from 1887 to 1914, 1.45 percent (0.92 percent) from 1914 to 1936, and −2.4 percent (−2.87 percent)

*Overview of modern economic development*   11

*Table 1.2* Industrial structure in modern China, Unit: %

| Year | Proportion of agriculture | Proportion of industrial sector | Proportion of service | GDP |
|---|---|---|---|---|
| 1840 | 70.8 | 9.6 | 19.6 | 100.0 |
| 1887 | 69.6 | 10.1 | 20.3 | 100.0 |
| 1894 | 68.4 | 10.1 | 21.5 | 100.0 |
| 1911 | 66.3 | 10.3 | 23.4 | 100.0 |
| 1914 | 68.2 | 13.2 | 18.5 | 100.0 |
| 1920 | 57.7 | 13.9 | 28.4 | 100.0 |
| 1936① | 58.0 | 13.2 | 28.8 | 100.0 |
| 1936② | 64.5 | 15.5 | 20.0 | 100.0 |
| 1940 | 70.8 | 9.6 | 19.6 | 100.0 |
| 1949 | 51.7 | 12.3 | 36.0 | 100.0 |

*Note:* The share of service sector is calculated based on the surplus remaining after the sum of agriculture and industry sectors.

*Data source:* For data for 1887, 1914, 1936 (2), and 1949, see Liu Foding et al. (1999); for the remaining data, see the Hitotsubashi University Economic Research Institute, Asian Long-term Economic Statistics Database Project. *Economic Statistics of the China Republic Period: Evaluation and Estimation* (2000).

from 1936 to 1949.[26] Although the economic growth rate in the more than 100 years is not high (it cannot compare with that after 1949 or with that of developed countries), it can be seen that there are differences from one period to the next. Before the Xinhai Revolution in 1911, the economic growth rate was not high, but there was some development. Some modern industries were introduced during this period, but large-scale industrialization did not take place because the growth was mainly driven by agriculture. The introduction and establishment of modern industry in China began with the Self-Strengthening Movement at the end of the 19th century, when military industries were imported from Europe primarily in the form of government-run factories, such as munitions factories, shipyards, and ironworks. The private sector began to introduce light industry factories such as spinning mills, matchstick factories, cigarette factories, and flour mills since the Republic of China period (1912–1949). As a result, the economic growth rate from 1912 to 1936 was relatively high, and this period is even called the "golden age of Chinese capitalism".[27] Thereafter, due to Japan's all-out invasion of China, China's economy was dealt a hammer blow. Coupled with the subsequent War of Liberation, the economic development plunged or even took a step backward.

Although it is not possible to draw conclusions based on the simple data, it is roughly believed that there was some economic growth during the Republic of China period, especially from 1912 to 1936. However, due to internal problems and external aggression, China did not initiate modern economic growth, and its economic development lagged behind. Of course, if, as Rostow put it, economic take-off requires political reforms, it was impossible during the Republic of China period. For example, the government's governance capacity, land system, and other issues had not been solved.

## 12  Preparatory investigation

Table 1.3 shows the real GDP and its industrial structure at some time points, which are made up of another set of data. In the more than four decades from 1890 to 1933, the industrial structure did not change obviously, and the primary industry accounted for about two-thirds of the total, and it did not decline until 1952. The proportion of the handicrafts sector remained largely unchanged, above 7 percent. The proportion of business, which is an important component of the tertiary industry, did not change much, remaining at about 9 percent. The government's share remained at a fixed level (2.8 percent), indicating that the government did not take up many resources. Although the proportion of the modern manufacturing sector, which is the most important, increased slightly in the long run, it was still very low, only increasing from 0.1 to 4.3 percent. Admittedly, it is defined too narrowly, and other sectors belonging to the manufacturing and secondary industries were separated. However, they were still very weak on the whole because it was insignificant even if those industries (such as mining, power, and construction) were added. Finally, the growth rate in this period is very low. The GDP increased from 21.283 billion yuan in 1890 to 29.980 billion yuan in 1933, an increase of only 41 percent in more than four decades, with an annual growth rate of only 0.95 percent. In contrast, Japan's growth rate was up to 3.6 percent.[28] Even if China's GDP increased to 31.695 billion yuan in 1952, the average growth rate was only 0.79 percent. Of course, the growth rate of emerging industries such as modern manufacturing sector was relatively fast, and some industries, such as electricity, mining, and finance, started from scratch.[29]

*Table 1.3* GDP structure of modern China, Unit: million yuan (%)

| Industries | 1890 | 1913 | 1933 | 1952 |
|---|---|---|---|---|
| Plantation, fisheries, forestry | 14,576 (68.5) | 16,769 (67.0) | 19,180 (64.0) | 17,664 (55.7) |
| | 1,646 (7.7) | 1,932 (7.7) | 2,220 (7.4) | 2,330 (7.4) |
| Handicrafts | 26 (0.1) | 156 (0.6) | 740 (2.5) | 1,350 (4.3) |
| Modern manufacturing | 45 (0.2) | 87 (0.3) | 230 (0.8) | 680 (2.1) |
| Mining | 0 (0.0) | 5 (0.0) | 160 (0.5) | 390 (1.2) |
| Electricity | 364 (1.7) | 420 (1.7) | 480 (1.6) | 960 (3.0) |
| Construction | 1,085 (5.1) | 1,150 (4.6) | 1,210 (4.0) | 1,210 (3.8) |
| Traditional transport and communications | 84 (0.4) | 208 (0.8) | 460 (1.5) | 880 (2.8) |
| | 1,747 (8.2) | 2,257 (9.0) | 2,820 (9.4) | 2,950 (9.3) |
| Modern transport and communications | 602 (2.8) | 692 (2.8) | 850 (2.8) | |
| | 64 (0.3) | 124 (0.5) | 220 (0.7) | 3,281 (10.0) |
| Commerce | 239 (1.1) | 293 (1.2) | 350 (1.2) | |
| Government | 805 (3.9) | 926 (3.8) | 1,060 (3.6) | |
| Finance | | | | |
| Personal services | | | | |
| Residential services | | | | |
| GDP aggregate | 21,283 (100.0) | 25,019 (100.0) | 29,980 (100.0) | 31,695 (100.0) |

*Note:* The data in the table are calculated at 1933 prices. The proportion is in parentheses, and the total amount is 100.

*Data source:* Maddison (2008) pp. 48, 156.

Table 1.4 shows the changes in China's GDP structure in the 1930s. Because the statistics for the 1930s are relatively abundant, the information in this period is more reliable.[30] For the hinterland in China, the primary industry (agriculture, forestry, animal husbandry, and fishery) had the largest share, accounting for close to 60 percent, with almost no changes. This was followed by the service sector, which accounted for over 20 percent, and it rose slightly. The proportion of industry declined slightly, but it was stable. The transport and communications sectors saw a significant decline in 1940. The share of other industries was small and did not change much. The proportion of mining, electricity, and gas rose modestly. The share of education and government also did not change much. The GDP barely increased, or even declined, indicating that there was no significant progress throughout the period. The same goes for all sectors. Some sectors saw zero growth and even decline, such as agriculture, forestry, animal husbandry and fisheries, industry, construction, transport, and communications. Only services and mining sectors realized growth to some degree. In short, although the 1930s, especially the period before 1936, was a period of sound economic development in China, there was still no obvious momentum of positive growth. Most sectors stagnated except for some sectors. If these data are accurate, it can be said that there was basically no growth in China's economy before 1949. The industrial structure did not change much. In other words, there was not much progress in terms of the concept of development.[31]

*Table 1.4* Changes in GDP structure, Unit: %

| Industries | Hinterland in China | | | Northeast region | | |
|---|---|---|---|---|---|---|
| | 1931 | 1936 | 1940 | 1932 | 1936 | 1940 |
| **Total** | 100.00 | 100.00 | 100.00 | 100.00 | 100.00 | 100.00 |
| Agriculture, forestry, animal husbandry, and fishery | 57.53 | 53.11 | 58.35 | 44.01 | 32.97 | 22.58 |
| Mining | 0.68 | 0.80 | 0.97 | 1.18 | 2.01 | 5.69 |
| Industrial sector | 12.55 | 12.34 | 11.46 | 3.98 | 9.22 | 13.01 |
| Construction | 1.95 | 0.92 | 0.87 | 1.12 | 2.23 | 1.52 |
| Electricity, gas | 0.70 | 0.84 | 0.85 | 1.37 | 2.14 | 2.71 |
| Transport and communications | 4.28 | 4.78 | 0.99 | 9.19 | 12.93 | 20.72 |
| Services | 20.23 | 22.29 | 23.37 | 34.27 | 30.92 | 27.26 |
| Education | 0.51 | 1.01 | 0.70 | 0.87 | 1.01 | 0.65 |
| Government | 2.39 | 4.78 | 3.32 | 3.98 | 6.60 | 5.89 |
| Attributable interest | 0.79 | 0.83 | 0.86 | – | – | – |

*Note:* China's hinterland government includes funding for the military. For the northeast region, the original document contains figures for two government departments and totals. The government (1) excludes the funding for the Japanese army and (2) includes the funding. The same is true of total (1) and total (2). The latter is used here, that is, including data on military spending.

*Data source:* Ryoshin Minami and Makino Fumio (2014), pp. 452, 516.

14   *Preparatory investigation*

The northeast region differed greatly from the hinterland in terms of industrial structure. The share of agriculture, which was lower from the beginning than that of other regions, fell to 22.58 percent in 1940, which is equivalent to the level in Japan in the 1920s. In other words, the share of the northeast region is at a level between that of other regions and that of Japan, even reaching the level of China around 1990. The proportion of industry was low at the beginning, at only 4 percent, but rose to 13 percent in fewer than 10 years, which can be said to be an improvement. Compared with other regions, the northeast region lagged far behind to begin with but then caught up. Although the share of the mining sector was low, it developed rapidly, rising from 1.18 to 5.69 percent. The transport and communications sector grew rapidly, doubling during the observed period, and the share of this sector had already been relatively high. It is particularly noteworthy that the high share of this sector is very special, which was higher than that of the hinterland and even Japan. The share of this sector in Japan was highest during World War II but only 12.5 percent (1938).[32] Electricity and gas sectors in the northeast region also developed to a certain extent. Due to the development of other sectors, the share of the service sector declined somewhat, which is a normal phenomenon in the economic development process of many countries and regions.

Table 1.5 shows detailed data on various sectors of national income from 1931 to 1946, and the service sector is wide-ranging. According to the criteria for dividing the three sectors, agriculture belongs to the primary sector. The proportion of the primary sector did not change much, basically remaining around 60 percent. The secondary sector includes mining, manufacturing, and construction. The proportion of mining was very low, with little changes. The proportion of construction sector was very low. Therefore, the secondary sector was mainly composed of manufacturing. In addition to the slight increase in 1946, the share of manufacturing rose

*Table 1.5* Structure of national income, Unit: %

| Industries | 1931 | 1932 | 1933 | 1934 | 1935 | 1936 | 1946 |
|---|---|---|---|---|---|---|---|
| Agriculture | 61.74 | 65.67 | 61.46 | 58.66 | 61.53 | 64.51 | 62.70 |
| Mining | 1.04 | 1.02 | 1.17 | 1.25 | 1.23 | 1.14 | 0.40 |
| Manufacturing | 7.77 | 8.14 | 9.22 | 9.39 | 9.55 | 9.60 | 7.20 |
| Construction | 0.81 | 0.61 | 1.08 | 1.35 | 0.91 | 0.76 | 0.10 |
| Transport | 3.95 | 3.85 | 4.50 | 5.16 | 5.02 | 4.04 | 3.70 |
| Business | 16.08 | 11.83 | 12.40 | 11.84 | 10.66 | 9.95 | 9.70 |
| Banking and insurance | 0.71 | 0.77 | 0.98 | 1.22 | 1.20 | 1.14 | 3.70 |
| Residential service | 3.77 | 4.07 | 4.56 | 4.84 | 4.46 | 3.62 | 3.60 |
| Freelance | 0.67 | 0.70 | 0.84 | 0.84 | 0.83 | 0.84 | 1.20 |
| Domestic service | 0.57 | 0.62 | 0.69 | 0.73 | 0.68 | 0.55 | 0.60 |
| Government service | 2.93 | 2.77 | 3.14 | 4.76 | 3.98 | 3.88 | 7.10 |
| Total | 100.00 | 100.00 | 100.00 | 100.00 | 100.00 | 100.00 | 100.00 |

*Data source:* Wu Baosan et al. (1947), pp. 20–21.

*Overview of modern economic development* 15

from 7.77 to 9.60 percent. Although this proportion was still very low, it proves that the secondary sector developed to a certain extent during this period. If we know the changes in the proportions of the primary and secondary sectors, we know the changes in the proportion of the tertiary sector. The transport industry and remaining entries in the table belong to the tertiary sector, with a total proportion of more than 20 percent, of which commerce, transport, residential service, and government service had a large share. The proportion of commerce gradually declined, from 16.08 to less than 10 percent, and little change was observed in several other industries. The rapidly increased share of government service in 1946 is questionable.

It is worth emphasizing that China was in the infancy of industrialization before 1949, with industry accounting for a low proportion of GDP, agriculture accounting for a relatively large proportion, and the service sector accounting for a small proportion. Under general circumstances, the service sector depended to a certain extent on the development of the industry and manufacturing sectors. The service sector would not have great development without the development of industry. Due to a low level of industrialization in China at that time, only a few cities began to develop some new industries, and most areas had traditional handicraft industry, which had the nature of a service sector. People usually sold their self-produced products such as sundry products or food at the stores along the street, while the processing sites were located at backyards. These are workshops rather than factories. A case in point is tofu mills, where tofu was sold in the front shop and processed in the backyard.

This practice should have been very common before 1949, and the modern machine manufacturing industry was scarce, not to mention modern service sector such as finance, insurance, securities, education, medical care, media, and transport. Even if there was a service sector, it was traditional. For example, Shanghai, Tianjin, and other big cities also introduced banks and securities markets, but most of the Chinese people did not have the opportunity and possibility of using and participating in these. The usual participants were local money shops, firms for the exchange and transfer of money, and other traditional financial institutions. The same is true of the transport industry. At the time, China could not make cars[33] and could barely produce trains. The network of roads and railways was limited. People relied more on traditional horse-drawn carriage. Shipping was more important in some regions with developed water systems in south China. Education, medical care, and other industries also developed alongside the development of the economy. At that time, the traditional service sector was overwhelmingly dominant in China. In terms of education, only a few people had access to education, let alone higher education. Some people studied in local private schools or under hired private teachers, and what they learned was traditional content such as "Four Books and Five Classics". This is not education in the modern sense, although the primary education system developed somewhat since the beginning of the Republic of China period. In terms of medical care, traditional Chinese medicine dominated in China, while Western medicine was rarely practiced. Peking Union Medical College Hospital, which was founded in the early 1920s, is the predecessor of modern regular hospitals. The vast majority of the Chinese people were treated by local

16　*Preparatory investigation*

traditional Chinese medicine doctors or by physicians trained in herbal medicine who travelled from place to place. New industries such as newspapers, broadcasting, and publishing were few and far between and could only be found in large cities, which were few at that time.[34] Therefore, before 1949, the traditional service sector (such as catering and commerce) was dominant in China, while new types of the service sector were rarely seen.

The industrial structure of the labor force is examined next. Table 1.6 shows the number and proportion of employees in the hinterland and northeast region in China by industry in the 1930s. In the hinterland in China, in terms of proportion, the primary sector had been absolutely dominant, employing approximately 80 percent of the labor force, and this did not change over time, which corresponds to GDP. The proportion of employees in the secondary sector did not change, basically remaining at 10 percent. The proportion of employees in the tertiary sector was slightly lower than that of the secondary sector. The three sectors were the same in one respect: there was no change. Data available only cover about 10 years, but they indicate that the economic structure of the hinterland in China did not change significantly. In other words, there was no transfer from the primary sector to the secondary and tertiary sectors. In today's China, the proportion of employees has changed to a certain extent every decade, particularly in the more than 40 years since the reform and opening up. This shows that the economic development at that time was at a standstill or that there was growth but no structural change. It merits further observation and analysis.

The number of employees in the northeast region was about one-tenth of that in the hinterland, but there was a difference in industrial structure. Although the share of agriculture was also relatively high, it was lower than that of the hinterland. What is important is that it gradually declined, which is in line with the law of industrial development. The proportion of the secondary sector was about 8 percent, slightly lower than that of the hinterland, only with a slight increase. The

*Table 1.6* Number and proportion of employed persons

| Year | Number of people (10,000 people) | | | | Proportion (%) | | | |
|---|---|---|---|---|---|---|---|---|
| | Total | Primary sector | Secondary sector | Tertiary sector | Total | Primary sector | Secondary sector | Tertiary sector |
| **Hinterland in China** | | | | | | | | |
| 1931 | 26,015 | 21,342 | 2,427 | 2,247 | 100.00 | 82.04 | 9.33 | 8.64 |
| 1935 | 26,787 | 21,263 | 2,868 | 2,656 | 100.00 | 79.38 | 10.71 | 9.92 |
| 1940 | 25,840 | 20,592 | 2,725 | 2,523 | 100.00 | 79.69 | 10.55 | 9.77 |
| 1944 | 25,833 | 21,328 | 2,339 | 2,166 | 100.00 | 82.57 | 9.06 | 8.39 |
| **Northeast region** | | | | | | | | |
| 1932 | 1,545.2 | 1,148.1 | 120.4 | 276.8 | 100.00 | 74.31 | 7.80 | 17.92 |
| 1937 | 2,041.9 | 1,511.8 | 162.2 | 367.9 | 100.00 | 74.04 | 7.95 | 18.02 |
| 1942 | 2,450.0 | 1,713.1 | 215.3 | 521.6 | 100.00 | 69.93 | 8.79 | 21.29 |

*Data source:* Ryoshin Minami and Makino Fumio (2014), pp. 362, 481–482.

*Overview of modern economic development* 17

proportion of the tertiary sector was significantly higher than that of the hinterland, which was mainly due to the difference in the share of the primary sector. Moreover, it was increasing. Overall, the employment structure in the northeast region was slightly better than that of the hinterland, indicating that the land was relatively abundant and that more labor was engaged in other industries. This proportion was roughly equivalent to that of Japan in the late 19th century (such as 1888) and to that of China in the 1970s and 1980s.[35] Overall, the labor force structure in the northeast region was better than that of the hinterland, but the proportion of the secondary sector was not high.

Table 1.7 shows the actual output per capita in China's two regions by three major sectors in the 1930s. In terms of the total, it had been rising in the hinterland until 1936 but very weakly. It declined thereafter, touching bottom in 1940. In other words, it hit the high point in 1936 and then fell to a lower point. This shows that the per capita output during this period did not increase as a whole, but with an increase in the middle. It declined because of the damage caused by the Japanese invasion. It was the lowest in agriculture among the three sectors and much lower than other industries, especially the tertiary sector, only equivalent to one-fourth or one-fifth of it. Furthermore, the primary sector had been moving horizontally, with no significant changes, indicating that the agriculture sector had stagnated. The secondary sector saw a decline; it was relatively high in the early 1930s and low in the later period. We believe that it was chiefly caused by Japan's invasion of China because the manufacturing sector was mainly concentrated in cities, the key targets of the Japanese invasion. Therefore, it dealt a severe blow to the manufacturing sector. In contrast, it had little impact on agriculture. The changes in the tertiary sector were also similar to the changes in the secondary sector, declining in the late 1930s. However, it was not as obvious as in the secondary sector, which is related to the characteristics of the tertiary sector.

*Table 1.7* Actual output per capita in the 1930s, Unit: 1,000 yuan

| Year | Total | Primary sector | Secondary sector | Tertiary sector | Total | Primary sector | Secondary sector | Tertiary sector |
|---|---|---|---|---|---|---|---|---|
| | Hinterland in China | | | | Northeast region | | | |
| 1931 | 7.53 | 5.28 | 12.25 | 24.50 | | | | |
| 1932 | 7.66 | 5.53 | 10.64 | 23.50 | 10.43 | 6.18 | 8.39 | 28.90 |
| 1933 | 7.92 | 5.54 | 11.24 | 24.46 | 10.96 | 6.03 | 12.14 | 31.38 |
| 1934 | 7.49 | 4.93 | 13.01 | 26.12 | 10.26 | 4.58 | 14.23 | 32.69 |
| 1935 | 7.84 | 5.26 | 10.83 | 25.90 | 11.16 | 5.21 | 16.57 | 34.11 |
| 1936 | 8.03 | 5.48 | 9.81 | 25.37 | 11.84 | 5.22 | 20.87 | 36.16 |
| 1937 | 7.32 | 5.15 | 7.47 | 23.12 | 12.25 | 5.30 | 20.78 | 37.02 |
| 1938 | 7.15 | 5.40 | 6.20 | 20.26 | 13.56 | 5.37 | 25.57 | 41.95 |
| 1939 | 7.17 | 5.08 | 9.31 | 21.20 | 15.31 | 4.98 | 37.03 | 48.18 |
| 1940 | 6.99 | 5.12 | 8.81 | 20.93 | 15.80 | 4.89 | 37.67 | 48.53 |

*Data source:* Calculated based on Ryoshin Minami and Makino Fumio (2014), pp. 362, 452, 481, 516–517.

## 18 *Preparatory investigation*

The changes in the northeast region were quite different. First, except for the primary sector, it did not decline but rose in the secondary and tertiary sectors, including the total, of course. Second, the level of the primary sector was almost the same as that of the hinterland. It was high and then low, more than that in the hinterland in the early stage but lower than that in the hinterland in the later stage. Third, except for the primary sector, it far exceeded that of the hinterland in other sectors. Importantly, it was not significant in the early stage but was much higher in the later stage. In general, the per capita output of the northeast region, except for the primary sector, was higher than that of the hinterland, and there was a clear upward trend.

### 1.4 Conclusion

As the first chapter of this book, this chapter primarily examines the general situation of China's economic development before 1949. We position the economic development and changes in this period as the background or preparatory stage because China did not initiate modern economic growth during this period but only introduced some modern industries and developed some industries in some cities without creating a comprehensive development trend. Although there were some modern sectors and the people had a better understanding of science and technology as well as industrial production systems imported from the West, normal growth was not achieved in terms of the economy as a whole. In addition to the constraints of the economy itself, the development of China's economy was also affected by politics, society, and international relations. There was political instability for a long time, with frequent government changes in the early Republic of China period and turmoil in the later period. Coupled with warlord dogfights and foreign aggression, China lacked a good environment for peaceful and stable economic development.

China only entered the so-called republic era in 1912. The imperial rule before then could not promote economic development in a real sense. Imperial rulers could not comprehend the meaning of modern economic development at all or recognize the great power of science and technology, as well as the meaning of the nation state. Their only consideration was how to maintain their rule against threat. No country in the world has achieved economic development under imperial rule. Although historians usually define China's modern history as beginning with the Opium War, in fact, it was nothing more than a relic of a declining dynasty rather than the beginning of a modern country until the Xinhai Revolution in 1911. China is wholly different from Japan in this regard.

Japan pursued the path of capitalist development since the Meiji Restoration in 1868, and China lagged behind Japan for more than 40 years. From this viewpoint alone, the gap between China and Japan in modern times is obvious. Japan started modern economic growth around 1886 after the Meiji Restoration. If China had developed normally, it should have achieved economic take-off in the 1930s. The facts also point to this trend. However, the Japanese invasion threw China's economic development off the track, and the economic development during the Republic of China period could only be seen as a "failed economic take-off".[36]

*Overview of modern economic development* 19

The gap between the Xinhai Revolution and the Meiji Restoration in time symbolizes the gap in economic development between the two countries. This gap even widened for a long time. It is only after China's reform and opening up that this gap has gradually narrowed, but the gap that is narrowing is one that had previously widened. There is still a gap of not less than 40 years between the two countries.

## Notes

1　For the explanation of concepts such as economic development and economic growth, see Guan Quan (2014).
2　Regarding the time of China's economic take-off, see Guan Quan (2019).
3　In premodern times, China was almost equal to foreign powers. In the traditional era, it requires strength to feed a big population. Such so-called strength is measured by land area and fertility, land productivity, the level of state governance, etc.
4　Taiwan and the northeast region became Japanese colonies in 1895 and 1931, respectively.
5　For issues about the emergence of capitalism in China, see Li Bozhong (2013).
6　In many Western writings, the year 1500 CE is used a starting point for discussing economic and social development in modern times. This is the case for history and economics, such as Kennedy (2006) and Kindleberger (2003).
7　Since then, it has declined. Western Europe's proportion in the world's population was 9.2 percent in 1973 and 6.4 percent in 2001.
8　In 1973 and 2001, Africa's proportion in the world's population was 10.0 percent and 13.4 percent, respectively.
9　This phenomenon indirectly verifies the Malthusian trap to a certain extent. In traditional societies, the population will increase if food yield increases. An increase in population will lead to a relative decline in food output (diminishing marginal returns). An expanding population will lead to a shortage of food because land productivity is largely constant unless there is technological progress.
10　According to Maddison statistics, this is the year when China had the lowest proportion in the world.
11　The world as a whole refers to Western Europe, North America, Japan, etc., excluding underdeveloped regions.
12　In 1973 and 2001, it accounted for 25.6 percent and 20.3 percent, respectively.
13　However, after World War II, the proportion of these countries and regions in terms of GDP changed differently. Russia fell to 3.6 percent in 2001, the United States remained around 21 percent after peaking in 1950, Latin America remained the same as in 1950 or slightly higher, and Japan jumped and reached 7.8 percent in 1973.
14　India's share of GDP picked up slightly in 2001, accounting for 5.4 percent, while Africa's share of GDP hovers at 3.3 percent.
15　Because the economy of these regions has developed rapidly since modern times, they did a good job in statistics.
16　It was different even in the 1930s.
17　Rawski (2009). It is called rapid growth because even today's developed countries have a long-term average rate of only 2 to 3 percent except for Japan, which did not achieve high growth rates in the process of economic development. See Kuznets (1999), Ryoshin Minami (1981).
18　Yeh (1979), Perkins (1975), Liu Foding et al. (1997).
19　Maddison (2009), Ryoshin Minami and Makino Fumio, eds. (2014).
20　Ryoshin Minami and Makino Fumio (2014), p. 360.
21　Liu Foding et al. (1997).
22　This is the case with the study by John K. Chang et al.; see Chang (1969).

## 20  *Preparatory investigation*

23  Since there is a lack of continuous data for the 1939–1948 period, it is impossible to see a big picture of economic changes in this period. At most, the data for 1949 or 1950 can only be compared with those in 1936 or 1938.
24  Maddison (2009) pp. 170–172.
25  For the long-term changes in the industrial structure of various countries, see Guan Quan (2014). The original data from Mitchell (2002).
26  In parentheses are the average annual growth rates of per capita income. Liu Foding et al. (1999), p. 66.
27  Bergere (1994).
28  Ryoshin Minami (1981), p. 26.
29  It is worth noting that some of the numbers here are calculated by Maddison on the basis of hypotheses. See Maddison (2008), p. 167.
30  For the data on 1933, there is also the study by Wu Baosan and others. It is not shown here for the sake of a unified standard. See Wu Baosan (1947).
31  It is for this reason that we have reservations about calling this period the "golden age of the Chinese bourgeoisie", but we (author of this book) agree to some degree because a lot of modern industries were introduced in this period, and an industrial base was established. In particular, the development of private enterprises made possible the subsequent economic take-off.
32  Ryoshin Minami (1981), p. 76.
33  In 1930, Shenyang produced trucks. Shanghai also carried out trial production, but they were not mature.
34  For the situation of cities, see Guan Quan (2018).
35  Regarding Japan, see Ryoshin Minami (2002), p. 203; regarding China, see *China Statistical Yearbook*.
36  For the basis of this view, see Guan Quan (2018).

# Part II
# Processes and characteristics

# 2 Changes in agriculture

## 2.1 Introduction

In modern China, agriculture was an important industry, but people could not do much about it. Agriculture is important for its function and role. In other words, it produces food and some industrial raw materials. Food is indispensable, regardless of how much of it is obtained. No one can live without food. Although it is not very important today in terms of industrial raw materials, it is also very meaningful. For example, cotton can be used to make clothing, and silk can be used to make silk cloth. People could not do much about it because its productivity was not as high as that of industry and services sectors, and its share and status in economic activities were declining. Given the basic fact that China's economy as a whole did not develop significantly in modern times, agriculture could only maintain the current status without any growth. The development of agriculture depends largely on the development of industry because a developing industry employs the surplus labor force from rural areas, produces the means of production for agriculture, and provides funding for agriculture.[1] Before 1949, China was an agrarian society without modern economic growth, and the vast majority of the people and labor force were engaged in agricultural production in rural areas. This means that rural areas had a huge surplus labor force, resulting in low agricultural productivity and living standards. This situation can only be changed through industrialization and urbanization, so that the surplus rural labor flows to these sectors, and more cultivated land is freed up for fewer farmers. In this way, agricultural productivity can be enhanced, thereby improving living standards.

Some basic statistical data are available for use regarding agriculture in modern China, but there are some problems and limitations. One is the *Agricultural and Commercial Statistics Table* produced during the Beiyang government period, which contains data for years from 1914 to 1920, but the data are poor in quality and contain many errors. The second is two surveys conducted by John Lossing Buck, an American scholar and professor at the University of Nanking: *Series of Classic Overseas Studies on Modern Chinese Culture* for the years from 1921 to 1925 and *Land Use in China* for the years from 1929 to 1933. The third is the *Report on Agricultural Situation*, prepared by the Central Agricultural Experiment Institute of the Ministry of Industry of the Republic of China Government, which

DOI: 10.4324/9781003410386-4

## 24 *Processes and characteristics*

contains data for the years from 1931 to 1937. There are other surveys on agriculture that cover a small scope. For example, after occupying North China, Japanese aggressors prepared the *Survey of Agricultural Produce in North China*, which contains data on North China for the years from 1939 to 1944. The author first briefly introduces agriculture in modern China. Then agriculture during the Republic of China period is discussed in chronological order: the 1910s, the 1920s, and the 1930s–1940s.

### 2.2 Overview of agriculture in modern China

Agriculture in the premodern era developed very slowly and sometimes took a step backwards. Due to protracted wars, frequent natural disasters, diseases, poor nutrition, and other reasons, the population of many countries sometimes dwindle, and some countries or nationalities will even disappear. In peacetime, the more important factor is whether agriculture can feed more people. If it develops well, the population will increase. Otherwise, the population will decrease or stagnate.[2] This has happened in countries around the world, notably the Black Death in Europe, the Napoleonic Wars, and the two world wars. China is no exception. The burst Yellow River, schistosomiasis, the Taiping Rebellion, warlord dogfights, the Japanese invasion of China, etc. decimated the population or aggravated famines. In modern times (mainly from 1846 to 1911), more than 60 disasters struck the Yellow River Basin and the Yangtze River Basin, with some degree of famine in almost every year.[3]

Table 2.1 shows several estimates of the population, the area of cropland, and the area of cropland per capita in modern times. Due to the different data and calculation methods used and different years, there are some differences, but they are close and can roughly reflect the changes during this period. On the whole, the population increased slightly, despite a decline in some periods, mainly in the 1870s to 1890s. There was a large increase in cultivated land, and it even doubled by the early 20th century according to some estimates. In this way, cultivated land per capita increased somewhat, mainly in the 19th century. It was basically stagnant after the 20th century. In other words, the increase in cultivated land was offset by the simultaneous increase in population, resulting in equilibrium to some extent. If this equilibrium is low and no technological progress is made, it is difficult to enhance the productivity of agriculture.

Table 2.2 lists the agricultural development in modern China estimated by Taiwan scholars. According to the estimates in the table, the average annual growth rate of China's agriculture from the 1880s to the 1930s was 0.6 percent, which was low and largely attributed to the population increase. Liu Foding et al. estimated the growth rate at 1.05 percent, higher than the estimate by Taiwan scholars, even if this figure is also not high.[4] It is particularly noteworthy that the data for 1957 are also listed in the table. Despite large fluctuations, a comparison shows that agricultural productivity did not improve much in the past 100 years, and some parts (average productivity and marginal productivity of labor) even declined.

Table 2.1 Various estimates of population, cultivated land, and cultivated land per capita in modern times

| Year | Population (100 million) | | | | Area of cultivated land (100 million mu , 1 mu equivalent to 0.07 ha) | | | | Area of cultivated land per capita (mu) | |
|---|---|---|---|---|---|---|---|---|---|---|
| | Ding Changqing et al. | Perkins | Wu Chengming | Xu Daofu | Ding Changqing et al. | Perkins | Wu Chengming | Xu Daofu | Ding Changqing et al. | Xu Daofu |
| 1840 | 4.13 | – | 4.13 | – | – | – | – | – | – | – |
| 1850 | 4.32 | 4.10 | 4.15 | – | 7.72 | – | – | – | 1.79 | – |
| 1863 | – | – | – | 4.05 | – | – | – | 7.52 | – | 1.86 |
| 1872 | – | 3.50 | 3.45 | 3.30 | 7.70 | 12.10 | 11.45 | 7.56 | – | 2.29 |
| 1883 | 3.78 | – | 3.62 | – | – | – | 9.46 | – | – | – |
| 1887 | – | – | – | 3.38 | – | – | – | 8.41 | – | 2.49 |
| 1893 | 4.21 | 3.85 | 3.80 | – | – | 12.10 | 11.89 | – | – | – |
| 1900 | – | – | – | 3.67 | – | – | – | 8.48 | – | 2.31 |
| 1910 | 4.38 | – | – | 3.69 | – | – | – | 14.55 | 3.19 | 3.95 |
| 1912 | – | 4.30 | 4.38 | – | 13.95 | – | 12.68 | – | – | – |
| 1916 | – | – | – | 4.10 | – | – | – | 12.77 | – | 3.12 |
| 1923 | 4.45 | – | 4.45 | – | – | – | – | – | – | – |
| 1933 | 4.50 | 5.00 | 4.50 | 4.62 | 13.74 | 14.70 | 14.05 | 12.28 | – | 2.66 |
| 1936 | 4.79 | – | – | – | – | – | – | – | 2.96 | – |
| 1943 | 4.55 | – | 4.56 | – | – | – | – | – | 3.07 | – |
| 1946 | 4.56 | – | – | 4.63 | 13.67 | – | 14.11 | 14.11 | 3.10 | 3.05 |
| 1949 | 5.42 | – | 5.42 | – | 14.24 | – | 14.81 | – | 2.71 | – |

Sources: Population: Ding Changqing, Ci Hongfei (2000), p. 22; Perkins (1984), p. 288; Wu Chengming (1989); Xu Daofu ed. (1983), p. 7. Cultivated land: Ding Changqing and Ci Hongfei (2000), p. 28; Perkins (1984), p. 325; Wu Chengming (1989); Xu Daofu ed. (1983), pp. 8–9.

26  *Processes and characteristics*

*Table 2.2* Agricultural production, average and marginal productivities in modern times

| Year | Agricultural production | | Average labor productivity (1,000 calories per person) | Average land productivity (1,000 calories per person) | Marginal productivity of labor (%) | Marginal productivity of land (%) |
|---|---|---|---|---|---|---|
| | Volume (1 billion calories) | Growth rate (%) | | | | |
| 1840 | 264,503 | 4.52 | 642.00 | 226.46 | 256.80 | 135.87 |
| 1850 | 272,282 | 2.94 | 660.88 | 225.03 | 264.35 | 135.02 |
| 1860 | 268,346 | −1.45 | 711.79 | 216.93 | 284.72 | 130.16 |
| 1870 | 260,316 | −2.99 | 727.14 | 216.57 | 290.86 | 129.94 |
| 1880 | 261,353 | 0.40 | 710.20 | 222.81 | 284.08 | 133.68 |
| 1890 | 275,070 | 5.25 | 723.87 | 222.73 | 289.55 | 133.64 |
| 1900 | 281,638 | 2.39 | 704.10 | 229.72 | 281.64 | 137.83 |
| 1910 | 306,220 | 8.73 | 723.92 | 228.35 | 289.57 | 137.01 |
| 1920 | 334,729 | 9.31 | 709.17 | 234.57 | 283.67 | 140.74 |
| 1930 | 353,368 | 5.57 | 722.63 | 234.48 | 289.05 | 140.69 |
| 1957 | 424,915 | 7.50 | 656.75 | 253.23 | 262.70 | 151.94 |

*Note:* For the sake of limited space, the lowest value is used here. The highest value is also listed in the original text.

*Data source:* Liu Foding et al. (1999), p. 125.

## 2.3  Agriculture in the 1910s

Precious statistical data are available for this period. The *Agricultural and Commercial Statistics Table* by the Ministry of Agriculture and Commerce is an survey and report on agriculture, industry and commerce prepared by the Beiyang government (Beijing government). It had been continuously compiled for 10 years (1912–1921). However, due to the influence of the domestic situation at that time and limited editorial experience, this material is seriously flawed in quality. Reports are missing in many areas primarily because of warlord dogfight, transport and other reasons.[5] In addition, the completion, preparation, editing and other work are replete with loopholes, which undermine the effectiveness of this material. Therefore, most economic historians do not use this data. Even if it is used, only the data for years 1912–1915 are used because of its relative integrity. Nevertheless, there are many problems. For example, the output and value of silk in 1915 in Table 2.3 are significantly deviated from the positive output value. It shows that the local government made an error in filling in the forms, or editors made a mistake. Nevertheless, we believe that this material is still irreplaceable and shall be introduced as an important reference.[6]

The statistics regarding agriculture in the *Agricultural and Commercial Statistics Table* began with the third (1914) survey, covering all aspects, such as the number of farmer households and the area of farmland, including paddy fields and dry land, areas for self-cultivation and rental, the size of cultivated land, and classification by the size of farmland. The total yield and yield per unit area of various agricultural

*Changes in agriculture* 27

products cover, in addition to grain, various cash crops, such as hemp, cotton, tea, tobacco, medicinal herbs, fruit, cotton, silkworms, as well as forestry, aquatic products, and livestock products.

Table 2.3 shows the number of agricultural households, the planting area, the average area per household, as well as silk and tea manufacturing from 1914 to 1919. Due to the limited data, the data for years after 1916 are not reliable. Especially for 1919, the data are significantly less than in previous years. Nevertheless, the information here is also illustrative because, if the national conditions at that time are considered, coupled with the fact that it is the only statistical data for national statistics during this period, its significance cannot be underestimated. Even if the data for the later years are not good, especially the total figures that are certainly incomplete, the average figures are still meaningful. The number of farming households was similar before 1918, with only slight reductions. It is relatively credible if the fact that some areas did not report in later years is taken into account. In other words, if we refer to the data for the previous one year or two for the unreported provinces, the subsequent changes can be conjectured. The total figures such as the number of farming households and the planting area were reduced, but the average area per household did not decrease, or even increased, indicating that the data on total figures do not necessarily affect the average figures. Of course, this does not mean that the average figures are necessarily reliable. It may be that the lack of raw data causes deviations.

It is noteworthy that silk was manufactured manually and mechanically. The manual method is traditional technology, while the machine method uses imported new technology. The number of households that adopted machinery (only about 1,500 households) is far less than the number of households that adopted the manual method (750,000–800,000) in 1914 and 1915. What is important are the advanced and reliable machinery-based silk reeling technology, as well as the better quality of products. China has a long history of silk reeling, but it adopted the traditional manual method. Machine silk reeling technology was introduced from Western Europe since the beginning of modern times. At the same time, Japan also introduced this advanced technology and improved it to compete against China in the international market. Due to poor industrial and economic development in China, Chinese products were not as competitive as Japanese products in the era of machine reeling and were repeatedly dwarfed by Japanese products in the international market.[7]

Table 2.4 shows the yield and yield per *mu* of the main crops. As mentioned, data for years after 1916 are unreliable due to statistical problems, especially regarding total yield. For example, the yield of rice was stable in 1914 and 1915 and was significantly higher than in later years. The yield of taro had been decreasing since 1914, as were the yields for potatoes, melons, vegetables, grapes, sugar cane, and hemp. However, the yield of some crops does not follow in this direction, such as wheat, sorghum, beans, peanuts, maize, and cotton. The yield per *mu* was more stable than the total yield. This shows that the yield per *mu* is calculated based on the total yield and the area of cultivated land. As long as the two are reported together, the data should be accurate. The agricultural products not listed

*Table 2.3* Basic state of agricultural production

| Year | The number of farming households and planting area | | | The number of silk manufacturing households | | | Silk output | | Tea making | |
|---|---|---|---|---|---|---|---|---|---|---|
| | *Number of farming households (10000 households)* | *Planting area (100 million mu)* | *Average area per household (mu)* | *Manual (10000 households)* | *Machines (household)* | *Total (10,000 households)* | *Quantity (5,000 kg)* | *Amount of money (10,000 yuan)* | *Number of tea-making households (10,000 households)* | *Output (5,000 kg)* |
| 1914 | 5,940.2 | 15.8 | 26.6 | 75.0 | 1,670 | 75.3 | 7,307.9 | 1,3926.5 | 93.5 | 72,677.0 |
| 1915 | 4,677.6 | 14.4 | 30.8 | 80.5 | 1,431 | 80.6 | 5,0432.8 | 1,94947.7 | 148.8 | 46,943.7 |
| 1916 | 5,932.3 | 15.1 | 25.5 | 59.5 | 707 | 59.5 | 5,453.8 | 19220.6 | 97.2 | 19,960.2 |
| 1917 | 4,890.8 | 13.7 | 27.9 | 62.1 | 361 | 62.1 | 3,583.9 | 2,0578.1 | 86.8 | 14,116.5 |
| 1918 | 4,393.5 | 13.1 | 29.9 | 64.8 | 168 | 64.8 | 3,025.0 | 1,9324.0 | 65.5 | 13,286.1 |
| 1919 | 2,954.9 | 9.4 | 31.7 | 59.7 | 137 | 59.7 | 3,035.5 | 20657.4 | 45.0 | 8,870.7 |

*Data source:* Ministry of Agriculture and Commerce, *Eighth Agricultural and Commercial Statistics Table*, pp. 3, 98–99, 103.

Table 2.4 Yield and yield per *mu* of major crops

| Year | Crop yield | | | | | | | |
|---|---|---|---|---|---|---|---|---|
| | *(100 million shi)* | *Wheat (100 million shi)* | *Beans (100 million shi)* | *Sorghum (100 million shi)* | *Peanuts (million shi)* | *Millet (million shi)* | *Maize (million shi)* | *Taro (50 million kg)* |
| 1914 | 21.3 | 3.5 | 1.3 | 1.1 | 37.5 | 18.4 | 43.6 | 62.1 |
| 1915 | 20.9 | 3.4 | 0.9 | 1.0 | 219.2 | 29.8 | 44.7 | 42.9 |
| 1916 | 5.4 | 4.6 | 1.1 | 1.0 | 56.5 | 21.4 | 38.9 | 37.9 |
| 1917 | 5.3 | 2.9 | 1.5 | 0.9 | 27.1 | 18.6 | 32.4 | 14.1 |
| 1918 | 3.0 | 4.3 | 1.8 | 2.8 | 33.3 | 45.2 | 57.2 | 17.3 |
| 1919 | 1.0 | 3.9 | 1.4 | 2.5 | 33.3 | 47.1 | 54.3 | 11.8 |
| Year | Per unit yield of crops (shi/mu) | | | | | | | |
| | *Rice* | *Wheat* | *Beans* | *Sorghum* | *Peanut* | *Millet* | *Maize* | *Taro (0.5 kg/mu)* |
| 1914 | 3.7 | 0.9 | 0.7 | 0.9 | 1.5 | 0.3 | 0.8 | 555.7 |
| 1915 | 5.2 | 1.0 | 0.7 | 0.9 | 9.4 | 1.0 | 0.7 | 384.6 |
| 1916 | 2.2 | 0.9 | 0.6 | 0.8 | 4.4 | 0.7 | 0.8 | 553.4 |
| 1917 | 2.2 | 0.6 | 0.7 | 0.9 | 2.1 | 0.8 | 0.8 | 242.2 |
| 1918 | 1.7 | 0.6 | 0.8 | 1.1 | 1.6 | 0.8 | 1.0 | 457.4 |
| 1919 | 1.3 | 0.7 | 0.8 | 1.2 | 1.7 | 1.0 | 1.1 | 597.1 |

(*Continued*)

*Table 2.4* (Continued)

| | Crop yield | | | | | | | |
|---|---|---|---|---|---|---|---|---|
| Year | Potatoes (100 million jin) (one jin equivalent to 0.5 kg) | Melons (100 million jin) | Vegetables (100 million jin) | Grapes (100 million jin) | Sugar cane (100 million jin) | Hemp (100 million jin) | Cotton (100 million jin) | Tobacco leaves (100 million jin) |
| 1914 | 95.8 | 183.0 | 207.3 | 96.4 | 81.2 | 15.2 | 15.7 | 22.0 |
| 1915 | 66.3 | 125.3 | 856.6 | 101.5 | 36.4 | 19.2 | 89.6 | 7.7 |
| 1916 | 53.7 | 175.4 | 217.8 | 25.4 | 12.8 | 3.8 | 19.5 | 12.4 |
| 1917 | 22.2 | 46.7 | 134.9 | 38.8 | 16.5 | 4.6 | 30.9 | 8.8 |
| 1918 | 52.1 | 51.5 | 225.9 | 49.1 | 7.6 | 5.1 | 23.7 | 13.0 |
| 1919 | 10.0 | 39.2 | 177.3 | 39.8 | 6.8 | 4.5 | 33.0 | 11.9 |

| | Per unit yield of crop (jin/mu) | | | | | | | |
|---|---|---|---|---|---|---|---|---|
| Year | Potatoes (jin/mu) | Melon (jin) | Vegetables (jin) | Grapes (jin) | Sugar cane (jin) | Hemp (jin) | Cotton (jin) | Tobacco leaves (jin) |
| 1914 | 1,381.7 | 1,416.5 | 931.7 | 73.9 | 1,637.4 | 191.6 | 55.4 | 416.7 |
| 1915 | 778.7 | 1,585.7 | 3,627.9 | 761.6 | 382.7 | 253.1 | 269.4 | 136.8 |
| 1916 | 500.1 | 2,164.0 | 1,180.7 | 141.9 | 213.3 | 77.3 | 48.6 | 342.0 |
| 1917 | 428.6 | 697.3 | 781.6 | 743.3 | 724.1 | 97.1 | 64.9 | 184.9 |
| 1918 | 1,346.9 | 687.7 | 944.2 | 982.2 | 614.2 | 109.6 | 45.9 | 124.1 |
| 1919 | 430.5 | 747.0 | 1,118.7 | 1,358.3 | 655.5 | 135.7 | 72.4 | 127.8 |

*Data source:* Ministry of Agriculture and Commerce, *Eighth Agricultural and Commercial Statistics Table*, pp. 62–80.

*Changes in agriculture* 31

here include silkworms, fruit, and medicinal herbs. Because there are only total yield and no planting area, the yield per *mu* cannot be calculated.

Table 2.5 shows the livestock yield. As mentioned earlier, although data for later years are missing, it is obvious for the year 1919. Given the lack of data for later years, the output of these livestock products should increase year by year or at least steadily. In other words, the yield of livestock during this period was relatively gratifying, without significant decrease, although the data show a decrease in the table. Of these, the yield of horses, donkeys, and sheep was better; the yield of cattle was reduced, and that of pigs was also significantly reduced. It is worth mentioning that horses, cattle, and donkeys are large livestock in rural areas and are means of production. In terms of economics, they are the capital stock because they are productive and can help farmers produce. Their increase and decrease mean, to some extent, changes in productivity. It is impossible to make an accurate judgment here because the purpose of these livestock is not known.

## 2.4 Agriculture in the 1930s–1940s

### 2.4.1 The hinterland in China

Beginning in the 1930s, a special situation occurred in China. After Japan occupied Northeast China and supported the "last emperor" Puyi in establishing Manchukuo, China was essentially in a divided state for the subsequent decade or so. Therefore, many statistics are also separate, and discussion here is made separately. Of course, this is not entirely the case. Some data are consolidated.

Table 2.6 shows the increase in agricultural production in China in the 1930s. It can be seen that the growth rate was very low or even negative in the hinterland. There was growth somewhat in the northeast region, and the growth rate was slightly lower than that of Taiwan (1.4 percent) at that time. For the sake of reference, the table lists the growth rates in Japan and North Korea for the same period. It was slightly higher in Japan than in North Korea. On average, the growth rate in North Korea was significantly higher than that in China. In short, the most reliable data for this period show that there was no significant increase in agricultural production in the hinterland in China, despite a high growth rate in individual years during this period. The rate of growth after Japan's full-scale invasion of China in

*Table 2.5* Livestock yield, Unit: 10,000 heads

| Year | Horse | Cattle | Donkey | Sheep | Pig |
|------|-------|--------|--------|-------|-----|
| 1914 | 493.4 | 2,199.7 | 439.4 | 2,218.6 | 7,681.9 |
| 1915 | 474.4 | 2,288.6 | 514.0 | 2,390.5 | 6,024.6 |
| 1916 | 442.5 | 1,822.1 | 366.2 | 2,272.6 | 5,068.4 |
| 1917 | 462.9 | 1,539.9 | 491.4 | 2,436.6 | 4,124.4 |
| 1918 | 430.3 | 1,240.5 | 497.2 | 2,330.6 | 3,786.3 |
| 1919 | 197.7 | 764.4 | 372.6 | 1,168.9 | 2,248.2 |

*Data source:* Ministry of Agriculture and Commerce, *Eighth Agricultural and Commercial Statistics Table*, pp. 214–218.

## 32  Processes and characteristics

*Table 2.6* Growth rate of actual value added in agriculture, Unit: %

| Year | Hinterland in China | Northeast China | Taiwan of China | Japan | North Korea |
|---|---|---|---|---|---|
| 1932 | 6.5 | – | 14.9 | 11.6 | 6.3 |
| 1933 | −2.4 | 7.0 | −7.3 | 10.2 | 3.1 |
| 1934 | −11.5 | −21.4 | 9.0 | −14.9 | −5.3 |
| 1935 | 7.5 | 18.5 | 5.6 | 5.5 | 10.6 |
| 1936 | 3.9 | 3.9 | 4.8 | 7.5 | −13.3 |
| 1937 | −9.6 | 4.4 | −1.4 | 2.4 | 35.1 |
| 1938 | 2.6 | 3.2 | 5.8 | −2.8 | −11.9 |
| 1939 | −3.5 | −6.3 | −1.6 | 7.7 | −29.6 |
| 1940 | 1.5 | −1.5 | 17.3 | −2.8 | 25.9 |
| Average | −0.6 | 1.0 | 1.4 | 2.7 | 2.3 |

*Note*: The 1933 price for China's hinterland, the 1935 price for Northeast China, the 1960 price for Taiwan, the 1934–1936 price for Japan, and the 1935 price for North Korea.

*Data source*: Ryoshin Minami and Makino Fumio (2014), p. 95.

1937 was significantly lower than before, despite large fluctuations in the latter period. The northeast region experienced fluctuations at a slightly different time than the hinterland. Except for large negative growth in 1934 and 1939 and negative growth in some years after 1940, it was positive growth for the other years in the northeast region.

Table 2.7 shows the changes in the production volume, input, and value added of the primary sector from the 1930s to the 1940s in China's hinterland. In terms of agriculture, both the production volume and the number of intermediate inputs and the value added show a trend of horizontal movement or slight decrease. Especially in the early 1940s, it decreased obviously and then rebounded. It is worth observing that in the early 1930s (before 1936), intermediate input showed an obvious trend of increase, which was different from the changes in production volume and value added. The forestry industry saw a rise and then a decline. It mainly declined in 1938 and then rebounded. The changes in the aquaculture industry were basically the same as those in agriculture, showing a horizontal movement as a whole, with a slight decline in the process. Since agriculture had the largest share of the primary sector, the overall change was basically the same as that of agriculture, that is, a slight decline amid horizontal movement.

Figure 2.1 shows the growth rate of agricultural value added and intermediate inputs in the 1930s and 1940s. First of all, it can be seen that the change trend of the three curves is basically similar (somewhat different in individual time periods), indicating that the value added and the input amount are closely linked. Second, the curve for the years from 1933 to 1936 fluctuated largely, both in terms of decline and increase, but there were no large fluctuations for other periods. Finally, the 1938–1942 period generally saw a very low level of growth, without major ups and downs.

*Table 2.7* Production volume, input, and value added of the primary sector in China's hinterland, Unit: million yuan

| Year | Agriculture | | | Forestry | | | Aquaculture | | | Total | | |
|---|---|---|---|---|---|---|---|---|---|---|---|---|
| | Production value | Intermediate input | Value added | Production value | Intermediate input | Value added | Production value | Intermediate input | Value added | Production value | Intermediate input | Value added |
| 1931 | 12,123.3 | 1,554.2 | 10,569.1 | 303.6 | 55.0 | 248.6 | 190.1 | 30.7 | 1,59.4 | 12,617.0 | 1,639.9 | 10,977.1 |
| 1936 | 12,880.4 | 1,654.1 | 11,226.3 | 323.1 | 58.6 | 264.5 | 204.9 | 33.1 | 171.9 | 13,408.4 | 1,745.8 | 11,662.7 |
| 1941 | 10,867.8 | 1,391.6 | 9,476.2 | 310.3 | 56.2 | 254.0 | 174.0 | 28.1 | 145.9 | 11,352.1 | 1,475.9 | 9,876.1 |
| 1947 | 12,161.5 | 1,416.6 | 10,744.9 | 334.3 | 60.6 | 2,73.7 | 197.6 | 31.9 | 165.7 | 12,693.4 | 1,509.1 | 1,1184.3 |

*Note:* The 1933 price is shown here. Due to space limitations, figures for all the years from 1931 to 1947 are not shown here.

*Data source:* Ryoshin Minami and Makino Fumio (2014), p. 377.

## 34  Processes and characteristics

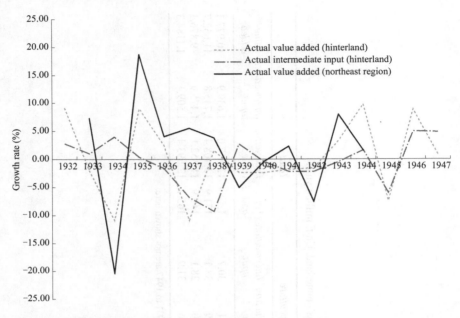

*Figure 2.1* Growth rate of actual value added and intermediate inputs in agriculture (%)
*Data source*: Calculated based on Ryoshin Minami and Makino Fumio (2014), pp. 377, 487.

Table 2.8 shows the output of major agricultural products in China's hinterland in the 1930 and 1940s. The production index of agricultural products in the last column changed basically in the same way as the production volume and value added of agriculture and primary sector as mentioned previously, showing a trend of horizontal movement and a slight decline. However, it increased slightly before 1936, was significantly lower from 1937 to 1943, began to rebound after 1944, but did not exceed the previous level. The changes in the major agricultural products were almost the same, with no change for a long time, a slight decline, and a slight increase for various produce. This shows China's stagnating agricultural production during this period. If we add the increase in population, the per capita output will be significantly reduced, indicating that people's living standards were reduced. If you take into account wars and natural disasters, the living standards of Chinese people at that time can only be imagined.

In terms of the per unit yield, the yields of the main agricultural products are shown in the table. The yield is divided by the planting area to obtain the yield per unit area. Because the planting area did not change much, the yield per unit area also did not change much. This indicator represents agricultural productivity, mainly land productivity, which is very important because it is associated with many factors, the first of which is whether there were technological advances. If new varieties with a higher yield were available during this period, the same planting area would increase yield. Agricultural varieties belong to biotechnology and can usually be improved and innovated in two ways. One is the traditional empirical improvement, whereby

*Table 2.8* Yield of major agricultural products and per unit yield in the hinterland, Unit: 1,000 metric tons

| Year | Rice | Wheat | Maize | Barley | Millet | Sorghum | Soybean | Peanut | Sweet potato |
|---|---|---|---|---|---|---|---|---|---|
| **Output (1000 metric tons)** | | | | | | | | | |
| 1931 | 78,122 | 18,570 | 12,344 | 6,167 | 10,181 | 10,557 | 5,653 | 2,051 | 20,745 |
| 1936 | 81,751 | 19,796 | 11,891 | 6,249 | 10,588 | 12,310 | 6,017 | 2,386 | 21,906 |
| 1941 | 66,914 | 15,435 | 10,568 | 4,749 | 8,612 | 8,894 | 4,951 | 2,094 | 24,539 |
| 1947 | 74,347 | 21,251 | 12,590 | 5,974 | 8,965 | 8,918 | 5,495 | 2,290 | 27,571 |

| Year | Potato | Taro | Rapeseed | Cotton | Tobacco | Sugarcane | Fruits | Vegetables | Production index of agricultural products |
|---|---|---|---|---|---|---|---|---|---|
| 1931 | 2,476 | 1,226 | 1,805 | 2,385 | 730 | 6,325 | 1,698 | 25,393 | 93.0 |
| 1936 | 2,509 | 1,604 | 1,997 | 3,372 | 955 | 6,679 | 1,976 | 26,814 | 100.2 |
| 1941 | 1,907 | 1,398 | 2,215 | 2,121 | 832 | 7,482 | 1,734 | 30,036 | 85.1 |
| 1947 | 2,398 | 1,617 | 3,344 | 2,743 | 963 | 8,406 | 1,896 | 33,748 | 96.7 |

| Year | Rice | Wheat | Maize | Barley | Millet | Sorghum | Soybean | Peanut | Sweet potato |
|---|---|---|---|---|---|---|---|---|---|
| **Per unit yield (kg/ha)** | | | | | | | | | |
| 1931 | 2,679.9 | 956.2 | 1,540.5 | 10,37.0 | 1,214.9 | 1,297.4 | 1,014.5 | 1,237.8 | 7,333.0 |
| 1936 | 28,97.5 | 986.7 | 1,481.6 | 11,18.7 | 1,315.4 | 1,641.6 | 1,127.4 | 1,635.4 | 6,901.7 |
| 1941 | 2,572.5 | 752.6 | 1,246.8 | 933.6 | 970.6 | 1,301.1 | 884.7 | 1,469.5 | 6,848.7 |
| 1947 | 2813.9, | 944.5 | 1,514.3 | 10,43.9 | 1,158.4 | 1,343.3 | 1,091.4 | 1,479.3 | 6,990.6 |

| Year | Potato | Taro | Rapeseed | Cotton | Tobacco | Sugarcane | Fruit | Vegetable | Raw tea |
|---|---|---|---|---|---|---|---|---|---|
| 1931 | 5,526.8 | 5,261.8 | 593.0 | 558.8 | 981.2 | 25,816.3 | 1,949.5 | 11,321.0 | 758.1 |
| 1936 | 5,959.6 | 7,160.7 | 605.9 | 672.0 | 1,339.4 | 24,287.3 | 2,579.6 | 10,657.4 | 1,038.8 |
| 1941 | 4,979.1 | 6,594.3 | 569.1 | 546.8 | 1,227.1 | 24,135.5 | 2,315.1 | 10,576.1 | 953.8 |
| 1947 | 5,563.8 | 7,030.4 | 724.9 | 565.3 | 1,310.2 | 24,651.0 | 2,329.2 | 10,795.9 | 1,014.2 |

*Note*: Due to space limitations, figures for all the years from 1931 to 1947 are not shown here.

*Data source*: Calculated based on Ryoshin Minami and Makino Fumio (2014), pp. 372–375.

## 36 Processes and characteristics

farmers identify or screen out excellent varieties after a long period of production practice. This mostly occurred before modern times. The other is the use of biotechnology, such as hybridization and updated genetic modification methods. These new technologies became available mainly after World War II, although there was some progress before the War. These mainly existed in developed countries and were not introduced to China on a large scale. Second, the yield can be increased by applying more fertilizers, watering, etc. Traditional farm manure is a biofertilizer and is generally relatively stable. Later, chemical fertilizers were invented, which not only replaced farm manure to some extent but also increased the yield. However, the use of chemical fertilizers requires progress in the chemical industry. As chemical fertilizer industry was basically nonexistent in China before 1949, it was impossible to increase yield by applying chemical fertilizers. Third is good weather for the crops. In addition to the fertility of land, agriculture relies heavily on the weather. In the event of a serious natural disaster, there will be a drop in crop yield, and farmers' income will decrease. In severe cases, there will be a crop failure. This is the biggest weakness of agriculture and basically cannot be solved.

Table 2.9 shows the quantity of livestock and poultry in China's hinterland in the 1930s and 1940s. In terms of livestock, large livestock are capital equipment as far as agriculture is concerned and are usually counted as capital stock because they are used as means of production. At a time when there were fewer means of production and no modern agricultural machinery, large livestock were the principal means of production. They play an important role even today. In a country that has not achieved agricultural mechanization, large livestock is an irreplaceable agricultural equipment. Except in countries with few people and a vast land, agricultural mechanization is usually only possible after the agricultural surplus labor is transferred to urban sectors, which was impossible in China before 1949. Agricultural mechanization has not been fully realized even in today's China.

On the whole, the number of domestic animals of all types decreased, and only the number of cattle increased in the early 1930s but then began to decline. We believe that this is likely to be associated with Japan's all-out invasion of China because the invasion began in the north, while the use of cattle for farming is mainly the mode of production in the south. As the Japanese invasion spread southward, the south was affected. In the case of poultry, there was across-the-board reduction,

*Table 2.9* Quantity of livestock and poultry in China's hinterland, Units: million heads, million pieces

| Year | Cattle | Horse | Mule | Donkey | Pig | Sheep | Goat | Chicken | Duck | Goose |
|------|--------|-------|------|--------|------|-------|------|---------|------|-------|
| 1930 | 32.1 | 4.4 | 3.5 | 9.2 | 68.9 | 40.5 | 18.4 | 303.7 | 56.1 | 12.9 |
| 1935 | 42.6 | 4.6 | 5.4 | 11.4 | 63.9 | 32.8 | 15.8 | 241.4 | 45.6 | 9.3 |
| 1940 | 33.4 | 3.5 | 3.2 | 8.4 | 51.4 | 22.1 | 9.2 | 191.3 | 38.0 | 6.3 |
| 1947 | 31.8 | 2.7 | 2.0 | 8.6 | 51.7 | 24.2 | 9.2 | 184.6 | 33.4 | 6.0 |

*Note:* Due to space limitations, figures for all the years from 1930 to 1947 are not shown here.

*Data source:* Ryoshin Minami and Makino Fumio (2014), p. 375.

*Changes in agriculture* 37

with no exception. We think this may be related to feed because food production stagnated but the population increased. Food that could have been used as feed was consumed by people, and as a result, poultry quantity was reduced.

### 2.4.2 Northeast China

As mentioned, Japan occupied Northeast China after the September 18 Incident in 1931. The following year, Japanese invaders assisted Puyi, the last emperor of the Qing Dynasty, in establishing the puppet state of Manchukuo, although it was not recognized by any other country. Nevertheless, Japan occupied Northeast China as a colony by dint of its military strength. In this way, Northeast China was actually controlled by Japan until the defeat of Japan in 1945, and various statistics were also compiled separately. Therefore, the study of this period has to be divided into two parts: China's hinterland and Northeast China.

Table 2.10 shows the actual production volume and value added of the primary sector in Northeast China. In terms of agriculture, there is a horizontal movement accompanied by a slight increase, indicating that agriculture developed to a certain extent during this period. This growth may be the result of territorial expansion or productivity gains. According to statistics, the planting area of almost all major crops expanded somewhat during this period. Another possibility is that the yield was increased as a result of technological advances or more efficient production, which is not verified by sufficient data. In terms of forestry, it shows a clear upward trend, indicating that forestry in Northeast China developed rapidly during this period. As we know, the northeast region is rich in forest resources, and one of the purposes of Japan's occupation of Northeast China was to plunder resources. Therefore, the rapid growth of the forestry industry in this period can be expected. The aquaculture industry saw a rise and then a decline, but slightly, and the reasons are unclear. On the whole, the changes in the production volume and value added of the primary sector showed a slight, steady increase, which contrasted with horizontal movement with a slight decline in the hinterland.

*Table 2.10* Actual production volume and value added of the primary sector in Northeast China, Unit: million Manchukuo yuan

| Year | Agriculture | | Forestry | | Aquaculture | | Total | |
|---|---|---|---|---|---|---|---|---|
| | Production value | Value added | Production value | Value added | Production value | Value added | Production value | Value added |
| 1932 | 1,243.3 | 1,104.8 | 17.0 | 14.0 | 7.6 | 6.3 | 1,268.0 | 1,125.1 |
| 1938 | 1,379.4 | 1,232.6 | 62.2 | 51.0 | 19.2 | 16.2 | 1,460.7 | 1,299.8 |
| 1944 | 1,330.9 | 1,183.7 | 93.7 | 76.8 | 14.7 | 12.3 | 1,439.2 | 1,272.9 |

*Note:* Manchukuo yuan at 1935 prices. Due to space limitations, figures for all the years from 1932 to 1944 are not shown here.

*Data source:* Ryoshin Minami and Makino Fumio (2014), p. 488.

## 38 Processes and characteristics

Table 2.11 shows the yield and per unit yield of agricultural products in the northeast region. In terms of the yield, it declined for some produce, such as upland rice; it rose for some, such as rice and maize; it rose first and then fell for others, such as soybeans, other beans, peanuts, wheat, and coarse cereals; it basically remained flat for still others, such as sorghum and millet with a slight increase. In terms of the per unit yield, it generally declined but rose for only a few agricultural products, such as rice. This shows that agricultural production in the northeast region did not have higher productivity during this period and that the increase in some agricultural products was more the result of expanded cultivated land. In this sense, agriculture in Northeast China during this period realized extensive development. In other words, the increase in the yield of some agricultural products was achieved by means of a vast territory with a sparse population and the increase in population.

Table 2.12 shows the real capital stock of Northeast China, including large livestock and agricultural machinery and implements. Compared with the hinterland, agricultural machinery and implements, as well as large livestock, are included here. The quantity of large livestock declined in the early 1930s, quickly rebounded, and eventually increased slightly, in contrast to the hinterland. Agricultural machinery and implements were divided into large trucks, local large agricultural tools, and imported agricultural machinery. The number of both large trucks and large local agricultural tools increased to a certain extent, indicating that the use of capital for agricultural production in Northeast China increased during this period. Of course, it refers to the total number, not the per capita indicator, and the population of Northeast China in this period also increased, even significantly faster than that of the hinterland.[8] Compared with local trucks and large agricultural implements, the quantity of imported agricultural machinery increased even faster. In particular, it started from scratch in the early 1930s and increased to a high level in a short time. It began to decline after hitting a high in 1941, which should be related to the Pacific War launched by Japan, because these agricultural machinery and implements were supposed to be used by Japanese migrants to Northeast China, and the war led to a decline in the number of these people. On the whole, the number of capital stock in the northeast rose slowly, in stark contrast to that in the hinterland. As a Japanese colony, the puppet state of Manchukuo developed in many ways in terms of agriculture, including population and planting area, as well as agricultural production equipment.

### 2.4.3 Comparison of the hinterland and Northeast China

Based on the preceding observation, we have a basic idea of the development and changes in agriculture in China's hinterland and Northeast China in the 1930s–40s. Strictly speaking, there was no real development in agriculture during this period, and therefore it should not be called development, but some changes are also real, e.g., the introduction of new agricultural machinery in Northeast China. This indicates progress in agricultural production, although these agricultural machinery and implements were used by a small number of people.[9] The hinterland also saw

*Table 2.11* Yield and per unit yield of major agricultural products in Northeast China

| Year | Soybeans | Other beans | Sorghum | Millet | Maize | Wheat | Rice | Upland rice | Coarse cereals | Peanuts |
|------|----------|-------------|---------|--------|-------|-------|------|-------------|----------------|---------|
| **Yield (1,000 metric tons)** | | | | | | | | | | |
| 1924 | 3,472 | 313 | 4,360 | 2,672 | 1,503 | 907 | 122 | 97 | 1,459 | 31 |
| 1929 | 4,869 | 386 | 4,707 | 3,371 | 1,731 | 1,303 | 139 | 157 | 1,830 | 71 |
| 1934 | 3,510 | 338 | 3,873 | 2,504 | 1,700 | 659 | 207 | 127 | 1,338 | 111 |
| 1939 | 3,952 | 383 | 4,929 | 3,621 | 2,451 | 899 | 752 | 103 | 1,346 | 114 |
| 1944 | 3,503 | 229 | 5626 | 4,001 | 4,212 | 340 | 701 | 36 | 1,173 | 43 |
| **Unit yield: kg/ha** | | | | | | | | | | |
| 1924 | 1,376.1 | 1,194.7 | 1,667.3 | 1,450.6 | 1,540.0 | 940.9 | 1,718.3 | 1,114.9 | 1,366.1 | 1,527.1 |
| 1929 | 1,258.8 | 1,046.1 | 1,585.9 | 1,485.7 | 1,745.0 | 1,013.2 | 1,805.2 | 1,427.3 | 1,339.7 | 2,164.6 |
| 1934 | 1,020.6 | 759.6 | 1,209.9 | 891.4 | 1,325.0 | 773.5 | 1,934.6 | 1,233.0 | 808.0 | 1,761.9 |
| 1939 | 935.6 | 704.0 | 1,246.3 | 992.3 | 1,251.8 | 654.3 | 2,523.5 | 953.7 | 782.1 | 1373.5 |
| 1944 | 1,028.2 | 698.2 | 1,236.8 | 999.3 | 1,286.5 | 643.9 | 2,130.7 | 857.1 | 667.6 | 1,343.8 |

*Note:* Due to space limitations, figures for all the years from 1932 to 1944 are not shown here.

*Data source:* Calculated based on Ryoshin Minami and Makino Fumio (2014), pp. 483–484.

## 40  *Processes and characteristics*

*Table 2.12* Actual capital stock for agriculture in Northeast China, Unit: 10,000 Manchukuo yuan

| Year | Large livestock | Agricultural machinery and implements | | | Total |
|---|---|---|---|---|---|
| | | Large trucks | Local large agricultural implements | Imported agricultural machinery | |
| 1932 | 311,436 | 10,831.0 | 10,319.6 | 1.9 | 52,296.1 |
| 1936 | 228,616 | 11,738.0 | 11,586.0 | 153.3 | 46,338.9 |
| 1940 | 258,359 | 13,845.7 | 13,500.7 | 433.6 | 5,3616.0 |
| 1944 | 263,508 | 14,421.8 | 14,161.4 | 344.1 | 55,278.1 |

*Note:* Due to space limitations, figures for all the years from 1932 to 1944 are not shown here. Manchukuo yuan at 1935 prices. Large livestock include cattle, horses, mules, and donkeys.

*Data source:* Ryoshin Minami and Makino Fumio (2014), p. 488.

an increase in livestock per hundred people, per capita production value, and per capita value added, despite a downward trend after 1937 (Table 2.13). In other words, agriculture developed somewhat in the hinterland before 1937, but this progress was reversed as a result of Japan's all-round invasion of China.

The situation in the northeast region is complicated. On the whole, the per capita capital stock declined, and the per capita large livestock also decreased, but the number of per capita local large agricultural implements remained basically flat, while there was rapid increase in the per capita imported large agricultural machinery. However, per capita production value and per capita value added declined, which we believe was mainly caused by the rapid population increase.

Figure 2.2 shows the changes in agricultural production in China's hinterland in the 1930sand 1940s. The number of livestock per hundred people and the per capita value added are used here as variables, and it is the approximate production function. In other words, theoretically, as the per capita capital stock increases, the per capita output will also increase. The number of livestock per hundred people here is equivalent to the capital stock because large livestock in the field of agricultural production are equivalent to agricultural machinery and can be used for a long time. At a time when there is no agriculture mechanization, large livestock plays a crucial role in agricultural production because it is more productive than agricultural laborers. The curve in the figure shows a rise and then a decline, indicating that there was some progress before 1936, but then it took a step backward, in a sense heading back to where it had been. We believe that this "quirky" change was primarily caused by the Japanese invasion of China, which is highly similar to the situation of industry during this period.[10] China's economy saw a rare momentum of development from the beginning of the Republic of China period to 1936, particularly the introduction of many emerging industries in some cities in the industry sector or new developments in traditional industries, such as the introduction of mechanized modes of production. Although industrial development as a whole

*Table 2.13* Agricultural per capita capital stock, per capita production value, and per capita value added, Units: yuan, head

| Year | Hinterland | | | Northeast China | | | | | |
|---|---|---|---|---|---|---|---|---|---|
| | Number of livestock per hundred people (head) | Per capita production value (yuan) | Per capita value added (yuan) | Total per capita capital stock (yuan) | Per capita large livestock (yuan) | Per capita local large agricultural implements (yuan) | Per capita imported large agricultural machinery (yuan) | Per capita production value (yuan) | Per capita value added (yuan) |
| 1931 | 23.06 | 59.12 | 51.43 | | | | | | |
| 1932 | 23.55 | 62.97 | 55.21 | 45.55 | 27.13 | 8.99 | 1.65 | 110.44 | 98.00 |
| 1933 | 25.01 | 63.38 | 55.36 | 39.26 | 21.70 | 8.59 | 4.52 | 107.00 | 95.67 |
| 1934 | 25.99 | 57.83 | 49.46 | 33.32 | 17.69 | 7.68 | 16.00 | 81.32 | 72.20 |
| 1935 | 28.58 | 61.93 | 53.58 | 32.29 | 16.05 | 7.97 | 58.85 | 90.76 | 81.96 |
| 1936 | 30.17 | 63.27 | 55.03 | 32.02 | 15.80 | 8.01 | 105.94 | 91.99 | 82.02 |
| 1937 | 29.66 | 58.82 | 50.86 | 31.68 | 15.51 | 7.93 | 198.57 | 93.12 | 82.84 |
| 1938 | 28.49 | 60.38 | 52.97 | 32.18 | 15.43 | 8.18 | 213.99 | 93.98 | 83.63 |
| 1939 | 23.84 | 57.84 | 50.42 | 32.62 | 15.59 | 8.27 | 247.32 | 87.64 | 77.01 |
| 1940 | 24.65 | 56.18 | 48.85 | 32.72 | 15.77 | 8.24 | 264.63 | 86.23 | 75.01 |
| 1941 | 23.37 | 54.66 | 47.55 | 32.82 | 15.69 | 8.33 | 286.59 | 87.02 | 76.03 |
| 1942 | 22.58 | 53.25 | 46.37 | 31.58 | 15.04 | 8.07 | 248.56 | 78.17 | 67.83 |
| 1943 | 22.06 | 54.99 | 48.11 | | | | | | |
| 1944 | 21.22 | 58.49 | 51.65 | | | | | | |

*Note:* Large livestock include cattle, horses, mules, and donkeys. There are data only on quantity but not on value for the hinterland; there are data only on value but not on quantity for the northeast region. The legal tender is used for the value in the hinterland and Manchukuo yuan for the northeast region.

*Data source:* Ryoshin Minami and Makino Fumio (2014), pp. 362, 375, 481, 488.

42  Processes and characteristics

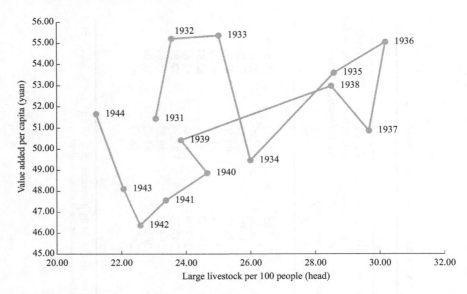

*Figure 2.2* Relationship between large livestock per 100 people and per capita value added in agriculture in mainland China

Data source: Calculated based on Ryoshin Minami and Makino Fumio (2014), pp. 375, 377.

suffered setbacks or there was no obvious growth, these new developments are a fact, which show signs of economic development. Similarly, agriculture developed to a certain extent before 1936 but took a step backward due to the Japanese invasion of China.

Next, the theory of production function is used to explain the changes in agriculture in the northeast region. Figure 2.3 shows two isoquant curves representing traditional and modern methods. In other words, agriculture in the Northeast in the 1930s can be divided into two sectors. One is the sector in which the Chinese people carried out production according to the traditional mode of production. The other is the sector in which the people represented by Japanese migrants conducted production using modern agricultural machinery. The two sectors were different from the outset. The traditional sector featured agricultural labor, which is a labor-intensive mode of production, as shown on the right side of the figure. The modern sector made greater use of agricultural machinery, which is characterized by being capital-intensive, as shown on the left side of the figure. Since their capital/labor ratios are different, they differ in productivity. In the 1930s, there was no obvious improvement in the mode of production in the traditional sector. Due to the massive increase in population, the agricultural labor force increased rapidly, which reduced per capita yield, as manifested in the movement from point A to point C in the figure. This situation is interesting because it rarely happens. This phenomenon is called "capital shallowing", meaning the use of people to replace capital, even though the population growth caused by immigration was not intended to replace

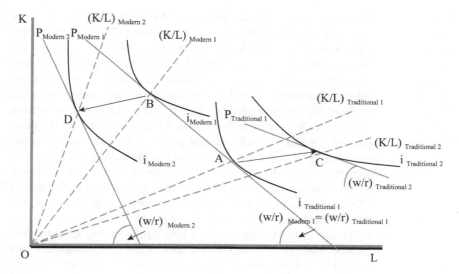

*Figure 2.3* Dual structure of agriculture in Northeast China in the 1930s

capital in the Northeast at that time. Nevertheless, this is the case in principle and is a fact. The opposite applies in the modern sector. Its capital/labor ratio increased significantly due to the greater use of modern agricultural machinery, resulting in an increase in productivity, as manifested in the movement from point B to point D in the figure. It means that this sector achieved technological progress to a certain extent and that it was capital-biased progress. It is noteworthy that this change in agriculture in the northeast region differed from that in industry. There are also two sectors in terms of industry: factories operated by the Chinese people and factories operated by the Japanese people. Although factories operated by the Chinese people were inferior to those operated by the Japanese people, they achieved progress to a certain degree.[11]

## 2.5 Conclusion

The development of China's agriculture was plagued by a host of disasters and difficulties. Before 1949, agricultural development was restricted or even stagnated, and farmers lived at the mercy of the weather due to the inherent problems of China (such as the small-scale peasant economy) and social turmoil, as well as slow industrialization, the failure to start modern economic growth, etc.

This observation shows that the reasons for the slow or even stagnant development of agriculture in modern China are legion and that factors such as institutions, government, society, economy, wars, and turmoil had a great impact. In terms of institutions, China was still under imperial rule in the second half of the 19th century, and it was difficult to achieve modern economic growth at the time. On the political front, it was politically unstable in the second half of the 19th century and the first

## 44   *Processes and characteristics*

half of the 20th century. Even after the successful Xinhai Revolution, the basic conditions for economic development were lacking because China was first ruled by the Beiyang government and later by the Chiang Kai-shek regime. In terms of society, some new thoughts and ideas were introduced from the West, but this only took place in some cities and coastal areas, and only a few intellectuals benefited. Society as a whole was not impacted, and the traditional backward habits persisted. On the economic front, the resource plunder made by the invaders and reparations for war deprived China of its economic foundation for development. On the other hand, low productivity, a lack of technological progress, coupled with frequent natural disasters, seriously impeded the development of agriculture in China.

Based on different perspectives and observations, scholars have drawn different conclusions from the study of the basic features of rural economy or agriculture in modern China. These views roughly fall into three categories: theory of recession, theory of growth, and theory of development. Those who hold the theory of recession are mainly Marxist scholars, who studied China's rural society from the perspective of semicolonial and semifeudal Chinese society and concluded that China was a society that had been descending. From the September 18 Incident to Japan's all-round invasion of China, half of China fell into enemy hands after the July 7 Incident, and there was no peace in China. Even if China made some progress in certain areas of the economy, such as the commodity economy and cottage craft industry, the incomplete development in specific periods under specific circumstances only reflected the deepening semicolonization, and it was bound to rapidly become bankrupt or semibankrupt. Those who hold the theory of growth argue that China's rural areas in modern times were in the transitional stage of modernization, that the rural economy indeed grew somewhat in some areas, but that this kind of economic growth was restricted by the shackles of the old system and fell into the equilibrium trap. External impact was needed to break the equilibrium and promote real economic development. This view is represented by the question of "the involution of the small-scale peasant economy" raised by Huang Zongzhi.[12] In short, the believers of the growth theory argue that China's rural economy in modern times "grew but did not develop". More scholars note that modern China started the process of modernization, although it ended up in failure. In this process, China's rural economy in modern times developed to a certain extent, and this is the theory of development. Wu Chengming, Ci Hongfei, Zhang Li, et al. hold this view,[13] and we quite agree with it.

### Notes

1  Of course, agriculture made a positive contribution in the early days of industrialization, including providing labor, food, capital, and markets for industrial and urban development and exporting agricultural products to earn foreign exchange. However, this role will diminish as industrialization progresses. See Guan Quan (2014).

2  This situation is often considered to be the so-called Malthusian trap. Societies in premodern times or before the start of modern economic growth can be considered to be basically in this situation.

3  Yuan Shuyi and Dong Conglin (2001), pp. 150–159.

*Changes in agriculture* 45

4 Liu Foding et al. (1999), pp. 121–122.
5 Regarding agricultural data, there is a lack of data on provinces mainly in the southwest region, such as Sichuan, Guangdong, Guangxi, Yunnan, as well as Rehe and Suiyuan.
6 For the issue and flaws of the data as well as ways of improvement, see Guan Quan (2011, 2018).
7 There is much literature on the evolution of the silk reeling industry and silk reeling technology in modern China and Japan, such as Kiyokawa Yukihiko (1995, 2009).
8 The population of the northeast had been increasing in the first half of the 20th century, from 17.184 million in 1907 to 23.158 million in 1920, to 30.289 million in 1930, and to 51.697 million in 1944. See Ryoshin Minami and Makino Fumioed (2014), p. 478.
9 In our view, such agricultural machinery was mainly used by Japanese immigrants and farmers associated with them.
10 For the development and changes in China's industry during this period, see Guan Quan (2018).
11 For industrial development and progress in the northeast region, see the relevant section of this book and Guan Quan (2018).
12 It refers to the phenomenon of increasing the total output at the cost of diminishing marginal returns per working day.
13 See Sheng Bangyue (2008), pp. 43–47.

# 3 Development of industry: part 1

## 3.1 Introduction

In a word, the development of China's industry before 1949 can be summarized as local development and overall stagnation.[1] When China was forced open by the Western powers in 1840, whether they wanted it or not, Chinese people realized the strength of the West in various forms and began to learn from them. This process has three climaxes. The first is the Self-Strengthening Movement in the late Qing Dynasty. Some military industry, heavy industry, and mining industry were introduced by those represented by the Self-Strengthening Movement. The second is the Republic of China period, which was mainly reflected in the development of the private sector of the economy. Modern textiles, flour, silk reeling, matchsticks, papermaking, pharmaceutical, and other light industries developed rapidly, and resource-based industries including mining also developed mainly through bureaucratic capital. Some describe this period (1912–1937) as the golden age of the bourgeoisie.[2] The third is the Japanese invasion and occupation of Northeast China. Through the establishment of puppet state of Manchukuo and colonial rule, the Japanese people developed and built mines and factories, and progress was made in transport and infrastructure. Although this process was forced by Japan to assert its rule, it objectively laid the groundwork somewhat for resource exploitation and industrial development in Northeast China.

Despite the aforesaid process of industrial development and learning as well as some achievements made, industrialization was not greatly deepened as a whole, and the all-round development of the economy was lacking. On the one hand, it was attributed to China's weak economic foundation and unstable political and social environment. On the other hand, the aggression of the great powers, especially the Japanese invasion, disrupted China's economic development and even resulted in stagnation and regression. China's economy could have taken off earlier if it had not been for Japanese Aggression.[3]

Industrial development in the Republic of China period is studied here. Because of the wide-ranging content, discussions are dealt with in two chapters. This chapter mainly conducts discussion in chronological order by region. In terms of chronological order, it covers the 1910s, 1930s, and 1940s. In terms of region, it covers the whole country and regions, depending on the data.

DOI: 10.4324/9781003410386-5

*Development of industry: part 1* 47

## 3.2 Industry in the 1910s

The only statistical data on the industrial development in this period is the *Agricultural and Commercial Statistics Table*, which states the industrial development in the decade or so from 1912 to 1921.[4] However, because of the complex national conditions and turmoil at that time, this statistical data seem to be rough and incomplete and are even replete with errors. As a result, the data have been regarded as rarely usable. We treated them appropriately so that they roughly reflect the situation in this period.[5] Table 3.1 gives an overview of industrial development during this period, including labor productivity, average scale, and growth rate. The following can be observed from the table. First, judging from labor productivity and average scale on the left, the average number of employees per household is very small but with a slight increase. Real labor productivity also increased slightly as a result of the significant increase in the number of employees during this period but a little increase in production value. Judging from the growth rate on the right, the number of manufacturing households, the number of employees, and the actual production value all had a high growth rate (5 to 7 percent), which can be called high-speed growth.

It is necessary to briefly discuss whether China's handicraft industry developed or reversed during this period. This issue is rarely studied, and it is not possible to draw a final conclusion. Wu Chengming et al. believe that China's handicraft industry developed considerably from the Opium War to around 1920 but then gradually declined. However, from the perspective of data on handicraft exports, it peaked from 1930 to 1931.[6] Recent studies conclude that the year 1912 was the

*Table 3.1* Overview of industry from 1912 to 1921

| Year | Labor productivity and average scale | | Period | Growth rate (%) | | |
|---|---|---|---|---|---|---|
| | Actual per capita production value (100 yuan) | Average number of employees per household (person) | | Number of manufacturers | Number of employees | Actual production value |
| 1912 | 5.19 | 3.87 | 1912–1913 | 7.92 | 4.94 | 4.94 |
| 1913 | 5.24 | 3.76 | 1913–1914 | 10.33 | 15.23 | 15.23 |
| 1914 | 4.51 | 3.93 | 1914–1915 | 7.57 | 6.52 | 6.52 |
| 1915 | 4.17 | 3.89 | 1915–1916 | −0.20 | 4.49 | 4.49 |
| 1916 | 3.94 | 4.07 | 1916–1917 | 5.72 | 2.00 | 2.00 |
| 1917 | 3.68 | 3.93 | 1917–1918 | 5.26 | 2.56 | 2.56 |
| 1918 | 3.53 | 3.83 | 1918–1919 | 7.47 | 8.58 | 8.58 |
| 1919 | 3.28 | 3.87 | 1919–1920 | 0.97 | 9.93 | 9.93 |
| 1920 | 2.94 | 4.21 | 1920–1921 | 2.69 | 3.64 | 3.64 |
| 1921 | 3.11 | 4.25 | 1912–1921 | 5.30 | 6.43 | 6.43 |

*Note:* The actual value of production is adjusted by the Tianjin Industrial Goods Price Index.

*Data source:* Guan Quan (2011).

## 48 Processes and characteristics

best period for the development of handicraft sector, but at least according to our data, it grew steadily and smoothly during the period from 1912 to 1921.

In addition to the data on cottage industry (handicrafts), the *Agricultural and Commercial Statistics Table* specifically investigated factories with more than 7 people. However, it only contains data on the number of factories, the number of employees, the number of prime movers and horsepower, wages, average working hours, coal consumption, as well as the number of factories by size and the number of factories by year of establishment. Factory production value is also included in the total figures. As there are no separate data on factory production value or on cost (such as price of raw materials), it is impossible to conduct a more detailed analysis. Only a brief introduction to the basic situation and simple discussions are made here. Since the data for years after 1916 are questionable, only the situation for the years from 1912 to 1915 is described here.

Table 3.2 shows the basic situation of factories from 1912 to 1915 (number of factories, number of prime movers and horsepower, and number of employees).

*Table 3.2* Overview of factories from 1912 to 1915

| Year | Number of factories | | | |
| --- | --- | --- | --- | --- |
| | Use of prime movers | No prime movers | Total | Proportion of factories using prime movers (%) |
| 1912 | 363 | 20,386 | 20,749 | 1.75 |
| 1913 | 347 | 21,366 | 21,713 | 1.60 |
| 1914 | 360 | 19,992 | 20,352 | 1.77 |
| 1915 | 478 | 18,843 | 19,321 | 2.47 |
| Year | Horsepower of prime mover | | | |
| | Steam engine (horsepower) | Electric motor (horsepower) | Total (horsepower) | Ratio of electric motors (%) |
| 1912 | 20,351 | 2,853 | 23,204 | 12.29 |
| 1913 | 43,448 | 20,198 | 63,646 | 31.74 |
| 1914 | 55,120 | 12,153 | 67,273 | 18.07 |
| 1915 | 53,311 | 13,067 | 66,398 | 19.68 |
| Year | Number of employees | | | |
| | Male workers (person) | Female workers (person) | Total (person) | Proportion of female workers (%) |
| 1912 | 421,994 | 239,790 | 661,784 | 36.23 |
| 1913 | 418,304 | 212,586 | 630,890 | 33.70 |
| 1914 | 391,126 | 233,398 | 624,524 | 37.37 |
| 1915 | 376,534 | 243,195 | 619,729 | 39.24 |

*Note:* "Other" is also included in the total horsepower of prime movers, which is not listed here.

*Data source:* Ministry of Industry and Commerce/Ministry of Agriculture and Commerce, *Agricultural and Commercial Statistics Table* (1st–4th editions).

*Development of industry: part 1*  49

The following can be observed. First, there was a total of about 20,000 factories, and there was no major change. Only 1 to 3 percent of factories used prime movers. In other words, factories at that time were basically manually operated or did not have much mechanical equipment. It shows that factories at that time were very backward but that the number of factories using prime movers increased slightly.[7] Second, the total number of prime movers increased somewhat. Specifically, the proportion of electric motors was tiny (except for 1913, which had about 15 percent), indicating that electric motors were not widely used during this period and that steam engines were still dominant.[8] Third, the number of employees was relatively stable, with no significant growth. An exception was the high proportion of female workers, possibly because factories at that time provided jobs considered suitable mostly for women, such as food and textiles. Fourth, the average number of factory employees is not listed, but it is easy to see that the number of people per factory was about 30, indicating that factories on average were not small in size. It also shows that factories at that time were labor-intensive.

When collecting the statistics related to industrial development during the Republic of China period, we found that there is almost no detailed data on the 1920s. The *Agricultural and Commercial Statistics Table* was last published in 1921, perhaps because of political instability, warlord dogfights, and social turmoil. In any case, data on this period are almost nonexistent. Fortunately, Du Xuncheng investigated the number of factories and the amount of capital for the years from 1912 to 1927. Although the data sources are diverse and the content is relatively simple, it is a somewhat of a supplement. The data show that the number of factories, the amount of capital, or the average amount of capital of factories in 1927 was almost the same as in 1912. However, these figures increased in some years. Development went relatively well from the later part of the early 20th century to the early 1920s, which is consistent with what is shown on the *Agricultural and Commercial Statistics Table*. In other words, it developed in the later part of the early 20th century.[9]

Table 3.3 shows the situation of factories by industry (number of factories and number of employees). In terms of industry distribution, of the more than 20,000 factories, the three industries of chemicals, weaving and dyeing, and food account for one-fourth each, accounting for three-quarters in total. Fabrics in the weaving and dyeing industry, ceramics, papermaking, and oil and wax making in the chemical industry, brewing in the food industry, and metals were the largest industries. The number of factories in these major industries exceeded 1,000, and even 3,000 for some industries. These were the main industries of this period. Very few of these industries really belong to modern industry. In particular, the machinery and appliance industry, a sign of modern industry, did not achieve sound development. The number of employees is slightly different, with nearly half of the more than 600,000 workers employed in the weaving and dyeing industry, followed by the food and chemical industries. In other words, the weaving and dyeing industry was more labor-intensive than the chemical and food industries, while the chemical industry was relatively labor-saving.

## 50  Processes and characteristics

*Table 3.3* Number of factories and number of employees by industry

| Industries | Number of factories | | | | Number of employees | | | |
|---|---|---|---|---|---|---|---|---|
| | 1912 | 1913 | 1914 | 1915 | 1912 | 1913 | 1914 | 1915 |
| Weaving and dyeing | 4,150 | 4,642 | 4,273 | 5,069 | 228,497 | 249,294 | 288,212 | 294,935 |
| Machinery and appliance | 2,393 | 2,524 | 2,182 | 1,643 | 33,267 | 36,697 | 37,515 | 25,183 |
| Chemicals | 7,567 | 6,030 | 6,909 | 6,373 | 154,621 | 94,745 | 118,066 | 113,115 |
| Food | 4,801 | 6,145 | 5,308 | 4,384 | 208,900 | 181,732 | 141,566 | 139,117 |
| Miscellaneous | 1,746 | 2,184 | 1,329 | 1,506 | 30,726 | 64,352 | 30,004 | 34,328 |
| Special factories | 92 | 158 | 350 | 346 | 5,773 | 4,040 | 9,161 | 13,051 |
| Total | 20,749 | 21,683 | 20,351 | 19,321 | 661,784 | 630,860 | 624,524 | 619,729 |

*Note:* Since no modification is made, some data are questionable from the order of realization. For the sake of space, only major industries are shown here. Special factories include electrical, gas, tap water, and metal refining factories. The metal refining industry was the largest, with 337 factories employing 12,490 people in 1915.

*Data source:* Ministry of Industry and Commerce/Ministry of Agriculture and Commerce, *Agricultural and Commercial Statistics Table* (1st–4th editions).

Next, the situation of textile factories is studied. Given the importance and special nature of textile factories, it was listed since the third edition of *Agricultural and Commercial Statistics Table*, and the data are relatively rich. In addition to the number of factories, the number of employees, the horsepower of prime movers, and coal consumption, it also contains data on the number of spindles, value of raw materials, and production value. The data quality in this area is slightly better than those of other types of factories because these factories were relatively large in size and few in number, and it was easy to conduct statistics. The number of factories increased slightly, particularly since 1918, but it was not remarkable as a whole. The horsepower of prime movers began to increase significantly in 1920, indicating a quantum leap in the use of motors in factories and the capital equipment. From the perspective of types, steam engines were dominant in the early stage, while the proportion of generators and other types of power was relatively small. This is also in line with technological advances at that time. However, key changes occurred in 1920, resulting in a significant increase in generators. If the data are accurate, electricity began to become the dominant driving force for textile factories. Except for a slight decrease in 1914, the number of spindles only increased slightly thereafter and did not increase significantly as prime movers did. The number of employees, except for a large increase in 1920, increased only slightly in other years, with fluctuations in the process. Both the value of raw materials and production value increased, but since such data take into account price changes, it is difficult to make a direct comparison. However, even irrespective of price factors, the value added (= production value – value of raw materials) of production value compared to raw materials in the same year is also very meager and was even negative in some years

(1918). Only 1914 (66.89 percent) was the year with a large proportion of value added, and the other years with a high value added were 1919 (33.44 percent) and 1918 (30.90 percent). According to these rough calculations, it can be judged that textile factories in this period as a whole made progress somewhat, but no substantial development was made. However, it was not easy to achieve such a scale in the early Republic of China period, a turbulent and chaotic period.

Figure 3.1 shows the approximate production function of textile factories from 1916 to 1920, with the horizontal axis representing the number of spindles per capita and the vertical axis representing the production value per capita. It is an approximate production function because statistics for that period are incomplete. For example, as there are no data on the per capita capital stock, but only the number of spindles and the horsepower of prime movers, only one of them is used as a substitute. Because the spindle is used as the basic device unit in the textile industry, the number of spindles per capita is used here. Of course, because the data on the horsepower of prime movers are not as complete as the number of spindles, it is not adopted here. Although the statistics cover the value of raw materials and production value, there are many outliers in the difference between the two (value added). For example, the value of raw materials is larger than or very close to the production value. If it is normal, it can be said that the value added rate is low. However, the situation at that time is abnormal, and it is difficult to calculate a reasonable value added. As a result, the per capita production value is used.

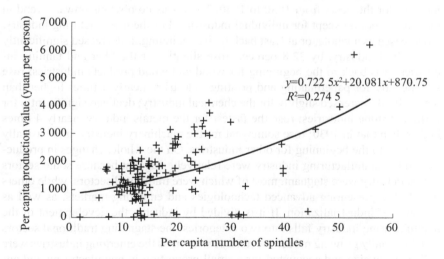

*Figure 3.1* Relationship between the number of spindles per capita and per capita production value from 1916 to 1920

*Note:* Data shown here cover the five years from 1916 to 1920, and the production value is influenced by the price factor. The production value for individual factories is replaced by the value of raw materials. Individual factories for which there are outliers were removed.

*Data source:* Ministry of Industry and Commerce/Ministry of Agriculture and Commerce, *Agricultural and Commercial Statistics Table* (5th–9th editions).

## 52 *Processes and characteristics*

According to the approximate production function curve in the figure, there is a one-to-one correspondence between the per capita capital stock and the per capita production value (approximate labor productivity). To put it another way, as per capita capital stock increases, per capita production value also increases markedly, which shows either the role of the market economy in resource allocation or the full utilization of resources. Furthermore, the textile industry has economies of scale. The larger the scale, the more the output generated by the same per capita capital, or higher labor productivity. This can be confirmed by the distribution of the two factories in the top right corner (upward).

### 3.3 Industry in the hinterland in the 1930s

As mentioned, there was a lack of complete statistics in the 1920s, but this improved since the 1930s. Although it left a lot to be desired, it can be used for preliminary observation and analysis. Of course, there is a problem: since Japan launched the September 18 Incident in 1931 to invade and occupy Northeast China, the hinterland and Northeast China were artificially separated, and their economic development and statistics were also separated. Statistics for the hinterland exclude the northeast region, the statistics of which was the responsibility of the Japanese rulers and the statistical department of the puppet state of Manchukuo. This will be discussed in the next section.

Table 3.4 shows the manufacturing production index, which was 100 in 1933 by industry for the years from 1930 to 1940. There was no obvious upward trend in the whole period except for individual industries. For the manufacturing industry, it decreased as a whole, or at least back to the beginning. It decreased significantly in the food industry, by 32.8 percent; rose slightly for the fiber and tanning industries; was back to the beginning for wood and wood products industries; rose significantly for papermaking and printing industries, nearly 4 times higher than that in 1930; increased slightly for the chemical industry; declined significantly for earth and stone industries; rose the fastest for the metals industry, nearly 4 times higher than that in 1930; rose somewhat for the machinery industry; and basically went back to the beginning for other industries. On the whole, changes in production in the manufacturing industry were relatively stagnant because some sectors in this industry were stagnant, most of which were traditional sectors, while others rose fast, representing advanced technologies and emerging markets, as well as the level of industrialization. If it is divided by industry, the development of the manufacturing industry falls into two categories: the stagnating traditional sectors and the rapidly growing modern sectors. However, as the emerging industries were still small in size and accounted for a small proportion in manufacturing and aggregate economic output, it did not represent overall development but rather was a development trend.

Table 3.5 shows the proportion of production value and value added of various sectors in the manufacturing industry from 1930 to 1940. Whether it be production value or value added, food and fiber occupied an absolute share. The food sector was the largest, followed by fiber. The two could sometimes account for nearly 90

*Table 3.4* Production index of various manufacturing sectors in the hinterland in the 1930s (1933 = 100)

| Year | Total | Food | Fiber and tanning | Wood and wood products | Papermaking and printing | Chemicals | Earth and stone | Metals | Machinery | Others |
|------|-------|------|-------------------|------------------------|--------------------------|-----------|-----------------|--------|-----------|--------|
| 1930 | 76.1 | 79.0 | 80.4 | 73.7 | 76.2 | 78.3 | 99.9 | 85.5 | 82.1 | 73.7 |
| 1931 | 92.5 | 91.9 | 92.5 | 105.1 | 100.1 | 93.2 | 99.7 | 73.2 | 87.8 | 105.1 |
| 1932 | 93.4 | 94.1 | 93.1 | 84.6 | 89.7 | 86.2 | 96.9 | 102.5 | 95.8 | 84.6 |
| 1933 | 100.0 | 100.0 | 100.0 | 100.0 | 100.0 | 100.0 | 100.0 | 100.0 | 100.0 | 100.0 |
| 1934 | 95.8 | 90.9 | 104.1 | 101.0 | 102.1 | 107.5 | 100.3 | 88.5 | 98.8 | 101.0 |
| 1935 | 95.1 | 89.7 | 104.2 | 91.5 | 102.2 | 108.7 | 116.4 | 93.4 | 101.2 | 91.5 |
| 1936 | 101.5 | 90.8 | 120.2 | 113.4 | 114.0 | 119.6 | 121.6 | 92.6 | 104.6 | 113.4 |
| 1937 | 73.6 | 69.1 | 75.0 | 109.6 | 123.1 | 72.3 | 72.9 | 111.7 | 97.1 | 109.6 |
| 1938 | 66.6 | 57.3 | 81.8 | 108.6 | 146.4 | 44.7 | 37.2 | 141.3 | 55.8 | 108.6 |
| 1939 | 97.2 | 88.2 | 112.4 | 68.1 | 238.6 | 68.0 | 51.7 | 346.8 | 96.6 | 68.1 |
| 1940 | 78.9 | 53.1 | 108.4 | 72.1 | 373.0 | 94.2 | 69.4 | 409.4 | 138.8 | 72.1 |

*Data source:* Ryoshin Minami and Makino Fumio (2014), p. 379.

## 54    *Processes and characteristics*

*Table 3.5* Proportion of production value and value added of the manufacturing industry in the hinterland in the 1930s

| Industries | Production value (million yuan) | | | Proportion of value added (%) | | |
|---|---|---|---|---|---|---|
| | 1930 | 1935 | 1940 | 1930 | 1935 | 1940 |
| Total | 7,809 | 9,790 | 7,981 | 100.00 | 100.00 | 100.00 |
| Food | 4,579 | 5,645 | 3,321 | 58.64 | 57.66 | 41.61 |
| Fiber and tanning | 2,352 | 3,034 | 3,038 | 30.12 | 30.99 | 38.07 |
| Wood and wood products | 135 | 168 | 132 | 1.73 | 1.72 | 1.65 |
| Papermaking and printing | 137 | 181 | 669 | 1.75 | 1.85 | 8.38 |
| Chemicals | 160 | 225 | 127 | 2.05 | 2.30 | 1.59 |
| Earth and stone | 124 | 145 | 87 | 1.59 | 1.48 | 1.09 |
| Metals | 33 | 36 | 158 | 0.42 | 0.37 | 1.98 |
| Machinery and hardware | 234 | 288 | 395 | 3.00 | 2.94 | 4.95 |
| Others | 55 | 68 | 54 | 0.70 | 0.69 | 0.68 |

*Note:* Based on 1933 prices.

*Data source:* Ryoshin Minami and Makino Fumio (2014), pp. 380–381.

percent, which shows the structure of China's industrial development at the time. This corresponds to the index shown in Table 3.4. Although some emerging industries such as metals and machinery grew rapidly, their share was very small and was not dominant in China's industry or even China's economy. Of course, there were some changes in the share of various sectors. In 1940, the production value of food and fiber and tanning accounted for 79.67 percent, which was a decline compared with nearly 90 percent in the preceding period. This shows that the share of other sectors increased and that these sectors were those emerging industries, which was encouraging. For example, the share rose from 0.42 to 1.98 percent for the metal sector, rose from 3.00 to 4.95 percent for machinery and hardware sector, and rose from 1.75 to 8.39 percent for the papermaking and printing sector, although the share is small. The value added also showed a similar trend of changes, with greater changes than those in production value.

A more specific study was conducted for the year 1933.[10] Table 3.6 shows the basic situation of this type of enterprises in 1933, including the number of factories, the amount of capital, horsepower, the number of employees, sales volume, and the value added. There was a total of 2,435 factories. There were 821 textile factories, which accounted for the largest proportion, followed by catering, machinery, and metals factories, all of which exceeded 300 respectively. The number of factories in the papermaking, printing, chemicals, clothing accessories, and earth and stone sectors exceeded 100. Judging from this, there were two kinds of industries with large factories in China at that time. One is traditional industries, such as catering, earth and stone, and clothing accessories. The other is modern industries, such as chemicals, machinery, metals, and textiles. In terms of the amount of capital, textiles had the largest share, accounting for more than 40 percent of the total, followed by catering, which accounted for about 17 percent. Others such as

*Table 3.6* Basic situation of factories

| Industries | Number of factories | Amount of capital (1,000 yuan) | Horsepower | Number of employees | Sales volume (1,000 yuan) | Value added (1,000 yuan) |
|---|---|---|---|---|---|---|
| Wood | 18 | 1,115.2 | 490.0 | 1,331 | 3,268.6 | 329.7 |
| Furniture | 12 | 419.5 | 33.5 | 2 002 | 1,519.6 | 846.7 |
| Smelting | 33 | 269.8 | 1,350.0 | 2,351 | 4,755.2 | 2,150.9 |
| Machinery and metals | 306 | 16,549.7 | 5,272.8 | 23,597 | 32,876.2 | 16,211.3 |
| Transport appliances | 55 | 19,004.4 | 8,534.4 | 16,973 | 22,352.2 | 10,203.7 |
| Earth and stone | 112 | 29,184.3 | 33,304.8 | 17,254 | 29,996.4 | 20,623.0 |
| Construction | 14 | 298.1 | 64.0 | 1,014 | 1,746.3 | 1,219.5 |
| Hydropower | 14 | 32,613.6 | 32,685.0 | 1,618 | 13,166.6 | 10,738.7 |
| Chemicals | 148 | 26,326.9 | 4,142.3 | 29,464 | 49,693.9 | 16,897.0 |
| Textile | 821 | 166,828.3 | 103,825.2 | 321,400 | 483,585.2 | 120,455.7 |
| Clothing accessories | 141 | 6,006.1 | 176.5 | 15,442 | 27,425.3 | 9,576.9 |
| Leather and rubber | 84 | 6,339.8 | 1,971.5 | 14,627 | 20,530.8 | 3,970.7 |
| Catering | 390 | 68,380.2 | 25,234.3 | 52,221 | 361,587.4 | 59676.5 |
| Papermaking and printing | 234 | 26,877.5 | 8,502.2 | 21,107 | 45,450.4 | 20,214.7 |
| Ornaments and instruments | 26 | 812.3 | 73.0 | 2,527 | 2,684.5 | 1,304.8 |
| Others | 27 | 2,426.0 | 419.0 | 2,397 | 3,335.8 | 2,321.7 |
| Total | 2435 | 403,451.67 | 226,078.52 | 525,325 | 1,103,974.31 | 296,741.58 |

*Data source: China Industrial Survey Report* (volume 2).

## 56 *Processes and characteristics*

hydropower, earth and stone, papermaking, printing, chemicals, transport appliances, machinery, and metals also had a relatively large share. The first two had a large production scale because of the huge market, with many factories and significant investment. The textile industry also needed a large investment. The latter few industries include machinery, metals, chemicals, and transport appliances, which rather belong to modern industries. These industries required much production equipment, most of which relied on imports at the time. Since these were imports, prices were very expensive. The horsepower of motors was the most prominent in textiles, accounting for about 46 percent of the total, with a higher share than the capital. It was far ahead of other industries, underscoring the importance of the textile industry in China at that time. The industries with a high share include earth and stone, hydropower, and catering. The first two require great power in the production process, while it was due to many factories for the latter.

In terms of the number of employees, textiles accounted for 61 percent of the total, showing that this industry needs many people as well as huge capital and is a neutral industry with two sides. Catering, chemicals, machinery and metals, papermaking and printing, and other industries also employed many people, although these industries were not comparable to the textile industry. The catering industry had many factories and employees, and other industries had many employees because of the large size of factories. In terms of sales volume, the textile industry accounted for 43 percent, and the catering industry accounted for 32 percent. These two industries accounted for a total of 75 percent, indicating that the market demand at that time was more for traditional food, clothing, shelter, and transportation. Especially for the former two (clothing and food), people tried to meet the essential needs as much as possible rather than seeking products with higher value added. The value added also exhibited this tendency. It was the highest in the textile industry, accounting for 44 percent of the total, followed by catering. It was much lower for other industries. This situation is similar to sales volume, showing the importance of these two market-dependent industries as well as the light-industry or labor-intensive nature of industry in China at the time. This is inevitable in a sense. In the early days of industrialization or economic development, it is usually the light industry that develops first. There is a shift to heavy industry after a certain accumulation has been realized.[11] The so-called accumulation here refers to the market, technology, capital, workers' experience in production, managers' management experience, etc., all of which are important for industrial development.

Table 3.7 shows indicators calculated based on Table 3.6. These represent the size of factories, the level of technology, productivity, capital intensity, and other concepts with economic significance. First, the average number of factory employees represents the size of a factory. The average was 216.77 employees, which is a sign of large enterprises.[12] Other surveys, including *China Industrial Survey Report* (volume 2), do not contain such an average. Although there were relatively small enterprises, the number of employees was 70 to 80. Large factories such as textile factories had about 400 employees, which show a large scale. Transport appliance factories were also relatively large in size. The average per capita capital was 770.82 yuan, but it was up to 20,000 yuan in the hydropower industry, far more

*Table 3.7* Characteristics of factories

| Industry | Average number of factory employees | Capital per capita (yuan/person) | Horsepower per 100 people | Per capita production value (yuan/person) | Labor productivity (yuan/person) | Labor distribution rate (%) | Proportion of male skilled workers (%) | Proportion of managers (%) |
|---|---|---|---|---|---|---|---|---|
| Wood | 73.94 | 837.85 | 36.81 | 2,455.75 | 247.73 | 82.22 | 8.52 | 6.01 |
| Furniture | 166.83 | 209.54 | 1.67 | 759.02 | 422.94 | 31.13 | 55.22 | 4.95 |
| Smelting | 71.24 | 114.74 | 57.42 | 2,022.61 | 914.89 | 22.49 | 13.01 | 5.57 |
| Machinery and metals | 77.11 | 701.35 | 22.35 | 1,393.23 | 687.01 | 26.52 | 32.04 | 7.85 |
| Transport appliances | 308.60 | 1 119.68 | 50.28 | 1,316.92 | 601.17 | 68.10 | 55.45 | 5.43 |
| Earth and stone | 154.05 | 1 691.45 | 193.03 | 1,738.52 | 1,195.26 | 18.94 | 31.08 | 5.18 |
| Construction | 72.43 | 294.00 | 6.31 | 1,722.21 | 1,202.67 | 14.46 | 20.35 | 6.02 |
| Hydropower | 115.57 | 20,156.75 | 2,020.09 | 8,137.58 | 6,637.04 | 9.23 | 33.38 | 12.24 |
| Chemicals | 199.08 | 893.53 | 14.06 | 1,686.60 | 573.48 | 23.18 | 13.04 | 5.92 |
| Textile | 391.47 | 519.07 | 32.30 | 1,504.62 | 374.78 | 38.31 | 41.54 | 3.96 |
| Clothing accessories | 109.52 | 388.94 | 1.14 | 1,776.02 | 620.18 | 34.37 | 28.76 | 1.11 |
| Leather and rubber | 174.13 | 433.43 | 13.48 | 1,403.62 | 271.46 | 83.75 | 13.84 | 0.77 |
| Catering | 133.90 | 1 309.44 | 48.32 | 6,924.18 | 1 142.77 | 16.07 | 36.20 | 6.54 |
| Papermaking and printing | 90.20 | 1,273.39 | 40.28 | 2,153.33 | 957.73 | 31.70 | 33.01 | 10.44 |
| Ornaments and instruments | 97.19 | 321.46 | 2.89 | 1,062.33 | 516.35 | 26.93 | 25.40 | 9.34 |
| Others | 88.78 | 1,012.10 | 17.48 | 1,391.67 | 968.57 | 14.18 | 7.29 | 10.39 |
| Average | 216.77 | 770.82 | 42.83 | 2,110.42 | 522.92 | 33.61 | 36.68 | 5.23 |

*Data source: China Industrial Survey Report* (volume 2).

## 58 *Processes and characteristics*

than that in other industries. It shows the capital-intensive nature of this industry, as well as economies of scale and external economy nature.[13] Other industries were relatively balanced, with a per capita capital ranging from more than 1,000 yuan to as low as a few hundred yuan. In terms of per capita horsepower, hydropower dwarfed other industries because this industry produces the power itself, and power production also needs power, whether it be thermal power or hydropower. From a modern viewpoint, electricity is actually included in the service sector, although it has a two-sided nature because of production and service. Power generation is a kind of production behavior, and power supply is a process of service. The gap between other industries is small.

Per capita production value and labor productivity (per capita value added) can be observed together. Both indicators were the highest in the hydropower industry, catering was close to hydropower in terms of per capita production value, and other industries were close to one another at a low level. Labor productivity was still the highest in hydropower, followed by construction, earth and stone, and catering. In terms of the labor distribution rate, the average was 33.61 percent, which is reasonable. It was high, more than 80 percent, in some industries. Generally speaking, the labor distribution rate is not very high in the early stage of economic development, and 33.01 percent is normal because there is surplus labor and wages are kept low. As industry further develops and the surplus labor force is employed by industry and services sectors, wages may rise, and the labor distribution rate may increase.[14] One of the features of this survey is the more detailed division of workers because it includes not only male and female workers but also staff and workers, as well as skilled workers and unskilled workers. This is very rare and valuable in industrial surveys conducted at that time. The ratio of male skilled workers to managers is listed here. The latter was relatively evenly distributed, mostly below 10 percent, and the average is about 5 percent. The average of the former is 36.68 percent, but there is a large gap between industries, ranging from more than 50 to less than 10 percent. This is obviously associated with the technology-intensive level of the industry. This technology is more manifested in the skills of laborers (workers). We can conclude that the higher the level is of modernization of an industry, the higher the proportion of skilled workers will be.

Figure 3.2 shows the relationship between the horsepower per 100 people and the per capita production value. The horsepower per 100 people is used as the proxy variable for the per capita capital stock. In other words, the horsepower of power is seen as a kind of capital stock. Although it is not shown in amount of money, nor is it the entire capital stock, machinery and equipment are indispensable for modern production, and every machine runs on power. Therefore, the horsepower is largely complementary to the size of machines and production efficiency.[15] The relationship shown here is very close. In brief, capital equipment as a whole corresponds to labor productivity because more machinery will lead to productivity gains. While this relationship is easy to identify in theory, it is not easy to obtain good results using cross-sectional data because there may be huge differences between industries. They do not belong to the same production function. Nevertheless, it is possible to keep a relatively close production function in the same period in the same

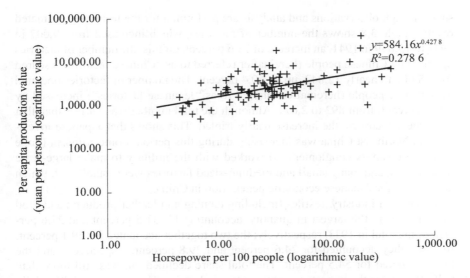

*Figure 3.2* Relationship between the horsepower per 100 people and the per capita production value in factories nationwide in 1933

Data source: *China Industrial Survey Report* (volume 2).

country despite differences between industries. For example, there is basically no large difference between traditional industries. There is not much technical difference between manual basket weaving and flour grinding, and they can basically be regarded as the same production function. In comparison, there may be large differences between modern industries. Steel, smelting, chemicals, etc. require much capital, while this is not necessarily the case in the machinery industry. In other words, division is possible for some industries, but it is not easy to divide other industries. The so-called segmentation means that production can be large-scale or small-scale. For steelworks, the larger the size, the more efficient it is. However, this is not necessarily the case for machinery factories.

### 3.4 Industry in the Northeast in the 1930s

In 1931, Japan launched the September 18 Incident and invaded and occupied the northeast region. In the following year, Puyi, the last emperor of the Qing Dynasty, was elected to power, and the puppet state of Manchukuo was founded. The northeast region was in the hands of the Japanese invaders for 14 years until Japan's surrender in 1945, and relevant statistical work was conducted separately. Based on the materials such as *Manchukuo Statistics of Factories*,[16] we estimated the overall situation at that time and obtained more complete data on various industries by the country of origin of the factory owners from 1933 to 1941. Due to space limitations, the following analysis is limited to industry classification. For the sake of space, owners in other countries are omitted here because figures for them are

## 60 Processes and characteristics

small. Rough observations and analysis are performed for the following estimated results. Table 3.8 shows the number of factories, which increased from 9,007 in 1933 to 15,639 in 1941, an increase of 73.6 percent. Of this, the number of factories operated by Chinese people (hereinafter referred to as "Chinese factories") soared from 8,006 to nearly 12,842, up by 60.4 percent. The number of factories operated by Japanese people (hereinafter referred to as "Japanese factories") increased by 199.4 percent, from 892 to 2,671. Although the total number was far less than that of Chinese factories, the increase nearly tripled. This shows that Japanese investment in Northeast China was increasing during this period. Some *zaibatsu* (large Japanese business conglomerates) worked with the military to make large-scale investments, and many small and medium-sized factories were established, which accelerated the Japanese economic penetration in China.

In terms of industry, textiles (including tanning and leather products) and food industries were the largest in quantity, accounting for 31.5 percent and 27.6 percent of the total in 1933, respectively; the two together accounted for 59.1 percent. In 1941, they accounted for 24.6 percent and 29.8 percent, respectively, and the two accounted for 54.5 percent. The total share declined but was still more than half, illustrating the importance of these two industries. They are essential for daily necessities, and therefore the demand was huge. Behind these two industries is machinery and appliances, which accounted for 11.8 percent of the total in 1933 and 13.7 percent in 1941. Other industries were similar, with no changes, slight increases, or slight declines for various industries.

Table 3.9 shows that the total number of employees in the manufacturing industry was 168,505 in 1933 but increased to 489,208 in 1941, up by 190.3 percent, more than the increase in the number of factories, indicating the expanding size of factories. Of this, the number of employees in Chinese factories jumped from 108,237 to 204,518, up by 88.9 percent. The number of employees in Japanese factories increased from 58,668 to 275,780, up by 370.1 percent. The growth rate of employees in Japanese factories far exceeded that of Chinese factories, indicating that the size of Japanese factories expanded faster. In terms of specific industries, textile accounted for 28.1 percent in 1933 and 20.9 percent in 1941, which was a sharp decline. The share of the food industry fell from 23.5 to 15.6 percent. The share of the combined textile and food industries fell from 51.6 to 36.5 percent, a larger reduction compared to the number of factories. This shows that the size of these two industries, especially food industry, did not expand and was even downsized. In other words, the share of factories did not decline much (it rose for the food industry), while the proportion of employees declined. It rose from 12.6 to 17.9 percent for the machinery industry. It rose from 1.7 to 6.6 percent for the metal industry, indicating the development speed and importance of this industry at that time. The proportion of employees rose from 15 to 20.7 percent for the kiln industry and rose from 6.8 to 6.9 percent for the chemicals industry. Overall, the rising share in the metals, kilns, and chemical industries means that these industries, which belong to the modern industry, grew rapidly, and exceeded traditional industries such as food and wood. In particular, a greater increase in the number of employees than the increase in the number of factories indicates that the scale of

Table 3.8 Number of factories

| Industry | Country of owner | 1933 | 1934 | 1935 | 1936 | 1937 | 1938 | 1939 | 1940 | 1941 |
|---|---|---|---|---|---|---|---|---|---|---|
| Total | Total | 9,007 | 8,120 | 6,861 | 8,418 | 9,384 | 10,350 | 12,247 | 13,927 | 15,639 |
| | Japan | 892 | 1,187 | 1,237 | 1,427 | 1,549 | 1,671 | 2,085 | 2,357 | 2,671 |
| | China | 8,006 | 6,857 | 5,572 | 6,917 | 7,747 | 8,576 | 10,056 | 11,453 | 12,842 |
| Textile | Total | 2,836 | 2,920 | 1,901 | 2,432 | 2,780 | 3,127 | 3,271 | 3,527 | 3,848 |
| | Japan | 101 | 144 | 125 | 150 | 177 | 203 | 277 | 336 | 404 |
| | China | 2,715 | 2,767 | 1,773 | 2,274 | 2,585 | 2,895 | 2,974 | 3,175 | 3,427 |
| Metals | Total | 193 | 199 | 216 | 275 | 320 | 364 | 370 | 365 | 382 |
| | Japan | 15 | 22 | 34 | 43 | 49 | 55 | 62 | 61 | 63 |
| | China | 178 | 175 | 181 | 231 | 268 | 305 | 307 | 302 | 317 |
| Machinery and appliances | Total | 1,063 | 1,161 | 1,122 | 1,373 | 1,388 | 1,403 | 1,688 | 1,913 | 2,142 |
| | Japan | 131 | 194 | 207 | 267 | 285 | 303 | 359 | 427 | 486 |
| | China | 928 | 953 | 909 | 1,094 | 1,090 | 1,086 | 1,303 | 1,462 | 1,633 |
| Kilns | Total | 652 | 602 | 481 | 652 | 694 | 735 | 1,042 | 1,364 | 1,691 |
| | Japan | 114 | 153 | 149 | 174 | 185 | 195 | 265 | 330 | 404 |
| | China | 535 | 444 | 331 | 477 | 509 | 540 | 776 | 1,032 | 1,284 |
| Chemicals | Total | 398 | 209 | 235 | 251 | 281 | 311 | 299 | 312 | 314 |
| | Japan | 62 | 79 | 80 | 81 | 88 | 95 | 131 | 137 | 143 |
| | China | 330 | 126 | 154 | 170 | 192 | 213 | 166 | 167 | 162 |
| Food | Total | 2,486 | 1,488 | 1,672 | 1,828 | 2,184 | 2,539 | 3,441 | 4,066 | 4,656 |
| | Japan | 268 | 320 | 366 | 400 | 441 | 481 | 578 | 635 | 718 |
| | China | 2,171 | 1,137 | 1,273 | 1,389 | 1,700 | 2,010 | 2,817 | 3,377 | 3,877 |
| Wood and wood products | Total | 651 | 691 | 585 | 722 | 823 | 924 | 1,036 | 1,180 | 1,325 |
| | Japan | 76 | 96 | 95 | 93 | 100 | 107 | 154 | 161 | 172 |
| | China | 572 | 594 | 488 | 626 | 721 | 816 | 881 | 1,016 | 1,150 |

(Continued)

*Table 3.8* (Continued)

| Industry | Country of owner | 1933 | 1934 | 1935 | 1936 | 1937 | 1938 | 1939 | 1940 | 1941 |
|---|---|---|---|---|---|---|---|---|---|---|
| Printing and binding | Total | 480 | 507 | 396 | 561 | 618 | 675 | 726 | 803 | 855 |
| | Japan | 95 | 126 | 125 | 164 | 178 | 192 | 209 | 212 | 218 |
| | China | 374 | 374 | 266 | 389 | 435 | 481 | 511 | 586 | 632 |
| Others | Total | 248 | 343 | 253 | 324 | 298 | 272 | 374 | 397 | 426 |
| | Japan | 30 | 53 | 56 | 55 | 48 | 40 | 50 | 58 | 63 |
| | China | 203 | 287 | 197 | 267 | 249 | 230 | 321 | 336 | 360 |

*Note:* Due to the omission of factory owners of other countries, the total number does not match the total of China and Japan.

*Sources: Manchukuo Statistics of Factories* over the years, *Kwantung Leased Territory Statistics of Factories.*

*Table 3.9* Number of employees

| Industry | Country of owner | 1933 | 1934 | 1935 | 1936 | 1937 | 1938 | 1939 | 1940 | 1941 |
|---|---|---|---|---|---|---|---|---|---|---|
| Total | Total | 168,505 | 189,788 | 176,743 | 225,478 | 281,130 | 336,781 | 439,783 | 451,892 | 489,208 |
| | Japan | 58,668 | 83,167 | 90,791 | 104,983 | 145,350 | 185,716 | 259,849 | 254,976 | 275,780 |
| | China | 108,237 | 102,923 | 80,882 | 114,754 | 130,924 | 147,094 | 173,809 | 189,456 | 204,518 |
| Textile | Total | 47,277 | 63,213 | 47,945 | 71,617 | 85,420 | 99,222 | 107,495 | 98,890 | 102,470 |
| | Japan | 9,919 | 14,447 | 14,873 | 21,382 | 26,025 | 30,668 | 42,586 | 38,478 | 45,319 |
| | China | 37,217 | 48,521 | 33,026 | 50,146 | 59,179 | 68,211 | 64,651 | 60,208 | 56,939 |
| Metals | Total | 2,937 | 4,779 | 8,995 | 10,587 | 16,494 | 22,401 | 32,902 | 29,190 | 32,045 |
| | Japan | 797 | 2180 | 6581 | 6945 | 12315 | 17685 | 25535 | 21728 | 24228 |
| | China | 2140 | 2546 | 2404 | 3632 | 4160 | 4688 | 7360 | 7448 | 7803 |
| Machinery and appliances | Total | 21,217 | 28,353 | 26,280 | 35,599 | 53,176 | 70,752 | 90,663 | 87,445 | 87,450 |
| | Japan | 12,468 | 18,876 | 17,550 | 24,171 | 40,335 | 56,498 | 72,443 | 64,014 | 58,898 |
| | China | 8,712 | 9,269 | 8,565 | 11,133 | 12,537 | 13,941 | 17,813 | 22,943 | 27,928 |
| Kilns | Total | 25,229 | 30,478 | 27,211 | 26,771 | 33,531 | 40,290 | 72,796 | 87,824 | 101,165 |
| | Japan | 14,235 | 20,198 | 20,880 | 16,654 | 22,358 | 28,061 | 48,741 | 56,193 | 63,232 |
| | China | 10,892 | 9,490 | 6,323 | 10,109 | 11,169 | 12,229 | 24,040 | 31,611 | 37,908 |
| Chemicals | Total | 11,408 | 10,408 | 13,313 | 14,835 | 18,187 | 21,539 | 28,964 | 30,005 | 33,768 |
| | Japan | 5,515 | 6,957 | 9,609 | 10,677 | 13,365 | 16,052 | 24,379 | 25,131 | 28,660 |
| | China | 5,755 | 3,330 | 3,699 | 4,158 | 4,814 | 5,469 | 4,574 | 4,801 | 4,998 |
| Food | Total | 39,675 | 25,355 | 32,810 | 37,075 | 39,699 | 42,323 | 57,656 | 66,547 | 76,087 |
| | Japan | 8,438 | 9,949 | 11,614 | 14,234 | 15,537 | 16,840 | 21,615 | 25,846 | 30,801 |
| | China | 30,420 | 14,221 | 16,427 | 17,920 | 20,228 | 22,536 | 31,348 | 34,815 | 38,138 |
| Wood and wood products | Total | 8,747 | 11,431 | 8,784 | 11,685 | 13,702 | 15,719 | 19,855 | 21,581 | 23,572 |
| | Japan | 3,253 | 4,110 | 4,196 | 3,929 | 5,451 | 6,972 | 9,295 | 8,664 | 8,313 |
| | China | 5,469 | 6,481 | 4,560 | 7,709 | 8,226 | 8,742 | 10,500 | 12,734 | 15,012 |

(*Continued*)

Table 3.9 (Continued)

64 Processes and characteristics

| Industry | Country of owner | 1933 | 1934 | 1935 | 1936 | 1937 | 1938 | 1939 | 1940 | 1941 |
|---|---|---|---|---|---|---|---|---|---|---|
| Printing and binding | Total | 9,169 | 10,159 | 8,294 | 12,453 | 15,020 | 17,587 | 20,237 | 22,893 | 25,330 |
| | Japan | 3,205 | 4,443 | 4,441 | 6,077 | 7,922 | 9,767 | 11,477 | 12,844 | 14,566 |
| | China | 5,755 | 5,605 | 3,814 | 6,215 | 6,865 | 7,514 | 8,391 | 9,700 | 10,415 |
| Others | Total | 2,846 | 5,612 | 3,111 | 4,856 | 5,902 | 6,948 | 9,215 | 7,517 | 7,321 |
| | Japan | 838 | 2,007 | 1,047 | 914 | 2,044 | 3,173 | 3,778 | 2,078 | 1,763 |
| | China | 1,877 | 3,460 | 2,064 | 3,732 | 3,748 | 3,764 | 5,132 | 5,196 | 5,377 |

*Note:* Due to the omission of factory owners of other countries, the total number does not match the total of China and Japan.

*Sources: Manchukuo Statistics of Factories* over the years, *Kwantung Leased Territory Statistics of Factories* over the years.

factories in these industries was large or expanding. A large scale means that the economies of scale effect is increasing.

Due to space limitations, the actual production value and actual value added are not shown here. Figure 3.3 shows the changes in actual production value and actual value added. In terms of the actual production value, it increased much faster in Japanese factories than in Chinese factories, although Chinese factories saw a remarkable increase from 1935, only to begin to decline since 1939. Japanese factories quickly grew nonstop. Regarding the value added, it was not as high as the production value in terms of absolute value, but the trend is similar. The value added of Japanese factories was not as high as the production value, especially after 1939, it saw a horizontal shift. Chinese factories generally did not grow as fast as Japanese factories, but they grew steadily, with a slight downward trend from about 1939 onward. According to these observations, both the production value and the value added grew faster in Japanese factories than in Chinese factories. However, Chinese factories also performed well, indicating that the industrial development as a whole in the northeast region during this period was good.

Figure 3.4 shows the index of actual production value and actual value added, that is, the production index. Since it is an index, it is easier to make comparisons because it focuses on the trend rather than the absolute value. It clearly shows that before 1937, the growth rates of the production value and the value added for both Chinese and Japanese factories were highly similar. After 1937, these began to decline in Chinese factories but kept rising in Japanese factories. Especially after 1939, the decline was more obvious in Chinese factories, while the production value of Japanese factories continued to rise, and the value added slowed down slightly.

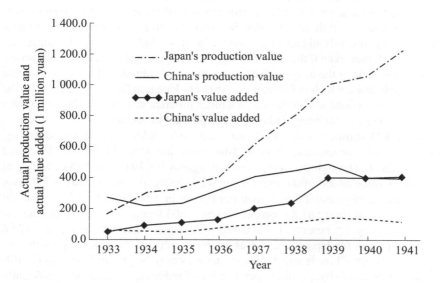

*Figure 3.3* Actual production value and actual value added by Chinese factories and Japanese factories

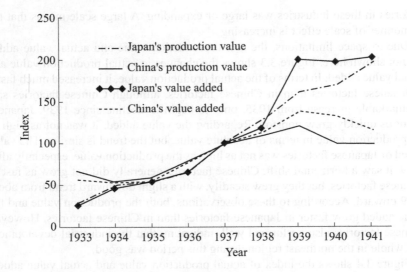

*Figure 3.4* Production index by Chinese and Japanese factories (1937 = 100)

The average figures are studied below. Table 3.10 shows the average number of factory employees. Overall, it increased slightly, from fewer than 20 to more than 30 employees and to 35 employees in individual years. From the perspective of industry, chemicals, metals, machinery, and appliances, kilns and other heavy industries had a large number of employees, far exceeding that in the light industries such as wood and wood products, food, textiles, printing, and binding. It shows the economies of scale characteristic of these industries. In terms of country of origin, Japanese factories were significantly higher than Chinese factories, indicating that Japanese factories were larger, even if they also belonged to traditional labor-intensive industries. Further, the scale of the heavy industries, as previously mentioned, far exceeded that of light industries, which in fact mainly existed in Japanese factories. In contrast, the average size of Chinese factories was not much different in various industries, with a slightly higher size for heavy industries than for light industries.

Table 3.11 shows that the actual per capita value added, or labor productivity, shows a nonlinear increase. It peaked for some industries in 1938 or 1939 and then declined. Through the comparison of figures for 1941 and 1933, the actual per capita value added of the manufacturing industry as a whole was 673.9 yuan per person in 1933 and 1,096.2 yuan per person in 1941, up by 62.7 percent. Of this, it increased from 561.8 yuan per person to 603.9 yuan per person for Chinese factories, up by 7.5 percent. It increased from 876.8 yuan per person to 1,472.8 yuan per person for Japanese factories, up by 68 percent. In terms of growth rate, the gap between Chinese and Japanese factories may be primarily due to the difference in productivity. From the perspective of industry, it increased significantly for the metals, chemicals, and other industries, increased slightly for textiles, food, kiln, and other industries, and even declined for some industries such as food. This shows a large gap between industries. Some modern industries obtained higher

*Table 3.10* Average number of factory employees

| Industry | Country of owner | 1933 | 1934 | 1935 | 1936 | 1937 | 1938 | 1939 | 1940 | 1941 |
|---|---|---|---|---|---|---|---|---|---|---|
| Total | Total | 18.7 | 23.4 | 25.8 | 26.8 | 30.0 | 32.5 | 35.9 | 32.4 | 31.3 |
| | Japan | 65.8 | 70.1 | 73.4 | 73.6 | 93.8 | 111.1 | 124.6 | 108.2 | 103.2 |
| | China | 13.5 | 15.0 | 14.5 | 16.6 | 16.9 | 17.2 | 17.3 | 16.5 | 15.9 |
| Textile | Total | 16.7 | 21.6 | 25.2 | 29.4 | 30.7 | 31.7 | 32.9 | 28.0 | 26.6 |
| | Japan | 98.2 | 100.3 | 119.0 | 142.5 | 147.5 | 151.1 | 153.7 | 114.5 | 112.2 |
| | China | 13.7 | 17.5 | 18.6 | 22.1 | 22.9 | 23.6 | 21.7 | 19.0 | 16.6 |
| Metals | Total | 15.2 | 24.0 | 41.6 | 38.5 | 51.6 | 61.5 | 88.9 | 80.0 | 83.9 |
| | Japan | 53.1 | 99.1 | 193.6 | 161.5 | 251.3 | 321.5 | 411.9 | 356.2 | 384.6 |
| | China | 12.0 | 14.5 | 13.3 | 15.7 | 15.5 | 15.4 | 24.0 | 24.7 | 24.6 |
| Machinery and appliances | Total | 20.0 | 24.4 | 23.4 | 25.9 | 38.3 | 50.4 | 53.7 | 45.7 | 40.8 |
| | Japan | 95.2 | 97.3 | 84.8 | 90.5 | 141.5 | 186.5 | 201.8 | 149.9 | 121.2 |
| | China | 9.4 | 9.7 | 9.4 | 10.2 | 11.5 | 12.8 | 13.7 | 15.7 | 17.1 |
| Kilns | Total | 38.7 | 50.6 | 56.6 | 41.1 | 48.3 | 54.8 | 69.9 | 64.4 | 59.8 |
| | Japan | 124.9 | 132.0 | 140.1 | 95.7 | 121.2 | 143.9 | 183.9 | 170.3 | 156.5 |
| | China | 20.4 | 21.4 | 19.1 | 21.2 | 22.0 | 22.6 | 31.0 | 30.6 | 29.5 |
| Chemicals | Total | 28.7 | 49.8 | 56.7 | 59.1 | 64.7 | 69.3 | 96.9 | 96.2 | 107.5 |
| | Japan | 89.0 | 88.1 | 120.1 | 131.8 | 151.9 | 169.0 | 186.1 | 183.4 | 200.4 |
| | China | 17.4 | 26.4 | 24.0 | 24.5 | 25.1 | 25.7 | 27.6 | 28.7 | 30.9 |
| Food | Total | 16.0 | 17.0 | 19.6 | 20.3 | 18.2 | 16.7 | 16.8 | 16.4 | 16.3 |
| | Japan | 31.5 | 31.1 | 31.7 | 35.6 | 35.3 | 35.0 | 37.4 | 40.7 | 42.9 |
| | China | 14.0 | 12.5 | 12.9 | 12.9 | 11.9 | 11.2 | 11.1 | 10.3 | 9.8 |
| Wood and wood products | Total | 13.4 | 16.5 | 15.0 | 16.2 | 16.6 | 17.0 | 19.2 | 18.3 | 17.8 |
| | Japan | 42.8 | 42.8 | 44.2 | 42.2 | 54.5 | 65.2 | 60.4 | 53.8 | 48.3 |
| | China | 9.6 | 10.9 | 9.3 | 12.3 | 11.4 | 10.7 | 11.9 | 12.5 | 13.1 |
| Printing and binding | Total | 19.1 | 20.0 | 20.9 | 22.2 | 24.3 | 26.1 | 27.9 | 28.5 | 29.6 |
| | Japan | 33.7 | 35.3 | 35.5 | 37.1 | 44.5 | 50.9 | 54.9 | 60.6 | 66.8 |
| | China | 15.4 | 15.0 | 14.3 | 16.0 | 15.8 | 15.6 | 16.4 | 16.6 | 16.5 |
| Others | Total | 11.5 | 16.4 | 12.3 | 15.0 | 19.8 | 25.5 | 24.6 | 18.9 | 17.2 |
| | Japan | 27.9 | 37.9 | 18.7 | 16.6 | 43.0 | 79.3 | 75.6 | 35.8 | 28.0 |
| | China | 9.2 | 12.1 | 10.5 | 14.0 | 15.1 | 16.4 | 16.0 | 15.5 | 14.9 |

*Note:* Due to the omission of factory owners of other countries, the total number does not match the total of China and Japan.

*Sources: Manchukuo Statistics of Factories* over the years, *Kwantung Leased Territory Statistics of Factories* over the years.

productivity through technological advances or economies of scale, while some traditional industries had stagnating or declining labor productivity because they were too small or had no technological progress. This is an inevitable law of economic development or industrial development.

Next is a study of power used at factories measured in horsepower. It is studied here as a proxy variable for capital stock because there are no data on capital stock in the statistics, only data on the horsepower of power. Since this period was an era of power, it progressed from a lack of power to the use of power, from the

68  *Processes and characteristics*

*Table 3.11* Actual per capita value added (at 1937 price, yuan per person)

| Industry | Country of owners | 1933 | 1934 | 1935 | 1936 | 1937 | 1938 | 1939 | 1940 | 1941 |
|---|---|---|---|---|---|---|---|---|---|---|
| Total | Total | 673.9 | 809.6 | 977.2 | 994.3 | 1,116.0 | 1,080.0 | 1,269.3 | 1,208.2 | 1,096.2 |
| | Japan | 876.8 | 1,107.8 | 1,203.7 | 1,252.0 | 1,386.2 | 1,273.0 | 1,550.3 | 1,552.5 | 1,472.8 |
| | China | 561.8 | 550.5 | 699.2 | 716.9 | 817.9 | 817.2 | 848.3 | 747.6 | 603.9 |
| Textile | Total | 374.3 | 456.8 | 409.1 | 438.5 | 625.3 | 540.1 | 693.1 | 504.3 | 500.4 |
| | Japan | 656.8 | 685.3 | 455.7 | 557.3 | 811.8 | 713.2 | 960.5 | 642.7 | 547.7 |
| | China | 297.7 | 368.5 | 385.7 | 386.8 | 542.8 | 463.2 | 517.6 | 416.1 | 462.3 |
| Metals | Total | 683.6 | 1,594.8 | 4,063.3 | 3,387.3 | 2,616.4 | 1,021.6 | 3,978.9 | 4,576.6 | 5,095.8 |
| | Japan | 993.2 | 2,776.2 | 5,301.3 | 4,691.7 | 3,302.7 | 1,195.3 | 4,923.0 | 5,602.2 | 6,309.6 |
| | China | 568.2 | 595.9 | 690.2 | 901.6 | 594.1 | 370.1 | 706.7 | 1,592.6 | 1,335.6 |
| Machinery and appliances | Total | 781.4 | 1,148.2 | 1,516.4 | 1,130.0 | 760.0 | 734.7 | 789.0 | 1,027.2 | 1,110.1 |
| | Japan | 846.6 | 1,438.2 | 1,625.6 | 1,263.8 | 737.3 | 770.8 | 790.0 | 1,122.1 | 1,325.3 |
| | China | 688.0 | 543.9 | 1,295.8 | 846.6 | 829.4 | 590.0 | 775.1 | 754.4 | 659.1 |
| Kilns | Total | 358.3 | 431.6 | 334.8 | 576.1 | 703.5 | 673.2 | 499.3 | 460.9 | 488.6 |
| | Japan | 503.7 | 536.8 | 331.2 | 757.9 | 911.0 | 830.5 | 554.1 | 549.0 | 552.5 |
| | China | 169.1 | 219.5 | 346.3 | 276.5 | 288.3 | 312.1 | 388.1 | 304.2 | 381.9 |
| Chemicals | Total | 881.7 | 1,149.7 | 1,046.5 | 1,118.8 | 1,960.4 | 2,830.0 | 2,142.8 | 2,168.2 | 1,373.9 |
| | Japan | 1,396.9 | 1,514.3 | 1,283.8 | 1,355.3 | 2,411.7 | 3,467.1 | 2,375.5 | 2,397.5 | 1,476.2 |
| | China | 388.2 | 291.6 | 430.3 | 511.6 | 709.8 | 968.3 | 903.5 | 981.5 | 801.9 |
| Food | Total | 1,205.3 | 1,742.9 | 1,198.6 | 1,730.3 | 2,133.0 | 2,762.4 | 2,463.3 | 1,928.9 | 1,103.4 |
| | Japan | 1,434.6 | 1,810.8 | 901.5 | 1,254.6 | 2,149.6 | 2,842.0 | 2,919.0 | 2,313.7 | 1,495.7 |
| | China | 1,149.7 | 1,715.5 | 1,362.2 | 2,041.0 | 2,331.4 | 2,790.2 | 2,318.1 | 1,791.2 | 886.6 |
| Wood and wood products | Total | 422.5 | 496.8 | 459.5 | 538.9 | 1,101.9 | 518.6 | 453.0 | 465.2 | 533.2 |
| | Japan | 747.2 | 972.8 | 579.4 | 888.8 | 2,049.6 | 816.1 | 676.9 | 709.4 | 659.5 |
| | China | 230.8 | 259.2 | 349.1 | 348.1 | 465.5 | 281.5 | 254.7 | 298.8 | 466.3 |
| Printing and binding | Total | 600.6 | 701.9 | 979.5 | 906.1 | 977.4 | 1,030.2 | 1,265.9 | 846.1 | 940.4 |
| | Japan | 1,076.8 | 1,104.2 | 1,289.2 | 1,159.4 | 1,400.4 | 1,512.4 | 1,813.8 | 1,190.7 | 1,189.7 |
| | China | 321.9 | 376.8 | 618.9 | 650.7 | 458.6 | 371.6 | 491.3 | 392.2 | 574.5 |
| Others | Total | 402.3 | 320.7 | 695.3 | 605.9 | 550.2 | 630.2 | 673.7 | 1,342.2 | 1,151.8 |
| | Japan | 854.8 | 368.5 | 1160.6 | 989.3 | 913.2 | 916.5 | 1023.6 | 2910.1 | 2437.7 |
| | China | 186.7 | 281.4 | 459.2 | 522.8 | 358.4 | 389.0 | 398.2 | 608.2 | 570.2 |

*Note:* Due to the omission of factory owners of other countries, the total number does not match the total of China and Japan.

*Sources: Manchukuo Statistics of Factories* over the years, *Kwantung Leased Territory Statistics of Factories* over the years.

*Development of industry: part 1*   69

traditional power source to the modern mechanical power source, and to internal combustion engines and electric motors.[17] In other words, the power system was popular in factory production at that time. However, this was only the case in foreign countries. China had not yet achieved full coverage of power use, and many small and medium-sized enterprises still used manual operation. In short, in the case of the use of power, the amount of horsepower can approximately, albeit not directly replace the function and efficiency of mechanical equipment.

Table 3.12 shows the size of horsepower per 100 people. It shows the data only for the puppet state of Manchukuo, excluding the Kwantung region. On the whole,

*Table 3.12* Horsepower per 100 people

| Industry | Country of owner | 1934 | 1935 | 1936 | 1938 | 1939 | 1940 |
|---|---|---|---|---|---|---|---|
| Total | Total | 28.6 | 72.4 | 62.3 | 134.8 | 159.8 | 136.4 |
| | Japan | 37.3 | 126.5 | 171.6 | 243.2 | 261.6 | 222.0 |
| | China | 25.5 | 47.5 | 34.3 | 31.9 | 38.9 | 44.5 |
| Textiles | Total | 21.7 | 45.7 | 28.4 | 36.2 | 111.0 | 99.1 |
| | Japan | 24.8 | 97.0 | 89.8 | 70.9 | 267.2 | 238.4 |
| | China | 21.6 | 41.5 | 20.6 | 24.3 | 14.5 | 19.4 |
| Metals | Total | 11.4 | 37.4 | 18.4 | 423.0 | 513.1 | 393.4 |
| | Japan | 76.0 | 94.2 | 59.4 | 626.6 | 745.8 | 556.6 |
| | China | 7.8 | 11.2 | 10.4 | 12.8 | 17.7 | 42.7 |
| Machinery and appliances | Total | 54.0 | 66.6 | 43.9 | 32.7 | 73.4 | 70.6 |
| | Japan | 103.2 | 98.4 | 92.2 | 35.1 | 84.5 | 89.5 |
| | China | 31.3 | 21.1 | 14.8 | 21.5 | 21.1 | 28.1 |
| Kilns | Total | 6.5 | 113.1 | 175.8 | 114.7 | 122.4 | 112.3 |
| | Japan | 8.8 | 137.9 | 365.1 | 164.3 | 181.4 | 166.5 |
| | China | 5.0 | 13.1 | 4.5 | 4.2 | 3.0 | 14.8 |
| Chemicals | Total | 64.5 | 106.6 | 107.1 | 519.0 | 239.6 | 266.3 |
| | Japan | 78.5 | 137.2 | 97.5 | 894.0 | 345.1 | 353.1 |
| | China | 59.6 | 82.6 | 104.6 | 71.7 | 77.6 | 118.4 |
| Food | Total | 151.5 | 183.8 | 203.4 | 143.0 | 205.6 | 166.4 |
| | Japan | 110.7 | 383.8 | 272.1 | 172.9 | 212.4 | 161.4 |
| | China | 140.8 | 144.5 | 187.9 | 121.8 | 204.7 | 172.9 |
| Wood and wood products | Total | 21.9 | 115.9 | 44.4 | 91.6 | 84.7 | 73.2 |
| | Japan | 96.3 | 148.5 | 159.0 | 158.1 | 145.7 | 138.2 |
| | China | 11.0 | 60.7 | 5.4 | 34.7 | 28.6 | 24.4 |
| Printing and binding | Total | 14.5 | 25.9 | 13.8 | 15.3 | 18.7 | 16.7 |
| | Japan | 28.2 | 32.9 | 16.0 | 16.8 | 19.9 | 15.5 |
| | China | 11.0 | 21.1 | 9.7 | 11.7 | 10.9 | 13.8 |
| Others | Total | 4.4 | 20.4 | 13.0 | 10.8 | 23.4 | 10.4 |
| | Japan | 19.7 | 24.6 | 31.5 | 20.3 | 69.3 | 18.3 |
| | China | 3.5 | 16.7 | 5.1 | 5.5 | 5.1 | 4.6 |

*Notes:* (1) Due to the omission of factory owners of other countries, the total number does not match the total of China and Japan. (2) Data for the year 1937 are missing.

*Data source: Manchukuo Statistics of Factories* over the years.

it showed a trend of increase, even if some industries performed differently, and the absolute value was relatively low. The differences between industries are also obvious. The figure was high for heavy industries that use more power and was relatively low for light industries that relied less on machinery and power. In addition, Japanese factories generally used more power than Chinese factories. It can also be considered that Japanese factories had a high level of mechanization and power use.

Figure 3.5 shows the relationship between horsepower per 100 people and per capita value added. The combined figures for 1934 and 1939 are shown here[18] because the relationship between the two is relatively clear with a good positive correlation; that is, as per capita horsepower (100 people) increases, the per capita value added will also increase. The horsepower per 100 people represents the capital stock (proxy variable), and the per capita value added represents the productivity of labor. The relationship between the two is actually a manifestation of the production function. This relationship is clearly present although it does not show a clear pattern of the law of diminishing marginal returns.

Growth rate is analyzed next. Table 3.13 shows various growth rates for years from 1934 to 1941, including those of the number of factories, the number of employees, actual production value, actual value added, and the per capita value. Overall, the growth rates of the number of factories, the number of employees, production value, and value added are relatively high, with some reaching 20 to 30 percent, while the growth rate of per capita value is low. In addition, the growth rate was far higher for Japanese factories than for Chinese factories, sometimes by

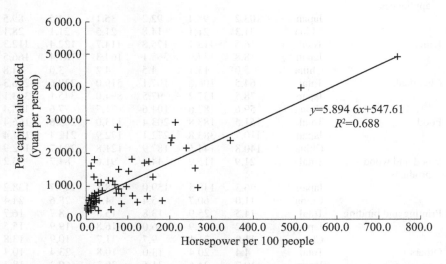

*Figure 3.5* Relationship between horsepower per 100 people and per capita value added (1934, 1939)

*Note:* The horsepower per 100 people here excludes the Kwantung region.

*Sources:* Manchukuo Statistics of Factories over the years, Kwantung Leased Territory Statistics of Factories over the years.

*Table 3.13* Growth rate (average, 1934–1941)

| Industry | Country of owner | Number of factories | Number of employees | Actual production value | Actual value added | Actual production value per capita | Actual value added per capita |
|---|---|---|---|---|---|---|---|
| Total for the manufacturing industry | Total | 7.93 | 14.93 | 18.21 | 22.85 | 3.32 | 6.88 |
| | Japan | 15.03 | 22.37 | 29.39 | 32.48 | 5.53 | 7.29 |
| | China | 7.13 | 9.64 | 6.65 | 10.85 | −1.57 | 1.78 |
| Textile | Total | 7.55 | 11.61 | 11.58 | 20.00 | −0.30 | 5.81 |
| | Japan | 23.57 | 21.14 | 16.52 | 26.78 | −4.34 | 2.10 |
| | China | 6.95 | 7.30 | 7.79 | 15.71 | 0.47 | 7.08 |
| Metals | Total | 2.76 | 23.34 | 49.44 | 74.63 | 21.35 | 36.47 |
| | Japan | 17.17 | 48.77 | 111.56 | 118.13 | 30.56 | 35.79 |
| | China | 1.35 | 8.66 | 6.09 | 23.26 | −0.75 | 15.72 |
| Machinery and appliances | Total | 18.52 | 24.68 | 27.58 | 36.48 | 3.78 | 12.57 |
| | Japan | 19.57 | 24.46 | 26.25 | 35.15 | 4.69 | 13.87 |
| | China | 18.35 | 28.16 | 38.36 | 46.34 | 8.33 | 15.60 |
| Kilns | Total | 14.55 | 21.32 | 30.39 | 27.37 | 9.34 | 7.58 |
| | Japan | 17.48 | 23.30 | 30.08 | 26.99 | 8.82 | 9.41 |
| | China | 14.52 | 22.71 | 36.29 | 34.79 | 14.09 | 13.62 |
| Chemicals | Total | 7.78 | 12.66 | 13.71 | 18.52 | 1.63 | 6.31 |
| | Japan | 14.25 | 26.07 | 27.69 | 27.43 | 0.93 | 0.80 |
| | China | 7.57 | 2.37 | 1.08 | 7.55 | 0.37 | 6.87 |
| Food | Total | 9.30 | 10.07 | 9.28 | 16.95 | 1.37 | 7.32 |
| | Japan | 13.55 | 17.37 | 22.20 | 32.82 | 4.71 | 13.05 |
| | China | 9.48 | 8.73 | 7.92 | 17.34 | 1.94 | 7.86 |
| Wood and wood products | Total | 9.56 | 14.15 | 17.92 | 28.17 | 2.09 | 11.37 |
| | Japan | 11.42 | 13.78 | 17.03 | 30.21 | 2.89 | 12.22 |
| | China | 9.58 | 15.58 | 22.95 | 31.00 | 8.62 | 14.93 |
| Printing and binding | Total | 7.84 | 12.33 | 16.64 | 21.76 | 4.17 | 12.15 |
| | Japan | 8.83 | 14.94 | 19.62 | 23.70 | 4.40 | 9.35 |
| | China | 8.30 | 11.92 | 15.02 | 20.78 | 4.80 | 16.31 |
| Others | Total | 6.46 | 16.42 | 26.26 | 27.80 | 11.63 | 10.75 |
| | Japan | 16.22 | 21.10 | 28.80 | 30.69 | 6.45 | 8.95 |
| | China | 5.68 | 14.27 | 23.77 | 26.06 | 11.15 | 10.45 |

*Note:* Due to the omission of factory owners of other countries, the total number does not match the total of China and Japan.

*Sources: Manchukuo Statistics of Factories* over the years, *Kwantung Leased Territory Statistics of Factories* over the years.

2 to 3 times. However, this is not entirely the case from the perspective of industry; indicators were higher for Chinese factories in some industries such as the per capita value for textiles, kilns, wood and wood products, printing and binding, and other industries.

Figure 3.6 shows the growth rates of several indicators, including the number of factories, the number of employees, actual production value, and actual value added. Overall, there is a pattern of a rise followed by a decline. The growth rate was low from 1934 to 1935, but it grew rapidly from 1936 to 1939 and then fell sharply after 1940. The initial low growth may be due to the fact that the various economic relationships were improper. When conditions matured after 1935, high growth followed. After 1940, the domestic and external situations deteriorated, with the economy of Manchukuo declining, and Japan's domestic economy in serious trouble. The outbreak of the Pacific War aggravated the situation, and even the *Manchukuo Statistics of Factories* was discontinued. Figure 13.4 shows that the growth rates of the number of factories and workers were lower than those of the production value and value added, although they reached a fairly high level. In other words, the growth rates of production value and value added were higher and can even be called super-high growth rates. We believe that this is mainly due to three reasons. First, the northeast region had abundant resources and good infrastructure. Given large investment, it could achieve rapid growth. Second, Japan made painstaking efforts to run this colony,[19] including launching large-scale immigration, investment from *zaibatsu* (especially emerging *zaibatsu*) companies, and the construction

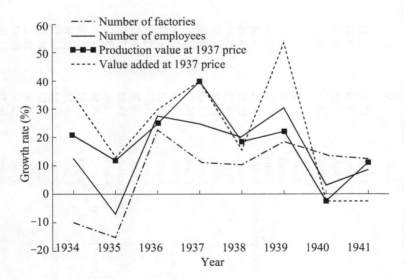

*Figure 3.6* Annual growth rates for years from 1934 to 1941

Sources: Manchukuo Statistics of Factories over the years, Kwantung Leased Territory Statistics of Factories over the years.

Development of industry: part 1    73

of infrastructure of all types. Third, the region was sparsely populated and rich in resources. It could easily achieve rapid growth as long as there was capital and technology, as well as immigrants.

Next is a study of the distribution of factories by scale. Figures 3.7 and 3.8 show the scales of Chinese and Japanese factories, respectively, which confirm the differences just mentioned. Chinese factories mainly had fewer than 30 people, and, in particular, the number of these factories is in the overwhelming majority. The number of employees changed basically in the same way as the number of factories but was slightly inclined toward medium-level or large factories. In other words, large factories had more workers. Production value also showed this tendency but not comparable to the number of employees. It was concentrated in factories with less than 100 people, while factories with 30 to 49 people produced more products.

Japanese factories were obviously different from Chinese factories, although the number of factories was relatively close for China and Japan. Although small factories did not have the largest share, factories with 5 to 9 people were in the vast majority, and they were evenly distributed, close to the distribution of the production value of Chinese factories. Japanese factories were completely different from Chinese factories in terms of the number of employees. The larger the Japanese factory, the more concentrated the employees. That is to say, large Japanese factories were prominent in terms of the number of employees. Although the production

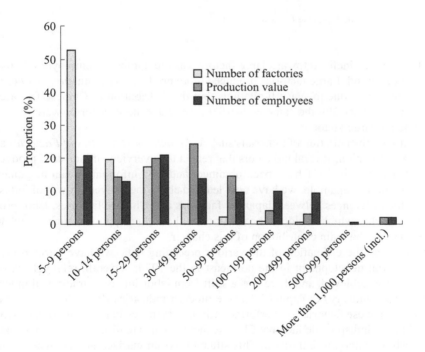

*Figure 3.7* Size of Chinese factories (1936)

74  *Processes and characteristics*

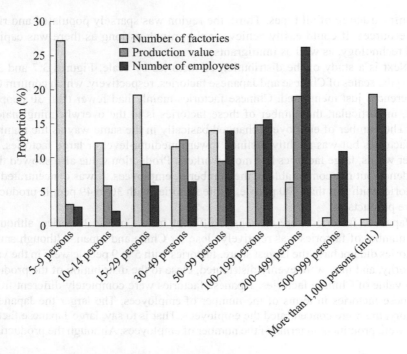

*Figure 3.8* Size of Japanese factories (1936)

value is not as inclined toward large factories as the number of employees, it also shows this trend. Large factories produced more products. The situation in 1940 is not shown here due to space limitations, but the distribution of Chinese factories by size was basically the same as in 1936, while Japanese factories were further inclined to large factories.

Through the collation of materials such as *Manchukuo Statistics of Factories* as well as estimation, several indicators that reflect the overview of industrial production from 1933 to 1941 have been obtained, and new information can be gained from them. For example, we have now learned about the uneven growth of industries, the differences between Japanese factories and Chinese factories, labor productivity, etc., which could not be obtained without the support of such complete data. This is the main contribution of this chapter.

Based on the estimation of the various preceding data, we have a rough idea of industrial development in the northeast in the 1930s. Overall, relatively rapid growth was achieved, and there was a shift from labor-intensive traditional industries (light industry) to capital-intensive modern industries (heavy industry). Although Japanese factories outperformed Chinese factories in terms of productivity, etc., it is an indisputable fact that Chinese factories also realized rapid growth, particularly in emerging industries. This situation is summarized and analyzed from the perspective of economics theory.

Development of industry: part 1    75

Figure 3.9 shows the relationship between the input of factors of production and the production quantity, which expresses the production function and is also a form of technological advance. It shows two aspects of industrial development in the northeast region: the growth of Japanese factories and progress made by Chinese factories. Let's suppose Japanese companies began to enter the Northeast in the initial period (such as 1931). Because Japan had better economic development than China at that time, Japanese factories were relatively capital-intensive from the outset. It is expressed as capital/labor ratio $(K/L)$ Japan 1 in the figure. It is on the far left relative to Chinese factories, and the production point is point $B$. At the same time, local Chinese factories already existed, but because China's economy as a whole was relatively backward, Chinese factories were more labor-intensive, expressed as $(K/L)$ China 1 in the figure, or closer to the right side, and the production point is point $A$. Compared with Japanese factories, Chinese factories used less capital and had low productivity and low wage rates. Thanks to the abundant resources in the northeast region, coupled with investment and development, the northeast saw rapid economic development. Both Japanese and Chinese factories made progress, represented as moving toward the origin in the figure.[20] However, this movement does not exactly point to the origin but to capital-intensity, that is, moving from point $B$ to point $D$ and from point $A$ to point $C$, respectively. The capital/labor ratio after the movement is $(K/L)$ Japan 2 and $(K/L)$ China 2, respectively. This is because the northeast is rich in resources, which is suitable for the development of heavy industry. In addition, Japan needed to exploit the resources in the northeast, either for the purpose of war or to supply the Japanese domestic market. Under these circumstances, both Japanese and Chinese factories were motivated to become capital-intensive.

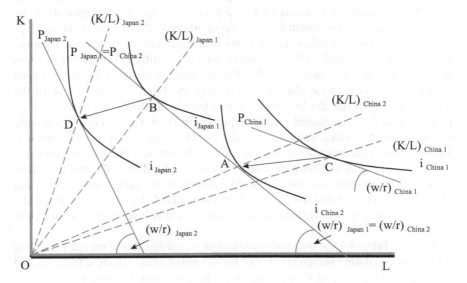

*Figure 3.9* Development of industry in the northeast in the 1930s

## 76 *Processes and characteristics*

From this point of view, the basic conditions of industry in the northeast were highly different from those in the hinterland. Natural resources in the hinterland are more dispersed, and capital was invested more in resource exploration and concentrated in a few coastal cities. In this case, it was difficult to promote overall development and was easier to lead to a dual structure. Although there was also a dual structure in the northeast, its population was relatively small and not as dense as that in the hinterland. Therefore, except for those engaged in agricultural production, people were more easily concentrated in cities in the northeast and participated in industrial development. Compared with the hinterland, the northeast region had better resource endowments for development in terms both agriculture and industry.

### 3.5  Industry in North China in the 1940s

As mentioned earlier, the survey of factories in North China focused on the years 1939 and 1942. The year 1939 was the eighth year after Japan's all-out invasion of China. As Mao Zedong put it, China entered a stage of strategic stalemate form this year onward. Japanese forces could roughly control north China, which became an occupied area. The Japanese began to investigate local industrial development either to provide a basis for future rule or to furnish war supplies.

Table 3.14 shows the basic situation of factories in North China in 1942. There were 6,352 factories, far more than that in 1939. Of these, Chinese factories were in the majority, nearly 5 times more than that of Japanese factories. The factories were primarily textiles and food factories, which together accounted for 58 percent of the total. Modern industries such as machinery and chemicals also developed considerably. In terms of horsepower, Japanese factories held an absolute advantage. Textiles factories accounted for 42.5 percent, while others, chemicals, food, machinery, etc. also accounted for a large proportion, indicating the rapid development of some modern industries. In terms of the number of employees, Japanese factories slightly outdid Chinese factories, which was different from that in 1939. It may be that Japanese factories had higher revenue, or the labor might have been forced. There were major changes in the industry. From the perspective of the number of employees, the kiln industry was the top employer, accounting for 67 percent of the total, compared to only 10 percent in 1939. The kiln industry usually includes cement, bricks, ceramics, refractory bricks, etc. In terms of production value, Japanese factories outperformed Chinese factories, with a production value about 1.6 times that of Chinese factories. In terms of industry, the textiles industry was still dominant, accounting for 40.3 percent of the total. Food, others, and chemicals also performed well. In terms of value added, Japanese factories held a large advantage, indicating that Japanese factories either had lower costs or higher productivity.

Further, Table 3.15 shows some indicators calculated based on the preceding data. In terms of the average number of factory employees, Japanese factories had far more employees than Chinese factories, by more than 6 times, but their factory size was larger overall. The proportion of factories with fewer than 30 people

Table 3.14 Overview of factories in North China in 1942 by industry

| Industry | Country of owners | Number of factories | Number of employees | Horsepower | Production value (1,000 yuan) | Value added (1,000 yuan) | Electrification rate (%) |
|---|---|---|---|---|---|---|---|
| Total | Total | 6,352 | 719,866 | 313,027.3 | 2,785,860.9 | 1,015,767.7 | 78.7 |
| | Japan | 1,127 | 391,501 | 194,968.1 | 1,528,184.5 | 626,857.7 | 79.6 |
| | China | 5,102 | 293,368 | 70,379.0 | 933,761.8 | 286,197.0 | 91.3 |
| Textile | Total | 1,848 | 99,941 | 133,066.1 | 1,121,833.5 | 361,504.0 | 75.7 |
| | Japan | 142 | 44,695 | 95,957.1 | 668,152.0 | 228,882.9 | 76.7 |
| | China | 1,685 | 44,152 | 16,613.7 | 303,462.8 | 97,033.3 | 97.8 |
| Metals | Total | 302 | 14,029 | 20,395.5 | 70,766.0 | 29,150.4 | 87.1 |
| | Japan | 41 | 8,728 | 17,820.7 | 47,478.6 | 20,984.4 | 85.3 |
| | China | 259 | 5,170 | 2,232.8 | 22,964.6 | 7,989.6 | 99.1 |
| Machinery | Total | 641 | 38,477 | 35,877.2 | 172,742.9 | 98,221.4 | 76.0 |
| | Japan | 155 | 15,895 | 17,004.9 | 85,254.5 | 44,216.4 | 89.4 |
| | China | 462 | 8,918 | 2,647.5 | 47,821.4 | 30,299.8 | 96.2 |
| Kilns | Total | 327 | 478,146 | 19,296.3 | 62,215.6 | 36,941.2 | 99.6 |
| | Japan | 101 | 271,417 | 3,817.5 | 16,786.1 | 10,222.6 | 100.0 |
| | China | 212 | 203,544 | 13,181.3 | 33,268.2 | 19,553.1 | 99.4 |
| Chemicals | Total | 598 | 21,132 | 43,555.4 | 339,712.5 | 118,851.2 | 78.0 |
| | Japan | 127 | 13,068 | 31,370.4 | 182,381.1 | 77,668.7 | 78.7 |
| | China | 451 | 6,737 | 9,013.9 | 141,108.8 | 35,290.3 | 76.1 |
| Food | Total | 1,839 | 20,817 | 42,273.0 | 527,548.4 | 123,786.8 | 68.9 |
| | Japan | 243 | 9,003 | 14,283.2 | 169,451.6 | 55,089.6 | 64.0 |
| | China | 1,572 | 9,912 | 23,697.1 | 297,801.4 | 60,153.5 | 83.6 |
| Wood | Total | 187 | 6,210 | 5,743.9 | 65,031.3 | 19,405.7 | 97.5 |
| | Japan | 106 | 4,512 | 4,112.8 | 54,514.9 | 16,789.2 | 99.2 |
| | China | 79 | 1,618 | 1,262.0 | 8,999.2 | 2,445.3 | 91.3 |
| Printing | Total | 226 | 6,713 | 1,567.8 | 38,429.9 | 16,895.3 | 99.0 |
| | Japan | 71 | 2443 | 506.3 | 15081.5 | 5789.3 | 100.0 |
| | China | 148 | 2916 | 663.6 | 14296.4 | 5627.6 | 97.7 |
| Others | Total | 384 | 34,401 | 11,252.3 | 387,580.8 | 211,011.7 | 92.1 |
| | Japan | 141 | 21,740 | 10,095.4 | 289,084.1 | 167,214.6 | 90.5 |
| | China | 234 | 10,401 | 1,067.4 | 64,039.1 | 27,804.5 | 99.7 |

Note: In addition to Chinese and Japanese owners, the total includes owners from other countries, including joint ventures.

Data source: Statistics of Factories in North China (1943).

*Table 3.15* Characteristics of factories in North China in 1942 by industry

| Industry | Country of owner | Average number of factory employees | Horsepower per 100 people | Per capita production value (yuan per person) | Per capita value added (yuan per person) | Proportion of factories with fewer than 30 people (%) | Proportion of employees in factories with fewer than 30 people (%) |
|---|---|---|---|---|---|---|---|
| Total | Total | 113.3 | 43.5 | 3,870.0 | 1,411.1 | 75.6 | 7.1 |
| | Japan | 347.4 | 49.8 | 3,903.4 | 1,601.2 | 45.0 | 2.0 |
| | China | 57.5 | 24.0 | 3,182.9 | 975.6 | 83.7 | 14.7 |
| Textile | Total | 54.1 | 133.1 | 11,225.0 | 3,617.2 | 70.6 | 18.2 |
| | Japan | 314.8 | 214.7 | 14,949.1 | 5,121.0 | 40.8 | 2.4 |
| | China | 26.2 | 37.6 | 6,873.1 | 2,197.7 | 73.9 | 38.8 |
| Metals | Total | 46.5 | 145.4 | 5,044.3 | 2,077.9 | 79.5 | 23.3 |
| | Japan | 212.9 | 204.2 | 5,439.8 | 2,404.3 | 36.6 | 2.6 |
| | China | 20.0 | 43.2 | 4,441.9 | 1,545.4 | 86.5 | 58.5 |
| Machinery | Total | 60.0 | 93.2 | 4,489.5 | 2,552.7 | 70.4 | 15.7 |
| | Japan | 102.5 | 107.0 | 5,363.6 | 2,781.8 | 41.3 | 6.7 |
| | China | 19.3 | 29.7 | 5,362.3 | 3,397.6 | 83.5 | 55.8 |
| Kiln | Total | 1,462.2 | 4.0 | 130.1 | 77.3 | 39.1 | 0.5 |
| | Japan | 2,687.3 | 1.4 | 61.8 | 37.7 | 10.9 | 0.1 |
| | China | 960.1 | 6.5 | 163.4 | 96.1 | 54.7 | 1.0 |
| Chemicals | Total | 35.3 | 206.1 | 16,075.7 | 5,624.2 | 78.6 | 23.4 |
| | Japan | 102.9 | 240.1 | 13,956.3 | 5,943.4 | 47.2 | 6.9 |
| | China | 14.9 | 133.8 | 20,945.3 | 5,238.3 | 89.6 | 58.6 |
| Food | Total | 11.3 | 203.1 | 25,342.2 | 5,946.4 | 93.1 | 46.9 |
| | Japan | 37.0 | 158.6 | 18,821.7 | 6,119.0 | 69.1 | 26.7 |
| | China | 6.3 | 239.1 | 30,044.5 | 6,068.8 | 97.6 | 73.0 |
| Wood | Total | 33.2 | 92.5 | 10,472.0 | 3,124.9 | 66.3 | 25.9 |
| | Japan | 42.6 | 91.2 | 12,082.2 | 3,721.0 | 56.6 | 19.3 |
| | China | 20.5 | 78.0 | 5,561.9 | 1,511.3 | 79.7 | 43.7 |
| Printing | Total | 29.7 | 23.4 | 5,724.7 | 2,516.8 | 72.1 | 34.5 |
| | Japan | 34.4 | 20.7 | 6,173.4 | 2,369.7 | 54.9 | 26.7 |
| | China | 19.7 | 22.8 | 4,902.7 | 1,929.9 | 83.1 | 56.8 |
| Others | Total | 89.6 | 32.7 | 11,266.6 | 6,133.9 | 53.6 | 9.0 |
| | Japan | 154.2 | 46.4 | 13,297.3 | 7,691.6 | 22.7 | 2.2 |
| | China | 44.4 | 10.3 | 6,157.0 | 2,673.3 | 73.9 | 24.8 |

*Note:* In addition to Chinese and Japanese owners, the total includes owners from other countries, including joint ventures.

*Data source: Statistics of Factories in North China* (1943).

and the proportion of employees are two indicators related to the factory size. The lower these two indicators are, the larger the factory size, and vice versa. In terms of the former, Chinese factories accounted for 83.7 percent, while Japanese factories were only about half. In terms of the latter, there was a gap of almost 7 times between Chinese factories and Japanese factories. That is to say, there were more small Chinese factories, while Japanese factories were usually larger. In terms of horsepower per 100 people, Japanese factories outdid Chinese factories by more than 2 times and even 6 times in some industries. However, the opposite was the case in some industries such as kiln. In terms of per capita production value and per capita value added (labor productivity), in general, Japanese factories were slightly better than Chinese factories, but it was the opposite in some industries.

We can obtain a data equivalent to the per capita capital stock. Because this is not the real capital stock but the horsepower, only a proxy variable can be used. However, machinery and equipment basically became popular in the 1930s, and one of the conditions for factories to be investigated was the use of power. Supposing that each device uses the corresponding horsepower, the data on horsepower can be regarded as a representation of capital equipment. At the same time, we can also calculate the value added and the per capita value added, with the latter being the labor productivity. The relationship between the per capita capital stock (horsepower) and the per capita value added (labor productivity) can be seen as an approximate production function relationship.

This relationship is shown in Figure 3.10, from which we can see an arc curve, which is the production function curve. In other words, as the per capita capital

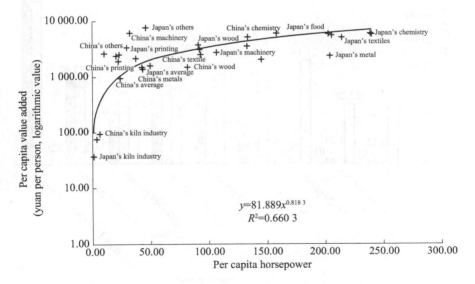

*Figure 3.10* Relationship between horsepower per 100 people and per capita value added in factories in North China in 1942

*Data source: Statistics of Factories in North China* (1943).

## Processes and characteristics

stock increases, the per capita value added (labor productivity) also increases. This mirrors the role of capital equipment per capita in labor productivity. Upon close inspection, most modern Japanese industries are seen located in the upper right corner, while China's traditional industries are located on the left. To put it another way, capital-intensive Japanese factories had higher productivity, while labor-intensive Chinese factories had lower productivity. Of course, there were also labor-intensive Japanese factories and capital-intensive Chinese factories, but the overall distribution indicates a big gap in capital equipment and productivity between Chinese and Japanese factories.

The gap between Chinese and Japanese factories can also be observed in terms of size. Figures 3.11 and 3.12 show the size distribution of Japanese and Chinese factories in 1942. In Figure 3.11, the size distribution of Japanese factories is close to the normal distribution, slightly skewed to the left but not completely inclined toward small factories. The number of employees is inclined toward large factories. Larger factories employed more employees. Production value is more inclined toward large factories, indicating that the productivity of large factories was far higher than that of small factories. Figure 3.12 shows the size distribution of

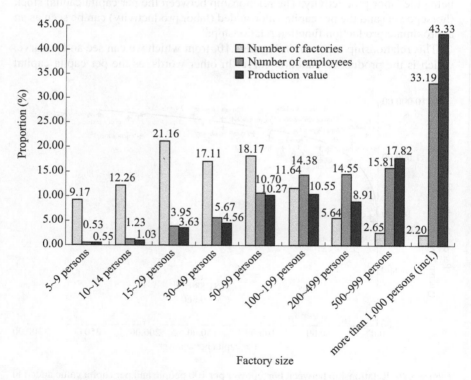

*Figure 3.11* Size distribution of factories in North China in 1942 (Japan)
Data source: *Statistics of Factories in North China* (1943).

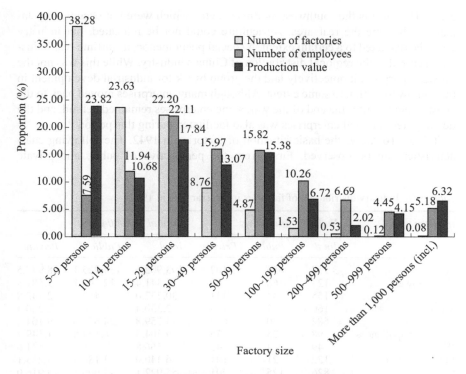

*Figure 3.12* Size distribution of factories in North China in 1942 (China)

Data source: *Statistics of Factories in North China* (1943).

Chinese factories, which obviously presents a different pattern compared to Japanese factories. To begin with, it was completely inclined to small factories in terms of the number of factories, the number of employees, and production value. The number of employees is slightly different, showing signs of normal distribution. The number of factories is completely one-sided because very few factories employed more than 100 people. Production value is basically distributed in this way. However, due to the high productivity of large factories, it shows a slightly different distribution pattern compared to the number of factories.

### 3.6 Industry in the rear in the 1940s

After the outbreak of the War of Resistance against Japanese Aggression, many enterprises in the occupied area began to migrate inland, which was a unique feature in the process of China's industrial development. During the War of Resistance against Japanese Aggression, China was divided into three regions. The first is the northeast region occupied by Japan earlier, where the puppet state of Manchukuo had already been established. The second is the vast region including North China and East China, which were gradually occupied by Japan and became occupied

## 82    Processes and characteristics

areas. The third is the southwest, northwest, etc., which were not occupied by Japan and became the rear area. Agriculture could not be relocated, but industry could be relocated to a certain extent. A special phenomenon, a wartime rear industry, occurred in the regional distribution of China's industry. While this was not the intended purpose, it objectively laid the groundwork for industrial development in the southwest region to some extent. Although many enterprises moved back to the coastal regions after the end of the war, some enterprises remained behind, and the development of local enterprises was also facilitated during this period.[21]

Table 3.16 shows the basic situation of factories in 1942. The following characteristics can be observed. First, from the perspective of public and private

*Table 3.16* Industry distribution of factories in the rear area in 1942

| Industry | Number of factories | | | Capital (10,000 yuan) | | |
|---|---|---|---|---|---|---|
| | Total | Public | Private | Total | Public | Private |
| Total | 3,758 | 656 | 3,102 | 193,902.6 | 134,925.1 | 58,977.5 |
| Hydropower | 123 | 60 | 63 | 14,341.4 | 12,760.1 | 1,581.3 |
| Smelting | 155 | 44 | 111 | 30,232.0 | 27,489.2 | 2,742.8 |
| Metals | 160 | 7 | 153 | 2,330.4 | 70.0 | 2,260.4 |
| Machinery | 682 | 50 | 632 | 33,759.8 | 24,655.6 | 9,104.2 |
| Electrical appliances | 98 | 23 | 75 | 9,304.5 | 8,154.8 | 1,149.7 |
| Wood | 49 | 4 | 45 | 566.8 | 25.2 | 541.6 |
| Earth and stone | 122 | 21 | 101 | 6,440.0 | 3,186.9 | 3,253.1 |
| Chemicals | 826 | 125 | 701 | 55,922.1 | 42,006.1 | 13,916.0 |
| Catering | 360 | 32 | 328 | 8,343.5 | 1,917.5 | 6,426.0 |
| Textile | 788 | 245 | 543 | 29,050.9 | 14,246.5 | 14,804.4 |
| Costume | 147 | 8 | 139 | 1,104.4 | 70.5 | 1,033.9 |
| Culture | 224 | 35 | 189 | 2,142.2 | 329.4 | 1,812.8 |
| Miscellaneous | 24 | 2 | 22 | 364.6 | 13.3 | 351.3 |

| Industry | Number of workers | | | Horsepower | | |
|---|---|---|---|---|---|---|
| | Total | Public | Private | Total | Public | Private |
| Total | 241,662 | 77,217 | 164,445 | 143,915.8 | 60,867.8 | 83,048.0 |
| Hydropower | 4,618 | 2,519 | 2,099 | 51,213.0 | 20,738.0 | 30,475.0 |
| Smelting | 17,404 | 6,657 | 10,747 | 9,659.0 | 8,351.0 | 1,308.0 |
| Metals | 8,291 | 1,791 | 6,500 | 2,064.0 | 1,107.0 | 957.0 |
| Machinery | 31,541 | 9,991 | 21,550 | 16,077.5 | 7,534.0 | 8,543.5 |
| Electrical appliances, | 7,197 | 4,985 | 2,212 | 8,561.5 | 7,158.0 | 1,403.5 |
| Wood | 1,839 | 379 | 1,460 | 582.0 | 65.0 | 517.0 |
| Earth and stone | 10,651 | 2,289 | 8,362 | 4,804.0 | 1,357.0 | 3,447.0 |
| Chemicals | 36,140 | 7,938 | 28,202 | 24,835.0 | 9,703.0 | 15,132.0 |
| Catering | 11,447 | 2,595 | 8,852 | 9,705.0 | 1,383.0 | 8,322.0 |
| Textile | 93,265 | 34,552 | 58,713 | 15,452.6 | 3,298.8 | 12,153.8 |
| Costume | 9,241 | 843 | 8,398 | 160.3 | | 160.3 |
| Culture | 7,320 | 2,615 | 4,705 | 657.0 | 173.0 | 484.0 |
| Miscellaneous | 2,708 | 63 | 2,645 | 145.0 | | 145.0 |

*Data source:* Division of Statistics, Ministry of Economic Affairs (1943) pp. 11–12.

*Development of industry: part 1* 83

enterprises, private enterprises accounted for up to 82.5 percent of the total number of enterprises, which is in line with the usual situation. In terms of capital, public factories accounted for 69.6 percent, while private factories accounted for slightly more than 30 percent. In other words, private factories were mostly businesses with small capital, while public factories were capital-intensive and needed more capital. In terms of the number of workers, private factories accounted for 68 percent, indicating that private factories were more labor-intensive and employed more workers. In terms of horsepower, private factories accounted for 60 percent, slightly more than that of public enterprises. This means that by 1942, power was generally adopted for industrial production in the rear area, with few factories that operated without power. This can be said to be significant progress.[22]

Second, the three industries of chemicals, textiles, and machinery had the largest number of factories. This shows a major feature of the rear industry: relatively developed heavy industry. Generally, the textile and food industries were absolutely dominant, followed by heavy industry. In contrast, in the rear area, which was a special region in a special era, the industrial structure showed a different picture. From the perspective of the amount of capital, the four industries of chemicals, machinery, smelting, and textile had a large share, which shows the capital-intensive nature of these industries. In particular, because the first three are heavy industries, they needed considerable capital. In terms of the number of workers, the textile industry was the top employer, followed by chemicals, machinery, and smelting, indicating that these industries might have large factories. It was a somewhat different picture in terms of horsepower. Hydropower accounted for 35.6 percent of the total, and chemicals, machinery, and textiles also accounted for a large share. Hydropower was the dominant industry in this region. Mountainous terrain and abundant water resources made it ideal to develop hydropower. Of course, the energy industry was also a basic industry with a crucial strategic position.

It is important to observe that the distribution of industries in the rear was inclined to heavy industry because light industry should come before heavy industry according to the normal order of development, both at home and abroad.[23] However, a special phenomenon occurred in the rear industry during this period – it was in a state of war economy at this time, and there was a need to produce a wealth of weapons and war-related materials. One outcome was that it advanced industrialization in this otherwise relatively backward area, at least to some extent.[24]

The basic data just provided are briefly analyzed next. Table 3.17 shows several analytical indicators: average factory capital, average number of factory workers, per capita capital, and per capita horsepower. From the perspective of industries, smelting, hydropower, electrical appliances, chemicals, earth and stone, machinery, and other industries had great advantages in terms of average factory capital, especially smelting and hydropower. These industries are obviously of a public nature, especially smelting and machinery, while capital was relatively even for private factories and was mostly far less compared to public factories. In terms of the average number of factory workers, textiles, smelting, and miscellaneous industries had more workers. This shows two different tendencies. One is large-scale factories such as smelting and textile factories. The other is labor-intensive factories, such

## 84 Processes and characteristics

as miscellaneous industry. This is an interesting observation and also accords with the principles of economics. An important reason why an enterprise is called "big" is that they employ more employees or workers. Usually, an important measure of large and small enterprises is the number of employees, although other criteria such as output and scale of investment are also used.[25] Hiring more workers is needed for production purposes or for the market. If there is a large market, large enterprises can leverage its strength in economies of scale, and their market share may be high. Of course, it also needs to take into account machinery and equipment. Large

*Table 3.17* Industry characteristics of factories in the rear area in 1942

| Industry | Average factory capital (1,000 yuan) | | | Average number of factory workers | | |
|---|---|---|---|---|---|---|
| | Total | Public | Private | Total | Public | Private |
| Total | 516.0 | 2,056.8 | 190.1 | 64.3 | 117.7 | 53.0 |
| Hydropower | 1,166.0 | 2,126.7 | 251.0 | 37.5 | 42.0 | 33.3 |
| Smelting | 1,950.4 | 6,247.5 | 247.1 | 112.3 | 151.3 | 96.8 |
| Metals | 145.7 | 100.0 | 147.7 | 51.8 | 255.9 | 42.5 |
| Machinery | 495.0 | 4,931.1 | 144.1 | 46.2 | 199.8 | 34.1 |
| Electrical appliances | 949.4 | 3,545.6 | 153.3 | 73.4 | 216.7 | 29.5 |
| Wood | 115.7 | 63.0 | 120.4 | 37.5 | 94.8 | 32.4 |
| Earth and stone | 527.9 | 1,517.6 | 322.1 | 87.3 | 109.0 | 82.8 |
| Chemicals | 677.0 | 3,360.5 | 198.5 | 43.8 | 63.5 | 40.2 |
| Catering | 231.8 | 599.2 | 195.9 | 31.8 | 81.1 | 27.0 |
| Textile | 368.7 | 581.5 | 272.6 | 118.4 | 141.0 | 108.1 |
| Costume | 75.1 | 88.1 | 74.4 | 62.9 | 105.4 | 60.4 |
| Culture | 95.6 | 94.1 | 95.9 | 32.7 | 74.7 | 24.9 |
| Miscellaneous | 151.9 | 66.6 | 159.7 | 112.8 | 31.5 | 120.2 |

| Industry | Per capita capital (1,000 yuan) | | | Per capita horsepower | | |
|---|---|---|---|---|---|---|
| | Total | Public | Private | Total | Public | Private |
| Total | 8.0 | 17.5 | 3.6 | 0.6 | 0.8 | 0.5 |
| Hydropower | 31.1 | 50.7 | 7.5 | 11.1 | 8.2 | 14.5 |
| Smelting | 17.4 | 41.3 | 2.6 | 0.6 | 1.3 | 0.1 |
| Metals | 2.8 | 0.4 | 3.5 | 0.2 | 0.6 | 0.1 |
| Machinery | 10.7 | 24.7 | 4.2 | 0.5 | 0.8 | 0.4 |
| Electrical appliances | 12.9 | 16.4 | 5.2 | 1.2 | 1.4 | 0.6 |
| Wood | 3.1 | 0.7 | 3.7 | 0.3 | 0.2 | 0.4 |
| Earth and stone | 6.0 | 13.9 | 3.9 | 0.5 | 0.6 | 80.4 |
| Chemicals | 15.5 | 52.9 | 4.9 | 0.7 | 1.2 | 0.5 |
| Catering | 7.3 | 7.4 | 7.3 | 0.8 | 0.5 | 0.9 |
| Textile | 3.1 | 4.1 | 2.5 | 0.2 | 0.1 | 0.2 |
| Costume | 1.2 | 0.8 | 1.2 | | | |
| Culture | 2.9 | 1.3 | 3.9 | 0.1 | 0.1 | 0.1 |
| Miscellaneous | 0.2 | 0.3 | 0.2 | 0.1 | | 0.2 |

*Data source:* Division of Statistics, Ministry of Economic Affairs (1943) pp. 11–12.

*Development of industry: part 1*   85

enterprises should own more advanced production equipment and even hire workers of a higher caliber. This will make enterprises more competitive. In addition, public factories had significantly more workers than private factories, indicating that there were more large enterprises among public factories and that industries were generally modern, whereas there were more small enterprises among private factories, and industries were generally traditional.

In terms of per capita capital, salient industry characteristics can be observed. Hydropower had the largest per capita capital, followed by smelting, chemicals, electrical appliances, and machinery. Per capita capital was lower in other industries. This is obviously determined by the characteristics of these industries, most of which are modern industries, and needed a larger number of more advanced capital equipment. They could perform efficiently with capital equipment. Furthermore, the capital advantage of public factories was obvious, especially in the chemical, hydropower, and smelting industries. Capital was far less in private enterprises. In terms of per capita horsepower, hydropower was most prominent, with more horsepower than other industries by many times. An interesting phenomenon is that private factories outdid public factories in this respect. It is special because factories that moved inland or that were built in times of war were relatively advanced, even if they were private factories, unlike factories in other regions that developed according to the law of natural development.

Thus was the situation of main industries in industrial categories, including the number of factories, the amount of capital, the number of workers, and horsepower of power equipment. On the whole, the industry in the rear showed a clear feature: heavy industry occupied a high position. It has twofold meanings: comparison with the existing level of industrialization of the region and comparison with the national average at the time. As mentioned, an analysis of the background to industries in the rear area shows that economic activities in this area had been mainly related to agriculture, while industry had been relatively backward. This region developed an industrial base during this period because of Japan's all-out invasion of China and the relocation of factories and enterprises in the occupied areas to the hinterland (rear area). This also needs to be understood in two areas. First, some of the relocated enterprises represented the best in China at that time. Second, they developed accordingly after relocation. Accordingly, we use economics theory to explain the characteristics of industry in the rear during this period.

Figure 3.13 shows the relationship between the input of factors of production and the production output. It is essentially an expression of the production function and also a manifestation of technological progress. Shown here is the situation of industry in the rear area before factories relocated inland from coastal areas (such as in 1937) and after (such as in 1945). Before the relocation, the industry here had been relatively backward, belonging to typical traditional industry and the labor-intensive system, as represented by the capital/labor ratio $(K/L)a$ in the figure. At that time, factories had used more labor instead of capital, and their productivity and wage rates had been relatively low. After the relocation, capital-intensive development took place, as represented by $(K/L)b$ in the figure. At this time, factories used more capital and less labor, with relatively high wage rates. It is noteworthy that

## 86 Processes and characteristics

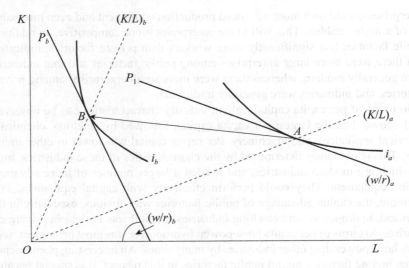

Figure 3.13 Changes in industry in the rear area

industrial development during this period was the result of two roles. First, as a result of factory relocation,[26] developed modern industries from coastal areas settled here, which led to the rapid development of heavy industry and capital-intensive industries. It is a form of technological diffusion. Second, due to the impact and promotion of wars, industries relocated here further developed, that is, with a focus on industry and capital-intensity.

### 3.7 Conclusion

This chapter examines the industry by period and region during the Republic of China period. Due to limited data and materials, it is only possible to make a rough judgment about industrial development and changes in this period. In other words, industry developed to a certain extent during the Republic of China period, at least compared with before. This was mainly attributed to the rapid rise and development of private enterprises, and considerable progress was made regardless of social chaos and political instability. This is mainly manifested in the following areas.

First, many enterprises were established in various places since the early Republic of China period, including almost all categories at that time, both emerging and traditional. Emerging industry was basically mechanized production, although it was of a small scale and the technical level was low. Such industries include matchsticks, tobacco, papermaking, chemicals, printing, and pharmaceuticals. Traditional industries were also mechanized production, such as textiles, flour, weaving, hardware, and leather.

Second, some industries and enterprises achieved a large scale, and the level of production was not high. Some could export products, and others developed great

*Development of industry: part 1*  87

strength. Industries such as textiles and machinery gradually built an industrial chain and could independently realize complex production, such as the trial production of trucks in Shenyang, Liaoning Province, in 1930.

Third, there were regional differences due to Japanese Aggression. After Japan invaded and occupied the northeast region in 1931, it became a Japanese colony until Japan's defeat in 1945. The northeast region developed independently for 14 years. After Japan's all-out invasion of China in 1937, many factories moved inland, and the southwest region became the rear area. During this period, the southwest region also developed independently, characterized by its war economy, as manifested in the high status of heavy industry.

Overall, the industrial development during the Republic of China period was a checkered history, with both success and failure. The so-called success primarily refers to the introduction and establishment of many emerging industries, as well as wide-ranging development. As for failure, Japan's invasion of China played havoc with normal economic development and impeded development during this period. Therefore, it was "failed take-off".

## Notes

1  This and the next chapters briefly discuss industry during the Republic of China. For a detailed study, see Guan Quan (2018) and Kubo Toru et al. (2000).
2  Bergere (1994).
3  For this issue, see Guan Quan (2018).
4  For details of this period, see Guan Quan (2011, 2018).
5  Guan Quan (2011, 2018) explained in detail the problems with the statistics.
6  Xu Dixin and Wu Chengming (1993), p. 900.
7  Changes for the years from 1912 to 1913 are not necessarily accurate.
8  Japan began to shift from steam engines to electric motors during this period, which lasted until the 1930s. For details, see Ryoshin Minami (1976) or Minami (1987).
9  Du Xuncheng (1991), p. 107.
10  For the data for this year, there is *China Industrial Survey Report*. For the details of this report, see Guan Quan (2018).
11  Economic development usually begins with light industry and then gradually transitions to heavy industry, as in Britain and Japan.
12  A factory of more than 200 people is a small factory by today's standards, but it was supposed to be a large factory at that time.
13  It is noteworthy that this industry is sometimes not included in the manufacturing industry and is somewhat special in nature.
14  In this regard, little data are available for international comparison. See Ryoshin Minami (2002), p. 227. Japan's experience rose from 40 to 80 percent.
15  For the role of horsepower, see Ryoshin Minami (1976) and Minami (1987).
16  For Manchukuo's *Factory Statistics Table* and its collation, development, and analysis, see Guan Quan (2005, 2018)
17  For the change in power technology, see Ryoshin Minami (1976) and Minami (1987).
18  The correlation coefficient for individual years is also high.
19  The northeast region in the occupied period was nominally independent but essentially a Japanese colony.
20  It indicates that the same quantity of product can be produced with less input.
21  For more information on industry in the rear area during the War of Resistance against Japanese Aggression, see Guan Quan (2018).

# 88 *Processes and characteristics*

22 For the issue of power used at factories, see Chapter 5 of this book, as well as Ryoshin Minami (1976) and Minami (1987). These documents studied the issue of the power used at factories in modern Japan and demonstrated that power was widely used in Japan in the late 19th and early 20th centuries, and electrification was realized in the 1920s.

23 It is worth mentioning that after 1949, China took a different approach and adopted the development strategy of prioritizing heavy industry, at least in the planned economy period. On the one hand, China followed the development model of the Soviet Union. On the other hand, China tried to catch up with Western developed countries faster.

24 The war economy has negative effects. On the one hand, the improper allocation of resources causes inefficiencies, and market principles may be abandoned for the sake of war. On the other hand, in most cases, depression comes in the wake of war because there is no market demand.

25 Before World War II, the criterion for measuring a large manufacturing enterprise in Japan was 300 persons. There was no fixed standard in China during this period.

26 In history, much technological progress was made during wars because people work hard to win wars at all costs.

# 4　Development of industry: part 2

## 4.1　Introduction

As a continuation of the previous chapter, this chapter further examines industrial development. This chapter comprises three parts: urban industry, mining production, and the development of some industries. In the first part, the development of industry in modern China was in large measure industrial development in cities, development especially of emerging modern industries. Of course, in modern China, traditional industries were always dominant, and emerging industries gradually spread to various places and cities. Therefore, it can be roughly said that the development of industry in modern China was development with a dual structure. On the one hand, it was traditional industry, mainly in rural areas and small towns. On the other hand, it was modern industry that developed rapidly in cities. The relationship between the two is also clear: traditional industries had a vast market and gradually became modernized by drawing on the technology and business philosophy of modern industries. Modern industries mainly relied on strong technology and funds to open up the market and to change people's ways of life, thus replacing traditional industries as the chief player.[1]

The second part is mining production during the Republic of China period. Mining is a very special industry. Given China's reality, Western powers first carried out geological exploration and mining and built a wealth of mines and factories in order to plunder resources. Later, national capital was involved, and a relatively large system was put in place. Because mining resources have the key characteristic of providing raw materials and fuel for industrial production, this industry was first plundered by foreign powers and, of course, also became the focus of competition for national capital. As a result, compared with other sectors such as agriculture and industry, mining statistics are relatively abundant, and it is possible to make long-term investigations from 1912 to 1949, while it is difficult to do the same for sectors such as agriculture and industry.

The third part deals with the drivers of industrial development. It is a complex and uncertain topic because the drivers are diverse and development is not the result of one or several factors. However, some factors play more important roles. A look at the history of economic development in various countries since the Industrial Revolution reveals that the factors contributing to success include several

DOI: 10.4324/9781003410386-6

## 90 *Processes and characteristics*

basic conditions: the level of development of agriculture and commerce; political factor, such as whether it is an independent state and whether the political decision-making process is reasonable; technical factor, such as whether there are technical reserves; market factor, such as whether there is a unified market and how the market functions; human resources factor, such as whether there are high-caliber workers and entrepreneurs. Here, the focus is on studying the role of the government, the market, and entrepreneurs in industrial development. It is specifically discussed through three industries with different characteristics. The first is the coal industry, which has the special nature of resources, particularly in the early stage of economic development. Many European countries that achieved industrial development early also developed the industrial foundation by means of the interaction between coal and steam engines. Because of this particularity, the government plays a far greater role than in other industries. This chapter also discusses this from this perspective. The second is the flour industry, which was an emerging industry introduced in modern times and also had a traditional base. In other words, it was a process in which mechanical production expanded and the traditional flour industry shrank. It is a typical industry that has developed in line with the laws of the market. Our discussion also centers around the market factor. The third is the textile industry, which was the largest industry in modern China. Like the coal and flour industries, the textile industry was also an industry introduced in modern times. There was also a competitive relationship with the traditional market, but their focus and degree of importance are different. Given the status of this industry and abundant materials, we discuss it from the perspective of entrepreneurship.

### 4.2 Overview of industrial development in cities

Before 1949, China's urbanization lagged because the country was far behind in terms of industrialization and economic development. In 1949, China's urban population accounted for only 10.64 percent of the total population, while the rural population accounted for 89.36 percent.[2] If this figure is used as a basis for estimating the situation before 1949, the level of urbanization at the time must be even lower. Other data show the population of various cities from the early 20th century to 1930. Although this is not the same as urbanization level, a glimpse can be gained based on the populations of these cities. If we assume that these data cover all the cities of China at that time, the degree of urbanization was very low based on the fact that the total population of China was about 400 million people (405 million in 1911 and 469 million in 1931).[3] The populations of large cities ranged from hundreds of thousands to millions of people. Such cities include Beijing, Baoding, Tianjin, Shanghai, Nanjing, Suzhou, Wuhan, Changsha, Chengdu, Chongqing, Hangzhou, Shaoxing, Fuzhou, Guangzhou, and Hong Kong.[4]

According to the research by Wang Yunwu, from the late 19th century to the early 1930s, the urban distribution of various industries was obviously centered on Shanghai, which occupied an invincible status.[5] Almost all industries could be seen in Shanghai, which was the main player in some industries. Shanghai had greater importance for industries with modern characteristics, such as spinning, weaving,

*Development of industry: part 2*   91

flour, and electrical appliances. These were also relatively concentrated in Tianjin, Wuhan, and Qingdao but were rarely seen in other cities. This shows that China's industry was in its infancy and had yet to spread to more places. Today's large cities such as Xi'an and Chengdu were invisible at the time in this regard.[6] The development of a city also has a process of popularization.

As mentioned earlier, cities are where industry develops. It can even be said that there is as much industry as there are cities and that the scale of industry depends on the size of a city, especially in the early stage of economic development. In the middle and late stages, the service sector will overtake industry and occupy a large proportion, especially in terms of employment. In terms of industrial distribution, it could be seen in almost all the major cities in China, but the number was very limited. Only those industries with more pronounced traditional characteristics, such as oil pressing, were distributed in more cities. Industries with modern characteristics, such as steel, were distributed in a few cities, or only in Wuhan in this case.

Table 4.1 shows the industrial distribution in 12 important cities in 1933 and 1947, including the number of factories, number of workers, amount of capital and net production, as well as the calculated average number of factory workers, per capita capital amount, and per capita net production value. These cities were quite representative, although they were not all-inclusive. These cities include large cities at the time such as Shanghai, Tianjin, Hankou, Guangzhou, Chongqing, Xi'an, and Nanjing, and most of them were cities with concentrated industries. It can be observed that Shanghai's position was invincible and growing. In Shanghai, the number of factories accounted for 36 percent of the total in 1933 and for 60 percent in 1947, and the proportion of number of workers rose from 53.3 to 60.8 percent for the same period. Although the data on the amount of capital and net production value were only available for 1933, their proportion exceeded that of the number of factories and number of workers, reaching 59.5 and 66.5 percent, respectively. Other important cities were Tianjin, Guangzhou, and Wuxi, while Qingdao and Hankou were also somewhat important. Conversely, cities with relatively backward industrial development, such as Xi'an, Fuzhou, and Shantou, had a large gap with developed cities in terms of the number of factories and number of workers. The average number of factory workers barely changed in more than a few decades, indicating that the factory size did not increase during this period. However, there were differences between regions, as well as changes. This index fell from 70.6 persons to 47.5 persons for Shanghai, increased from 28.4 to 47.6 for Tianjin, soared from 67.6 to 155.6 for Qingdao, increased from 29.1 to 53 for Guangzhou, increased by about the same extent for Chongqing, jumped from 15.1 to 85.7 for Xi'an, and fell from 202.4 to 60 for Wuxi. On the whole, the factories in Beijing, Nanjing, and Fuzhou were small, indicating that modern industries in these cities were not developed enough, because modern industries have economies of scale.

We next take a look at the amount of capital and net production value in 1933 as well as their per capita values. In terms of the absolute number, Shanghai obviously occupied an absolute advantage. In terms of the capital amount, it was followed by Guangzhou, Tianjin, Qingdao, Wuxi, and Beijing. In terms of net production value, Guangzhou was second only to Shanghai but came before Wuxi and Tianjin.

## 92 Processes and characteristics

Table 4.1 Overview of industry in 12 cities (1933, 1947)

| City | Number of factories | | Number of workers | | Average number of factory workers | | Amount of capital (1,000 yuan) | Net production value (1,000 yuan) | Capital per capita (yuan) | Net production value per capita (yuan) |
|---|---|---|---|---|---|---|---|---|---|---|
| | 1933 | 1947 | 1933 | 1947 | 1933 | 1947 | 1933 | 1933 | 1933 | 1933 |
| Shanghai | 3,485 | 7,738 | 245,948 | 367,433 | 70.6 | 47.5 | 190,870 | 727,726 | 776.1 | 2,958.9 |
| Tianjin | 1,224 | 1,211 | 34,769 | 57,658 | 28.4 | 47.6 | 24,201 | 74,501 | 696.1 | 2,142.7 |
| Qingdao | 140 | 185 | 9,457 | 28,778 | 67.6 | 155.6 | 17,650 | 27,098 | 1,866.3 | 2,865.4 |
| Beijing | 1,171 | 272 | 17,928 | 7,833 | 15.3 | 28.8 | 13,029 | 14,181 | 726.7 | 791.0 |
| Nanjing | 687 | 888 | 9,853 | 9,118 | 14.3 | 10.3 | 7,486 | 23,438 | 759.8 | 2,378.8 |
| Hankou | 497 | 459 | 24,992 | 21,048 | 50.3 | 45.9 | 8,816 | 26,309 | 352.8 | 1,052.7 |
| Guangzhou | 1,104 | 473 | 32,131 | 25,085 | 29.1 | 53.0 | 32,131 | 101,569 | 1,000.0 | 3,161.1 |
| Chongqing | 415 | 661 | 12938 | 34367 | 31.2 | 52.0 | 7345 | 10496 | 567.7 | 811.3 |
| Xi'an | 100 | 69 | 1505 | 5913 | 15.1 | 85.7 | 161 | 413 | 107.0 | 274.4 |
| Fuzhou | 366 | 176 | 3,853 | 3,067 | 10.5 | 17.4 | 2,612 | 7,773 | 677.9 | 2,017.4 |
| Shantou | 175 | 121 | 4,555 | 5,233 | 26.0 | 43.2 | 2,198 | 4,084 | 482.5 | 896.6 |
| Wuxi | 315 | 646 | 63,764 | 38,764 | 202.4 | 60.0 | 14,070 | 77,264 | 220.7 | 1,211.7 |
| Total | 9,679 | 12,899 | 461,693 | 604,297 | 47.7 | 46.8 | 320,569 | 1,094,852 | 694.3 | 2,371.4 |

Data source: China Industrial Survey Report (volume 2).

In terms of the per capita amount of capital, Qingdao and Guangzhou performed well, followed by Shanghai, Nanjing, Beijing, Tianjin, and Fuzhou. In terms of per capita net production value, Guangzhou, Shanghai, and Qingdao occupied leading positions. In terms of capital and production value, relatively backward cities (such as Xi'an) lagged far behind developed cities. It can be seen that West China (especially Northwest China) at that time was seriously backward.

Figure 4.1 shows the relationship between per capita capital amount and per capita net production value in the aforesaid 12 cities and shows a certain degree of positive correlation between the two, indicating that per capita output increases as per capita capital increases. Although this is not a production function in the strict sense and the amount of capital per capita is not the capital stock, it can be roughly seen as this relationship. Essentially, the production technology and production patterns vary from industry to industry. Moreover, due to the differences between regions, even if better production function data are used for calculation, the results are not necessarily very good. In other words, the production function used here, although rough, is in line with economic theory.

Table 4.2 shows the situation of industry in major cities in 1947. Shown here are the number of factories, the number of employees, horsepower, and electricity consumption by industry, as well as the indicators calculated according to these basic data. In terms of the number of factories, there were a total of 14,078 factories, of which 3,312 factories conformed to the factory law, accounting for 23.53 percent, and 10,766 did not conform to the factory law, accounting for 76.47 percent. These data are an improvement over 1933, despite a lapse of more than a decade and the outbreak of war. From the perspective of industry, textile factories were the most common, followed by clothing accessories, papermaking, printing, chemicals,

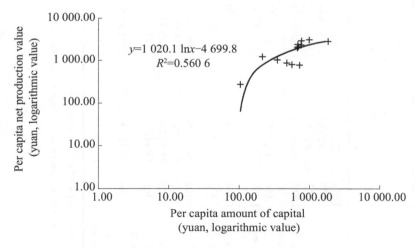

*Figure 4.1* Relationship between the amount of capital per capita and the per capita net production value of industry 12 cities in 1933

*Data source:* China Industrial Survey Report (volume 2).

*Table 4.2* Overview of industry in major cities in 1947 (1) (industry)

| Number of factories | Total | Number of enterprises that conformed to factory law (proportion) | Number of enterprises that did not conform to factory law (proportion) | Number of workers (1,000 people) | Horsepower (1,000 hp) | Electricity used (kWh) | Average number of factory workers | Horsepower per 100 people | Per capita electricity used |
|---|---|---|---|---|---|---|---|---|---|
| Total | 14,078 | 3,312(23.5) | 10,766(76.5) | 771.6 | 827.3 | 16,827.5 | 54.8 | 107.2 | 218.1 |
| Food | 1,379 | 326(23.6) | 1,053(76.4) | 108.3 | 74.7 | 1,750.0 | 78.5 | 68.9 | 161.6 |
| Textile | 3,773 | 1,089(28.9) | 2,684(71.1) | 337.7 | 329.2 | 7,640.1 | 89.5 | 97.5 | 226.2 |
| Clothing accessories | 1,783 | 290(16.3) | 1,493(83.7) | 52.0 | 8.5 | 104.8 | 29.2 | 16.3 | 20.2 |
| Wood | 156 | 42(26.9) | 114(73.1) | 4.5 | 4.7 | 41.6 | 28.8 | 104.4 | 92.4 |
| Papermaking, printing | 1,669 | 251(15.0) | 1,418(85.0) | 38.6 | 56.6 | 1,410.5 | 23.1 | 146.8 | 365.4 |
| Chemicals | 1,553 | 410(26.4) | 1,143(73.6) | 78.9 | 80.4 | 1,346.4 | 50.8 | 101.9 | 170.6 |
| Earth and stone | 152 | 67(44.1) | 85(55.9) | 15.7 | 117.7 | 2,882.4 | 103.3 | 748.1 | 1,836.0 |
| Smelting | 494 | 108(21.9) | 386(78.1) | 28.7 | 65.8 | 475.3 | 58.1 | 228.8 | 165.6 |
| Hardware | 682 | 217(31.8) | 465(68.2) | 21.9 | 26.7 | 381.1 | 32.1 | 122.2 | 174.0 |
| Machinery | 1505 | 223(14.8) | 1282(85.2) | 36.4 | 20.7 | 339.9 | 24.2 | 56.8 | 93.4 |
| Electrical equipment | 303 | 130(42.9) | 173(57.1) | 16.2 | 7.1 | 134.4 | 53.5 | 43.8 | 83.0 |
| Traffic equipment | 269 | 47(17.5) | 222(82.5) | 12.4 | 4.8 | 79.9 | 46.1 | 39.1 | 64.4 |
| Miscellaneous | 360 | 112(31.1) | 248(68.9) | 20.3 | 30.4 | 241.1 | 56.4 | 149.5 | 118.8 |

*Note:* The numbers in parentheses are proportions.

*Data source:* National Economic Survey Commission of the Ministry of Economic Affairs, *Summary of the Preliminary Report on the Survey of Major Urban Industries in China* (1948).

*Development of industry: part 2* 95

machinery, and food factories. Modern industries like chemicals and machinery also developed to a certain extent.[7] Judging from the proportion of enterprises that conformed to and did not conform to the factory law, the proportion of earth and stone and electrical equipment factories was the highest, exceeding 40 percent, which is not a low figure, indicating that factories in these industries were large in scale and used power. In terms of the number of workers, textiles factories ranked at the top, followed by food, chemicals, clothing accessories, and other industries. The large number of workers in the first two industries (also including clothing accessories) means that China's industrial labor force was still concentrated in light industries during this period, while chemicals, machinery, metals, and other heavy industries were not developed enough.

The horsepower of power is not the same as the number of factories and workers. Textile factories still ranked at the top, but food was ranked after earth and stone, and chemicals. Following behind were smelting, papermaking, and printing factories. This reflects the technical differences among industries. There are issues in several respects. First, industries of a modern nature such as chemicals, smelting, papermaking, and printing needed to use more power, while traditional industries such as food and clothing accessories used less power, which should theoretically undermine their productivity. Second, what is shown here is the absolute value, which is affected by the number of factories. Of course, it is also an issue about the size of the industry. If there were more factories, more power would be used, for example in the textile and food industries. If there were few factories, less power would be used, for example in wood, transport, appliances, and electrical equipment industries. Third, the rate of motorization at factories was different, as was the quantity of power used. For the same number of factories, the horsepower of power was high if the rate of motorization was high. Otherwise, it was low. However, although Table 4.3 does not provide data on the rate of motorization, it can be speculated from other data that the rate of motorization in China in this period was relatively high. Nevertheless, it varied greatly from industry to industry. This can also be seen from the proportion in Table 4–3 of the number of factories that conformed to factory law and factories that did not conform to factory law. Factories that conformed to the factory law must use power, and those that did not conform to the factory law did not necessarily reject the use of power. In this sense, it can be roughly estimated that the rate of motorization is 40 to 50 percent.[8]

The amount of electricity used by factories indicates the production situation of factories. Of course, this is assumed under the premise of the use of electricity in factories. Electricity used in factories consists of two parts: the electricity used for lighting and the electricity used for power. The former is needed even if there is no power, while the latter is needed for both. If it is a factory that used power, the electricity used for power should be the principal part. In terms of the amount of electricity used, textiles factories still ranked first, followed by earth and stone and food. Papermaking, printing, and chemical factories also had a large share. This situation reflects both differences in the industry and differences in the use of power. Textile factories have both at the same time. In other words, there were a large number of factories, which require lighting on a large scale and also use

## 96 *Processes and characteristics*

power, with huge electricity consumption for driving power. Earth and stone is a typical electricity guzzler, as it is a characteristic of this industry. Food factories consumed a great deal of electricity because of the large number of factories, not the use of more power. The papermaking, printing, and chemicals industries were more inclined to use electricity for driving power.

Now, let's take a look at a few average values: average number of factory workers, the horsepower of power per 100 people, and electricity consumption per capita. For the former, the average value for the manufacturing industry is 54.8 people, which should be a high figure because it includes factories that did not use power and did not conform to the factory law. From the perspective of industry, the earth and stone industry ranked at the top, with more than 100 people, followed by textiles and food industries. Textiles and food industries are labor-intensive and did not necessarily use much capital equipment, but the number of people was large, especially in the textile industry. It is followed by the smelting, electrical equipment, chemicals, and transport appliances industries, which are of a modern nature and capital-intensive. The number of factories in these industries is small, but the scale is significant. In contrast, the scale of the clothing accessories, wood, machinery, papermaking, printing, and hardware industries is small, about half of the average. It is divided into two kinds of industries. One is the typical traditional industries, such as clothing accessories. The other is the machinery, hardware, papermaking, and printing industries, which are of a modern nature but belong to the divisible industries. In other words, the scale of a factory can be large or small, and production links can be divided. For example, machining can process a part of the entire machine instead of producing full-fashioned products, so that they can be manufactured separately and then assembled, such as bicycles, cars, and ships.

The second indicator can represent the per capita capital equipment ratio or the capital/labor ratio. Although the capital data are not complete and horsepower represents only a part of it, it has such a meaning. In particular, this indicator also symbolizes the level of technology – the higher the per capita capital is, the higher the productivity. The earth and stone industry ranked first, far ahead of other industries, followed by smelting. This is easy to understand because smelting requires much power. Miscellaneous, papermaking, printing, hardware, wood, chemicals, etc. all exceed or approach the manufacturing average. These industries use more power, although the number of factories in these industries is not large. Clothing accessories, transport appliances, machinery, electrical equipment, etc. ranked low because their production is more manual. Finally, in terms of per capita electricity consumption, the earth and stone industry ranked far ahead of other industries and can be seen as a special industry. There is little difference between other industries except clothing accessories. This shows that enterprises used electricity based on market principles and did not waste electricity because electricity is a key component of production costs. The clothing accessories industry rarely used electricity because this industry basically adopted manual operations, such as sewing clothing. Workers at most used irons, and the remaining electricity was used for lighting, including heating or night duty.

Table 4.3 shows the same indicators as those in Table 4.2, but divided by city. From the perspective of the number of factories, Shanghai still had a large

*Table 4.3* Overview of industry in major cities in 1947 (2) (industry)

| Number of factories | Total | Number of enterprises that conformed to factory law | Number of enterprises that did not conform to factory law | Number of workers (1,000 people) | Horsepower | Electricity used | Average number of factory workers | Horsepower per 100 people | Per capita electricity used |
|---|---|---|---|---|---|---|---|---|---|
| Total | 14,078 | 3,312 (23.5) | 10,766 (76.5) | 771.6 | 827.5 | 16,827.4 | 54.8 | 107.2 | 218.1 |
| Nanjing | 888 | 36 (4.1) | 852 (95.9) | 12.0 | 18.1 | 397.2 | 13.5 | 150.5 | 331.0 |
| Shanghai | 7,738 | 1,945 (25.1) | 5,793 (74.9) | 406.4 | 325.3 | 7,017.3 | 52.5 | 80.0 | 172.7 |
| Beiping | 272 | 49 (18.0) | 223 (82.0) | 10.0 | 13.3 | 294.8 | 36.8 | 132.9 | 294.8 |
| Tianjin | 1,211 | 215 (17.8) | 996 (82.2) | 65.7 | 110.5 | 1,727.4 | 54.3 | 168.1 | 262.9 |
| Qingdao | 185 | 96 (51.9) | 89 (48.1) | 31.5 | 34.4 | 854.8 | 170.3 | 109.2 | 271.4 |
| Chongqing | 661 | 96 (14.5) | 565 (85.5) | 37.7 | 11.7 | 154.7 | 57.0 | 31.1 | 41.0 |
| Shenyang | 275 | 117 (42.5) | 158 (57.5) | 36.9 | 189.5 | 3,504.0 | 134.2 | 513.0 | 949.6 |
| Xi'an | 69 | 24 (34.8) | 45 (65.2) | 7.1 | 3.7 | 69.6 | 102.9 | 51.6 | 98.0 |
| Hankou | 459 | 86 (18.7) | 373 (81.3) | 23.9 | 10.2 | 698.4 | 52.0 | 42.6 | 292.2 |
| Guangzhou | 473 | 269 (56.9) | 204 (43.1) | 30.0 | 10.0 | 136.9 | 63.4 | 33.4 | 45.6 |
| Taiwan | 985 | 205 (20.8) | 780 (79.2) | 67.0 | 80.5 | 1,707.0 | 68.0 | 120.1 | 254.8 |
| Lanzhou | 39 | 17 (43.6) | 22 (56.4) | 3.2 | 2.0 | 24.7 | 82.1 | 61.5 | 77.2 |
| Shantou | 121 | 15 (12.4) | 106 (87.6) | 5.9 | 0.3 | 3.1 | 48.8 | 4.5 | 5.3 |
| Fuzhou | 176 | 17 (9.7) | 159 (90.3) | 3.7 | 3.3 | 66.3 | 21.0 | 89.0 | 179.2 |
| Kunming | 66 | 30 (45.5) | 36 (54.5) | 7.5 | 5.3 | 108.4 | 113.6 | 70.2 | 144.5 |
| Guiyang | 83 | 48 (57.8) | 35 (42.2) | 5.6 | 1.3 | 20.6 | 67.5 | 23.4 | 36.8 |
| Changsha, Hengyang | 216 | 23 (10.6) | 193 (89.4) | 10.3 | 4.0 | 3.6 | 47.7 | 39.3 | 3.5 |
| Nanchang, Jiujiang | 161 | 24 (14.9) | 137 (85.1) | 7.2 | 4.1 | 38.6 | 44.7 | 56.4 | 53.6 |

*Note:* The figures in parentheses are proportions.

*Data source:* National Economic Survey Commission of the Ministry of Economic Affairs, *Summary of the Preliminary Report on the Survey of Major Urban Industries in China* (1948).

## 98 Processes and characteristics

proportion, accounting for 55 percent of the total. Factories that conformed to the factory law accounted for 58.7 percent, and those that did not conform accounted for 53.8 percent. This proves that Shanghai still occupied half of China's industry at this time. It was followed by Tianjin, Taiwan, Nanjing, and Chongqing. This ranking is interesting.[9] Except in Taiwan, the urban industry on the mainland underwent some changes compared with the 1930s, but it was not so prominent in Nanjing and Chongqing, indicating that after the War of Resistance against Japanese Aggression and the development of industry in the rear area, these two cities grew faster than other cities. Like the number of workers and number of factories, Shanghai still accounted for 52.7 percent, far outpacing other cities.[10] This indicator exceeds the proportion of the number of factories, and even the proportion of the number of employees in Tianjin is not as large as the proportion of the number of factories. This shows that Shanghai's factories were large in both number and size and had many workers. Although these were similar in terms of proportion, it was more scattered in other cities that had no large factories. If the size of a factory is related to production efficiency (economies of scale), factories in Shanghai were more efficient than those in other cities. It is a pity that this data does not include the production value that represents productivity, let alone production cost. Therefore, it is impossible to calculate productivity. Shanghai ranked first in terms of horsepower, closely followed by Shenyang, Tianjin, and Taiwan. In particular, the gap between Shenyang and Shanghai is not large. However, Shanghai was still far ahead of other cities, such as Guiyang, Xi'an, Lanzhou, Shantou, and Fuzhou. After the period when the northeast fell, Shenyang developed rapidly in terms of heavy industry, as notably manifested in the use of power. This can also be seen from electricity consumption – Shanghai ranked at the top, followed by Shenyang, Tianjin, and Taiwan. Electricity consumption in Shanghai was twice as large as that in Shenyang, which was twice as much as that in Tianjin and Taiwan. This situation was unimaginable in 1933. It can be seen that Shenyang rose dramatically during this period, especially in terms of horsepower.[11]

In terms of the average number of employees, Qingdao ranked first, followed by Shenyang, Kunming, and Xi'an. Shanghai and Tianjin only reached the national average. This shows that factories in the top-ranking cities were large in size, possibly including many modern industries. The reason for this is clear: Shenyang developed after the northeast was occupied, while Kunming and Xi'an might have benefitted from the industrial development in the rear area during the War of Resistance. Qingdao is also a city that was occupied by Japan for a long time and is similar to Shenyang in many ways. Shenyang ranked top in terms of the horsepower per 100 people, several times higher than that of other cities, indicating the city's heavy industry and capital-intensive nature. Ranking behind are Nanjing, Tianjin, Beiping, Taiwan, and Qingdao, while Shanghai was still inconspicuous. Finally, Shenyang was still ahead of other cities in terms of electricity consumption. Ranking behind Shenyang were many cities such as Nanjing, Beiping, Hankou, Qingdao, Tianjin, and Taiwan. It should be noted that there were also third-tier cities in this regard, such as Changsha and Shantou. The gap between cities was very large.

*Development of industry: part 2* 99

## 4.3 Development of the mining industry

The endowment of natural resources often plays a crucial role in the economic development of a country. Therefore, governments, of course, strive to improve statistics in this regard. However, due to well-known reasons, mining statistics before 1949 were not complete, and even geological surveys were first conducted by foreigners. For example, the geological data on coal was collected by the German F.P.W. Richthofen in 1861 and 1868. He published estimates of China's coal reserves after returning to Germany. According to his estimates, there were 1,890 billion metric tons in Shanxi province alone, which, based on the level of consumption at that time, could serve the world for 1,300 years.[12] This figure was obviously exaggerated and was later refuted after several surveys. The American N.F. Drake, then a professor at Beiyang University, reported at the International Geological Congress in Canada in 1913 that China's coal reserves were 996.613 billion metric tons. Inoue Kinosuke from the Geological Survey of Japan estimated it at 39.565 billion metric tons. Later, China carried out some surveys and provided more accurate results.

Important materials about this period are introduced next. First, after the Xinhai Revolution in 1912, China established an independent survey body to conduct geological surveys, and the survey results were published in the *Summary of China's Mining Industry* (hereinafter referred to as the "*Summary*"). The *Summary* was published seven times from 1921 to 1945 as a relatively credible source of survey data. Second, the *Agricultural and Commercial Statistics Table* is the earliest statistical data compiled by the Chinese government based on the earliest surveys in modern times. It provides statistics on the industry and mining, agriculture, and commerce sectors from 1912 to 1921. However, because the political, economic, and social conditions were not mature for such statistical surveys, its accuracy is so low that it has no use value. However, some parts still have reference value. In addition to the aforesaid firsthand data, there are also secondhand data for use or reference. For example, the Central Party Headquarters (1937) made a record of the output, unit price, and output value of the mining industry from 1925 to 1934, and the data were mainly obtained from the *Summary*. The Institute of East Asian Studies (1942) recorded some data collected from European and American statistics from 1925 to 1940, and its sources are mainly the *Summary* and *Customs Statistics*.[13] Tan Xihong and Wu Zongfen (1948) recorded the output of major metallic mineral products. Cao Chengke (1946) recorded the output of major metallic minerals such as copper, tin, and lead. The Statistics Department of the Accountant Bureau of the Nationalist government (1947) recorded the figures for the whole country in the 1940s. The Investigation and Statistics Office of the Northeast Financial and Economic Commission (1949) recorded the figures for the northeast region in the early 1940s. In addition, works of industry history by Wu Chengluo (1929) and Yang Dajin (1940) et al. also recorded some data. The *Chronicle of China's Industry* (5 provinces) also provided data on mining.[14]

The aforesaid statistics on China's mining production during the Republic of China period are incomplete to varying degrees. Therefore, it is necessary to

## 100   *Processes and characteristics*

supplement and correct the data that are incorrect. To date, no comprehensive revision has been conducted, but there have been some studies on some periods or some projects. Shown next are a few of these studies. First is an estimation by Yan Zhongping et al. Strictly speaking, Yan Zhongping (1955) is not an estimate but a collection of data. However, the editorial notes of this book state that "most of the figures published here are processed by us".[15] While processing methods are not detailed in the book, it can be believed that the editor conducted corresponding technical treatment. However, we know that Yan Zhongping et al. (1955) was the first book after 1949 to comprehensively sort out the relevant statistics before 1949 and is of pioneering significance for subsequent researches, at least providing relatively comprehensive economic statistics data. Second are estimates by John K. Chang. Chang (1969) conducted quantitative analysis of modern industries during the Republic of China period, and the most important contribution was the production index of industry from 1912 to 1949, which is also the most comprehensive production index of industry in this period to date. He used 15 kinds of industrial and mining products – coal, iron ore, pig iron, steel, antimony, copper, gold, mercury, tin, tungsten, cotton and silk, fabric, cement, crude oil, and electricity, and nine of these belong to mineral products. If you add pig iron, steel, and cement, it brings the total to 12. Because of the excessive emphasis on mineral products, his industrial production index is often criticized because the share of mining in industrial and mining production should be relatively small.[16] Moreover, the study of China's industrial development in modern times (or during the Republic of China period) with a focus on mining has a more significant problem: the mining industry grew faster while other industries grew more slowly, leading to an illusion that China's industry as a whole grew rapidly. As we all know, China in modern times was carved up by Western powers, especially in the field of mineral resources. Therefore, the mining industry developed faster than other industries. In addition, there are two kinds of research estimates. One is the study of individual products, such as the estimation of coal by the Compilation Group of the History of Coal Mines in Modern China (1990) and the estimation of flour by the Institute of Economics Chinese Academy of Social Sciences (1966) and Shanghai Municipal Grain Bureau etc. (1987). The other is research on some years, such as estimation by Wu Baosan et al. (1947) on China's economy as a whole and in individual sectors in 1933, including the mining industry; Liu and Yeh (1965); Wu Chengming (1990, 1993); and others. These studies have their respective features, but the latter is more important for this chapter. These valuable research results can be used as objects of our comparison and reference. However, although the former is an estimate, it provides the method and basis for estimation.

We make estimates in order to learn about the basic situation of China's mining production in modern times, especially during the Republic of China period, including production value. With these reliable and continuous data, we can compile the mining production index and learn about growth and changes over the entire period. Specifically, it is necessary to calculate the output, output value, and value added in the long term according to product categories. Since the aforesaid materials contain more data on output than on output value, it is convenient to first estimate the output. Moreover, compared with the output value, the output has the advantage of not being affected by price changes. If the output can be calculated, the output value and the value added can be calculated by multiplying the output by price. Therefore, estimating the output is the most basic and important work. Because our purpose is to have a comprehensive and detailed knowledge of the production of mineral products as much as possible, 37 products are selected from the most informative *Summary* (5th edition).[17] It can be seen from Schedule 1 of this chapter that there are more data on metal products than on nonmetallic products.[18]

Figure 4.2 shows the John K. Chang index and our estimated value added index. The John K. Chang index is characterized by the small scope of trend growth, but it was relatively stable before 1942 and declined slightly after 1942. The index used in this chapter shows great fluctuations. It peaked around 1942 but declined considerably. At the same time, the pre-1933 high is also higher than the John K. Chang index. It should be noted that the manufacturing sector is not included in the index used in this chapter, while the John K. Chang index contains several modern industries.

## 4.4 Development of some industries

### 4.4.1 The role of the government: coal industry

The relationship between the coal mining industry and the government is studied here. This industry is chosen for several reasons. First, coal mining is a basic industry for modern industries and was irreplaceable in the energy industry before

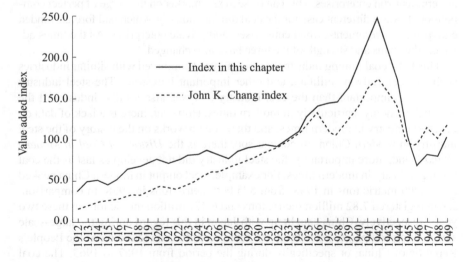

*Figure 4.2* Industrial and mining production index from 1912 to 1949

Note: Here is the value-added index.

Data source: See Chang (1969) for John K. Chang Index; see Guan Quan and Makino Fumio (1999) and Guan Quan (2018) for the index used in this chapter.

## 102 *Processes and characteristics*

oil became the most important energy source. Although Britain's Industrial Revolution began with the invention and application of steam engines and textile machines, coal is in fact indispensable for the operation of all modern industries. The steam engine itself runs on coal, and the more machinery and equipment driven by the steam engine, the more coal is needed. Even during the Second Industrial Revolution that began in the late 19th century, electric motors and internal combustion engines began to gradually replace steam engines, and coal was needed to generate electricity. As people's living standards improve and urbanization deepens, there is a growing demand for coal.[19] Although the status of coal declined in the age of oil after World War II, it is still an important energy resource for many countries, particularly those that lack oil. In fact, more countries lack oil than have it.

Second, the coal mining industry can better represent China's national circumstances in modern times, which is a special period. This is also the research perspective of this chapter – the competition between government-run enterprises, private enterprises, and foreign-funded enterprises. China in modern times was a semicolonial and semifeudal country, bullied by foreign powers. The influx and even monopoly of foreign investment was largely a normal phenomenon. Moreover, due to the conditions and the degree of development at that time, government-run enterprises had been involved in this industry from the beginning, although they might be mismanaged or had an ulterior motive. Nevertheless, government-run enterprises were always present, overtly or covertly, and private enterprises were sandwiched between foreign-funded enterprises and government-run enterprises. Of course, it also depends on the industry. Some industries that were not so important, such as rice milling and printing, as well as the flour industry discussed here,[20] had few foreign-funded enterprises and government-run enterprises. This can be seen as a market on the verge of perfect competition. It was a different case for the coal mining industry, which had foreign-funded enterprises, government-owned enterprises, and private enterprises. As the times advance, the status and strength of the three have also changed.

Third, the coal mining industry can be analyzed compared with similar industries such as steel, railway, military, and other important industries. The steel industry was no less important than the coal industry and was also a pillar industry of the national economy, particularly in modern times. However, there is a lack of data on the steel industry in modern times, and there are no works on the history of the steel industry in modern China. In comparison, there is the *History of Coal in Modern China*,[21] and, more importantly, the steel industry did not develop as fast as the coal mining industry in modern times. For example, steel output in modern China peaked at 923,000 metric tons in 1943, from 875,000 metric tons in 1938. In comparison, Japan registered 7.82 million metric tons and 6.472 million metric tons in these two years, respectively. China caught up with Japan in this regard during the large-scale steelmaking campaign and subsequent few years after the founding of the People's Republic of China, or specifically during the period from 1957 to 1963. The coal industry is different. Coal output peaked at 58.374 million metric tons in 1942, and Japan's coal output peaked at 56.472 million metric tons in 1941. The two countries were on a par in this regard.[22] In another example, railway belongs to the transport industry, not the manufacturing industry. Even under a broadened definition, railway

*Development of industry: part 2*    103

does not belong to any industry, and only the railway locomotive manufacturing and repair belongs to the manufacturing industry. The military industry is highly important. Perhaps because this industry is so important, it is not representative, since it does not reflect the development process of most industries.

Given the importance of the coal mining industry, bureaucratic capital entered this field almost at the same time as foreign investment or even slightly earlier. In 1875, Li Hongzhang developed the Zhili Cizhou Coal Mine, although it failed. In the same year, Sheng Xuanhuai and Li Mingchi founded Hubei Coal and Iron Mining Company. In 1876, Shen Baozhen and Ye Wenlan founded the Keelung Coal Mine in Taiwan. In 1877, Yang De and Sun Zhenquan built the Chizhou Coal Mine in Anhui Province. In the same year, Li Hongzhang and Tang Tingshu established the Zhili Kaiping Coal Mine. In 1879, Sheng Xuanhuai built Jingmen Coal Mine in Hubei Province, and so on. By 1934, there were 68 government-related coal mines. There were also coal mines invested and operated by foreign investors. These cover all the important coal mines in China at the time. These coal mines were run in two ways. One is government operation via bureaucracy or the government directly funding and operating coal mines. The other is commercial operation under government supervision; coal mines were funded by businessmen and operated by the government.

At that time, China's important coal mines included Shandong Luda Coal Mine, Zhongxing Coal Mine, Zhongyuan Company, Kailuan Mining Bureau, Jingxing Mining Bureau, Fushun Coal Mine, Yantai Coal Mine, Benxihu Coal Mine, and Beipiao Coal Mine. About half of these were foreign-funded or joint ventures, government-run or government–business joint enterprises. Another half were purely operated by business. The proportion of coal mines operated by businesses in the early 1930s increased considerably, indicating that as China's industry developed, private commercial capital was also able to enter the coal mining industry. Another important issue is that the early government-run coal mines basically went bankrupt because those bureaucrats had no knowledge of technology or management. The problem is that many so-called commercially run coal mines were actually government-run coal mines under a commercial guise.

Table 4.4 shows the output and proportion of coal mines operated by bureaucratic capital among machinery-based coal mines. The total output here does not include the part by foreign-invested coal mines. First, the combined proportion for bureaucratic capital plunged from almost 80 to 40 percent, which reflects the growth of real private capital. Conversely, the proportion of private capital jumped from 20 to 60 percent, which should be progress. On the one hand, the management policy under bureaucratic capital is rigid and bureaucratic and could hardly meet the needs of the market. On the other hand, the expanding market and fierce competition also necessitated reforms. Second, the proportion of coal mines that were government-run in name only with bureaucratic capital declined rapidly, from more than 40 percent in the early days to less than 5 percent. The nominal government–business joint enterprises were rarely seen in the early days, account for less than 5 percent, but increased to account for about 25 percent. The proportion of nominal commercially run coal mines did not change much, typically accounting for 35 percent, except in a few years.

104　*Processes and characteristics*

*Table 4.4* National capital in coal mines in modern times

| Year | National mining volume (10,000 metric tons) | Bureaucratic capital (10,000 metric tons, %) | | | |
|---|---|---|---|---|---|
| | | *Nominal government-run* | *Nominal government– business partnership* | *Nominal commercially run* | *Total* |
| 1912 | 41.66 | 7.23 (17.3) | 2.00 (4.8) | 25.00 (60.0) | 34.23 (82.2) |
| 1913 | 54.10 | 7.06 (13.0) | 2.20 (4.1) | 25.00 (46.2) | 34.26 (63.3) |
| 1914 | 82.60 | 37.90 (45.9) | 1.80 (2.2) | 24.84 (30.1) | 64.54 (78.1) |
| 1915 | 87.57 | 41.54 (47.4) | 3.00 (3.4) | 17.48 (20.0) | 62.02 (70.8) |
| 1916 | 187.60 | 58.45 (31.2) | 44.87 (23.9) | 45.54 (24.3) | 148.86 (79.3) |
| 1917 | 215.60 | 54.50 (25.3) | 35.44 (16.4) | 64.16 (29.8) | 154.10 (71.5) |
| 1918 | 252.20 | 69.48 (27.5) | 45.46 (18.0) | 76.02 (30.1) | 190.96 (75.7) |
| 1919 | 312.22 | 68.42 (21.9) | 89.31 (28.6) | 86.15 (27.6) | 243.88 (78.1) |
| 1920 | 327.98 | 43.78 (13.3) | 75.13 (22.9) | 104.77 (31.9) | 223.68 (68.2) |
| 1921 | 322.10 | 58.60 (18.2) | 58.46 (18.1) | 101.69 (31.6) | 218.75 (67.9) |
| 1922 | 305.99 | 0.77 (0.3) | 67.53 (22.1) | 111.58 (36.5) | 179.88 (58.8) |
| 1923 | 358.36 | 13.84 (3.9) | 87.41 (24.4) | 123.27 (34.4) | 224.52 (62.6) |
| 1924 | 115.03 | 6.83 (1.5) | 120.58 (27.1) | 147.09 (33.1) | 274.50 (61.7) |
| 1925 | 445.78 | 8.41 (1.9) | 104.11 (23.4) | 148.90 (33.4) | 261.42 (58.6) |
| 1926 | 338.14 | 16.19 (4.8) | 50.14 (14.8) | 108.45 (32.1) | 174.78 (51.7) |
| 1927 | 418.38 | 12.68 (3.0) | 108.33 (25.9) | 52.32 (12.5) | 173.33 (41.4) |

*Note:* (1) The national mining volume does not include the part by foreign-funded coal mines.

(2) The so-called nominal commercially run coal mines were founded by the big bureaucrats who held political power at that time in the name of individuals and who enjoyed many privileges.

*Data source:* Yan Zhongping et al. (1955), p. 154.

The development of the coal mining industry in modern China was studied from the perspective of the government, and several inspiring conclusions can be drawn. Because of China's national conditions in modern times, the coal mining industry actually includes other modern industries, such as railway, steel, military, shipbuilding, and other heavy industries, in which the government dominated. Although this fact is somewhat significant, it brings many problems. On the one hand, the government at that time was inefficient, and some bureaucrats only looked after their own interests rather than the national interest. On the other hand, owing to the rigid administration and a lack of basic scientific literacy, it was difficult to run modern enterprises well.

### 4.4.2　*The role of the market: flour industry*

The flour industry was originally a traditional industry, which existed extensively because it concerned the livelihood of all people. However, as new European technologies spread, flour mills equipped with machinery gradually appeared in China. The flour produced by them was called "foreign flour". A wealth of traditional workshops still existed, and their products were called "local flour". Because of the good quality of foreign flour and the high productivity, flour mills equipped

Development of industry: part 2    105

with machinery quickly spread in cities. In modern China, a mode of hybrid production of the two emerged: machine mill or small flour mill, which improved the traditional production method and was driven by power from electric motors or diesel engines. This mode of production is called "compromise technology" or "intermediate technology" in the sense of technological advance and often appears in the early days of industrialization or economic development.[23] Because there was a lack of capital, technology and personnel for adopting modernized mode of production at the time, such technology improvement would be made in many villages or small cities. It is a technological innovation in line with a country's national conditions. What we called "starting with indigenous methods" belongs to this technology.

If what has been just mentioned refers to the supply side, the other side of the flour industry is the demand side because this industry is directly related to the lives of all people. In particular in modern China, economic development was limited, and people's living standards were low, with most people living in a traditional and low-end life. The Engel coefficient was very high, and a considerable number of people relied on self-sufficient economy.[24] However, with the introduction of the opening up policy, the development of international trade, the influx of foreign investment and foreign cultures, as well as the progress of transport, particularly urbanization, the commodity economy developed at a faster clip, and the supply and demand relationship featuring urban residents underwent new changes. The development of the flour industry, particularly the machine-based flour industry, basically depended on the aforesaid national conditions.

Similar to many other modern industries, the development of China's machine-made flour industry came as a result of the opening up. In 1863, British merchants set up the first machine-made flour mill in Shanghai. In 1878, the first machine-made flour mill with national capital investment appeared in Tianjin. New flour mills were established every year from the beginning of the 20th century. From 1896 to 1912, 90 new flour mills were set up nationwide, including 47 with national capital investment. Of course, foreign investment still had an advantage in terms of technology and scale. World War I brought opportunities to China's economy. From 1913 to 1921, 123 mills were established, of which 105 were invested in with national capital, with a production capacity accounting for more than 80 percent. However, as Western European and Russian power exited, Japanese capital entered on a large scale. Foreign investment was involved in 18 out of the 123 flour mills, including 15 flour mills with Japanese capital.[25]

After the end of World War I, foreign investors entered China on a larger scale. Coupled with the warlord dogfight in China, the flour industry declined, with only 85 factories newly built from 1922 to 1931, including 82 with national capital. After the outbreak of the September 18 Incident in 1931, the flour industry lost a large market and important production areas of raw materials, and the flour mills invested by national capital in the northeast region (accounting for 35.5 percent of the total number of factories in China) were also controlled by the Japanese puppet regime.[26] Of the 52 flour mills newly built nationwide from 1932 to 1936, 12 were foreign-funded mills, but their production capacity accounted for half of the total. Except for 11 mills, which were opened by Japanese investors or forcibly purchased from Chinese enterprises, only 26 new factories were established in the region in the hinterland. During the War of Resistance against Japanese Aggression, the flour mills invested by national capital in the occupied areas met disasters of unprecedented magnitude, and half of them were either placed under Japanese military control or forced to be operated by Japanese businessmen. Due to the sharp increase in the population of migrants and the demand for army provisions in the rear area, there appeared a short-term boom, with a total of 89 flour mills established, accounting for half of the total in the period. However, their scale was relatively small, with a production capacity accounting for only 23.4 percent of the total. From 1937 to 1945, 180 flour mills were newly built nationwide, including 23 in the northeast, 68 in the occupied area in the hinterland, and 89 in the rear area under Kuomintang rule. Of the 180 factories, 143 involved private capital, 14 involved bureaucratic capital, and 23 were foreign-funded and Sino-foreign joint ventures. Sixty-nine factories suspended production during the same period. After the victory of the War of Resistance against Japanese Aggression, the flour industry saw an unprecedented boom, with a large number of factories built. A total of 131 factories were newly built from 1946 to 1949, which were primarily located in large cities, such as Wuhan, Shanghai, Tianjin, Chongqing, and Xi'an.[27]

Figure 4.3 shows the situation of new factories with national capital investment and existing factories (cumulative). Although the absolute number of factories was small, it shows the establishment of factories in rapid succession. The figure peaked

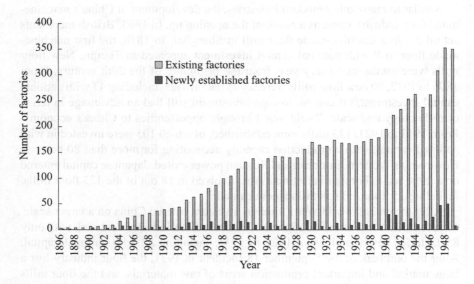

*Figure 4.3* Number of newly established and actual number of flour mills invested by national capital

Data source: Based on pp. 32–35 of the Institute of Economics, Chinese Academy of Social Sciences et al. (1966).

*Development of industry: part 2* 107

twice during this period. An average of more than 10 flour mills was built per year from 1913 to 1921. Although it was not active from 1922 to 1935, almost 7 to 8 flour mills were set up every year. It became active after 1936, especially from 1940 to 1948, when more than 20 factories were built every year. This figure was even close to 50 from 1947 to 1948, but these newly established factories were mostly small in size. This change was obviously associated with the national conditions at that time. Despite the warlord dogfight in the early Republic of China period, that is, during the Beiyang government, the core areas of the flour industry were not much affected. Machine-made flour mills were mainly located in large cities, such as Shanghai, Harbin, Tianjin, Wuhan, and Qingdao. This period coincided with World War I in Europe, and some foreign investors exited the Chinese market. As a result, Chinese investors had greater room for development. Due to the sluggish world economy in the mid- to late 1920s, foreign investors and foreign flour entered China in a big way, and the domestic flour industry developed slowly. The outbreak of the War of Resistance against Japanese Aggression worsened this situation. Some enterprises moved inland and developed somewhat in the rear area, but they were severely restricted by the level of economic development. A large part of the most developed areas in China were occupied by Japan at this time or were in a state of stalemate, while the rear area was mostly economically underdeveloped and had no basis for supporting the development of the machine-made flour industry. Other enterprises in the occupied areas were controlled by Japan and could not truly develop.

Nevertheless, after decades of development and accumulation of experience, flour enterprises developed considerably, and the actual number of enterprises increased from a few to hundreds of enterprises. Despite a slight increase in the size of enterprises, the increase in number shows a development trend, such as its coverage in many regions. Despite its setbacks and difficulties, the flour industry in modern China should be a success story on a par with the textile industry among the food or light industries.

### 4.4.3 *Entrepreneurship: textile industry*

#### 4.4.3.1 *Problems*

The problem of entrepreneurs is studied next. This is a difficult issue, especially for modern China, for the following reasons. To begin with, what is an enterprise? Who are the entrepreneurs? That's a problem. These are not problems for contemporary people. Anyone with common sense knows what a business and an entrepreneur are. Even if you have no idea, you can learn about these by consulting the dictionary or searching online. For example, enterprises are for-profit organizations of varying sizes. Unlike factories, enterprises are divided into joint-stock enterprises, family enterprises, state-owned enterprises, and township and village enterprises.[28] It is slightly difficult to define an entrepreneur, and its definition arouses controversy. Are all people who run businesses called entrepreneurs? There are divergent views. J.A. Schumpeter argues that only business operators who are constantly innovating can be called entrepreneurs. This is obviously too strict a definition.[29]

## 108 *Processes and characteristics*

From the perspective of innovation, however, this is indeed the best definition because if a company is to survive in the market, it must constantly innovate. The market is ruthless and reasonable. Only those who dare to innovate can survive in the marketplace. We can only promote social progress by constantly introducing new products or new production processes.[30]

However, from another viewpoint, operators who provide products (or services) in the market and contribute to society should also be called entrepreneurs. Of course, those who make counterfeit and shoddy products and fish in troubled waters should be ruled out. The process of an enterprise ranging from establishment to operation to development is a tough process because it is subject to a host of factors such as capital, personnel, technology, market changes, and government policies. More importantly, an enterprise must always compete with competitors. Otherwise, it will be easily overtaken by others and may go downhill. Therefore, anyone who founds an enterprise and keeps it a going concern can be called an entrepreneur. In particular, in the infancy of economic development, it is hard on business owners if they are required to show independent innovation. What is more important is their vision and capability. The so-called vision is the ability to observe market trends and to know what kind of commodities sell well. The so-called capability is the ability to run an enterprise, including the management of staff, funds, and properties, as well as the establishment of corporate culture. There is also the need for good coordination ability because business owners must also deal with others, especially corporate peers, government officials, and consumers, as well as having the ability to run a business independently.

Regarding entrepreneurs in modern China, it shall be noted that due to the special national conditions at that time, there were not only private enterprises but also government-run enterprises and foreign-funded enterprises. Foreign-funded enterprises at the time differed from today's foreign-funded enterprises. Today's foreign-funded enterprises enter the Chinese market based on the principle of mutual benefit and reciprocity, with a view to participating in China's economic development through equal competition and contributing to China while securing their own profits. For example, they create jobs in China, bring new technologies and management methods, and provide funds.[31] This is not the case for foreign-funded companies in modern times, which capitalized on their powerful political, military, and diplomatic forces to enter the Chinese market in a way similar to forcible entry and occupied the best resources. In other words, Chinese-funded and foreign-funded enterprises could not compete equally in modern China, with Chinese enterprises, especially those funded by private capital, always at a disadvantage. Due to such foreign relations, the growth of Chinese enterprises and entrepreneurs was greatly crippled.

### 4.4.3.2 *Enterprises and entrepreneurs*

As mentioned, it is hard to give an accurate definition of entrepreneur. Given the national conditions of modern China, all those who run an enterprise are called entrepreneurs, or at least most of them can be called entrepreneurs or entrepreneurs under specific circumstances. As a result, we can measure the frequency and quantity of entrepreneurial activity based on the establishment of an enterprise or factory. If many enterprises or factories are established in a given period, it means that the market environment or other conditions in this period are conducive to the emergence of entrepreneurs and that the conditions for economic development in this period are favorable because the establishment of an enterprise requires both a good environment, such as political stability, social peace, and economic prosperity, and the support of funds, technology, personnel, infrastructure, etc.

In modern China, there was a lack of complete and continuous statistics on the number of factories like Japan's *Factory Statistics Table*, except for rough data on individual years or individual industries.[32] Discussions can only be made based on data on the textile industry, the largest industry in China at that time. Figure 4.4 shows the change in the number of cotton mills in the modern textile industry. Chinese businesspeople began to introduce this modern mode of production in the late 19th century, and there was a trend of increase in early 20th century. This period should be called a "stage of experimentation". It was followed by a process of slow increase until around 1919, and this period can be called the "stage of adaptation". Thereafter, it saw rapid increase until 1936, and this process can be called a "stage of development". Due to a lack of data for the years after 1937, it is not listed here, but it can be conjectured that the textile industry would have developed better if it had not been for the war.[33]

Next, we examine the issue of foreign investment that could not be avoided in China at that time. There were few foreign-funded enterprises except Japanese-funded enterprises, and there was no increase or development. However, Japan was a different case. Although Japanese-funded enterprises were inconspicuous before

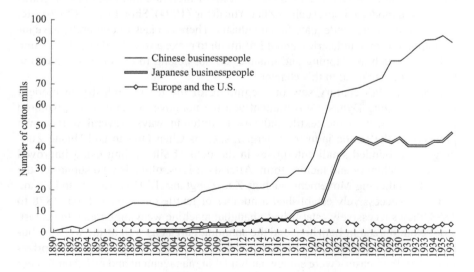

*Figure 4.4* Number of cotton mills by country from 1890 to 1936

Data source: Based on pp. 436–437 of *History of Textile in Modern China* (1997) (volume 3).

110    *Processes and characteristics*

1917, they changed basically in sync with Chinese-funded enterprises, only that the number of enterprises was far smaller. After World War I, the number of Chinese-funded enterprises increased, and so did Japanese-funded enterprises, especially before 1925. Thereafter, they remained at a high level, but their number did not increase. It can be said that the number of Japanese-funded enterprises during this period did not increase as much as Chinese-funded enterprises, but Japanese-funded enterprises as a whole accounted for about half of the enterprises in China. Further, the so-called foreign capital in this period was basically Japanese capital, while very few factories were invested by investors from other countries. It should be pointed out that the discussions focus on the number of enterprises or factories, without paying attention to their scale and connotation, such as production equipment, factory size, and production output. Generally speaking, foreign-funded enterprises at that time outperformed Chinese-funded enterprises in terms of these characteristics.[34]

Anyway, if the establishment and existence of these cotton mills are a manifestation of entrepreneurship, the activities of entrepreneurs in China's textile industry before 1939 are commendable. The establishment of such enterprises and their production contribute to China's economy as a whole and also benefit from the economic development. When the economy as a whole developed, people's income increased, and their spending power rose. As a result, their demand for clothing grew, which in turn stimulated the development of the textile industry.[35]

### 4.4.3.3 Emergence of entrepreneurs

With regard to the study of entrepreneurs in modern times, the textile industry is selected as a case due to a lack of information, the status of the industry, as well as the limitation of space. In fact, there are a lot of literature and materials on entrepreneurs in modern times, such as Zhao Yunsheng (1994), Shou Leying (2006), etc. However, these are inadequate for an industry. There is a lack of comprehensive information on some industries, and it is difficult to make a sound judgment. As some industries (such as shipping and finance) do not belong to the industry category, they are not discussed in this chapter.

The late 19th century saw the beginning of the textile industry in modern times. The Qing Dynasty government and the nongovernmental sector explored the development of the textile industry in different ways. Several well-known pioneers of the textile industry emerged, such as Chen Qiyuan and Huang Zuo-qing, who founded small enterprises in the field of silk reeling using improved Western machinery and factory form. After the 1870s, officials who supported the Self-Strengthening Movement, such as Zuo Zongtang, Li Hongzhang, and Zhang Zhidong, successively established a number of textile enterprises. From 1878 to 1898, they successively established Shanghai machine weaving bureau, the Gansu wool cloth bureau in Lanzhou, and the spinning bureau as well as the weaving bureau, silk reeling bureau, and the hemp-making bureau in Hubei. These enterprises funded by the treasury were somewhat feudal in management and relied on foreign technicians for technology. They all ended in failure. However, they introduced Western power-driven textile machinery and equipment by dint of their respective

Development of industry: part 2    111

power and financial resources, which served as precursor for the development of the textile industry in modern times.[36]

After China was defeated in the Sino-Japanese War of 1894–1895, some enlightened bureaucrats and gentlemen began to save the nation by engaging in industry. Most of them belonged to the literati and officialdom class. They leveraged their political power and social influence to secure the support of the government while raising private funds to open various modern enterprises and public institutions in the late Qing Dynasty and the early Republic of China period, a period of radial social changes. The textile industry became the focus of their investment due to the small investment required, abundant raw materials and labor, and a broad market. Yang Zonghan, who had been an aide of Li Hongzhang, had been in overall charge of Shanghai machine weaving bureau and the Hubei weaving bureau. In 1895, he raised funds to establish Yeqin Cotton Factory, one of the earliest private cotton mills in his hometown of Wuxi, Jiangsu province. Xue Nanming was a successful candidate in the imperial examinations at the provincial level and served as a candidate magistrate of the County. In 1896, he set up Yongtai Silk Factory in Shanghai. In 1894, Zhang Jian became the Number One Scholar outside the official imperial examination system and was awarded the title of court historiographer at the Hanlin Academy. Later, he established Dasheng Textile Enterprise Group in his hometown of Nantong. Nie Yuntai was a grandson of Zeng Guofan, an eminent Han Chinese official and military general. In 1909, Nie Yuntai and his family bought Huaxin Company and renamed it New Hengfeng Textile Bureau. Unlike the enterprises run by the officials who supported the Self-Strengthening Movement, the textile enterprises founded by these industrialists kept developing. Zhang Jian and Nie Yuntai became leaders in the textile and industrial circles, and their practices were valuable experience for the development of the textile industry. In a sense, this process can be compared with the "trend of going into business" that occurred in China in the early days of reform and opening up. One is a period of change in the old era, while the other is a period of change in the new era. The common denominator between the two is the word "market". The market brings business opportunities, leads to the emergence of talents, and makes possible career success.

China's national textile industry ushered in a so-called golden age during World War I and the several years that followed. It occupied a key position in modern industry and competed fiercely with international capitalism. During this period, a wealth of influential people emerged, including entrepreneurs, technical experts, and education experts. Some professional personnel who had received scientific and technological education in modern times became the pillar of the textile industry. They came from all walks of life, including the Rong brothers, Wu Linshu, and Liu Guojun, who were businesspeople; Su Taiyu, who was a staff member; the Guo brothers who were overseas Chinese businessmen; Zhou Xuexi, who was a bureaucrat; Yan Yutang, who was as a comprador; and Ji Mutao, Mu Ouchu, Zhu Wenqi, etc., who were students trained by new-style education.

Because market competition posed a heightened demand for enterprise management and technical level after the 1920s, the number of so-called student-type personnel increased, gradually becoming the mainstay of textile entrepreneurs,

## 112  *Processes and characteristics*

such as Cai Shengbai, Xue Shouxuan, Li Guowei, Li Shengbo, Zhu Jisheng, Tong Runfu, and Song Peiqing. Some were textile technology-expert-turned entrepreneurs, such as Zhu Xianfang, Wang Fuli, Shi Fengxiang, Lu Shaoyun, Wu Weijing, Zhang Wenqian, and Wang Ruiji. Entrepreneurs of this period shared the patriotic enterprise spirit of the earlier industrialists. They accumulated capital and scaled up expanded production by means of prudent decision making and flexible operations at a time of domestic strife and foreign aggression, and they established many enterprise groups of a considerable scale. At the same time, these entrepreneurs placed a higher emphasis on the internal management of enterprises. For example, Mu Ouchu translated the American Frederick Taylor's *Scientific Management Theory* and implemented it in the enterprise. Despite a host of obstacles, Wang Fuli abolished the foreman system, allowed students to run the factory, and adopted the standard work methods at New Hengfeng Textile Bureau and Shenxin Third Factory, as well as compiled the *Thoughts on Work at Mills* and *Standards on Gauze Factory Operation*. Thanks to the efforts of these student-type entrepreneurs, new financial rules, methods of employment, wage system, and work standards were popularized in a dozen years.

As the textile industry developed, a group of experts with a high academic caliber stood out, such as Zhu Xianfang, Lei Binglin, Wang Fuli, Shi Fengxiang, Lu Shaoyun, Zhu Mengsu, Huang Yunkui, Wu Shihuai, Luo Yangzhi, Zhang Wenqian, Zheng Jiapu, Qian Zichao, Zhang Fangzuo, Zhang Hanwen, Liu Chijun, and Wang Ruiji. They played a key role in introducing and drawing on Western technology and equipment as well as imitation production. After the 1920s, they replaced foreign technicians in technical management, and some technical experts also participated in corporate decision making, becoming excellent entrepreneurs. They performed important technological transformation and inventions in light of national conditions. For example, Lei Binglin invested Lei-style long draft for spinning and dual-horn thread tubes for roving frames; Du Jinsheng developed made-made photographic weaving method; Feng Yunhe invented the chemical degumming method of ramie; Zhang Fangzuo et al. developed new-style agricultural spinning machines; Liu Chijun and Wang Ruiji developed the perfection-style spinning machines; Zou Chunzuo developed a three-step ironwood spinning machines; Mu Ouchu organized the development of and promoted the July 7 spinning machine.[37]

The preceding discussion briefly introduces the background to the modern textile industry and some facts about entrepreneurship. The situation of Japanese entrepreneurs in modern times can be summarized as follows. First, China and Japan in modern times shared some similarities: in the face of strong pressure from advanced Western European countries, both countries needed to seek the road to survival as soon as possible. Therefore, from the perspective of enterprises and entrepreneurs, the two had similarities. Second, both Japanese entrepreneurs and Chinese entrepreneurs saw a shift from government-run enterprises to privately run enterprises in the process of enterprise development in modern times. Third, entrepreneurs in China and Japan in early years exhibited patriotism. On the one hand, patriotism was needed in the face of Western challenges. On the other hand, it is also a sense of responsibility and mission because entrepreneurs were in the

*Development of industry: part 2*    113

minority at the time, and most of them received a good traditional education and knew that their countries lagged behind other countries. Fourth, Chinese and Japanese entrepreneurs experienced a process of moving from simple passion to reliance on knowledge and rules and regulations in terms of business management. Modern enterprises were the result of the Industrial Revolution in Western Europe. Enterprises could be directly put into production through purchase, but in order to improve efficiency and make technological progress, it would take a long time to learn this and even to cultivate talents through public education and in-house education. Fifth, there are also differences between Chinese and Japanese entrepreneurs. The environment of the two countries in modern times was different. Although Japan was also suppressed by Western powers, it quickly got out of this situation and began to suppress China as a second-rate power. China could not get rid of this situation due to institutional and other reasons and was even surpassed by Japan, which had previously lagged behind China. This made it more difficult for entrepreneurs to run their own enterprises.[38]

### 4.4.3.4   Evaluation of entrepreneurs

Due to limitations of space, this discussion briefly introduces how textile entrepreneurs emerged and their general situation. A simple summary will be made here. First of all, the entrepreneurs introduced here lived in the early years, mostly figures who were active in the first 30 years of the 20th century. There is a basis for this because this period is a time when China's textile industry took shape and developed a good foundation and when it developed smoothly. During the War of Resistance against Japanese Aggression and the Liberation War period, China's economy as a whole was disrupted, and it was hard to engage in normal corporate activities. Entrepreneurs were busily saving the nation or were mired in turmoil. Entrepreneurs in the early years built the basic pattern of China's textile industry and made more contributions and had more distinctive characteristics compared with entrepreneurs who emerged later. Although later entrepreneurs had more know-how and an international vision, many of them just inherited the business founded by their predecessors.

Second, despite different backgrounds, entrepreneurs in modern China had one thing in common: vision. They had the most basic attribute required of an entrepreneur – the ability to discover markets (business opportunities) because the top priority of running a business is to understand the market. What is needed in the market? What products sell well? The aforesaid figures are outstanding in this regard. China had just opened up to the outside world at the time, and foreign new industries and new technologies began to be introduced to China. With the introduction of new industries, cities began to develop, and people's demand for clothing grew. Entrepreneurs decided to establish textile enterprises because they were optimistic about the development prospects of this industry. Why didn't Chinese entrepreneurs engage in mines, military, or shipbuilding industries? Since these industries need a lot of funds and the power of government and foreign capital was strong, it was difficult for private capital to survive, and the market could not be

## 114 *Processes and characteristics*

guaranteed. An industry similar to the textile industry is the flour industry, in which private capital was huge and also successful. For example, the Rong brothers also ran flour enterprises.[39]

Third, in addition to having a vision, these entrepreneurs had other entrepreneurial qualities, such as respecting knowledge, valuing talents, and having an international perspective. The first generation of entrepreneurs might not have been experts, but they were aware of the importance of specialized knowledge and the value of talents. They either hired experts or pinned high hopes on their offspring by sending them to study abroad. This is a shared characteristic of private entrepreneurs after China's reform and opening up. Most of the first-generation entrepreneurs received little schooling and lacked expertise and therefore could only engage in some simple industries. However, they knew that it was impossible to develop the enterprise and gain a foothold in the fierce competition without professional knowledge. Therefore, most of them sent their children to universities, and some sent their children abroad for study.

Finally, regarding the weakness of this generation of entrepreneurs, they were subject to the national conditions at the time and could not ensure the long-term development of enterprises. The national conditions mentioned refer to political instability and the unfavorable conditions for development. Entrepreneurs look to future development. If there is no future, no entrepreneur is willing to invest in running enterprises, especially in the manufacturing industry. The manufacturing industry needs production equipment, and equipment involves purchase, installation, maintenance, depreciation, aging, etc. If a society is in turmoil or the market has no prospects, equipment may be idle or inefficient, which is a taboo in running a business. Such an environment prevailed in China at that time. Entrepreneurial activities previously mentioned focused on the pre-1937 years because business activities were disrupted during the period of the War of Resistance against Japanese Aggression and the Civil War between the Kuomintang and the Communist Party of China. At that time, Shanghai, China's largest industrial city, was home to the most enterprises and entrepreneurs. Some were relocated a long distance away to the inland areas with a poor transport network. Even if they were settled, the production efficiency declined significantly because Shanghai had a far better environment as a whole. Some remained in Shanghai where they had to cooperate cautiously with Japan. How was it possible to give full play to entrepreneurship?

## 4.5 Conclusion

This chapter examines the issues of development of urban industry, mining, and some industries in modern China. Industrial development in cities is the mainstream type of industrial development because industry contributes to the formation of cities, which in turn promotes the development of industry. It is natural to study the industrial development in cities. The preceding observations show that there was a low level of industrialization in cities in modern times. There were problems of unbalanced and biased development in terms of both industry and region.

*Development of industry: part 2* 115

For example, industry was excessively concentrated in the big city of Shanghai, while there was a low level development in other cities. In terms of industry, light industries such as textiles and food were absolutely dominant, while the status of heavy industry was negligible, showing the fragile and low-level China's industrial development at the time. As a result, cities that had these industries were inevitably immature and fragile.

For the study of the mining industry during the Republic of China period in this chapter, various statistical data were used to estimate the production volume and production value of the mining industry and to calculate the mining production index. Compared with the studies by others such as John K. Chang, our research focuses on the mining industry rather than on manufacturing. This is a major feature of our research. Another feature is that our study covers mining production from 1912 to 1949, which is impossible for the manufacturing industry due to a lack of continuous statistics.

This chapter also examines the factors that promote industrial development, with a focus on the three factors of government, market, and entrepreneurs. The following conclusions have been drawn. First, the government played a relatively big role in the early days of economic development. The government's guidance and demonstration were needed for, say, the establishment of government-run enterprises and the preparation of laws and regulations at the time because there were no new enterprises, and the market was not yet perfect. However, in many cases, government-run enterprises failed. This situation also occurred in Japan during the early Meiji Restoration period. Nevertheless, the early government-run enterprises were still of some significance. First, they contributed to the diffusion of new technologies. Generally, new technologies require huge funds and are not technically mature. Few locals master these technologies. Only the government has the resources to hire highly skilled personnel and make investments. Second, operating a business usually requires a learning process. The experience and lessons learned by government-run enterprises provided a model for subsequent private enterprises. However, as the market matures, the role of the government should be to maintain the market order rather than directly participating in market activities. Few countries perform well in this regard.

Second, industrial development and economic development are essentially market behavior, while competition is needed in a market. A key issue is how to create a good market. In the course of economic development, many countries have met difficulties in industrialization and economic development because the market is not sound or developed enough. Of course, problems must be analyzed on a case-by-case basis. Some industries are better directly run by the government, such as the public service sector, but such industries are few. More industries must compete in accordance with market principles. A market without a competition mechanism will lead to inefficiency and even monopoly and distortion, which undermine economic development. The government and the market are always in a contradictory position. If the government is not involved at all, the market is prone to failure. If the government intervenes too much, it is easy to cause government failure.

## 116 *Processes and characteristics*

Finally, entrepreneurs play a great role in economic development, especially in the early days of economic development. Because there is a lack of a good market mechanism and laws and regulations in the early days of economic development, the market is vulnerable to cutthroat competition or speculation, which affect the sound development of the market. As a result, ambitious and capable entrepreneurs with a vision are needed to develop and establish good market rules. Entrepreneurs in the early days also had limitations and weaknesses. They might be government officials with no knowledge of the market, and collusion between officials and businessmen was likely to occur. They might be businesspeople with shrewd minds, but they lacked the experience and wisdom to run a business. They were prone to take risks because many opportunities were available in the early stage of economic development, and they were prone to go to extremes. They might be ignorant about technology and were prone to blind management without the momentum of development. Nevertheless, entrepreneurs also grew up amid fierce market competition. Entrepreneurs will emerge as long as there is a good market.

## Notes

1 For a detailed discussion on urbanization during the Republic of China period, see Guan Quan (2018).
2 National Bureau of Statistics (1999).
3 Zhao Wenlin and Xie Shujun (1988), p. 543.
4 Due to space limitations, it is not shown here. See Jiang Tao (1993) and Guan Quan (2014).
5 Wang Yunwu (1934), p. 8.
6 The development of industry extends from central cities to other cities. Guan Quan (1997) studied the relationship between modern cities and industrialization in Japan through the power revolution.
7 Regarding the situation of factories in the 1930s, see Guan Quan (2018).
8 Regarding the use of power at Chinese factories in the 1930s, see Guan Quan (2018). For the use of power in Japan, see Ryoshin Minami (1976) and Minami (1987).
9 It is worth noting that Taiwan is not a city but a region, but it is described as such in the original text.
10 For the situation in the 1930s, see Guan Quan (2018).
11 For the economic development of the northeast region, especially industrial development during this period, see Guan Quan (2005, 2017, 2018).
12 Hu Rongquan (1935), p. 4.
13 For statistical sources, see Institute of East Asian Studies (1942).
14 For the *Chronicle of China's Industry*, see Guan Quan (2018).
15 Yan Zhongping et al. (1955), p. 1.
16 According to Wu Baosan et al. (1947), of the gross national product (GNP) in 1933, mining was 238 million yuan, and the modern manufacturing industry was 498 million yuan. Mining was almost half of the modern manufacturing industry. Moreover, the mining industry also includes traditional production. Therefore, the proportion of modern mining in the modern industry is even lower.
17 Regarding pyrite and gems in the original materials as well as graphite, construction stone, apatite, mica, etc. in other materials, it can only be abandoned due to a scarcity of data.

*Development of industry: part 2*  117

18 For the overall situation of mining development during the Republic of China period, see Guan Quan and Makino Fumio (1999) and Guan Quan (2018).
19 Many of today's developed countries in Western Europe were major coal-producing powers before World War II, such as Britain and Germany. See Institute of East Asian Studies (1942).
20 In fact, there were also foreign-funded enterprises in the flour industry, especially in the early days. See Institute of Economics Chinese Academy of Social Sciences, etc. (1966) and the Shanghai Municipal Grain Bureau, etc. (1987).
21 Compilation team of *History of Coal Mines in Modern China* (1990). In the steel industry, there are only data on individual enterprises, such as Xie Xueshi and Zhang Keliang (1984).
22 Mitchell (2002).
23 Ryoshin Minamiand and Kiyokawa Yukihiko (1987) studied Japan's experience in introducing foreign technologies in modern times.
24 Liu Foding et al. studied the Engel coefficient in modern China. It fell from 74.34 percent in 1917 to 63.40 percent in 1936. See Liu Foding (1999), p. 330.
25 When we discuss industrial development in modern China, it is necessary to consider it together with Japan in many situations. For example, World War I mainly occurred in Europe, and Western European countries had no time for East Asian affairs. Both China and Japan benefited from this. As Japan developed earlier than China, it was more likely to have more opportunities.
26 The flour industry in the northeast was concentrated in Harbin and introduced by the Russians.
27 These figures come from the Institute of Economics Chinese Academy of Social Sciences et al. (1966) and Shanghai Municipal Grain Bureau (1987).
28 In the early days of China's reform and opening up, people disagreed over whether there were enterprises in China because these were called factories, not enterprises. As the Japanese economist Komiya Ryutaro put it, "China only has factories, but not enterprises". See Komiya Ryutaro (1989).
29 Schumpeter believed that the process of capitalist development was an ongoing process of "creative destruction". Only business operators that make constant innovation can be called entrepreneurs. See Schumpeter (1999).
30 Schumpeter has his own unique view on innovation, which is also well-known. See Schumpeter (1990) and Guan Quan (2014).
31 As for the merits and demerits of normal foreign investment to host countries, Appleyard and Field (2003) present comprehensive discussions.
32 When the northeast region was occupied, the *Statistics Table of Factories in Manchukuo* (1933–1941) was compiled in imitation of Japan's *Factory Statistics Table*. For details, see Guan Quan (2005, 2018).
33 Regarding the overall situation of the textile industry in modern times, see the Editorial Board of the *History of Textile in Modern China* (1997) and Fang Xianting (1934), Yan Zhongping et al. (1955). The Japanese scholar who conducted the study is Mori Tokihiko (2010).
34 This can be obtained by comparing data on Northeast China and North China in the 1930s. See Guan Quan (2018).
35 Although what is observed here is the trend of the textile industry, it can be roughly seen as the change in the industry as a whole. That is to say, the period from the early Republic of China period to before 1937 saw good development. This confirmed the statement of the "golden age of Chinese capitalism" and also laid the groundwork for the hypothesis we put forward later. If Japan had not launched its full-scale invasion of China, China might have achieved economic take-off in this period. See Guan Quan (2018).
36 A similar situation occurred in Japan in the same period. After the Meiji Restoration, enlightened government officials in Japan built many government-run factories and

# 118 *Processes and characteristics*

advanced technologies were introduced from Western Europe, including military, textile, silk reeling, and shipbuilding technologies. However, the vast majority of them were sold cheaply due to mismanagement to the government businesspeople (family businesses with intimate ties to the government, such as Mitsui and Mitsubishi), bringing opportunities for development to these companies. The Tomioka Silk Mill, the largest silk reeling factory imported from France at the time, has now become a World Heritage Site. Regarding issues about the operation of the Tomioka Silk Mill, see Kiyokawa Yukihiko (1995).

37 This introduction is obtained from the Editorial Board of *History of Textile in Modern China* (1997) (volume 1).

38 For Japanese entrepreneurship in modern times, see Kiyokawa Yukihiko (1995).

39 For the situation of the government and the market, as well as the coal mining and flour industries, see Guan Quan (2018).

# 5 Population, labor force, and urbanization

## 5.1 Introduction

The population grows according to a certain law in the course of economic development. Before the start of modern economic growth, the population growth stagnated or was slow or even fell into the so-called Malthusian trap. When modern economic growth begins, population growth begins to pick up. When economic development reaches a certain level, population growth begins to slow down. Some developed countries today even experience negative population growth. Therefore, the rate of population growth shows an "inverted U" in the long term. China did not become a populous country in a short period of time. China was a populous country even in ancient times, which is directly linked to China's vast territory as well as its developmental pattern. If China had developed a large number of small states with a single nationality like Europe, it would not be what it is today. According to records, China's population during the Han Dynasty (202 bce–220 ce) was 30 million to 40 million, and in some years (2–13 ce) reached 58 million to 59 million. The population remained at 50 million during the Eastern Han Dynasty (25–220). After a relatively glorious period, the population began to decline, to about 20 million during the Three Kingdoms period (220–280). Although the population increased somewhat during the Sui and Tang Dynasties (581–907), it sometimes plunged. The population remained at 20 million to 60 million at the time. Since the Northern Song Dynasty (960–1127), China's population began to climb steadily from 40 million to 100 million during the Southern Song Dynasty (1127–1279). At the end of the Southern Song Dynasty, the population fell to 54 million. It began to increase steadily during the Yuan Dynasty (1271–1368), continued to increase during the Ming Dynasty (1368–1644), approaching 100 million at the end of the Ming Dynasty. It increased steadily from about 90 million in the early years of the Qing Dynasty (1636–1912), reaching 300 million in the last year (1795) of the Qianlong period. It kept rising thereafter, reaching 440 million in the early years of the Xianfeng period (1851–1861). It then fell and hovered between 350 million and 400 million before increasing to 400 million in the first year (1912) of the Republic of China period and to 540 million in 1949.[1]

After introducing the quantitative changes in the population, the author tries to explain the reasons for the long-term changes in the population. As can be seen

DOI: 10.4324/9781003410386-7

120    *Processes and characteristics*

from the introduction, China's population remained constant for a long time, indicating that the population did not see appropriate growth due to wars, famines, diseases, etc. On the other hand, China's big population remained constant thanks to many favorable factors, such as the expansion of territory, increase in cropland, and the progress of technology. On the whole, historical changes in China's population show the following characteristics. First, it is relatively stable in the long run, with a trend of steady growth. Second, the population size fluctuated greatly in all dynasties, sometimes increasing markedly and sometimes plunging sharply. Third, China's population increased rapidly three times. The first increase occurred in the period from the Song Dynasty to the Ming Dynasty, with the population increasing from 50 million to 100 million. The second increase occurred in the first half of the Qing Dynasty, with a net population increase of 200 million from the beginning of the Kangxi period to the end of the Qianlong period (about 130 years). This can be said to be a miracle. The third increase occurred in the period from 1949 to 1980, with the population growing from 540 million to nearly 1 billion, nearly doubling in about 30 years.

China's population growth had been very slow for a long time and even declined several times, a pattern that is associated with the economy, government, society, and culture at the time. However, from the perspective of economic development, it is in fact the so-called Malthusian trap that shows the paradox between population growth and per capita income (or productivity): Population growth is bound to lead to more food consumption, and when productivity cannot meet the needs of the population, the population decreases. As Malthus put it, this decrease is caused by wars, famines, or diseases. When technology is improved to a certain extent (such as rice rotation and intensive cultivation), productivity improves, and more people can be fed. As a result, the population grows. This cycle was the norm due to substantial technological progress (such as the Industrial Revolution) in the premodern era. This situation occurred in both China and the vast majority of countries.

This chapter also studies urbanization, which usually refers to the concentration of rural population and labor in cities. Urbanization comes as a result of industrialization or economic development. Although cities existed in ancient times in countries worldwide and sometimes performed an important role, such as in southern Europe, this situation is not the same as urbanization in a modern sense because it usually reflected the cultural characteristics of a given region such as ports and commerce, as well as the developed handicrafts industry. Usually, many people were gathered in a small area. Urbanization is accompanied by industrialization because industry has an agglomeration effect, and there is a close link among many industries. In particular, as industrialization deepens, the link among industries becomes closer. The more complex the industrial product, the more parts and components are needed. An automobile consists of tens of thousands of parts. Another feature of industry is the high degree of division of labor, which can improve efficiency. The more complex the product, the greater the need for division of labor because no one manufacturer holds an advantage in the production of all parts. Moreover, some service industries progressed alongside the development of industry, especially the producer service industries, including finance, insurance,

*Population, labor force, and urbanization* 121

consulting, accounting, and design. Some traditional service industries, such as transport and warehousing, also expanded as the industrial sector developed. Some service industries, such as accommodation, catering, and commerce, developed as urbanization deepened. In modern China, due to little progress in industrial development, the level of urbanization was very low, only 10 percent in 1949. As little headway was made in urbanization, there was a lack of motive for labor mobility, and, if there was motivation, it was not necessarily a flow from rural to urban areas. It has a touch of tragedy if we consider the movement of population and labor caused by wars and famine. In short, due to anemic economic development in modern China, urbanization and labor mobility were backward, or at least there was no perceptible change in the modern sense.

## 5.2 Demographic changes

### 5.2.1 Population increase

The discussion here focuses on the population during the Republic of China period. Population statistics were fragmented and inaccurate due to the national conditions at that time. Despite the many types of statistics, none of them are reliable for at least three reasons. First, there was a problem with the integrity of the country. Second, government capacity was inadequate. Due to the frequent changes of government, it was difficult to cover all areas, not to mention conducting a population census. Although the first census was conducted in 1909, no national census in a strict sense was conducted from 1912 to 1949.[2] Third, it was difficult to calculate the population due to war and other reasons. Many people were displaced, and there were large-scale refugees and migrants, which all affected the demographic census.

Table 5.1 shows several estimates of the population during the Republic of China period. The population size increased from more than 400 million in the early days of the Republic of China period to about 540 million in 1949. It increased by more than 100 million or about one-fifth in less than 40 years, which was a fast growth rate. If we consider that China's economic growth during this period was slow, and wars often broke out, it is no exaggeration to describe it as a miracle, although this growth rate is not as fast as that in the period from 1949 to 1980. Closer observation reveals that the population grew mainly in the period from 1912 to 1936, or before Japan's full-out invasion of China. It increased from 400 million to 440 million to about 500 million in 1936. Thereafter, it increased only slightly, obviously as a result of the war. It is worth mentioning that the statistics given by domestic scholars are relatively low: the population increased from more than 400 million around 1912 to about 450 million in 1946, which is not a high growth rate. However, it is impossible to account for the increase from only about 450 million in 1946 to about 540 million in 1949. The estimates given foreign scholars are far higher, which stand to reason and better reflect the national conditions at that time.

However, the estimates given domestic scholars better reflect the development of China's economy. As a result of the slow or even stagnant economic

## 122  *Processes and characteristics*

*Table 5.1* Population during the Republic of China period, Unit: 10,000 people

| Year | Maddison estimate | Hitotsubashi estimate | Yang Zihui estimate | Estimate by Zhao Wenlin and Xie Shujun | Hou Yangfang estimate |
|---|---|---|---|---|---|
| 1911 | 42,766.2 | – | – | 40,543.4 | – |
| 1912 | 43,237.5 | 43,918 | 40,581.1[①] | 40,961.4 | 41,964.0 |
| | – | – | – | 41,964.1[②] | – |
| 1919 | 46,685.5 | 45,898 | 42,767.9 | 44,039.0 | – |
| 1920 | 47,200.0 | 46,192 | 43,609.5[①] | – | – |
| | – | – | – | 45,620.0[②] | – |
| 1930 | 48,900.0 | 49,808 | 41,995.7 | – | – |
| | – | – | – | 47,478.7 | – |
| 1931 | 49,264 | 50,357 | – | 46,884.2 | 41,628.7 |
| 1935 | 50,529.2 | 53,220 | 44,000.8[①] | – | – |
| | – | – | – | 44,665.0[②] | – |
| | – | – | – | 46,215.3[③] | – |
| 1936 | 50,795.9 | 53,999 | 46,136.4[①] | 46,961.8 | 47,908.5 |
| | – | – | – | 46,508.6[②] | – |
| | – | – | – | 47,908.5[③] | – |
| 1940 | 51,877.0 | 53,982 | 44,889.0[①] | – | – |
| | – | – | – | 45,831.3[②] | – |
| | – | – | – | 46,323.0[③] | – |
| 1946 | 53,541.8 | 55,093 | 44,558.2 | – | 46,100.6 |
| 1949 | 54,394.1 | 55,900 | 47,403.3[①] | 54,806.6 | – |
| | – | – | – | 54,167.0[②] | – |

*Note*: The superscripts ①, ②, and ③ in the table indicate that different types of statistics are given in Yang Zihui's *Research on Demographic Data in All Dynasties in China* (1996). Some figures are used here, such as 11 kinds in 1930. For details, see pp. 1285–1289 in Yang Zihui as editor-in-chief (1996). Hou Yangfang's 1946 is the data for the year 1947.

*Sources*: Maddison (2009); Ryoshin Minami and Makino Fumio (2014); Yang Zihui (1996); Zhao Wenlin and Xie Shujun (1988); Hou Yangfang (2001).

development in China at that time, the population would not grow so fast theoretically. However, this contradicts the data for 1949. If the data for 1949 is accurate, the data for years before 1946 will not make sense. Wars broke out in a large part of China from 1946 to 1949, and the population was unlikely to grow rapidly. If we accept the data given by foreign scholars, it will be difficult to account for the development of China's economy, let alone the frequent wars and disasters. We refer to this situation as the "Trilemma" for the population during the Republic of China period: if the population grew but the economy did not develop, it means that China fell into the Malthusian trap during this period. If there was little population growth, and the economy did not grow much, how come the population increased by 100 million in 1949? If the population did not grow significantly but the economy developed, how come China's per capita income did not increase? That is to say, the preceding three assumptions have flaws that are difficult to explain.

*Population, labor force, and urbanization* 123

### 5.2.2 Demographic transition

As there are few data and viewpoints on the demographic transition during the Republic of China period, only a brief introduction is made here. Some said that China underwent demographic transition in the 1920s and entered the second phase and that its population growth began to pick up.[3] There is a lack of continuous data on demographic transition for the Republic of China period, except incomplete data on birth rate, mortality rate, and natural growth rate for several time points. Because the census conducted at that time was incomplete and inaccurate, it is difficult to make an accurate judgment. Nevertheless, the data available present a rough idea of the demographic developments at the time.

The earliest investigation of China's birth and mortality rates was the population census conducted in 1912. However, the results are not reliable. The data vary greatly from region to region, with a high birth rate and a low mortality rate in some areas, a high mortality rate and a low birth rate in other areas, as well as balanced rates. The natural growth rates also varied greatly. According to the demographic transition theory, the first stage features a high birth rate, high mortality rate, and a low natural growth rate, which was the case in Fujian, Hunan, Shanxi, Jiangsu, Suiyuan, and other regions in 1912. The second stage is characterized by a high birth rate, a low mortality rate, and a high natural growth rate, which was the case in Yunnan, Sichuan, and other regions. The third stage features a low birth rate, a low mortality rate, and a low natural growth rate. This situation is theoretically unlikely in China, although there are signs of such a situation in some regions. This can only be attributed to inaccurate census data.[4]

There are some data on the birth rate, mortality rate, and natural growth rate for the years from 1918 to 1949 during the Republic of China period, but these data only cover some regions. For example, data for some regions from 1918 to 1928 show that the birth rate averaged 38.81 per thousand, the mortality rate averaged 26.57 per thousand, and the natural growth rate averaged 12.24 per thousand. For some regions from 1929 to 1936, the average birth rate averaged 38.64 per thousand, the mortality rate averaged 30.43 per thousand, and the natural growth rate averaged 8.22 per thousand. For some regions from 1937 to 1943, the birth rate averaged 27.98 per thousand, the mortality rate averaged 31.60 per thousand, and the natural growth rate averaged −3.62 per thousand. For some regions from 1946 to 1949, the birth rate averaged 30.70 per thousand, the mortality rate averaged 16.19 per thousand, and the natural growth rate averaged 14.51 per thousand.[5] The regions covered by these data are mostly rural areas, generally based on the unit of counties. These regions can be considered to be in the first stage of demographic transition at the time: a high birth rate, a high mortality rate, and a low natural growth rate.

There are also population data for some cities. For example, regarding Beiping City from 1929 to 1936, the birth rate averaged 17.13 per thousand, the mortality rate averaged 17.73 per thousand, and the natural growth rate averaged −0.60 per thousand. There was no trend of change from the perspective of time, with neither significant increase nor significant decrease. For the Chinese-controlled districts in Shanghai from 1929 to 1936, the birth rate averaged 12.77 per thousand, the

## 124 *Processes and characteristics*

mortality rate averaged 10.51 per thousand, and the natural growth rate averaged 2.26 per thousand, which also showed no obvious trend of change. For Beiping City from 1938 to 1945, the birth rate averaged 9.93 per thousand, the mortality rate averaged 16.1 per thousand, and the natural growth rate averaged −6.68 per thousand; the birth rate showed a clear downward trend, at least compared with the 1929–1936 period. For Tianjin from 1938 to 1945, the birth rate averaged 4.59 per thousand, the mortality rate averaged 6.30 per thousand, and the natural growth rate averaged −1.71 per thousand, which was similar to that of today's developed countries and is not reasonable.[6]

We can find out the birth rate, mortality rate, and natural growth rate after 1949 by urban and rural areas. For example, in 1954, the birth rate was 42.45 per thousand, the mortality rate was 8.07 per thousand, and the natural growth rate was 34.38 per thousand for cities; for rural areas, the corresponding figures were 37.51 per thousand, 13.71 per thousand, and 23.80 per thousand, respectively. This came as a result of widespread availability of medical treatment, medicines, etc. That is to say, during this period, China began to enter the second stage of demographic transition, with a large population increase and a bigger population in urban areas than in rural areas. In 1978, the birth rate was 13.56 per thousand, the mortality rate was 5.12 per thousand, and the natural growth rate was 8.44 per thousand in cities; in rural areas, the corresponding figures were 18.91 per thousand, 6.42 per thousand, and 12.49 per thousand, respectively. The rate of China's population growth fell to a low level.[7]

On the whole, the dynamic demographic data for the Republic of China period show that China did not enter the second stage of demographic transition at that time but was still in the first stage. Even if the data were not accurate, there was no evidence showing a demographic transition in China. This corresponds to the situation of China's economy and society at that time. China's economy had basically not developed, nor did the population. A demographic transition occurs as a result of the fundamental factor of economic development. Although a demographic transition might occur in some cities or enter the second stage, if you consider that China's urbanization rate was only 10 percent at that time, it is sure that China was still in the first stage during the Republic of China period, with a high birth rate and a high mortality rate.

### 5.2.3 *Demographic structure*

There are rich survey data on the age composition of the population during the Republic of China period. Despite the degree of inaccuracy, the data can give a rough idea of the situation at that time. The 1912 census covered the age structure for the first time and was the only national investigation on age groups before 1947. The age structure was not covered in other censuses covering other periods, such as the 1928 census, 1943 census (nonwar zone), and 1946 census. This also goes for censuses in other regions. This is attributed to the national situation at the time and basically reflects the actual situation.

Figure 5.1 shows the proportion of age groups in various censuses during the Republic of China period. The following can be observed from the figure. First,

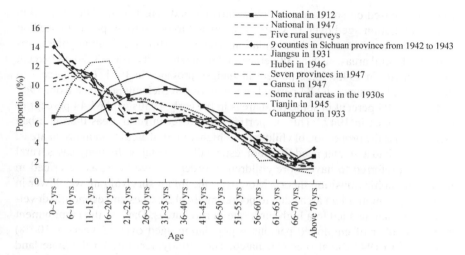

*Figure 5.1* Age structure of the population during the Republic of China period

Note: The age groups for various censuses vary slightly. For example, some include the age group of 20 to 24 years, and some include the age group of 21 to 25 years.

Data sources: Yang Zihui (1996), pp. 1364–1372; Hou Yangfang (2001), pp. 315–340.

there are generally two tendencies: a linear decline and a curved decline. The former indicates a large proportion of infants and adolescents. The latter indicates a low proportion of infants and young children and a large proportion of adults, as shown in the 1912 national census, 1933 Guangzhou census, and 1945 Tianjin census. However, a structure with this tendency is a special case, caused by the special circumstances of a city or by inaccurate census. At that time, the vast majority of the Chinese people lived in rural areas, who had a traditional view of fertility and living conditions. Therefore, having many children was a normal phenomenon. Second, the proportion of people aged 16 to 50 years is relatively stable, was evidenced by the results of various censuses. Fifty years of age is chosen because the proportion of people over 50 years old is small in view of the life expectancy at that time. In particular, the number of people aged over 70 years accounted for only 1.6 to 3.6 percent, indicating a low average life expectancy for the Chinese people at that time. Third, there are various reasons, as well as special circumstances. For example, the proportion of adults surveyed in 9 counties in Sichuan province from 1942 to 1943 is significantly lower than that of other censuses. The reasons are unknown, and these are only used for reference here.

## 5.3 Labor force

### 5.3.1 Labor supply

There is a scarcity of data on the labor supply during the Republic of China period, and the proportion of the number of people aged over 15 years can only be

126   *Processes and characteristics*

calculated based on some demographic statistics and census data. The proportion of the population aged over 15 years is calculated to be 60 to 80 percent based on the data on age structure of the population. This proportion was high in cities compared with rural areas, such as 80 percent in Guangzhou city in 1933, 70.48 percent in Tianjin city in 1945, 70.06 percent in Jiangsu province in 1931, 65.5 percent in the five rural censuses, 62.84 percent in 9 counties in Sichuan province from 1942 to 1943, 65.08 percent in some rural areas in the early 1930s, and 64.44 percent in Gansu province in 1947.[8] This proportion was lower in rural areas than in urban areas because the proportion of children was higher in rural areas than in urban areas. Rural areas had a greater need for labor, especially male labor. In many cases, rural residents preferred to have more children in order to have boys, as described in the demographic transition theory. Moreover, the infant survival rate was lower in rural areas than in urban areas due to poorer medical services and economic development, which also led to a high birth rate in rural areas. Data on the employment rate (= number of employed persons ÷ population aged over 15 years × 100%) from 1931 to 1944 can also be calculated. The employment rate for the hinterland fell from 87.3 percent in 1931 to 82.7 percent in 1944, which accorded with the national conditions at the time, generally the state of underdeveloped countries. If the puppet state of Manchukuo at that time was included, it fell from 89.1 percent in 1932 to 82.3 percent in 1942, which is consistent with the basic trend in the hinterland.[9]

The statistics on industrial workers in modern China are scarce. Therefore, a brief introduction is made here. In 1894, there were 91,900 to 98,100 industrial workers, including 19,600 in the machine silk reeling industry, 10,100 in the shipbuilding and machine ironmaking industry, 9,100 to 10,800 in the military industry, 9,100 to 9,600 in the cotton ginning and cotton textiles industry, 7,900 to 9,600 in the coal mining industry, 7,400 in the tea making industry, 6,300 to 8,200 in the metal mining industry, 3,400 in the matchstick industry, 3,000 in the ironmaking industry, 2,800 in the papermaking and printing industry, 1,800 to 2,200 in the iron ore mining industry, 1,400 in the public utilities industry, and 10,000 in other industries. In 1913, after nearly two decades of development, there were 1,176,400 industrial workers, including 630,900 factory workers (including 249,300 in the dyeing and weaving industry, 181,700 in the food industry, 94,700 in the chemicals industry, 64,400 in other light industries, 36,700 in the mechanical appliances industry, 3,700 in the metal smelting industry, and 400 in the electrical and tap water industries), 407,200 mining workers, 57,300 railway workers, 11,000 postal workers, and 70,000 seafarers. In 1920, there were 1,946,400 industrial workers, including 702,500 Chinese factory workers, 320,000 foreign factory workers in China, 597,000 mining workers, 23,200 postal workers, 10,700 telecommunications workers, 143,000 railway workers, and 150,000 seafarers. In 1927, this figure reached 2,750,000, including 540,000 mine workers, 300,000 transport wharf workers, 280,000 cotton mill workers, 250,000 municipal works workers, 250,000 salt workers, 160,000 silk mill workers, 160,000 seafarers, and 120,000 railway workers. In 1935, there were a total of 2,271,400 industrial workers, of whom 1,432,400 were in areas ruled by the Kuomintang, primarily including 941,900

*Population, labor force, and urbanization*   127

factory workers, 255,900 mine workers, 81,400 railway workers, 38,500 postal workers, and 14,500 telecommunications workers. There were 839,000 industrial workers in the northeast region occupied by Japan, mainly including 119,500 factory workers, 104,200 mine workers, 77,800 transport workers, 37,400 post and telecommunications workers, 320,000 foreign factory workers in China, and 180,000 seafarers. In 1944, there were a total of 2,166,500 industrial workers, including 1,376,700 workers in enemy-occupied areas, 400,000 workers in Kuomintang-ruled areas, 120,000 workers in the liberated areas, 20,000 seafarers, and 249,800 railway and post and telecommunications workers. In 1947, there were a total of 2,265,200 workers, of whom 979,500 workers were in the liberated areas and 1,285,700 workers in Kuomintang-ruled areas, including 682,400 workers engaged in the industrial sector, 323,900 railway workers, 199,400 seafarers, and 80,000 post and telecommunications workers.[10]

Table 5.2 shows the occupation composition of the rural population by gender in the late 1920s and early 1930s. They are divided into agricultural and nonagricultural workers. In terms of the difference between men and women, male agricultural workers accounted for 45.2 percent, while women accounted for only 9.2 percent. In contrast, male nonagricultural workers accounted for only 20.0 percent while women accounted for 58.9 percent. Obviously, there are large differences between men and women in terms of occupation, with men considered more suited to or more engaged in agricultural activities and women more suited to nonagricultural activities. It is noteworthy that both agricultural and nonagricultural workers also engaged in other activities. For example, 27.4 percent of male agricultural workers also engaged in other activities, and this figure is 20.4 percent for women. The other activities mainly refer to housework. 13.8 percent of men and 18.9 percent of women were engaged in housework. Other activities also include business running, in which men accounted for 6.0 percent and women accounted for only 0.1 percent, indicating that more men did business. Men engaged in manufacturing part-time accounted for 2.7 percent, while the figure was almost zero for women (0.1 percent in South China). Among nonagricultural workers, 8.6 percent of men and 0.8 percent of women were engaged in specialized professions. Men dedicated to housework accounted for 5.4 percent while women accounted for 55.1 percent. In addition, 2.8 percent of men were engaged in business, while women only accounted for 0.2 percent. Men engaged in manufacturing accounted for 1.8 percent, while only 0.1 percent of women worked in manufacturing.

Table 5.3 shows the proportion of occupations in the census in the first half of the 20th century. Due to the unclear time points, it is difficult to judge the changes in occupations, and only a simple introduction based on the figures can be made. In addition to the unemployed (accounting for 49.77 percent), agriculture employed the largest number of people, accounting for 26.00 percent, followed by industry at 11.80 percent, personnel services at 4.72 percent, commerce at 3.37 percent, public servants at 2.12 percent, and transport at 1.46 percent. In terms of the difference between men and women, the proportion of men engaged in agriculture (37.79 percent) is far higher than that of women (13.35 percent). Women mainly worked in industry sector (15.95 percent) and personnel services (7.39 percent). Of

*Table 5.2* Proportion of the rural population by occupation from 1929 to 1933

| Occupation | Males | | | Females | | |
|---|---|---|---|---|---|---|
| | Nationwide | Northern China | Southern China | Nationwide | Northern China | Southern China |
| Reported population (person) | 48,235 | 27,085 | 21,150 | 42,615 | 24,078 | 18,537 |
| Agriculture (%) | 45.2 | 41.7 | 49.7 | 9.2 | 10.7 | 7.2 |
| Agriculture and other occupations (%) | 27.4 | 29.6 | 24.5 | 20.4 | 17.9 | 23.6 |
| Housework | 13.8 | 15.7 | 11.3 | 18.9 | 17.3 | 21.0 |
| Business | 6.0 | 7.0 | 4.8 | 0.1 | – | 0.1 |
| Manufacturing | 2.7 | 2.3 | 3.2 | – | – | 0.1 |
| Transport | 1.9 | 1.8 | 2.2 | – | 0.0 | – |
| Specialized occupation | 1.1 | 1.2 | 0.9 | – | – | – |
| Cottage industry | 1.0 | 1.1 | 0.9 | 1.3 | 0.6 | 2.2 |
| Fisheries | 0.5 | 0.1 | 1.2 | – | 0.0 | – |
| Public servant | 0.3 | 0.4 | 0.1 | 0.0 | 0.0 | 0.0 |
| Mining | 0.0 | 0.0 | 0.0 | 0.0 | 0.0 | 0.0 |
| Unknown | 0.1 | 0.1 | – | – | – | – |
| Nonagricultural (%) | 20.0 | 21.2 | 18.4 | 58.9 | 59.8 | 57.7 |
| Specialized occupation | 8.6 | 9.0 | 8.0 | 0.8 | 0.8 | 0.8 |
| Housework | 5.4 | 5.7 | 5.0 | 55.1 | 57.2 | 52.5 |
| Business | 2.8 | 3.6 | 1.8 | 0.2 | 0.2 | 0.2 |
| Manufacturing | 1.8 | 1.4 | 2.2 | 0.1 | – | 0.1 |
| Public servants | 0.6 | 0.8 | 0.5 | 0.0 | 0.0 | 0.0 |
| Transport | 0.4 | 0.3 | 0.5 | – | 0.0 | 0.1 |
| Cottage industry | 0.3 | 0.3 | 0.2 | 2.7 | 1.6 | 4.0 |
| Fisheries | – | 0.0 | 0.1 | – | 0.0 | – |
| Mining | 0.0 | 0.0 | – | 0.0 | 0.0 | 0.0 |
| Unknown | – | – | – | – | – | – |
| Persons who are idle all year round | 7.3 | 7.4 | 7.3 | 11.3 | 11.2 | 11.3 |
| Unknown | 0.1 | 0.1 | 0.1 | 0.3 | 0.4 | 0.2 |

*Data source*: Buck (1941), Table 9.

*Population, labor force, and urbanization* 129

*Table 5.3* Proportion of occupations in the census in the first half of the 20th century, Unit: %

| Occupation | Males | Females | Total |
|---|---|---|---|
| Agriculture | 37.79 | 13.35 | 26.00 |
| Mining | 0.31 | 0.00 | 0.16 |
| Industrial sector | 7.92 | 15.95 | 11.80 |
| Business | 5.58 | 1.00 | 3.37 |
| Transport | 2.75 | 0.07 | 1.46 |
| Public servants | 3.75 | 0.36 | 2.12 |
| Freelancers | 0.50 | 0.18 | 0.35 |
| Personnel services | 2.23 | 7.39 | 4.72 |
| Others | 0.42 | 0.04 | 0.24 |
| Unemployed | 38.73 | 61.63 | 49.77 |
| Unknown | 0.01 | 0.02 | 0.02 |

*Note*: The data on the counties surveyed are enumerated in the original data. Only the aggregate results are shown here.

*Data source*: Statistics Bureau of the Comptroller Office of the Republic of China, *Statistical Yearbook of the Republic of China* of 1948, Table 30.

course, there were far more unemployed women than unemployed men, and the unemployed mainly did housework. Twice as many women worked in the industry sector as men. This phenomenon deserves studying. It is estimated that industry at that time was basically the handicraft industry, such as embroidery and tailor work, which were at the time more suited to women. The proportion of unemployed men was low, which occurred in industry, commerce, public service, and transport sectors. It was relatively evenly distributed.

### 5.3.2 Labor mobility

Urbanization should be a process in which the labor force gradually moves from rural areas to cities in search of higher income as the economy develops and industrialization deepens. Since China did not undergo industrialization before 1949, what are the characteristics of population movement? Even in the absence of industrialization and urbanization, people usually migrate for the following reasons. First is migration due to marriage. If a couple living in two places want to get married, one party must migrate, and this is normal migration. Second is migration due to development needs. Due to backward technology, a poor transport network, cold climate, lack of access to information, etc. in the early days of economic development, coupled with historical and political reasons, people need to migrate between densely populated areas and sparsely populated areas. In addition, some areas had been sparsely populated because people had not noticed the economic value there. When certain resources were discovered or exploited, the population would begin to concentrate there. Third are refugees displaced by famine and wars. This often occurred in old China. The flooding of the Yellow River, droughts, or wars would lead to a large-scale migration of people. What's more, these unfavorable factors interacted in some years and periods, resulting in economic, political, and social chaos in China.

130   *Processes and characteristics*

According to research, inward and outward migration of rural populations in various regions from 1929 to 1933 took place mainly for the following reasons. For outward migration, the first reason is a lack of jobs, which accounted for 48.8 percent nationwide. The second is marriage, which accounted for 23.2 percent. The third is "other", accounting for 17.3 percent. The fourth is a scarcity of food, accounting for 7.3 percent. Drought, war, bandits, and other reasons accounted for a very low proportion. Regarding the reasons for hinterland migration, the first is "others", accounting for 45.2 percent. The second is marriage, which accounted for 34.9 percent. The third is a lack of jobs, accounting for 15.0 percent. Drought, war, bandits, and other reasons accounted for a very low proportion.[11] This is largely the case nationwide, albeit with slight differences. This shows that there was a surplus labor force in rural areas who hoped to go out in search of work. Although it was not due to a lack of food, this factor cannot be wholly denied. According to the theory of modern labor mobility as well as practices, as long as there is surplus labor, there must be jobless people or a shortage of jobs. In other words, there is a lack of jobs, and the input made by the surplus labor does not produce more output. This population is called the "disguised unemployed", and their marginal productivity is zero.

Migration from the regions inside Shanhaiguan Pass to the northeast region in the first half of the 20th century was the largest in scale during this period. According to statistics, from 1912 to 1946, more than 19 million people moved to the three northeastern provinces from the provinces inside Shanhaiguan Pass; of that number, 10.7 million people returned in the same year, with 8.3 million people settling there. An average of 237,000 people settled in three northeastern provinces each year. Table 5.4 shows the overview of the period, covering the number of migrants, returnees, the number of people who settled there, and their respective proportions. Although it varied from period to period, more than half of the migrants returned to their original locations, and about 40 percent settled there.

The following can be observed from these incomplete data. First, before 1949, China's population movement was more from rural areas to rural areas rather than from rural areas to cities. Obviously, there was no really modern economic growth, and the scale of urban industry was small during this period in China. Therefore, cities did not need a wealth of rural surplus labor, and there was basically no large-scale migration of the rural population to cities. Second, the motivations for the population movement can be divided into two types. First, people moved passively as a result of natural and human-made disasters such as famines and war, which is also one of the reasons for population decline. Due to displacement and extreme hardships, the population, particularly children and women, died because of diseases, malnutrition, emergencies, etc. in the process of migration or after arrival at their destination. Second, people actively migrated because of marriage or the search for virgin land. The movement of people because of marriage is a normal movement and even contributed to the cross-circulation of the population and optimized the population quality. In traditional societies, marriages mostly occurred between locals or even between fellow villagers. Some couples came from the same clan with the same surname, leading to the problem of inbreeding,

Table 5.4 Migration of people from regions inside Shanhaiguan Pass to three northeastern provinces from 1917 to 1944

| Year | Length of interval years | Number of migrants (10,000 people) | Average number of migrants per year (10,000 people) | Number of returnees (10,000 people) | Proportion of the number of returnees to migrants (%) | Number of people who settled there (10,000 people) | Proportion of the number of people who settled there to migrants (%) |
|---|---|---|---|---|---|---|---|
| 1917–1923 | 7 | 231.3 | 33.0 | 93.6 | 40.47 | 137.7 | 59.53 |
| 1924–1930 | 7 | 535.9 | 76.5 | 281.6 | 52.55 | 254.3 | 47.45 |
| 1931–1937 | 7 | 348.0 | 49.7 | 294.1 | 84.51 | 53.9 | 15.46 |
| 1938–1944 | 7 | 575.2 | 82.2 | 299.1 | 52.00 | 276.1 | 48.00 |
| Total | 28 | 1690.4 | 60.4 | 968.4 | 57.29 | 722.0 | 42.71 |

Data source: Yang Zihui (1996), p. 1407.

## 132   *Processes and characteristics*

which would lower the population quality. The population movement caused by the search for virgin land, including the famous "brave the journey to Northeast", is an pioneering undertaking. Although it belonged to movement from rural areas to rural areas, it was no less important than the movement from rural areas to cities. Thanks to rapid economic development or industrialization, the economy of Northeast China in the early 20th century grew significantly faster than that of other regions. Alongside the construction of mines, railways, and factories, cities were gradually built and expanded.

### 5.4   Urbanization

Before 1949, urbanization lagged due to a lack of industrialization and economic development in China. In 1949, the urban population accounted for only 10.64 percent of the total population, while the rural population accounted for 89.36 percent.[12] Based on this figure, the level of urbanization would be lower than this for the years before 1949. The situation of urbanization from the mid- to late 19th century to the early 20th century can be seen from the incomplete data.

According to research, the rate of urbanization in the period from the mid-19th century (1843) and the late 19th century (1893) did not change much, inching only from 5.1 to 6.0 percent. Of course, there are still some differences for various regions. The rate of urbanization was higher in the lower reaches of the Yangtze River, rising from 7.4 to 10.6 percent. In the Lingnan region (south of the Five Ridges in South China), it climbed from 7.0 to 8.7 percent. It rose from 5.8 to 6.4 percent for southeast coastal areas, rose from 4.9 to 5.4 percent for the northwest region, rose from 4.5 to 5.2 percent for the middle reaches of the Yangtze River, rose from 4.2 to 4.8 percent for northern China, rose from 4.1 to 4.7 percent for the upper reaches of the Yangtze River, and rose from 4.0 to 4.5 percent for the Yunnan-Guizhou region.[13] In other words, it did not change much for the central and western regions, remaining at 4 to 6 percent. Obviously, this proportion is very low, and there was no urbanization to speak of. This also reflects the situation of China's economic development at the time. If it is a country that has started modern economic growth or a country that has begun to industrialize, there should be many modern factories, and cities will be formed, where the labor force and population will be concentrated. Judging from this viewpoint, China at that time was in a relatively traditional state without modern economic growth.

Table 5.5 shows the populations of cities with more than 100,000 people in 1918. It was ranked according to the size of population. The top-ranking cities, or most populous cities, were Guangzhou and Shanghai, with a population of more than 1.5 million each. These were indeed large cities at the time. The populations of Tianjin and Beijing were also close to 1 million. If these cities are regarded as "first-tier cities" according to today's standards, Hangzhou, Fuzhou, Suzhou, Hong Kong, Chongqing, Chengdu, Nanchang, Foshan, Ningbo, and Shaoxing can be seen as "second-tier cities", with a population of more than 400,000 each. Coming behind these are Hankou, Jinan, Nanjing, Yangzhou, and other cities with a population of more than 200,000, such as Changsha, Xi'an, and Ganzhou. These

*Population, labor force, and urbanization*  133

*Table 5.5* Cities with a population of more than 100,000 in 1918, Unit: 10,000 people

| City | Population | City | Population | City | Population | City | Population | City | Population |
|---|---|---|---|---|---|---|---|---|---|
| Guangzhou | 160.0 | Nanchang | 48.0 | Chaozhou | 25.0 | Changde | 18.0 | Changzhou | 12.5 |
| Shanghai | 150.0 | Foshan | 45.0 | Shenyang | 25.0 | Huai'an | 18.0 | Xuzhou | 12.5 |
| Tianjin | 90.0 | Ningbo | 45.0 | Wuchang | 25.0 | Wuhu | 17.5 | Xuzhou | 12.0 |
| Beijing | 85.0 | Shaoxing | 40.0 | Xi'an | 25.0 | Jiangmen | 16.8 | Ji'an | 12.0 |
| Hangzhou | 65.0 | Hankou | 35.0 | Changsha | 22.9 | Hanyang | 15.0 | Shaozhou | 12.0 |
| Fuzhou | 62.5 | Jinan | 30.0 | Ganzhou | 20.0 | Wuxi | 15.0 | Shunqing | 12.0 |
| Suzhou | 60.0 | Nanjing | 30.0 | Harbin | 20.0 | Wenzhou | 14.0 | Xiamen | 11.4 |
| Hong Kong | 52.5 | Yangzhou | 30.0 | Jining | 20.0 | Xiaolan | 14.0 | Lanzhou | 11.0 |
| Chongqing | 52.5 | Kaifeng | 28.0 | Xinhui | 20.0 | Qingjiangpu | 13.0 | Wanxian | 11.0 |
| Chengdu | 50.0 | Zhenjiang | 26.0 | Zhoujiakou | 20.0 | Quanzhou | 13.0 | Total | 1686.7 |

*Data source*: China Continuation Committee (1987), Appendix 7.

## 134 *Processes and characteristics*

cities can be regarded as "third-tier cities". Cities with a population of less than 200,000 can be regarded as "fourth-tier cities". Of course, this judgment is merely a description. Due to the degree of urbanization and urban functions at that time, it was unlikely for larger cities to form, nor was it possible to form today's so-called urban clusters because the level and scale of industrial production were woefully inadequate, and there was even no industrialization or modern economic growth. Furthermore, the total urban population was 16.867 million, accounting for less than 5 percent of the total population of over 400 million at that time. It indicates a low degree of urbanization. There were many cities with populations of less than 100,000. There were a total of 288 cities with a population of 25,000 to 100,000 each, and their total population size reached 13,980,100. Coupled with cities with populations of more than 100,000, the total urban population was 30,846,600, with an urbanization rate of about 7.29 percent.[14]

According to other statistics, there were 18 cities with a population of more than 100,000 in 1934, including Guangzhou, Changsha, Chengdu, Zhenjiang, Fuzhou, Hangzhou, Hankou, Hong Kong, Nanjing, Ningbo, Beiping, Shanghai, Suzhou, Tianjin, Jinan, Qingdao, Wanxian, and Wenzhou. Their total population reached 12.0144 million, accounting for 4.5 percent of China's total population.[15] In addition, the *China Land Use Survey* conducted by a scholar based on the data provided by John Lossing Buck and other data estimated that in China's 19 provinces, the population in cities accounted for 10 percent, the population in small towns (including rural parts) accounted for 11 percent, and the population in rural areas accounted for 79 percent.[16] Dwight H. Perkins cited Morris B. Ullman's estimates of China's urban population in the book *Agricultural Development in China*. According to this estimate, the population in cities from 1900 to 1910 was 16.851 million, accounting for 4.32 percent of the total population. In 1938, the urban population was 27.323 million, accounting for 5.25 percent of the total population.[17] In other words, China made little headway in urbanization in three decades from the early 20th century to 1938.

### 5.5 Conclusion

This chapter examined the issues such as population growth and demographic transition as well as population policy in modern China, found some demographic problems that distinguishes China from other countries, and analyzed the relationship between population and economic development. "A large population and a weak economy" set China apart from other countries. The population problem has been the biggest problem for China, which is a country steeped in history. Especially in modern times, China did not yet start modern economic growth, and the economy was largely in a state of stagnation, despite the rapid development of emerging industries in some cities. The population as a whole increased somewhat, but the demographic structure did not change much due to political instability and social turmoil. In addition, because the census statistics were incomplete and inaccurate, we can only gain a general idea of the population situation at that time.

*Population, labor force, and urbanization*  135

The chapter also examined labor issues, including labor supply and labor mobility. The supply of labor is related to both demographic changes and the degree of economic development. Given the underdeveloped economy in modern times, people could only engage in agricultural production, and few people worked in industry and commerce. During the Republic of China period, many new industry and commerce sectors emerged in cities, and a considerable number of the rural labor force became urban laborers as a result, which laid the groundwork somewhat for industrialization after 1949. However, due to the limited economic development, this groundwork is also limited. Labor mobility has existed throughout the history and is not a phenomenon that only occurred after modern times. However, labor mobility in a traditional sense is essentially different from the labor mobility caused by industrialization and urbanization since modern times. Traditional labor mobility is more characterized by the movement from rural to rural areas, such as women migrating to another place because of marriage. Of course, the migration of people due to famine and wars was frequent in the past in China. However, according to the preceding statistics, these factors are not the principal reasons for population and labor migration in the early 1930s.

This chapter also examined urbanization during the Republic of China period. In view of China's slow economic development during this period, it was unlikely to make much progress in urbanization because the rate of urbanization in 1949 was only 10 percent. As mentioned earlier, urbanization must be underpinned by industrialization. Despite a certain degree of industrial development in this period, modern industry was still limited to large cities, while traditional handicrafts and commerce sectors dominated small and medium-sized cities. Overall, China's urbanization advanced slowly during the Republic of China period, and many regions remained in a traditional state. New industries and occupations emerged in coastal areas and some central cities. Cities were developing, and the number of urban workers also increased. However, this was the initial development, which did not drive economic development and social progress as a whole. Nevertheless, such small-scale urbanization made a pioneering contribution to the subsequent development of China's economy.

## Notes

1 For the long-term changes in China's population, see Zhao Wenlin and Xie Shujun (1988), Yang Zihui editor-in-chief (1996), and Guan Quan (2014).
2 In fact, many sample surveys of varying sizes and censuses of small areas have been conducted. See Hou Yangfang (2001), p. 9.
3 Hou Yangfang (2001).
4 For details, see Hou Yangfang (2001), pp. 355–356.
5 Yang Zihui, editor-in-chief (1996), p. 1301.
6 Yang Zihui, editor-in-chief (1996), pp. 1304–1305.
7 *China Statistical Yearbook 1984.*
8 Yang Zihui, editor-in-chief (1996), pp. 1363–1375.
9 Ryoshin Minami and Makino Fumio eds. (2014), p. 362.
10 These figures are from the Department of Social Statistics of the National Bureau of Statistics (1987), pp. 251–256.

136  *Processes and characteristics*

11  Qiao Qiming (1945), pp. 136–137.
12  National Bureau of Statistics (1999).
13  Jiang Tao (1993), p. 286.
14  Calculated based on the total population of 423 million. Hou Yangfang (2001), p. 482.
15  Hou Yangfang (2001), p. 482.
16  Hou Yangfang, p. 483.
17  Hong Kong is not included here. Perkins (1969), pp. 292–296.

# 6 Changes in consumer prices and living standards

## 6.1 Introduction

This chapter examines the issue of consumer prices and living standards, as well as income distribution. Consumer prices are a signal of economic activities because trends in economic activities as well as the reasons can be observed from consumer prices. Microeconomics is also called price theory, highlighting the importance of consumer prices in a market economy. Price is the overall embodiment of market activity. Changes in the supply of and demand for production and services are reflected in prices as long as there is competitive market or there is no obvious distortion (such as monopoly). In terms of the scope of discussions in this book, prices rise as the economy develops and grows for at least the following reasons. First, an economy does not grow or develop in a linear way but is accompanied by fluctuations or business cycle. When the economy is good, the effective demand increases, and consumer prices rise accordingly. Conversely, when the economy is bad, consumer prices fall due to a lack of demand. Second, the cost of production affects price fluctuations. If wage rise exceeds labor productivity, the labor cost per unit rises, leading to an increase in consumer prices. Third, the money supply affects price changes. If the money supply increases significantly, the currency value decreases relatively, or the purchasing power of the currency per unit decreases, constituting substantial inflation. Conversely, if the money supply decreases, the currency value rises relatively, and the purchasing power of the currency per unit rises, which easily causes price retrenchment.

This chapter also discusses changes in the living standards. The purpose of economic development is to raise people's living standards. As long as people's living standards are raised, there is in large measure economic development. Conversely, if the rate of economic growth is high, but the living standards are rarely enhanced, such economic growth is questionable or at least problematic. For example, the economy usually grows during a war because there is a need to produce a wealth of weapons. There must be growth as far as the GDP is concerned. Moreover, during a war, the people usually work harder out of patriotism and often create more wealth, but such wealth is not in the form of consumer goods because they are spent in the war. As a result, the people's living standards are not improved. For another example, China's economy also grew rapidly during the planned economy period,

DOI: 10.4324/9781003410386-8

although not as well as in the reform and opening up period. However, the results of economic growth were rarely reflected in people's living standards but were generally used for investment. Admittedly, a relatively complete industrial system was put in place through investment, which laid the foundation for subsequent development. However, the living standards of people at the time did not improve much. Moreover, owing to the institutional problems at the time, many investments were inefficient.

Finally, the issue of income distribution is studied. Usually, income distribution was relatively equal at a time when there was no modern economic growth because people had relatively low income at this time. The vast majority of countries fall into the Malthusian trap. As the economy develops, incomes begin to increase. People's different abilities, coupled with increased opportunities, lead to income disparity. Some people's income increases quickly, while others' income rises slowly. As the economy further develops, people receive more education and become more skilled, and the level of social welfare has also improved. Institutional support is also provided. As a result, the income gap will gradually narrow. This is what Simon Smith Kuznets calls the "Inverted U-hypothesis" for income distribution. Since China had not started modern economic growth in modern times, income distribution was not greatly expanded.

## 6.2 Changes in consumer prices

Figure 6.1 shows the rural consumer price index, which includes the index for individual regions in Jiangsu. It includes both wholesale and retail prices for the

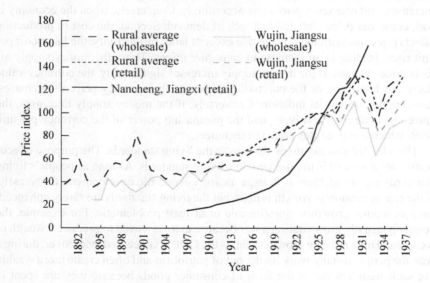

*Figure 6.1* Consumer price index in rural areas (1926 = 100)
*Data source:* Ryoshin Minami and Makino Fumio (2014), pp. 417–418.

years from 1890 to 1937. In the long term, the changes in the consumer price index between the early 20th century and the 1930s showed a slow and steady upward trend, particularly after the Xinhai Revolution. The rise before this period was slow, accompanied by great fluctuations. There were two significant increases in the last decade of the 19th century, indicating social and economic instability somewhat during this period. The slow increase after 1912 was driven by economic growth because many modern industrial sectors began to be introduced to China, and the private sector developed well during this period. Consumer prices fluctuated sharply in rural areas in the 1930s, and prices in 1937 were back to the level in the early 1930s. The sharp decline in this period can be seen as a result of the Great Depression (1929–1933).[1] In November 1935, the Nationalist government introduced an inconvertible legal tender system, which led to inflation and an increase in consumer prices.

Price changes in the cities are examined next. Figure 6.2 shows the wholesale price index from 1913 to 1937. Similar to the changes in the rural consumer price index, it also showed an upward trend before 1930 and a significant decline in the early 1930s before rising again. The trend of changes for mineral products is slightly different from that for agricultural products and industrial products. After a considerable increase in the early days of the Republic of China period, it fell rapidly and then rose steadily, but not as high as that of agricultural products and industrial products. The changes for mineral products after the 1930s were largely similar to those for agricultural and industrial products. By 1937, it surpassed others due to the low price levels in the early 1930s. It is also noteworthy that before the 1930s, the rise for agricultural products exceeded that for mineral products and also industrial products, especially after the 1920s. This indicates that there

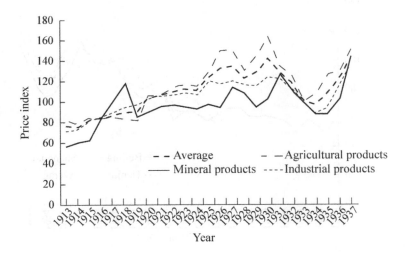

*Figure 6.2* Wholesale consumer prices index for cities (1933 = 100)

*Data source:* Ryoshin Minami and Makino Fumio (2014), p. 413.

140  *Processes and characteristics*

might be a shortage of agricultural products in cities or that the urban population expanded too fast.

We then take a look at the changes in the retail price index for cities. Figure 6.3 shows the retail price index for Beijing, Tianjin, Shanghai, and the average. The trend of changes in the consumer price index in various cities is similar and is also close to the changes in wholesale price indexes and rural consumer price indexes, as mentioned earlier. The consumer price index in Beijing could be extended until 1900, but the change before 1913 was stable, with a slight increase. This is broadly the same as the rural consumer price index in the same period as mentioned earlier, but it was more stable. The trend of changes after 1913 is basically consistent with that of urban wholesale price index and the rural consumer price index – rising significantly before 1929, then declining, and then rebounding again.

The following can be observed from the trend of changes in the aforesaid price indexes: First, price indexes for both rural and urban areas, as well as the wholesale price index or retail price index, show a highly similar trend of changes. In other words, there was a stable but slight increase before 1913, a rapid rise from 1913 to 1929, and a significant decline from 1930 to 1934 before rebounding again. This general trend basically reflects the overview of the Chinese economy during this period. To put it another way, consumer prices generally rose from the early 20th century to 1937, except that the Great Depression affected the economy in the early 1930s. On the whole, it reflects a certain degree of progress and growth in China's economy, although the price increase was not entirely the result of economic growth.

Second, the changes were highly similar for rural areas and cities, indicating that there was largely linkage in China's economy at that time. In other words,

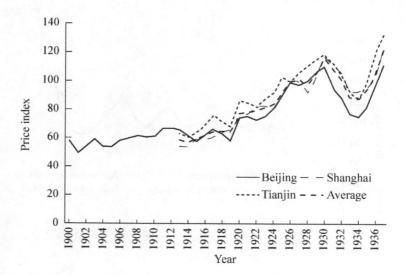

*Figure 6.3* Retail price index for cities (1926 = 100)

*Data source:* Ryoshin Minami and Makino Fumio (2014), p. 421.

*Changes in consumer prices and living standards* 141

urban and rural areas were connected through the market. Price changes in cities affected rural areas, which in turn affected cities. Of course, this view is still our assumption. If it is true, it will be a significant change. If rural areas and cities are independent of each other, it is not conducive to economic development. Economic development necessitates the reallocation of resources, and the existing resource structure will be restructured. Reallocation will lead to efficiency gains. For example, economic development requires industrialization, which needs huge capital and a wealth of labor. Because there is a lack of capital and industrial labor in underdeveloped countries, these must be obtained from agriculture and rural areas. It is difficult to reallocate resources in the absence of capital and labor market.

As a result of Japan's all-out invasion of China in 1937, consumer prices rose rapidly in China, especially after 1940. The War of Liberation erupted in the wake of the end of the War of Resistance against Japanese Aggression, and consumer prices rose further, even soaring as never seen before. In 1948, the consumer price index in Shanghai rose by 2.55 million times compared with 1937, and the consumer price index in Tianjin rose by 1.62 million times in the same period. This shows the enormous and far-reaching negative impact of the war on the economy and society.[2]

A situation similar to that of China also occurred in some Latin American countries in the 1970s and 1980s. In many countries such as Brazil and Argentina, the international debt crisis caused serious inflation, resulting in severe economic stagnation and recession. Therefore, although consumer prices are only a phenomenon, it involves many internal and external factors. Generally, prices do not rise or fall without a reason, but prices fluctuate as a result of economic cycles and some temporary reasons in normal economic performance. For example, the impact of weather anomaly on crop growth and yield, the shortage of certain important resources, and a strained situation caused by human intervention will lead to sharp fluctuations in the prices of related resources. As a result of the oil crisis of 1973, crude oil prices suddenly rose several times, which played havoc with the economic growth of oil-import-dependent countries. Japan was the hardest hit by the crisis because the oil crisis even directly brought an end to the era of rapid economic growth in Japan. Oil price is still one of the price changes of the greatest concern even today. Any disturbance in the world will put all countries on edge, and they will be prepared to take measures against the adverse effects on their economies.

## 6.3 Living standards

There is a lack of statistics in modern China, especially the data that can mirror people's everyday life. The time sequence data are available for only a few fields (such as goods import and export). Therefore, it is difficult to judge whether people's living standards improved or not during this period. Of course, it is possible to make conjectures based on indirect data. For example, data for certain time points or for certain regions can be compared with data for the early 1950s and thereafter in order to draw general conclusions.

From 1922 to 1925, the Department of Agricultural Economics of Jinling University investigated the income and living expenses of 2,854 rural households in 13

142 *Processes and characteristics*

places in 6 provinces, including Hebei. From 1926 to 1929, another scholar conducted a survey in the outskirts of Beiping and Dingxian County, Hebei Province. The proportions of various household expenditures can be analyzed according to the living conditions of rural households calculated from these surveys.[3] The proportion (Engel coefficient) of food, which ranked top, was close to 60 percent on average. If we consider the subsequent living standards of Chinese households, this proportion is not high. In some areas, it was as high as 93.90 percent, and the lowest was 48.68 percent. Of course, if measured by today's standards of living, this proportion should belong to absolute poverty. In turn, these figures verify the level of China's economic development at that time: China had no modern economic growth at the time. Other items include rent (4.55 percent on average), clothing (7.10 percent), fuels (10.43 percent), medicines (0.91 percent), life improvement (9.35 percent), hobbies (4.29 percent), apparatus and equipment (0.78 percent), and miscellaneous (2.64 percent).[4]

Another statistic on the Engel coefficient (see Table 6.1) shows that in 1930, it was between 39.04 percent (Xiamen) and 76.76 percent (Jiangdu) for the urban working class, with an average of 54.16 percent. In other words, the Engel coefficient for most areas was relatively low, in contrast to the preceding data. The Engel coefficient was slightly lower in cities than in rural areas. More importantly, the Engel coefficient during this period was lower than that in a certain period after 1949 – at least not higher than that during the planned economy period before the reform and opening up. What is the reason for this? A possibility is either that the data for this period are not accurate or that the sample size is not large enough. A few samples for some cities and deviations may occur. Another possibility is that the living standards of the Chinese people did not improve, at least not significantly, in modern China and during the planned economy period.

However, an explanation is needed here, especially for the situation after 1949, because China implemented a low wage system during the planned economy period, in which wages were not adjusted according to market principles, and consumer prices were specified according to the plan and basically remained unchanged for a long time. In other words, the government implemented a strategy in which the surplus brought by growth was used more for investment under the condition of meeting the basic living needs of the population, in order to build a complete industrial system in an all-round way as soon as possible. To this end, it was necessary to lower the living standards of the people. Although the goal was achieved, the people's living standards were not improved for a long time. In other words, it is the type of industrialization at the expense of not improving (or lowering) people's quality of life. Anyway, it is an indisputable fact that people's living standards did not improve significantly during the planned economy period.

The table also shows an intriguing situation that in many cities (about one-third of the total), the average household expenditure exceeded the average household income. That is to say, the phenomenon of negative savings existed. The savings surplus in those cities where average household income exceeded the average household expenditure was also low, indicating that the people's living standards at that time were low and that there was basically no room for savings. Another

*Table 6.1* Composition of living expenses of workers' households in 30 cities in 1930

| City | Number of households surveyed | Average number of people per household (person) | Average household income (yuan) | Average household expenditure (yuan) | Consumption composition (%) | | | | |
|---|---|---|---|---|---|---|---|---|---|
| | | | | | Catering | Clothing | Rent | Fuel | Miscellaneous |
| Shanghai | 300 | 4.5 | 28.10 | 30.41 | 56.82 | 7.60 | 9.08 | 7.33 | 19.17 |
| Suzhou | 22 | 3.2 | 22.12 | 24.63 | 54.06 | 6.44 | 8.75 | 8.95 | 21.80 |
| Wuxi | 159 | 3.7 | 23.51 | 31.14 | 49.98 | 9.51 | 6.98 | 7.61 | 26.92 |
| Wujin | 43 | 3.4 | 23.68 | 22.02 | 52.23 | 10.47 | 8.19 | 12.72 | 16.39 |
| Zhenjiang | 10 | 3.0 | 24.60 | 27.36 | 61.77 | 5.54 | 10.71 | 6.03 | 15.95 |
| Jiangdu | 1 | 2.1 | 14.00 | 18.24 | 76.76 | 11.40 | 1.81 | 8.22 | 1.81 |
| Nantong | 21 | 3.3 | 25.85 | 24.89 | 64.73 | 7.28 | 6.23 | 7.36 | 14.40 |
| Yixing | 18 | 2.7 | 23.88 | 13.47 | 60.03 | 8.31 | 6.65 | 11.17 | 13.84 |
| Nanjing | 56 | 3.7 | 27.49 | 35.35 | 62.37 | 2.09 | 2.90 | 8.33 | 24.31 |
| Wuxing | 84 | 3.1 | 21.73 | 21.49 | 59.77 | 6.06 | 10.31 | 9.86 | 14.00 |
| Hangzhou | 45 | 2.9 | 30.00 | 28.03 | 56.33 | 8.35 | 10.96 | 7.53 | 16.83 |
| Jiaxing | 8 | 3.9 | 44.25 | 27.74 | 44.16 | 10.24 | 11.04 | 7.89 | 26.67 |
| Anqing | 192 | 3.3 | 15.82 | 18.81 | 51.77 | 7.65 | 16.18 | 12.38 | 12.02 |
| Wuhu | 3 | 4.0 | 48.66 | 32.34 | 54.62 | 12.83 | 10.31 | 8.76 | 13.48 |
| Bengbu | 2 | 3.1 | 36.67 | 33.46 | 44.83 | 7.45 | 30.63 | 8.46 | 8.63 |
| Nanchang | 7 | 5.3 | 39.71 | 30.08 | 54.62 | 3.78 | 16.14 | 16.14 | 9.32 |
| Jiujiang | 15 | 3.2 | 24.23 | 21.99 | 46.69 | 10.95 | 15.62 | 11.53 | 15.21 |
| Hankou | 34 | 3.5 | 31.78 | 29.61 | 53.72 | 8.48 | 13.08 | 9.28 | 15.44 |
| Hanyang | 25 | 3.4 | 40.32 | 39.73 | 45.60 | 6.00 | 12.89 | 7.54 | 27.97 |
| Wuchang | 119 | 3.6 | 27.59 | 27.85 | 54.03 | 6.69 | 9.30 | 11.66 | 18.32 |
| Daye | 14 | 4.7 | 20.63 | 31.01 | 68.64 | 7.69 | 3.57 | 6.22 | 13.88 |
| Qingdao | 8 | 4.6 | 33.75 | 35.69 | 41.86 | 14.00 | 6.85 | 8.06 | 29.23 |
| Guangzhou | 199 | 2.8 | 30.24 | 27.08 | 53.55 | 6.78 | 20.63 | 8.67 | 10.37 |
| Foshan | 49 | 3.2 | 22.25 | 23.44 | 53.21 | 4.65 | 14.71 | 13.05 | 14.38 |
| Chao'an | 2 | 5.5 | 40.00 | 39.35 | 45.75 | 5.29 | 10.16 | 8.89 | 29.91 |
| Shantou | 44 | 3.9 | 47.02 | 46.29 | 46.89 | 5.54 | 11.51 | 7.81 | 28.25 |
| Wuzhou | 13 | 3.9 | 30.76 | 31.94 | 54.66 | 4.95 | 14.21 | 9.51 | 16.67 |
| Fuzhou | 136 | 3.0 | 21.99 | 21.62 | 54.92 | 5.53 | 10.49 | 12.64 | 16.42 |
| Xiamen | 7 | 3.4 | 36.57 | 32.78 | 39.04 | 10.42 | 19.61 | 6.97 | 23.96 |
| Sanduoao | 2 | 3.6 | 56.00 | 52.45 | 45.77 | 3.95 | 22.87 | 18.11 | 9.30 |
| Average | 1638 | – | 26.03 | 27.22 | 54.16 | 7.16 | 11.70 | 9.50 | 17.41 |

*Data source:* The Ministry of Industry and Commerce, Fifth Table of the *National Comprehensive Report on Survey and Statistics on Workers' Life and Industrial Production* (1930).

unexpected situation is that the average size of households is fewer than 4 persons, which was unthinkable for 1930, because it is close to the current situation in China's rural areas, and family planning has been in place for decades now.

We next observe the change in wages. If wages rose faster, consumer prices also rose, and the two cancel each other out, or there is surplus wage, it means that the living standards improved somewhat. Figure 6.4 shows the data on wages in some regions and some industries. Although the data on wages vary from industry to industry, the upward trend can be roughly observed. The benchmark year selected for the consumer price index above is different, and it is difficult to make a direct comparison, but it can be assumed that their trends of changes were close. As consumer prices rose, so did wages, and the increase margin in various industries are relatively close. Despite differences between industries, they are close in general, especially before the 1920s. Thereafter, the gap between industries began to widen. In particular, wages at Kailuan coal mine rose sharply, while the two modern industrial sectors in Shanghai saw a similar increase in wages as the agricultural industry. After the 1930s, wage increase in the flour processing industry was slower than that of agriculture, and its gap with the textile industry also began to widen, indicating that the flour processing industry met problems during this period either because of excessive competition or poor market prospects.

Due to a lack of relevant data for modern China, the information related to the preceding consumer prices and living standards is mostly concerned about a certain period or is limited to certain regions and industries, and it can hardly represent the

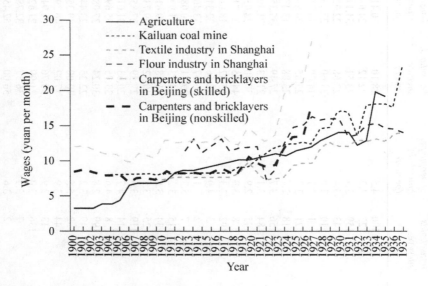

*Figure 6.4* Monthly wages in some industries

*Note:* Wages of agricultural sector and Beijing's masonry and carpentry industry are calculated based on the daily wage multiplied by 30.

*Data source:* Ryoshin Minami and Makino Fumio (2014), pp. 428–432.

*Changes in consumer prices and living standards*   145

situation of the country and the period as a whole. Therefore, it is difficult to judge whether the living standards in modern China improved or declined. Of course, we can judge the relationship between economic development and people's living standards during this period based on other materials, and we can conclude that living standards during this period did not improve. Of course, this does not exclude the possibility that the living standards of the relevant people and households in some areas and industries improved somewhat, as did the living standards for people in some emerging industries and emerging cities, while the living standards did not improve in traditional industries and rural areas.

## 6.4   Income distribution

There is a scarcity of systematic statistics on China's economy in modern times, especially continuous time sequence data. It is therefore very difficult to find out the actual situation of economic growth and income distribution. The research power is very weak because we can only rely on individual statistics and bits and pieces of research. According to estimates by some scholars,[5] the national income per capita at several time points in the 100 years from 1850 to 1949 can be roughly observed. From 1850 to 1887, the rate of economic growth was negative (−0.38 percent), the national income fell from 18.164 billion yuan to 14.343 billion yuan, and the per capita income also declined from 43.8 yuan to 38 yuan. This shows that during this period, China's economy registered negative growth, and the people's living standards worsened. Of course, it was caused by more than one reason, but foreign invasion upset the peace in China, caused instability, and even sent China into protracted wars. From 1887 to 1914, there was slight economic growth, although by only 0.3 percent, and the per capita income also increased slightly (41.22 yuan). This period was mainly under the Qing government rule, but at the end of the 19th century, China showed a clear trend of opening up as well as of change, and the Self-Strengthening Movement was launched. China introduced some advanced technologies from the West, built some modern factories, and also initiated economic activities such as exploiting mines and building railways. The years from 1914 to 1936 were a relatively good period for China's economic development and is called by some as the "golden age of the Chinese bourgeoisie". Despite a low growth rate (0.9 percent), the economy developed somewhat, and the per capita income increased to 50.51 yuan. During this period, more government-run factories were built, the private sector also made investment, and a wealth of factories in the textile, weaving, silk reeling, matchstick, tobacco, food, and other industries were built. China exhibited signs of economic take-off during this period, but the all-out invasion by Japan broke this trend, inflicting heavy losses on China's economy. As a result, it was natural that the growth rate from 1936 to 1949 was negative (−2.87 percent), and per capita income fell again. In short, in modern China, the economy was in tatters, and the masses had no means to live for a host of reasons. Some good signs, if there were any, were eliminated by foreign aggressors. According to the table, the average income of Chinese people in 1949 was back to the level in the late 19th century or even fell to its lowest level.

## 146   *Processes and characteristics*

Here, Maddison's estimates are used to further observe the changes in the GDP per capita in modern China, which was 600 yuan in 1850 (in 1990 international dollars for this and the following data), 530 yuan in 1870, 545 yuan in 1890, 552 yuan in 1913, 562 yuan in 1929, 580 yuan in 1937, and 448 yuan in 1950.[6] From the data on these specific time points, it can be seen that China's economy did not grow and even took a step backward in the 100 years from 1850 to 1950. Of course, this does not mean an across-the-board regression because there is the factor of population growth: China's population was 412 million in 1850, and reached 547 million in 1950. The problem is that output decreased from 247.20 billion yuan (1990 international dollars) in 1850 to 244.985 billion yuan in 1950. Although it was higher than in 1950 in some periods (reaching 303.433 billion yuan in 1936), it did not compensate for the decline caused by the increase in population (508 million in 1936).[7] This result is consistent with these estimates, indicating weak economic growth in modern China. Coupled with the population growth and the deprivations caused by war, the living standards of Chinese people declined somewhat.

Experts in economic history such as Liu Foding deduced from historical data that the period from the 1880s to the 1930s has the following characteristics. First, the proportion of the income of the wealthy to the total national income significantly declined, and the share of the income of the masses increased slightly. In 1887, the income of the wealthy, who accounted for 2 percent of China's total population, accounted for 21 percent of the total national income. In 1933, the income of the richest, who accounted for 1 percent of the country's population, accounted for only 4.7 percent of the total national income, and the rich, who accounted for 6.5 percent, accounted for 23.6 percent of the total national income. In 1887, the income of ordinary residents, who numbered 98 percent of the total population, accounted for 79 percent of the total national income. In 1933, the income of ordinary residents, who accounted for 93.5 percent of the total population, accounted for 76.4 percent of the total national income. Second, the gap between the high-income group and the lower-middle-income group narrowed significantly. In 1887, the per capita annual income of the high-income group, who accounted for 2 percent of the country's total population, was about 90 taels, while the average annual income of the remaining 98 percent was only 6.8 taels. The former is about 13.2 times more than that of the latter. In 1933, the wealthy, who accounted for 1 percent of the country's total population, had an annual income of 222 yuan, and the remaining 99 percent had an annual income of 46 yuan. The former is only 4.8 times more than that of the latter. Third, the absolute value of the per capita annual income of the wealthy declined significantly, while the annual income of ordinary residents rose markedly. If the figures for 1887 are converted into the 1933 currency value, it can be deduced that the per capita annual income of the wealthy in 1887 was 397 yuan, which is about 1.8 times the highest income of 222 yuan for the top 1 percent in the country in 1933. In 1887, the per capita annual income of ordinary residents was 30 yuan, which was equal to 65 percent of the per capita income of 46 yuan for middle- and low-income class, who accounted for 99 percent of the total population, in 1933.[8] Based on a rough comparison of the two time points, it can be seen that the income gap during this period narrowed somewhat, but due to a lack of

*Changes in consumer prices and living standards* 147

continuous data with time series, it is difficult to make an accurate judgment. This can only be used for reference.

As for the reasons for this change, Liu Foding et al. explained as follows.[9] First, an increase in labor productivity and economic growth are the basic conditions for raising the living standards of the middle- and low-income classes. If the gross national product (GNP) in 1887 is converted into the currency value in 1933, it is about 14.1 billion yuan, while the GNP in 1933 is 20.044 billion yuan, up by 42 percent in more than 40 years. Per capita national income rose from 37.6 yuan to 46 yuan, up by 22.3 percent. The annual income of ordinary residents, who accounted for more than 90 percent of the country's total population, increased from 30 yuan to 39 yuan, up by 30 percent. Second, the loss of feudal privileges changed the composition of the high-income class, causing their incomes to decline. A basic feature of China's long-term feudal society is the monetization of political rights. The wealthy classes in successive dynasties were dominated by the imperial families and officials at all levels, who exploited their political status and power to amass immense wealth by fair means or foul. When there was regime change or a political bloc and individuals lost power, the wealth they accumulated would also be gone, and the sources of various incomes would be cut off. The income of 681.35 million taels for the gentry class, who accounted for 2 percent of the country's total population, in 1887 consisted of the following: (1) salary of officials and remuneration from other professions totaling 207.75 million taels, (2) the land and house rent totaling 360 million taels, and (3) commercial profit totaling 113.6 million taels. When the Qing Dynasty collapsed in 1912, the first type of income of the gentry class who topped the national income was lost. Only some of them exploited their political and military privileges to keep and increase their wealth by becoming dignitaries during the Beiyang government period. By the 1930s, the Kuomintang bureaucracy led by Chiang Kai-shek began to amass private wealth by monopolizing the financial sector, but the annual income of this cohort of people in 1933 was lower than that of the gentry class in the 1880s. In 1933, the high-income bracket, in addition to the new bureaucracy, mainly comprised the comprador class and the middle and upper classes of the bourgeoisie who began to emerge since the second half of the 19th century, as well as the despotic gentry and landlord class, but their annual income was only about half that in 1887 if calculated based on the same proportion of people. Third, the modern industrial, mining, and transport sectors developed as a result of the change from the traditional economy to the modern economy, and the gap of national income distribution between the wealthy class and ordinary residents narrowed accordingly. Judging from the history of developed countries, as the economy develops, the share of wage income in total income will increase gradually, while the share of other income will decrease.

Table 6.2 shows such a situation in national income in 1933. The table shows that the more modern the sector is, the higher the proportion of wages and salaries and the lower the proportion of non-wage income. In comparison, the more backward the economic sector (such as agriculture) is, the lower the proportion of wages and salaries and the higher the proportion of non-wage income.

148   *Processes and characteristics*

*Table 6.2* Composition of national income in 1933

|  | *Wage and salary income (%)* | *Other income (%)* |
|---|---|---|
| Agriculture | 38.5 | 61.5 |
| Mining and metallurgy | 57.9 | 42.1 |
| Manufacturing | 78.0 | 22.0 |
| Transport | 75.9 | 24.1 |
| Business | 69.1 | 30.9 |
| Financial industry | 33.6 | 66.5 |

*Data source:* Wu Baosan et al. (1947), p. 14.

We have indirectly observed the issue of income distribution based on the data on economic growth, the composition of national income, etc. in modern times, but this obviously falls short of the goal because data and indicators that directly reflect income distribution, such as the Gini coefficient, are not used. However, there are still research results in this regard. Guan Yongqiang (2012) used some data available at that time to calculate the Gini coefficient. For example, he used the data from the *Reality of China's Rural Economy* to calculate the Gini coefficients for some counties in Zhejiang, Jiangsu, Anhui, and Zhili provinces in 1923, with an average of 0.56 and 0.69. He calculated the gap in the income distribution for rural households in 16 provinces in 1934 using the *Outline of the National Land Survey Report*, and the Gini coefficient ranged from 0.33 to 0.63, with an average of 0.42. He used a full variety of other data to calculate the Gini coefficient for Hebei from 1922 to 1949, Shanxi from 1934 to 1944, Shandong from 1922 to 1942, Shaanxi from 1928 to 1948, Henan and northern Anhui from 1932 to 1947, Jiangsu from 1922 to 1946, Zhejiang from 1922 to 1948, Guangdong from 1919 to 1933, Anhui for the years before 1937 and for 1940, Fujian in 1933, Jiangxi from 1933 to 1950, Northeast China from 1925 to 1946, Guangxi from 1929 to 1934, Yunnan from 1928 to 1950, and Sichuan from 1935 to 1950.[10] It mostly reached a high level (0.45 to 0.65) and as high as 0.80 for some regions. It was relatively low only in some parts of Shaanxi. These calculations are clearly inconsistent with the laws of economic development and our experience. In particular, given that the data mostly cover rural areas, these data are even more incredible. In other words, such a large inequality in income distribution is usually impossible in a country that did not yet start modern economic growth or showed signs of modern economic growth. It is because either the data contain errors or the calculation method is problematic. Therefore, the data can only be used as a reference. It also shows the limitations of the Chinese economy at that time.

## 6.5 Conclusion

This chapter examined changes in consumer prices and the living standards in modern China, including income distribution. There was only scarce information regarding these areas before 1949, but it can also be concluded that the relationship

*Changes in consumer prices and living standards* 149

between price changes and the living standards at that time should be consistent with each other. Specifically, consumer prices were closely associated with the standard of living before 1937, but after 1937, consumer prices soared, and the people's living standards actually worsened due to the wars.

Despite the economic development, the living standards of the people did not improve significantly, and it was not easy to meet the basic needs of living. People's living standards did not improve significantly for a host of reasons (such as explosive population growth, inefficiency caused by the planned economy, and the development of light industry and agriculture impeded by development strategies) even after 1949, not to mention in the years before.

In an era without modern economic growth, there was no large gap in income distribution, even if industries and bourgeoisie emerged during the Republic of China period. Except for a very small minority, the vast majority of the population and labor force lived in rural areas, and the wealth disparity in rural areas was small. The income gap in China did not widen greatly until after the reform and opening up at the end of the 20th century or as the economy grew rapidly.[11]

## Notes

1 See Jia Xiuyan and Lu Manping (1992), pp. 55–57.
2 See Kong Min, editor-in-chief (1988) and Wang Yuru (1997), p. 25.
3 Similar studies include those by Guan Yongqiang (2012).
4 Hou Yangfang (2001), pp. 566–567.
5 The following estimates are calculated at the currency value in 1936. See Liu Foding et al. (1999), p. 66.
6 Maddison (2009).
7 Maddison (2009).
8 Liu Foding et al. (1999), pp. 314–319.
9 Liu Foding et al. (1999), pp. 314–319.
10 Guan Yongqiang (2012), pp. 13, 15, 83–103.
11 Regarding this, see Guan Quan (2019).

# 7 Imbalance in regional development

## 7.1 Introduction

This chapter examines the imbalance in regional development. This issue varies from country to country, depending on the size of the country. China is a big country, and there are great differences between regions. To begin with, the big country has a vast territory, and resources are unevenly distributed, easily causing differences. For example, due to climatic differences, northern China is suitable for growing wheat and whole grains, while southern China is suitable for planting rice. Because of the landform that is high in the west and low in the east, water conservancy resources are concentrated in the west but less in the east. The distribution of minerals is even more uncertain, with coal and oil resources mostly distributed in northern China. Second, given the geographical location, the eastern coastal areas are very prone to influence by foreign cultures and engage in international exchanges in the context of opening up, which is beneficial to economic development. As the west is dominated by vast plateaus and deserts, it lacks the necessary conditions for economic development. Finally, a big country is often a multiethnic country. There are 56 ethnic groups in China, leading to cultural differences. It is difficult to fully realize cultural identity, and misunderstanding and disagreement may easily result. In this regard, China is better off than other big countries because the Han Chinese, who account for more than 90 percent of the total population, can dominate in terms of culture.

In addition to geographical location and the cultural diversity, regional development is also highly associated with economic development. If a country's economy develops fast, the regional differences narrow, expand, and narrow again, in a way similar to income disparity between groups and classes. In modern China, due to a lack of economic development, the regional differences were mainly caused by factors such as geographical location, natural resources, factor endowment, transport, and the governance capability. The relatively developed areas in modern China were mainly coastal areas, particularly the lower reaches of the Yangtze River as well as the northeast region after the 1930s. Of course, each region had their respective advantages. Some areas were developed in agriculture, some were industrially developed, and some enjoyed abundant natural resources. Sometimes, political factor led to the rapid development of an area, such as the relocation of the capital or the development of a central city.

DOI: 10.4324/9781003410386-9

*Imbalance in regional development* 151

## 7.2 Population, agriculture, services

### 7.2.1 Population

In China's long history, successive dynasties gathered statistics on the movements of the population. Coupled with the need for tax collection, there is no shortage of statistics on China's population. Population statistics even date to back more than 2,000 years. However, as a result of reasons such as wars and famine, the population statistics are inaccurate, especially for the statistics by administrative divisions. This is also the case for statistics for the Republic of China period. Table 7.1 shows the population of each province (including special cities at the same level as a province such as Peiping and Shanghai) from 1910 to 1947. Despite their inaccuracy, the figures for and changes in the population of each province can be basically observed from these statistics. First, China's total population size was relatively stable except in 1910, despite some fluctuations, such as the total population in 1931 being lower than that in 1928. That is to say, China's political situation and society during this period were unstable, the government was weak, and statistical work, including work for demographic statistics, was inadequate, but reasonable statistics can still be obtained. Second, except for statistical deviations, the population of each province was stable. This is particularly the case in densely populated provinces (also provinces with developed traditional agriculture and commerce), such as Hebei, Shanxi, Shandong, Jiangsu, Anhui, Zhejiang, Hubei, Hunan, Guangdong, Guangxi, Sichuan, Shaanxi, and Gansu. In contrast, the population in relatively remote areas, especially in the northeast region, increased significantly, perhaps due to the phenomenon of "braving the journey to Northeast". Finally, due to changes in administrative divisions and the statistical scope, the population size in some areas changed significantly. The population of a certain region was sometimes included in neighboring areas or the statistics were incomplete, such as for Mongolia before 1928.

### 7.2.2 Agriculture

The regional distribution of agriculture is studied next. Because of the special nature of agriculture, it is difficult to measure it using the same criteria. Agriculture has special features that industry and commerce do not have on account of the geographical location, land characteristics, climate, etc. A case in point is that northern China is suitable for growing wheat and whole grains, while southern China is suited for rice. Crops such as potatoes, sweet potatoes, and grapes prefer sandy land, and tropical crops (such as sugar cane, bananas, and coffee) cannot survive in northern China. Therefore, even if we have the relevant statistics, it is difficult to directly compare regions, such as in terms of productivity. Of course, a comparison of time sequence in the same region is valuable because we can observe changes in productivity, such as increase in per unit yield (yield per *mu*).

The changes in cultivated land in provinces between 1893 and 1933 are briefly introduced here. As a basis for judging the agricultural situation as a whole, Table 7.2 shows that the national average population index increased significantly, while

## 152  Processes and characteristics

*Table 7.1* Changes in population in provinces during the Republic of China period, Unit: 1,000 people

| Province | 1910 | 1912 | 1928 | 1931 | 1936 | 1947 |
|---|---|---|---|---|---|---|
| Hebei | 26,721 | 26,658 | 31,232 | 29,681 | 28,644 | 32,020 |
| Shanxi | 10,090 | 10,082 | 12,228 | 11,567 | 11,601 | 15,222 |
| Shandong | 29,557 | 30,989 | 30,336 | 35,853 | 38100 | 40,076 |
| Jiangsu | 25,883 | 32,283 | 34,126 | 32,137 | 36,469 | 41448 |
| Anhui | 16,229 | 16,229 | 21,715 | 21,600 | 23,354 | 22,293 |
| Zhejiang | 18,072 | 21,440 | 20,643 | 20,332 | 21,231 | 19,221 |
| Fujian | 12,500 | 15,849 | 9,744 | 11,862 | 11,756 | 11,110 |
| Jiangxi | 16,977 | 23,988 | 18,108 | 18,724 | 15,805 | 12,472 |
| Henan | 26,110 | 35,900 | 29,090 | 32,636 | 34,290 | 29,254 |
| Hubei | 26,647 | 29,590 | 26,699 | 26,960 | 25,516 | 21,663 |
| Hunan | 23,403 | 27,617 | 31,501 | 28,847 | 28,294 | 25,948 |
| Guangdong | 28,011 | 28,011 | 31,433 | 27,431 | 32,453 | 29,149 |
| Guangxi | 7,789 | 7,790 | 8,741 | 10,930 | 13,385 | 14,603 |
| Sichuan | 44,140 | 48,130 | 54,010 | 42,679 | 52,706 | 48,108 |
| Xikang | 464 | – | 521 | – | 968 | 1,651 |
| Yunnan | 7210 | 9,468 | 12,665 | 11,767 | 12,042 | 9,029 |
| Guizhou | 8,703 | 9,665 | 12,692 | 8,222 | 9,919 | 10,490 |
| Shaanxi | 8,054 | 12,364 | 11,802 | 10,750 | 9,780 | 10,471 |
| Gansu | 4,700 | 4,199 | 6,403 | 5,453 | 6,716 | 6,978 |
| Qinghai | 328 | 368 | 368 | 638 | 1,196 | 1,346 |
| Ningxia | – | 303 | – | 403 | 978 | 774 |
| Xinjiang | 2,085 | 2,098 | 2,552 | 2,578 | 4,360 | 4,047 |
| Heilongjiang | 1 859 | 2 029 | 3 725 | 3,749 | 3,751 | – |
| Jilin | 5,538 | 5,580 | 6,102 | 7,339 | 7,355 | – |
| Liaoning | 11,019 | 12,133 | 15,233 | 15,254 | 15,254 | – |
| Rehe | 3,166 | 4,630 | 4,372 | 2,185 | 2,185 | 6,197 |
| Mongolia | 15 | 340 | 17 | – | 6,160 | 4,047 |
| Chahar | 111 | 1,623 | 1,997 | 1,809 | 2,036 | 2,150 |
| Suiyuan | 249 | 630 | 2,124 | 2,083 | 2,084 | 2,230 |
| Tibet | 1,161 | 1,161 | 1,303 | – | 3,722 | 1,000 |
| Beiping | – | 725 | – | 1,488 | 1,551 | – |
| Nanjing | – | – | – | 654 | 1,019 | – |
| Shanghai | – | – | – | 1,866 | 3,727 | – |
| Qingdao | – | – | – | 391 | 515 | – |
| Tianjin | – | – | – | – | 1,218 | – |
| Weihaiwei | – | – | – | 189 | 222 | – |
| Total | 366,791 | 421,872 | 441,482 | 428,057 | 470,362 | 422,997 |

*Note:* In addition to the figures for 1936, there are 206,000 people in Xijing, 680,000 people in Dongsheng Special Region, and 7,839,000 overseas Chinese.

*Data source:* Data for 1910, 1928, and 1947 from Xu Daofu (1983), pp. 2–5; data for 1912 and 1931 from *Yearbook of Internal Affairs by* the Ministry of the Interior during the Republic of China period; data for 1936 from the *Household Statistics* (National Household Statistics Table) by the Statistics Department of the Ministry of the Interior during the Republic of China period; data for 1947 from the *National Household Statistics* (National Household Statistics Table) by the Ministry of the Interior during the Republic of China period.

*Imbalance in regional development* 153

*Table 7.2* Rural population and cultivated land area index in modern China (1873 = 100)

| Province | 1893 | | 1913 | | 1933 | |
|---|---|---|---|---|---|---|
| | Population | Cultivated land | Population | Cultivated land | Population | Cultivated land |
| Chahar | 114 | 104 | 144 | 112 | 160 | 104 |
| Suiyuan | 139 | 95 | 172 | 93 | 175 | 88 |
| Ningxia | 143 | 100 | 101 | 102 | 88 | 99 |
| Qinghai | 167 | 169 | 161 | 175 | 172 | 203 |
| Gansu | 115 | 116 | 129 | 117 | 117 | 118 |
| Shaanxi | 94 | 98 | 99 | 95 | 96 | 91 |
| Shanxi | 77 | 103 | 82 | 110 | 88 | 110 |
| Hebei | 112 | 98 | 122 | 100 | 140 | 98 |
| Shandong | 119 | 103 | 122 | 105 | 128 | 99 |
| Henan | 104 | 99 | 110 | 117 | 104 | 115 |
| Jiangsu | 108 | 101 | 128 | 102 | 150 | 110 |
| Anhui | 122 | 106 | 146 | 107 | 166 | 107 |
| Zhejiang | 102 | 102 | 107 | 73 | 123 | 78 |
| Fujian | 92 | 96 | 93 | 92 | 88 | 81 |
| Guangdong | 123 | 101 | 142 | 101 | 157 | 102 |
| Jiangxi | 100 | 99 | 100 | 93 | 93 | 91 |
| Hubei | 105 | 104 | 116 | 109 | 145 | 128 |
| Hunan | 118 | 88 | 129 | 89 | 144 | 88 |
| Guangxi | 109 | 105 | 149 | 117 | 164 | 123 |
| Sichuan | 118 | 102 | 135 | 104 | 157 | 110 |
| Yunnan | 135 | 111 | 179 | 133 | 237 | 331 |
| Guizhou | 106 | 115 | 118 | 121 | 128 | 130 |
| Whole country | 108 | 101 | 117 | 101 | 131 | 101 |

*Data source:* Zhang Youyi (1957), (volume 3), pp. 907–908.

the area of cultivated land remained unchanged. Of course, it was not exactly the same for all regions. The area of cultivated land increased in some regions, such as Qinghai, Hubei, Guangxi, Yunnan, and Guizhou. The area of cultivated land shrank in some provinces in some years, such as Suiyuan, Ningxia, Shaanxi, Shandong, Zhejiang, Fujian, and Jiangxi. This is also true of the population, with increases in some regions and decreases in other regions. The populations of Ningxia, Fujian, and Jiangxi declined, although they accounted for a small proportion in the total population. On the whole, however, China's population and area of cultivated land changed slightly from the late 19th century to the 1930s, or, to be exact, the population increased, while the area of cultivated land remained basically unchanged. It can be said that a fixed area of cultivated land fed a larger population. There are two possible reasons. One is technological progress. The productivity of land was improved as a result of biological or chemical technologies, but this possibility was unrealistic during this period. The other is a decline in living standards. Due to the decrease in per capita land owned, the number of people fed by per unit land increased. In the absence of other supplements, the standard of living inevitably declined. We think the second is more likely.

154  *Processes and characteristics*

### 7.2.3 Service sector

The situation of the service sector is difficult to pin down not only in China but also in other developed countries in the early stages of economic development. It is usually defined as the sector other than agriculture and industrial sectors for obvious reasons. First, the service sector had been vaguely defined for a long time, and it was not clearly defined until after World War II. Second, the service sector is too complex to be accurately defined because it includes the traditional catering and commerce industries, as well as modern financial and consulting industries. Third, especially in the early stages of economic development, some industries had the characteristics of the manufacturing and service sector. For example, in the catering and traditional handicraft industries, products were usually manufactured in the backyard and were then sold in the storefront shops. The traditional tofu mills, blacksmith's shops, traditional Chinese medicines shops, and jewelry stores belong to this type.

Table 7.3 shows the situation of personnel and capital of shops in various provinces in 1933, from which we can learn about commercial prosperity in various regions. There were many shops in Zhejiang, Jiangsu, Fujian, Jiangxi, Hebei, Shanxi,

*Table 7.3* Distribution of shops by province in 1933

| Province | Number of employees | | | Capital | | |
|---|---|---|---|---|---|---|
| | Number of stores | Number of employees | Average number of employees | Number of stores | Capital amount (10,000 yuan) | Average capital amount (yuan) |
| Jiangsu | 13,724 | 90,948 | 6.63 | 14,220 | 1,361.90 | 958 |
| Zhejiang | 28,297 | 13,66811 | 4.83 | 35,481 | 4,740.20 | 1336 |
| Anhui | 5,633 | 31,123 | 6.05 | 5,598 | 2,691.60 | 4,808 |
| Jiangxi | 19,131 | 76,448 | 4.00 | 18,895 | 1,848.28 | 978 |
| Hubei | 12,902 | 62,184 | 4.82 | 12,902 | 3,418.73 | 2,650 |
| Hunan | 1,477 | 4,726 | 3.20 | 5,718 | 1,300.15 | 2,274 |
| Fujian | 14,235 | 53,273 | 3.74 | 21,466 | 7,843.50 | 3,654 |
| Guangdong | 1,237 | 15,276 | 12.35 | 1,237 | 392.90 | 3,176 |
| Guangxi | 4,287 | 12,396 | 2.89 | 19,758 | 713.32 | 361 |
| Guizhou | – | – | – | 377 | 771.00 | 20,451 |
| Hebei | 22,131 | 123,787 | 5.59 | 49,735 | 8,137.90 | 1,636 |
| Shandong | 3,390 | 33,951 | 10.02 | 13,055 | 13,711.76 | 10,503 |
| Shanxi | 22,016 | 133,185 | 6.05 | 22,016 | 1,666.07 | 757 |
| Shaanxi | 2,417 | 13,125 | 5.43 | 4,628 | 675.94 | 1,461 |
| Suiyuan | 238 | 3,034 | 12.75 | 354 | 117.70 | 3,325 |
| Gansu | – | – | – | 2,986 | 1,490.68 | 4,992 |
| Whole country | 151,115 | 790,137 | 5.23 | 228,426 | 50,881.63 | 2,227 |

*Note:* The difference in the number of stores in the employees and capital columns is due to the difference in statistical caliber.

*Data source:* Wu Baosan, et al. (1947), pp. 103–104.

*Imbalance in regional development* 155

Guangxi, Shandong, Hubei, etc., indicating that these provinces might have a big population, as well as relatively developed local economy. Of course, the number of shops is only a sign of quantity. The scale is also important. The number of employees, particularly the average number is a good indicator. The average number of employees was highest in Suiyuan and Guangdong, followed by Shandong. On the whole, the sizes of shops were small, averaging 5.23 persons per store in the country. In other words, shops were mostly small in size. This is normal because there were basically small grocery stores run by individuals, while department stores were few. The total amount of capital was the largest in Shandong, followed by Hebei, Fujian, Zhejiang, Hubei, etc. The average capital amount was the highest in Guizhou, followed by Shandong, while other provinces hovered around the national average. Since these data refer only to one time point, it is difficult to observe the changes, and the data can only be used as a reference.

## 7.3 Industrial sector

### 7.3.1 *Distribution of industrial sector in the 1910s*

The industrial development of this period is detailed in the *Agricultural and Commercial Statistics Table*. The situation of these statistic data can be learned through other literature, while only the distribution of industrial development by region at that time is briefly introduced here.[1] Due to data limitations, only the number of factories and the number of employees, as well as the number of factories, in order of scale can be analyzed. Due to space limitations and the questionable quality of the data for the years after 1916, only the two years of 1912 and 1915 are studied here.

Table 7.4 shows the regional distribution of factories in both years, including factories that used power, those that did not use power, and the ratio of power use. The distribution is highly uneven, with many factories in some areas but few in others. In 1912, Zhejiang and Guangdong ranked first in terms of the number of factories, followed by Jiangxi, Shanxi, Fengtian, Sichuan, Fujian, Jiangsu, Hubei, Hunan, and Zhili. There were also many in Shandong and Henan, but few in Heilongjiang, Gansu, Guangxi, Yunnan, Guizhou, etc. There were no factories in some regions. This distribution largely continued in 1915; the number of factories in some areas increased significantly and doubled in Zhili. Some regions such as Fengtian, Hubei, Hunan, and Guangdong saw a decrease. Factories were built from scratch in some regions, such as in Xinjiang, Rehe, and Chahar.[2] In terms of the ratio of power use, which is the proportion of factories that used power, it averaged only 1.18 percent in 1912 and increased to only 2.47 percent in 1915, a situation of basically zero use of power. In this regard, China lagged far behind Japan, which had a ratio of power use of 28.4 percent in as early as 1909 and up to 65.2 percent in 1920.[3]

We next examine the number of employees and the average number of factory employees. In terms of the total, it exceeded 600,000 in both years, slightly less in 1915. From the perspective of region, in 1912, Jiangsu and Hubei had the largest

## 156  Processes and characteristics

*Table 7.4* Situations of factories in various regions in 1912 and 1915

| Region | 1912 | | | | 1915 | | | |
|---|---|---|---|---|---|---|---|---|
| | Number of factories | Ratio of power use (%) | Number of employees | Average number of factory employees | Number of factories | Ratio of power use (%) | Number of employees | Average number of factory employees |
| Jingzhao | 321 | 1.87 | 5,382 | 16.77 | 222 | 2.70 | 6,483 | 29.20 |
| Zhili | 1,012 | 0.20 | 25,691 | 25.39 | 2,267 | 1.15 | 43,183 | 19.05 |
| Fengtian | 1,331 | 4.13 | 20,970 | 15.76 | 783 | 3.07 | 12,908 | 16.49 |
| Jilin | 311 | 0.64 | 4,401 | 14.15 | 637 | 0.94 | 10,911 | 17.13 |
| Heilongjiang | 142 | 1.41 | 2,716 | 19.13 | 276 | 0.00 | 3,751 | 13.59 |
| Shandong | 909 | 1.10 | 22,662 | 24.93 | 936 | 12.93 | 24,774 | 26.47 |
| Henan | 903 | 0.11 | 10,577 | 11.71 | 842 | 0.36 | 14,891 | 17.69 |
| Shanxi | 1,655 | 0.00 | 19,829 | 11.98 | 1,294 | 0.08 | 14,047 | 10.86 |
| Jiangsu | 1,215 | 9.38 | 98,017 | 80.67 | 1,288 | 11.57 | 142,678 | 110.77 |
| Anhui | 343 | 0.00 | 4,731 | 13.79 | 386 | 0.00 | 24,680 | 63.94 |
| Jiangxi | 1,678 | 0.00 | 39,302 | 23.42 | 1,610 | 0.00 | 60,802 | 37.77 |
| Fujian | 1,320 | 0.00 | 28,989 | 21.96 | 1,129 | 0.00 | 23,095 | 20.46 |
| Zhejiang | 2,583 | 0.15 | 70,551 | 27.31 | 2,501 | 0.52 | 73,739 | 29.48 |
| Hubei | 1,218 | 0.74 | 94,288 | 77.41 | 532 | 3.20 | 36,790 | 69.15 |
| Hunan | 1,199 | 1.58 | 72,583 | 60.54 | 686 | 0.87 | 22,661 | 33.03 |
| Shaanxi | 364 | 0.00 | 4,299 | 11.81 | 465 | 0.00 | 5,058 | 10.88 |
| Gansu | 106 | 0.94 | 2,342 | 22.09 | 234 | 0.00 | 2,329 | 9.95 |
| Xinjiang | – | | | | 31 | 0.00 | 417 | 13.45 |
| Sichuan | 1,310 | 0.00 | 31,116 | 23.75 | 1,955 | 0.20 | 38,201 | 19.54 |
| Guangdong | 2,426 | 5.61 | 78,653 | 32.42 | 856 | 11.80 | 54,181 | 63.30 |
| Guangxi | 181 | 0.00 | 18,847 | 104.13 | 74 | 0.00 | 953 | 12.88 |
| Yunnan | 102 | 0.98 | 4,260 | 41.76 | – | | | |
| Guizhou | 120 | 0.83 | 1,578 | 13.15 | 17 | 0.00 | 606 | 35.65 |
| Rehe | – | | | | 173 | 0.58 | 1,586 | 9.17 |
| Chahar | – | | | | 127 | 0.00 | 1,001 | 7.88 |
| Total/average | 20,749 | 1.18 | 661,784 | 21.52 | 19,321 | 2.47 | 619,725 | 32.08 |

*Note:* Ratio of power use = number of factories that used power ÷ total number of factories × 100 percent.

*Data source:* Ministry of Agriculture and Commerce, *Agricultural and Commercial Statistics Table* (1st, 4th).

*Imbalance in regional development* 157

number of employees, followed by Guangdong and Hunan. In 1915, Jiangsu saw a significant increase, while Guangdong saw a significant decline, which is highly questionable. The average number of factory employees was 21.52 in 1912 but increased to 32.08 in 1915. It was encouraging progress because a bigger size of the factory helps to improve the economies of scale effect, introduce advanced equipment, and improve the factory management. Of course, it varied from region to region, with some regions barely meeting the standard (more than 7 people)[4] and some having up to 100 employees. The dereference indicates a gap in the level of development between regions.[5]

These simple observations show that the distribution of Chinese factories by region from 1912 to 1915 exhibits several characteristics. First, there was uneven regional distribution, with concentrated factories in some areas and few in others. Second, power was very rarely or not used at factories. Third, the number of factory employees was very small, with fewer than 30 people for the vast majority of factories. It shows that China's industrialization was in its infancy.

### 7.3.2 Industrial distribution in the 1930s

Except for the *Agricultural and Commercial Statistics Table* published in the first decade of the Republic of China period, there was a lack of statistics on the industrial sector in the 1920s, which can be said to be a mystery. How come there was a lack of statistics for a whole decade? In fact, this is also the case for other industries. We believe that this is linked to the political turmoil at that time, such as frequent warlord dogfights, incompetent government, and people living on the edge of starvation. It was impossible to conduct statistical surveys, as evidenced by the quality of the *Agricultural and Commercial Statistics Table* published in the last 5 years at the time.[6]

In the early 1930s, relatively good survey data became available, including the *China Industrial Survey Report* and *Chronicle of China's Industry*, as well as the *Statistics Table of Factories in Manchukuo* for the northeast region ruled by Japan. Due to space limitations, only the first one is introduced here. In the early 1930s, the Kuomintang Resource Committee commissioned the Shanghai Institute of Economic Statistics led by director Liu Dajun to survey factories nationwide. The survey was the most exhaustive and accurate one at the time, despite many loopholes and errors. We only discuss the geographical distribution of factories, while the analysis of various industries is conducted separately.[7]

Table 7.5 shows the characteristics of factories nationwide based on the *China Industrial Survey Report* (volume 2). In terms of the number of factories, it reached 18,725, far more than the 2,435 factories stated in *China Industrial Survey Report* (volume 2). In other words, the *China Industrial Survey Report* (volume 3) has a wider coverage, which helps us to learn about the basic situation of factories across the country. However, it was not prominent in terms of the number of employees, only 0.5 times more than the former (527,845 employees), indicating that factories were small in size. The amount of capital was 406,872,600 yuan in the former survey and 481,606,300 yuan in this survey, indicating that factories covered by

*Table 7.5* Overview of factories by province and city

| Province and city | Number of factories | Amount of capital (1,000 yuan) | Number of employees | Production value (1,000 yuan) | Average number of factory employees | Amount of capital per capita (yuan/person) | Per capita production value (yuan/person) |
|---|---|---|---|---|---|---|---|
| Nanjing | 678 | 7,486.0 | 9,853 | 23,437.6 | 14.5 | 759.8 | 2,378.7 |
| Shanghai | 3,484 | 190,870.3 | 245,948 | 754,515.9 | 70.6 | 776.1 | 3,067.8 |
| Beijing | 1,171 | 13,029.0 | 17,928 | 14,181.2 | 15.3 | 726.7 | 791.0 |
| Tianjin | 1,224 | 24,201.4 | 34,769 | 74,500.6 | 28.4 | 696.1 | 2,142.7 |
| Jiangsu | 2,036 | 53,928.7 | 147,743 | 202,231.1 | 72.6 | 365.0 | 1,368.8 |
| Zhejiang | 1,801 | 16,296.7 | 65,420 | 70,324.4 | 36.3 | 249.1 | 1,075.0 |
| Shandong | 938 | 31,685.8 | 36,436 | 79,311.7 | 38.8 | 869.6 | 2,176.7 |
| Hebei | 174 | 30,245.0 | 17,415 | 41,039.0 | 100.1 | 1,736.7 | 2,356.5 |
| Henan | 256 | 8,987.5 | 12,703 | 28,457.9 | 49.6 | 707.5 | 2,240.2 |
| Shanxi | 126 | 16,271.8 | 13,374 | 19,633.5 | 106.1 | 1,216.7 | 1,468.0 |
| Guangdong | 1,975 | 19,062.4 | 59,940 | 134,539.7 | 30.3 | 318.0 | 2,244.6 |
| Sichuan | 2,101 | 10,519.8 | 43,044 | 19,817.7 | 20.5 | 244.4 | 460.4 |
| Anhui | 748 | 2,961.7 | 8,069 | 10,899.9 | 10.8 | 367.0 | 1,350.8 |
| Hubei | 835 | 34,529.0 | 50,657 | 81,133.4 | 60.7 | 681.6 | 1,601.6 |
| Hunan | 233 | 4,978.8 | 6,570 | 15,957.3 | 28.2 | 757.8 | 2,428.8 |
| Jiangxi | 277 | 5,469.9 | 6,712 | 12,237.0 | 24.2 | 814.9 | 1,823.1 |
| Shaanxi | 104 | 181.1 | 1,565 | 777.6 | 15.0 | 115.7 | 496.9 |
| Fujian | 415 | 8,008.9 | 4,906 | 9,817.3 | 11.8 | 1,632.5 | 2,001.1 |
| Guangxi | 127 | 1,927.8 | 1,754 | 2,639.9 | 13.8 | 1,099.1 | 1,505.1 |
| Chahar | 6 | 13.8 | 471 | 384.2 | 78.5 | 29.2 | 815.7 |
| Suiyuan | 16 | 951.1 | 483 | 1,064.8 | 30.2 | 1,969.2 | 2,204.5 |
| Total/average | 18,725 | 481,606.3 | 785,760 | 1,596,901.5 | 42.0 | 612.9 | 2,032.3 |

*Note:* Some provinces and cities are integrated based on the original statistics, such as Qingdao City under Shandong Province and Tianjin City listed separately.

*Data source: China Industrial Survey Report* (volume 2).

*Imbalance in regional development* 159

this survey were more labor-intensive, while the former shows capital-intensive factories. The gap in the average number of factory workers is even wider, with 216.77 in the former and only 42 in this survey. There is also a gap in the amount of capital per capita, but the gap is smaller. It is noteworthy that the amount of capital mentioned here does not refer to the capital stock but to the amount of investment. Therefore, it does not represent the production capacity of fixed capital. Besides, the number of employees in the latter is not significantly larger, and therefore the gap in per capita value is not large. Interestingly, there is virtually no gap in per capita production value, possibly because small and medium-sized enterprises dominated traditional markets with large market potential.

Next is a comparison of the differences between factories in each region. Shanghai had the largest number of factories, followed by Sichuan, Jiangsu, Guangdong, Zhejiang, Tianjin, and Beijing. In terms of the amount of capital, Shanghai was far ahead of other provinces and cities; it was followed by Jiangsu, Hubei, Shandong, Hebei, Tianjin, and Guangdong. In terms of the number of employees, Shanghai still ranked at the top, followed by Jiangsu, Guangdong, Hubei, and Sichuan. In terms of the production value, Shanghai, Jiangsu, and Guangdong occupied the top three places, followed by Hubei, Shandong, Tianjin, and Zhejiang. In terms of the average number of factory employees, Shanxi and Hebei were prominent, followed by Chahar, Jiangsu, and Shanghai, while it was relatively small in other regions. In terms of the amount of capital per capita, Suiyuan, Hebei, Fujian, Shanxi, and Guangxi were prominent. In addition to Shanghai, the per capita production value was also high for many provinces and cities, such as Hunan, Hebei, Nanjing, as well as Henan, Guangdong, Suiyuan, Tianjin, and Shandong, with a small gap among them.

Overall, there are visible differences between provinces and cities. Some developed regions had visible advantages in both quantity and quality and basically met the conditions for industrial development, which laid the groundwork for future development. Other backward areas had a few factories, and the quality was also not good. Therefore, it can be said that these areas lacked the conditions for industrial development during this period.

Figure 7.1 shows the relationship between per capita capital amount and per capita production value by province and city. It basically shows an approximate production function. As per capita capital amount increases, the per capita production value also gradually increases, indicating one-to-one correspondence. In other words, under the theory of the production function, labor productivity is determined by per capita capital amount. Specifically, although Shanghai's per capita capital amount was not very high, its per capita production value was very high, indicating that Shanghai achieved more output with less capital. In general, provinces and cities above the regression line yielded more output with less capital. On the contrary, provinces and cities below the regression line might have a relatively large capital scale but little output. In other words, the productivity was lower.

We further examine factories in more regions, that is, approximate production function for factories in provinces and cities by region. Figure 7.2 shows the relationship between per capita capital amount and per capita production value of

## 160  Processes and characteristics

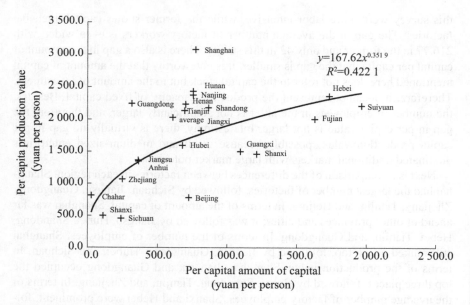

*Figure 7.1* Relationship between per capita capital amount and per capita production value
Data source: China Industrial Survey Report (volume 2).

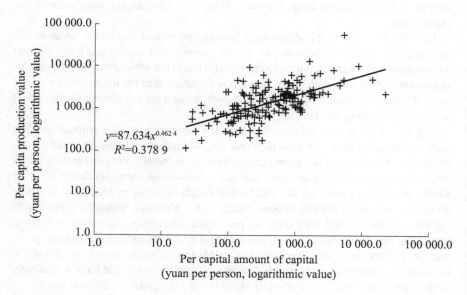

*Figure 7.2* Relationship between per capita capital amount and per capita production value (provinces and cities)
Data source: China Industrial Survey Report (volume 2).

factories by region (province or city). The number of samples here exceeds 160 (the regions of each province and city), showing that it is a representative sample. Figure 7.2 also shows correlation. The positive correlation between per capita capital amount and per capita production value is obvious.

The approximate production function relationship shown in the figures can also be shown by the division of industries. Figure 7.3 shows the relationship between the per capita capital amount and per capita production value of factories by industry in provinces and cities nationwide. Shown here are more than 550 samples (industry classification in provinces and cities), with the characteristics of a large sample. The results show that the per capita capital amount and the per capita production value of factories by industry also have a strong positive correlation. In other words, as per capita capital amount increases, the per capita production value also increases. Such analysis of the approximate production function basically illustrates the problem, albeit not in a rigorous way.

Figures 7.1 to 7.3 analyzed all the factories covered by the data from various provinces and cities, while the characteristics of factories in various regions are examined here. Because of data limitations and the differences in industrial development, only the industry of the main regions is studied here. The previous section shows a general picture of various provinces and cities, while the situation in cities and counties below the provincial level is not studied. Except Nanjing, Shanghai, Tianjin, and Beijing, it does not separately examine other important cities but includes them in the provinces to which they belong. For example, Qingdao,

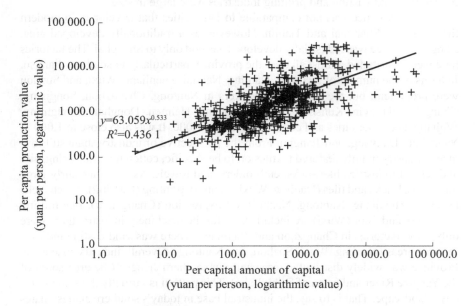

*Figure 7.3* Relationship between per capita capital amount and per capita production value (industries in provinces and cities)

*Data source:* China Industrial Survey Report (volume 2).

## 162   *Processes and characteristics*

Guangzhou, Wuhan, Chengdu, and Chongqing also had many factories and had a fairly developed industrial base. Moreover, the industry situation in cities including Nanjing, Shanghai, Tianjin and Beijing was not studied. Therefore, it is necessary to conduct further investigation from the perspective of cities and counties below the provincial level as well as the industry.

As the most industrially developed city in China, Shanghai has symbolic significance for its industry, although it is not a province. Shanghai's industrial sector is all-inclusive, including virtually all traditional and modern industries, such as the most state-of-the-art machinery, metals, electrical appliances, shipbuilding, locomotives, glass, cement, acid, alkali, and salt, and instruments and apparatus, as well as traditional industries like textiles and garment, food, and miscellaneous. Of course, the production process used in some traditional industries might be mechanized, such as in the textile industry. On the whole, Shanghai is unrivalled when it comes to the comprehensive and advanced industry.

Like Shanghai, Tianjin is an industrial and commercial city that has developed in modern times based on its port, but it was slightly smaller than Shanghai in size. Tianjin's industry mainly featured textiles but also had modern emerging industries such as machines. It also had fairly large-scale industries such as electrical appliances, locomotives, glass, bicycles, matchsticks, and printing. Compared with Tianjin, Beijing lagged far behind Tianjin in terms of the industry categories, especially in modern times, although Beijing had many factories too. Modern industries in Beijing include sand casting, smelting, glass, matchsticks, and printing. In particular, the sand-casting and printing industries were large in size.

Jiangsu Province was not comparable to large cities that developed in modern times such as Shanghai and Tianjin. However, as a traditionally developed area, Jiangsu province was industrially developed, second only to Shanghai. The factories here were distributed almost all over the province, particularly in southern Jiangsu. In terms of the number of factories, Nanjing, Nanhui, Zhenjiang, Wuxi, and Suzhou were prominent, but the number of workers in Nantong, Changzhou, Songjiang, Changshu, Jiangyin, Kunshan, Qidong, Taicang, Haimen, Donghai, Chongming, Wujiang, and other cities and counties exceeded 1,000. It was also close to 1,000 in Yangzhou, Danyang, and Jiangpu. From the perspective of industry, Jiangsu Province's industry mainly featured textiles or, to be specific, cotton manufacturing, silk and related industries like socks, embroidery, and towels. As for other fairly large industries, bricks and tiles (Nanjing, Wuxi, Nanhui), printing (Nanjing), matchsticks (Suzhou, Zhenjiang, Nantong, Nanhui), oil expression (Changzhou), rice milling (Nanjing), and flour (Wuxi) are included. As for the machinery industry, there were only some factories in Changzhou and Zhenjiang. There was sand-casting industry in some areas (Nanjing, Wuxi, Suzhou, and Nantong). Overall, industry in Jiangsu Province was widely distributed, especially in southern Jiangsu (the area south of the Yangtze River and north of Taihu Lake). This pattern is virtually the same as today's landscape. That is to say, the industrial base in today's southern Jiangsu dates back to the early 20th century, or at least there is relevance.

Zhejiang Province, which is adjacent to Jiangsu Province, is also a place of affluence. It previously had developed agriculture and commerce and has also shown

*Imbalance in regional development* 163

new developments after modern times. The industry here was highly similar to that of Jiangsu Province, featuring textiles and silk reeling, supplemented by other industries. From the perspective of geographical area, Hangzhou played a leading role, and developed industries were also wide distributed in Wenzhou, Ningbo, Huzhou, Shaoxing, Jiaxing, as well as Haining, Yuyao, Deqing, Xiaoshan, and Fenghua. In terms of the industry, Hangzhou, Ningbo, and Wenzhou developed some modern industries, such as locomotives, sand casting, matchsticks, and soap. The industries were mainly textile and silk as well as other traditional industries. Therefore, Zhejiang Province was similar to Jiangsu Province in terms of industry because the two provinces had fairly developed industrial bases in the silk and cotton weaving industries.

Guangdong Province, which is geographically different from Jiangsu and Zhejiang provinces, saw rapid development in industry thanks to the opportunity presented by opening up in modern times and even during the Qing Dynasty. The industrial distribution centered on Guangzhou, with many workers also in Shunde, Nanhai (Foshan), and Shantou. Guangzhou had relatively complete industries, covering both traditional and modern industries, although the textile industry dominated. It was similar to Shanghai and Tianjin in this regard. Shunde, Shantou, Nanhai, etc. mainly featured the textile industry, supported by the food industry. During this period, Guangdong Province only had industries in coastal areas open to the outside world.

Another large hinterland industrial province, Sichuan Province, is not to be underestimated. The industry in Sichuan Province was concentrated in Chengdu and Chongqing, and, to a lesser extent, Luzhou and Jiading, indicating that the industry in Sichuan Province as a whole was not developed, and industry was nonexistent in most areas. As the largest industrial city in Sichuan Province at the time, Chengdu had more factories than Chongqing by three times and more workers by about two times. In both Chengdu and Chongqing, the textile and silk industries were dominant, with modern industries include printing, matchsticks, and sand-casting. Chongqing also had industries such as batteries, shipbuilding, and glass.

Shandong Province also had a fairly developed industry, although not as developed as those in the aforesaid provinces and cities. In terms of area, the industry was mainly distributed in Qingdao and Jinan, which were evenly matched in terms of the number of factories and workers. Furthermore, Changshan, Linqu, Yantai, Qingzhou, and Weixian also had an industrial base to a degree. In terms of industry, Jinan and Qingdao both had traditional industries (such as textiles) and modern industries (such as machines, locomotives, sand-casting, and matchsticks). Yantai had a developed clock and watch industry, Changshan had a large-scale textile industry, and Linqu was the production base of the silk reeling industry. On the whole, Shandong's industry centered in two core cities, with industries of different characteristics in other cities and counties.

Hubei Province's industry was mainly distributed in the three towns of Wuhan but rarely in other areas, except for a certain scale in Shashi. Wuhan was an industrial powerhouse that had realized rapid development since modern times. Its geographical location is also highly important. Despite being an inland city, it had

164    *Processes and characteristics*

the pattern of a large city thanks to its developed transport network, and its industry was also comprehensive and modern. For example, in addition to traditional industries such as textiles and rice milling, it also had fairly developed industries like railway locomotives, sand-casting, military uniforms, printing, and shipbuilding.

Other provinces also realized a certain degree of industrial development, albeit at a lower level. Some provinces exhibited obvious characteristics. The industry in Hebei Province was mainly concentrated in Tangshan and also developed somewhat in other cities and counties such as Shijiazhuang, Baoding, and Gaoyang. In terms of industry, Tangshan featured the cement, textile, and railway locomotives industries. Shijiazhuang and Gaoyang featured the textile industry. The railway locomotive industry was prominent in Changxindian. The industry in Henan Province was mainly in Zhengzhou, Kaifeng, Anyang, Jixian (renamed Weihui City in 1988), Xinxiang, etc. Zhengzhou and Anyang featured the textile industry, while cotton weaving and printing industries were prominent in Kaifeng. The industry in Shanxi Province was primarily distributed in Taiyuan, Xinjiang, and Yuci. In terms of industry, Taiyuan had the machine industry in addition to the textile and military uniform industries. Xinjiang and Yuci mainly had the cotton spinning industry. Furthermore, industries were also somewhat developed in cities such as Wuhu in Anhui Province, Jiujiang and Nanchang in Jiangxi Province, Changsha in Hunan Province, Chang'an in Shaanxi Province, and Fuzhou (tea making) in Fujian Province.

The following conclusions can be drawn from these discussions. The first concerns the continuation and development of traditional industries. As a result of economic development since modern times, particularly since the Republic of China period, traditional industries were given a new life, and a dual structure was established. In some areas, the traditional mode of production, or a mode of production that mainly relies on manpower, still existed. At the same time, Western modern technologies emerged in some large cities such as open ports, such as those in the modern textile and flour industries. These industries had traditional markets. As the economy developed and urbanization advanced, there were broad market prospects.

Second is the rise and development of emerging industries. The so-called emerging industries are primarily those industries that applied modern production technologies imported from the West before modern times, such as medicine, machines, metals, electrical appliances, matchsticks, tobacco, shipbuilding, clocks and watches, as well as tap water and power generation. These industries are characterized by a high level of mechanization, the use of power (steam engine, internal combustion engine, and electric motor), and high productivity. More importantly, there is a linkage effect. In other words, an industrial chain was established. The upstream area produced materials or energy, such as coal, steel, and chemicals, while the downstream area produced high-value-added manufactured products, such as machine tools, automobiles, locomotives, ships, and clocks and watches.

Third is the emergence of central industrial and commercial cities. Following the opening of ports and the invasion of foreign forces in modern times, coastal port cities represented by Guangzhou, Shanghai, Tianjin, and Qingdao developed at a

Imbalance in regional development 165

fast clip. These cities benefited from commerce and trade in their development and also introduced modern industries, which laid the foundation for the subsequent development of these industries in China. The development of these industries also led to the emergence of many skilled workers and managers knowledgeable about modern engineering technologies and enterprise management, who contributed to the establishment and running of more industrial enterprises.

Fourth is the formation of a dual structure. Since modern times, modern industries began to emerge in China. In particular, military industrial enterprises and resource-based industrial enterprises represented by the Self-Strengthening Movement at the end of the 19th century, as well as enterprises run by foreign investors are the prototype of industry in modern times, but most of these industrial enterprises belonged to the government, and a few were private enterprises. Private enterprises mainly emerged after 1912, and many emerging industries and new-type traditional industries began to become popular as of this period. Importantly, these industries first started in coastal cities or central cities, such as Shanghai, Guangzhou, and Tianjin, and individual industries developed in inland areas, such as Sichuan and Shanxi provinces. In this way, what Lewis called a dual economy or a binary structure gradually took shape in China during this period. In other words, a few modern industries represented by machinery coexisted with most traditional industries based on handicrafts.

To learn more about the binary structure of China's industry around 1933, theoretical discussions are conducted next based on the principle of production function. Figure 7.4 depicts the dual structure of China's industrial development in modern times. Two production functions are shown in the figure. A high production

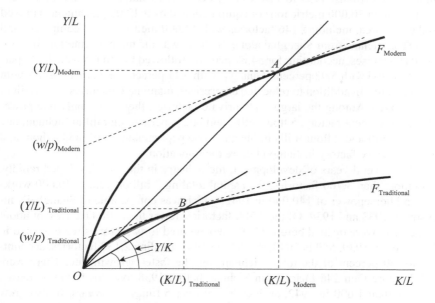

Figure 7.4 Binary structure of China's industry in 1933

## 166 *Processes and characteristics*

function refers to modern industries featuring the introduction of technology. It needs a high capital/labor ratio $(K/L)_{modern}$. As shown on the vertical axis, it has a high per capita output $(Y/L)_{Modern}$. They are represented by open large cities, as shown in point $A$. In contrast, many traditional industries existed in many parts of China, represented as a low production function in the graph. They are basically characterized by a low capital/labor ratio $(K/L)_{Traditional}$ and a low per capita output $(Y/L)_{Traditional}$, as shown in point $B$. In other words, due to a lack of sufficient capital equipment and workers related to such equipment, the per capita output of traditional industries was low. The increase in capital equipment in modern industries as well as the laborers related to such equipment contributed to the increase in per capita output. Correspondingly, the capital productivity $(Y/K)$ is also different, which was higher in modern industries than in traditional industries because the quantity and performance of capital equipment directly affect output. In other words, the value created by capital is different. This is vitally important for economic development because it largely symbolizes technological advance and production efficiency. If much capital is invested but the output is small, it means waste and inefficiency. If the capital is highly productive, it means that capital is efficient. Moreover, the rates of wage are also different, which were high for modern industries but low for traditional industries.[8]

### 7.3.3 *Industry in the rear area during the War of Resistance against Japanese Aggression*

A significant part of the industry in the rear area was moved from coastal regions, mainly from August 1937 to July 1940. According to statistics, a total of 448 enterprises with 70,000 metric tons of equipment and over 12,000 technicians moved to the rear area, including 146 factories with 14,600 metric tons of equipment and 2,500 technicians from Shanghai alone. Sichuan was the main destination for relocated enterprises, accounting for 54.67 percent, followed by Hunan with 29.21 percent, Shaanxi with 5.92 percent, Guangxi with 5.11 percent, and other regions with 5.11 percent.[9] In addition to relocated enterprises, many new factories were built in the rear area. Among the large-scale private factories, there were only one power plant, one cement factory, 5 flour mills, and one papermaking mill in Sichuan, one spinning mill and 2 flour mills in Shaanxi, one papermaking mill in Guizhou, and one machinery factory in Jiangxi before the relocation.

After several years of development, the industry in the rear developed rapidly, with more than 3,700 factories, the capital totaling 2 billion yuan, 240,000 workers, and horsepower of 140,000 in 1942, which was comparable to Shanghai's industry in 1933 and 1934. Of the 3,700 factories, fewer than 600 factories, or about 15 percent, were opened before 1938. Two hundred forty factories were opened in 1938, 466 in 1939, 589 in 1940, and 843 in 1941, totaling 2,138 factories, accounting for 60 percent of the total. Sichuan saw the fastest growth rate. There were a little more than 240 factories in Sichuan before 1938, but this figure increased to more than 1,600 in 1942, an increase of over 5 times in 5 years. It also grew rapidly in Hunan, which had more than 90 factories before 1938, but it increased

*Imbalance in regional development* 167

by 4 times in 5 years. It was followed by Shaanxi, Yunnan, Guizhou, and Gansu provinces. Previously, China's industry was concentrated in the coastal regions, with Shanghai accounting for half of the total alone. There had been basically no modern industry in the hinterland. This was not the case during the comprehensive War of Resistance against Japanese Aggression, and industry developed rapidly in the hinterland. Sichuan developed the fastest, with the number of factories accounting for 44 percent, followed by Hunan with 13.34 percent, Shaanxi with 10.24 percent, Guangxi with 7.77 percent, Yunnan with 2.82 percent, Guizhou with 2.98 percent, and Gansu with 3.64 percent. In terms of capital, Sichuan's industrial capital accounted for 58.00 percent of the total, Yunnan 10.80 percent, Guangxi 7.89 percent, Shaanxi 5.43 percent, Zhejiang 4.71 percent, Hunan 3.91 percent, Gansu 3.19 percent, and Guizhou 3.38 percent.

Table 7.6 shows the numbers of factories and workers as well as the average capital amount and average number of workers in the rear area in 1942. Sichuan was dominant in terms of the number of factories, accounting for 44 percent, followed by Hunan and Shaanxi. It means that factories in Sichuan accounted for nearly half of the total in this region. In terms of the number of workers, Sichuan accounted for up to 45 percent, followed by Hunan, which accounted for 13 percent. The proportion of the number of workers is relatively close to that of factories. Overall, from the perspective of regional distribution, Sichuan had a large share or even accounted for "half of the total in the rear area". This situation had an important impact on the subsequent economic development. Sichuan still was an important development force after 1949, particularly during the "third-front construction" period in the 1960s.

The table also shows the distribution of the average value by region. In terms of the average capital of factories, Yunnan, Zhejiang, and Qinghai occupied the top three places, followed by Sichuan, Guangxi, Gansu, and Guizhou. It was significantly higher for public factories than for private factories. In terms of the average number of factory workers, Yunnan and Ningxia ranked first, followed by Jiangxi and Zhejiang, and then Hubei, Sichuan, Hunan, and Shaanxi. Public factories also outperformed private factories in this area. There is no clear rule to go by because, although Sichuan ranked at the top, there might be one or more very important factories in some regions, and this raised the overall ranking for the local regions.

## 7.4 Conclusion

This chapter examines the issue of imbalanced regional development. In modern China, regional development was not seriously imbalanced because China had yet to start modern economic growth at the time. Usually, as the economy develops, the gap between regions widens. The income gap for individuals also widens as the regional gap widens. In traditional times, the differences between regions were determined by natural conditions or factor endowments. If a region had fertile land, a fair climate, a small population, and convenient access to transport, the productivity would be high, the shipment of goods would be significant, and the living standards would be high. In a region with barren land, an inclement climate, and

## 168    *Processes and characteristics*

*Table 7.6* Overview of factories in the rear in 1942

| Region | Number of factories | | | Number of workers | | |
| --- | --- | --- | --- | --- | --- | --- |
| | Total | Public | Private | Total | Public | Private |
| Total | 3,758 | 656 | 3,102 | 241,662 | 77,217 | 164,445 |
| Sichuan | 1,654 | 156 | 1,498 | 108,205 | 20,374 | 87,831 |
| Xikang | 12 | 10 | 2 | 393 | 301 | 92 |
| Guizhou | 112 | 20 | 92 | 4,578 | 2,023 | 2,555 |
| Yunnan | 106 | 43 | 63 | 18,094 | 11,433 | 6,661 |
| Guangxi | 292 | 51 | 241 | 15,987 | 6,842 | 9,145 |
| Guangdong | 69 | 15 | 54 | 2,594 | 664 | 1,930 |
| Fujian | 88 | 26 | 62 | 6,204 | 2,498 | 3,706 |
| Hunan | 501 | 53 | 448 | 31,574 | 7,639 | 23,935 |
| Jiangxi | 102 | 65 | 37 | 9,127 | 6,469 | 2,658 |
| Zhejiang | 70 | 33 | 37 | 6,039 | 4,575 | 2,064 |
| Jiangsu | 3 | – | 3 | 194 | – | 194 |
| Anhui | 83 | 20 | 63 | 773 | 678 | 95 |
| Shaanxi | 385 | 62 | 323 | 23,510 | 5,997 | 17,513 |
| Gansu | 139 | 32 | 107 | 7,888 | 4,022 | 3,866 |
| Qinghai | 1 | 1 | – | 11 | 11 | – |
| Ningxia | 14 | 7 | 7 | 1,448 | 1,060 | 388 |
| Suiyuan | 7 | – | 7 | 217 | – | 217 |
| Hubei | 17 | 11 | 6 | 1,201 | 1,027 | 174 |
| Henan | 88 | 40 | 48 | 2,479 | 1,241 | 1,238 |
| Shanxi | 15 | 11 | 4 | 546 | 363 | 183 |

| Region | Average capital amount of factories (1,000 yuan) | | | Average number of factory workers | | |
| --- | --- | --- | --- | --- | --- | --- |
| | Total | Public | Private | Total | Public | Private |
| Total | 515.97 | 2,056.79 | 190.13 | 64.31 | 117.71 | 53.01 |
| Sichuan | 683.20 | 4,559.85 | 279.49 | 65.42 | 130.60 | 58.63 |
| Xikang | 274.83 | 316.80 | 65.00 | 32.75 | 30.10 | 46.00 |
| Guizhou | 413.08 | 1,968.25 | 75.00 | 40.88 | 101.15 | 27.77 |
| Yunnan | 1,976.41 | 4,645.61 | 154.57 | 170.70 | 265.88 | 105.73 |
| Guangxi | 524.42 | 2,597.86 | 85.64 | 54.75 | 134.16 | 37.95 |
| Guangdong | 133.73 | 438.81 | 48.99 | 37.59 | 44.27 | 35.74 |
| Fujian | 127.14 | 308.69 | 51.01 | 70.50 | 96.08 | 59.77 |
| Hunan | 151.70 | 539.42 | 105.84 | 63.02 | 144.13 | 53.43 |
| Jiangxi | 326.83 | 438.33 | 130.94 | 89.48 | 99.52 | 71.84 |
| Zhejiang | 1,304.11 | 2,690.82 | 67.32 | 86.27 | 138.64 | 55.78 |
| Jiangsu | 20.00 | – | 20.00 | 64.70 | – | 64.70 |
| Anhui | 13.68 | 29.15 | 8.77 | 9.31 | 33.90 | 1.51 |
| Shaanxi | 273.53 | 703.36 | 191.03 | 61.06 | 96.73 | 54.22 |
| Gansu | 445.37 | 1,681.68 | 74.79 | 56.75 | 125.69 | 36.13 |
| Qinghai | 1,000.00 | 1,000.00 | – | 11.00 | 11.00 | – |
| Ningxia | 67.88 | 42.90 | 92.86 | 103.43 | 151.43 | 55.43 |
| Suiyuan | 19.29 | – | 19.29 | 31.00 | – | 31.00 |
| Hubei | 121.56 | 183.31 | 8.33 | 70.65 | 93.36 | 29.00 |
| Henan | 33.31 | 27.57 | 38.11 | 28.17 | 31.03 | 25.79 |
| Shanxi | 18.86 | 19.91 | 16.00 | 36.40 | 33.00 | 45.75 |

*Data source:* Statistical Office of the Ministry of the Economy (1943), pp. 13–14.

*Imbalance in regional development* 169

underdeveloped transport network, the living standard will not be high, even if the population is small. If modern economic growth was initiated after modern times, resources would be concentrated in profitable areas, and the same goes for talents. As a result, there would be inequality. However, China did not start modern economic growth in modern times, but some emerging industries and cities arose, and some sectors began to develop, which led to some imbalance.

According to these observations, it is worthwhile to summarize in at least the following three areas. First, the economic development between regions during the Republic of China period was unbalanced. Some coastal regions saw rapid economic development, especially in Shanghai, Tianjin, Qingdao, Wuxi, Wuhan, Guangzhou, and Beijing. This to some extent caused the differences among regions in the subsequent period, at least during the Republic of China period and for a long period after 1949. Second, Japan launched the September 18 Incident in 1931 to invade and occupy Northeast China and founded the puppet state of Manchukuo, where it ran the economy of Northeast China for more than a decade. During this period, Japan exploited the mineral resources in the northeast region and built a full variety of factories, making the northeast region another central region in China's economic development. Third, Japan's all-out invasion of China in 1937 directly played havoc with China's economy and led to a large-scale migration. On the one hand, it torpedoed the economy of the occupied areas. On the other hand, it led to the inland relocation of a wealth of factories, resulting in the rear economy and changing the regional landscape of China's economy during this period.

## Notes

1 For a detailed description of industrial development in this period, see Guan Quan (2011, 2018).
2 Chahar and Rehe were established as special administrative regions in 1913 and 1914, respectively, and became provinces in 1928.
3 Regarding the issue of the use of power in Japan, see Ryoshin Minami (1976) and Minami (1987).
4 It was stipulated that it was called a factory if there were more than 7 people or a handicraft workshop if fewer than 7 people. For details, see Guan Quan (2011, 2018).
5 However, the reliability of data may be in question. For example, the average number of factory workers in Guangxi was up to 104.13 in 1912 but 12.88 in 1915 because Guangxi was not an economically developed region. This figure increased from 80.67 in 1912 to 110.77 in 1915 for Jiangsu province, which is more credible.
6 For issues about the *Agricultural and Commercial Statistics Table*, see Guan Quan (2011, 2018).
7 For details of this survey report, see Guan Quan (2018).
8 For a comparison of production rate between different countries in a similar way to this book, see Weil (2011), p. 149.
9 Statistical Office of the Ministry of the Economy (1943). For the issue of relocating factories to the hinterland, see Sun Guoda (1991), Xu Dixin and Wu Chengming (1990), Zhang Shouguang (2008, 2012), and Guo Qin (2013).

# Part III
# Conditions and causes

# 8 Natural resources and human resources

## 8.1 Introduction

This chapter deals with natural resources and human resources, which do not seem to fall into the same category but which are actually essential for economic development. Natural resources are determined by geographical conditions and are largely natural, usually remaining unchanged.[1] Despite the link to geographical conditions, human resources are largely acquired and can be improved. Human resources usually refer to the size of the population, the length of schooling received, as well as the health of the people, skills of the labor force, entrepreneurship, government capability, etc.

In China, its vast territory and big population are ideal conditions for economic development. In fact, the two are contradictory. The vast territory belongs to natural resources and, in a sense, the more the better. A big population is not necessarily a good thing because a large population consumes more resources, including food and natural resources, although it can boost productivity. More importantly, if the population is little educated, they are unproductive and cannot make good use of natural resources, as verified by the economic development in many countries. Some resource-rich countries are under the "resource curse"[2] due to a lack of human resources, which is the case in most of the oil-producing countries in the Middle East. This is also the case in the majority of today's African countries, which can only export resources to other countries and which fall into the "comparative advantage trap"[3] economically. On the contrary, some resource-poor countries and regions have leveraged their abundant human resources to become affluent and developed economies, notably Japan and the so-called Four Asian Tigers.

Another problem is that after China was subjected to the great powers in modern times, a wealth of resources were plundered, and few were used by the Chinese people. On the one hand, foreign powers invested in China's resource exploitation to meet their own needs. On the other hand, Chinese people did not have such high spending power at that time. Judging from the experience of developed countries, the consumption of resources will increase as the economy develops and income rises. Human resources were also underdeveloped, primarily because of the underdeveloped economy as well as political and social instability. Despite some gains in education during the Republic of China period, the progress is still elementary and

DOI: 10.4324/9781003410386-11

174    *Conditions and causes*

negligible from a modern viewpoint. Because the economy was underdeveloped, people naturally had poor health, with an average life expectancy of only about 35 years, 40 years less than today's average of 76 years. This point alone illustrates the importance and significance of economic development.

## 8.2   Utilization of resources

### 8.2.1   Resource exploitation

With regard to the use of natural resources and the environment in modern China, these problems were not very serious, as shown by the state of China's economic development in this period. However, the large-scale migration caused by domestic strife and foreign aggression caused a certain degree of damage to areas that had not been developed. Of course, migration had a positive effect on the economic development in underdeveloped areas, which is not a bad thing. Moreover, China's population in modern times grew within a moderate range.

Table 8.1 shows the output and net export volume of some metal ores from 1912 to 1937. The output fluctuated only slightly. What is important is the large export volume of these mineral products, particularly tungsten and antimony. These two minerals are China's competitive mineral products, occupying a key position in the world. Therefore, their exports accounted for a large share of the output, sometimes even close to 100 percent. Tin was also abundant in China and in some countries in the Indochinese Peninsula, and a considerable proportion of the output was exported. China's tin ingot exports accounted for about half of the output and for 100 percent in individual periods. Part of iron sand was also exported, but the exports declined, from almost the full output in 1912 to a small proportion in 1937. From the output and exports of these mineral products, we can conclude that a significant proportion of China's resources flowed overseas due to China's small demand at that time or due to plunder by foreign countries. This is highly similar to what happens in some of today's developing countries that fall into the comparative advantage trap, because they cannot use their own resources, or they have to export them in return for foreign exchange.[4]

*Table 8.1* Output and net exports of major metal ores, Unit: metric ton

| Year | Tungsten ore | | Pure antimony | | Tin ingot | | Mercury | | Iron sand | |
|---|---|---|---|---|---|---|---|---|---|---|
| | *Output* | *Export* | *Output* | *Export* | *Output* | *Export* | *Output* | *Export* | *Output* | *Export* |
| 1912 | – | – | 15,992 | – | 9,695 | 6,351 | 7 | – | 221,280 | 204,579 |
| 1915 | – | – | 21,870 | – | 8,928 | 5,481 | 188 | 30 | 505,140 | 288,577 |
| 1920 | 6,856 | 4,223 | 15,618 | 13,495 | 12,368 | 8,266 | 83 | 17 | 133,6285 | 662,632 |
| 1925 | 7,474 | 5,962 | 18,383 | 19,809 | 9,936 | 5,600 | 408 | – | 101,9021 | 822,161 |
| 1930 | 6,844 | 8,724 | 17,963 | 17,492 | 7,334 | 3,322 | 41 | 39 | 177,3536 | 849,033 |
| 1937 | 1,3991 | 1,6518 | 1,4951 | 1,2520 | 1,3004 | 1,3077 | 61 | – | 3,409,991 | 586,530 |

*Data source:* Yan Zhongping et al. (1955), pp. 139–140.

*Natural resources and human resources* 175

Table 8.2 shows China's steel output and imports from the end of the 19th century to 1937. China had no steel industry at the end of the 19th century but began to produce steel in early 20th century. China saw significant development after 1910, and the annual output reached nearly 500,000 metric tons in 1920. The steel industry further developed in the 1930s, and its output reached 1.515 million metric tons by 1937, which is no mean achievement. However, it is noteworthy that pig iron dominated in this period, while the output of steel was limited. A significant increase after 1935 was mainly attributed to production in the northeast region, such as Benxihu Coal and Iron Company and An'shan Steelworks. The volume of imports also increased steadily. A rapid increase in the 1920s indicates China's growing demand for steel, which can also be observed from the data on consumption. Before 1905, China's steel consumption was less than 200,000 metric tons but exceeded 400,000 metric tons in 1910, 860,000 metric tons in 1920, 1 million metric tons in 1930, and 2 million metric tons in 1937. These data show that China's economy grew somewhat from 1910 to 1937. It should be pointed out that this does not show the big picture of China's economic development. In other words, the industrial sector developed somewhat in modern times, while the traditional sector stagnated.

Similar to other sectors (such as agriculture and industrial sector), China's mining industry lacked accurate data on its production before 1949,[5] mainly due to a lack of systematic statistics. More importantly, political turmoil, social disturbance, and weak economic development in old China made it impossible to conduct continuous and accurate surveys. As a result, it is difficult to gain a real understanding of China's economy at that time and to accurately portray the history of China's subsequent economic development. Therefore, it is vitally important to figure out how to collect and analyze the historical materials of the time, particularly the data, so that the process, characteristics, and problems regarding economic changes at that time can be described in a systematic manner.

*Table 8.2* National steel output and import volume from 1896 to 1937, Unit: metric ton

| Year | Output | | | Import | Consumption |
|---|---|---|---|---|---|
| | Total | Pig iron | Steel | | |
| 1896 | – | – | – | 123,006 | 123,006 |
| 1900 | 25,890 | 25,890 | – | 64,360 | 90,250 |
| 1905 | 32,314 | 32,314 | – | 174,830 | 207,144 |
| 1910 | 169,509 | 119,396 | 50,113 | 259,064 | 428,573 |
| 1915 | 385,016 | 336,649 | 48,367 | 125,658 | 510,674 |
| 1920 | 497,808 | 429,548 | 68,260 | 366,622 | 863,835 |
| 1925 | 393,836 | 363,836 | 30,000 | 405,266 | 799,102 |
| 1930 | 513,306 | 498,306 | 15,000 | 527,428 | 1,040,734 |
| 1937 | 1,515,030 | 958,683 | 556,347 | 644,077 | 2,159,107 |

*Note:* Consumption is the sum of output and imports.

*Data source:* Yan Zhongping et al. (1955), pp. 141–142.

## 176 Conditions and causes

Although China lay in tatters at that time, and there was a lack of complete statistics, it is still possible to see a roughly real situation by making appropriate additions and corrections to existing data. Mining was a highly specialized industry before 1949. Because of the national circumstances at that time, the Western powers conducted geological surveys and mining, and built a wealth of mines and factories in order to plunder resources. Later, national capital was involved, and a relatively large system was established. That is to say, mining resources have the key characteristics of providing raw materials and fuels for a host of industries, which means that this industry was the first to be the object of plunder by Western powers, as well as the focus of rivalry for national capital. As a result, compared with other sectors such as agriculture and industry, the mining industry has relatively rich statistics, or at least its surveys covering the years from 1912 to 1949 could be conducted. In comparison, it is difficult to acquire data on the agriculture, industrial sector, transport, and other industries.[6]

Table 8.3 shows the overview of mining production during the Republic of China period. Shown here are only several of the time points, from which the following can be observed. First, the production value and the value added in other regions of China (except the northeast region) increased in the early 20th century but stagnated or even declined in the 1930s and 1940s. The production index also shows such signs – an increase before the Japanese invasion of China but stagnation or decline thereafter. Second, the northeast region grew rapidly in a linear fashion, indicating that mining production in this region consistently showed a good momentum of growth. On the one hand, foreign forces, represented by Japan, invested heavily here. On the other hand, it shows the fact that this region abounds with minerals. Third, the differences in growth between the rest of China (except

*Table 8.3* Real production value, value added, and production index of the mining industry

| Year | China's hinterland | | | Northeast region | | |
|---|---|---|---|---|---|---|
| | *Production value (1,000 yuan)* | *Value added (1,000 yuan)* | *Production index* | *Production value (1,000 yuan)* | *Value added (1,000 yuan)* | *Production index* |
| 1912 | 72,336 | 58,384 | 46.6 | 12,359 | 10,377 | – |
| 1915 | 97,144 | 79,127 | 62.6 | 19,109 | 16,049 | – |
| 1920 | 152,690 | 124,962 | 98.4 | 27,204 | 22,874 | – |
| 1925 | 156,909 | 128,632 | 101.2 | 47,689 | 39,997 | 62.2 |
| 1930 | 146,216 | 120,627 | 94.3 | 80,618 | 66,633 | 86.9 |
| 1935 | 210,372 | 174,065 | 135.6 | 115,114 | 94,372 | 124.5 |
| 1940 | 209,790 | 173,706 | 135.3 | 218,438 | 178,191 | 235.9 |
| 1944 | 188,323 | 158,295 | 121.4 | 252,723 | 205,709 | 271.5 |

*Note:* (1) Data on only some years are selected here. The original document covers the years from 1912 to 1944.
*(2) The data for 1925 for the northeast region is actually the data for 1926. Due to few varieties before that, the production index for the northeast region only covers the period after 1926.*

*Sources:* Guan Quan and Makino Fumio (1999); Makino Fumio and Guan Quan (2007).

*Natural resources and human resources* 177

the northeast) and the northeast led to significant quantitative changes. The northeast produced less than the rest of China in the second and third decades of the 20th century but overtook the rest of China after the 1940s.

Before 1949, the mining industry developed relatively rapidly even though China's industrial development was insignificant. The reasons for this are crystal clear. First, as a raw material for the industrial sector, the mining industry should develop first. This is also the case for the industrialization of developed countries in Europe and the United States, or at least the industrial sector and mining industry develop simultaneously. Many countries in Western Europe used coal as a source of power for industrialization. Japan also supported its industrial development by exploiting coal resources in Hokkaido and Kyushu in modern times. Second, one of the goals of the foreign powers invading China was to loot resources, and therefore the priority development of mining was an inevitable trend. It shows that foreign capital was involved in almost all large mines. In particular, Japanese investors laid more emphasis on resource exploitation in China. Third, the government and bureaucratic capital also saw the value of resource development, and therefore more attention was paid to the development of mining than to other industries. Of course, private capital was also extensively involved in mining development, albeit small-scale mining or in a subordinate position. In brief, compared with the industrial sector, the mining industry in modern China developed rapidly, except for some looted by the foreign powers. This development objectively laid the groundwork for economic development.[7]

Figure 8.1 shows the actual production value and value added of the mining industry. The two indicators changed in the same way, indicating small changes in production costs. Therefore, it can be roughly seen that the two indicators changed simultaneously, with differences in only the amount. Overall, mining production exhibited an upward trend in the more than three decades from 1912 to 1944. Of course, it can be divided into the following stages: the first stage is the years before 1920, with a more obvious upward trend. The second stage, from 1920 to 1933, witnessed fluctuations, and the upward trend was not obvious. In the third stage, from 1933 to 1938, it rose first and then declined, mainly as a result of Japan's invasion of China. The fourth stage, from 1938 to 1944, saw greater fluctuations, peaking in 1942 before declining. Overall, mining production was on the rise and at a fast speed at that.

The preceding can be verified by the mining production index. Figure 8.2 shows the mining production index in the northeast and the rest of China. The situation in the rest of China is basically consistent with that shown in Figure 8.1. In other words, there was a steady rise before 1933, particularly before 1920, but it fluctuated thereafter, although with a high growth rate. The situation for the northeast region shows a different pattern. Despite a late start, it showed a tendency to rise in a linear way. In particular, it basically rose in a linearly without fluctuations after 1932, which is very rare. It can be conjectured that Japan stepped up efforts to exploit the resource of the northeast region since the establishment of puppet Manchukuo in 1932. As a result, mining production in the northeast region kept rising until Japan surrendered.

178  *Conditions and causes*

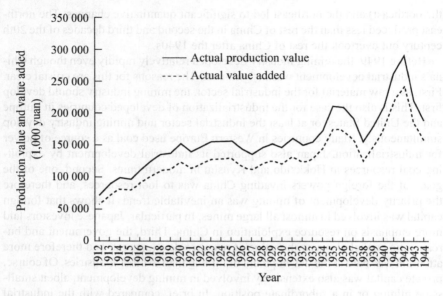

*Figure 8.1* Actual production value and value added of the mining industry
Data source: Ryoshin Minami and Makino Fumio (2014), p. 382.

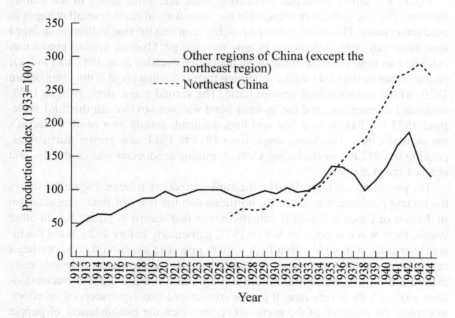

*Figure 8.2* Mining production index
Data source: Ryoshin Minami and Makino Fumio (2014), p. 382.

*Natural resources and human resources* 179

### 8.2.2 International comparison

In order to get a full picture of the modern mining industry, especially the development of the global mining industry after the 20th century, the author observed the world mining production index from 1913 to 1939. Table 8.4 shows this situation, enumerating the production indexes of 15 mineral products as well as the composite index. The combined index shows a clear upward trend, and it nearly doubled in 1939 compared to 1913, indicating that mining production during this period developed rapidly. This period covers World War I. In theory, more resources are needed in a war, but the index did not increase in 1920, and the consumption of the vast majority of mineral products except aluminum and oil did not increase significantly. Growth began in the 1930s or after the 1920s. If the growth in this period was not the result of preparations for war, it was needed for normal economic growth, or the world's mining industry was just developing rapidly during this period.

Next, the differences between China and Japan are examined through the production of several mineral products important for economic development.[8] Table 8.5 shows the situation of some industrial and mineral products as well as infrastructure, which shows an obvious gap. In terms of absolute value, Japan was ahead of China in terms of almost all products and infrastructure, except iron ore. This is easy to explain because iron ore is just a raw material, which was also exactly what the Western powers wanted to acquire and which was also a key export commodity for China. Coal is also similar in this sense, and China was close to Japan in this regard. It is worth mentioning that Japan also exported coal in the early days of economic development (during the Meiji period) because Japan was unable to export more industrial products. It needed to export primary products to obtain foreign exchange and to import machinery and equipment. During the Meiji period, Japan mainly exported grain, potatoes, tea, aquatic products, tobacco, ginseng, sulfur, camphor, Japanese paper, coal, ceramics, copper, Japanese umbrellas, and lacquerware.[9] China and Japan were also close in terms of the number of knitting spindles,

*Table 8.4* World mining production index

| Year | Total index | Coal | Petroleum | Pig iron | Manganese | Chromium | Tungsten | Copper |
|---|---|---|---|---|---|---|---|---|
| 1913 | 87 | 101 | 37 | 114 | 90 | 42 | 56 | 75 |
| 1920 | 86 | 100 | 65 | 91 | 71 | 59 | 79 | 74 |
| 1930 | 117 | 107 | 134 | 116 | 136 | 142 | 114 | 119 |
| 1939 | 152 | 115 | 197 | 153 | 217 | 236 | 260 | 164 |

| Year | Lead | | Zinc | Aluminum | Tin | | Phosphates | Gold | | Silver | Diamond |
|---|---|---|---|---|---|---|---|---|---|---|---|
| 1913 | 90 | | 95 | 38 | 95 | | 94 | 101 | | 98 | 139 |
| 1920 | 89 | | 69 | 70 | 87 | | 87 | 74 | | 81 | 72 |
| 1930 | 127 | | 133 | 148 | 135 | | 142 | 92 | | 117 | 152 |
| 1939 | 131 | | 158 | 373 | 131 | | 156 | 179 | | 124 | 250 |

*Note:* 1913–1937 = 100. Potassium is also included in the total index but is not listed here.

*Data source: Institute of East Asian Studies* (1942), pp. 2–3.

## 180   Conditions and causes

which is a production tool and a kind of capital equipment. It indicates that China's cotton manufacturing industry developed to a certain extent. China was also close to Japan in terms of the length of railway. As China is far bigger than Japan, there is no need to directly compare the length of railways. Nevertheless, the long railway built in China provided support for economic development and other economic activities. It needs to be pointed out that the railway was also an important project for the Western powers (including Japan) to loot China's resources, and that this industry was also most valued by all parties in modern times. Many Sino-foreign joint ventures centered on the railway, and a host of disputes and even wars also broke out because of the railway because, in the absence of railway, resources could not be exploited, or, even if these were developed, they could not be transported.

Second, shown here is an absolute number rather than per capita value. If the difference in population between China and Japan is considered, the gap is even greater. The figures on population in several key years are given here for reference. China's population in 1900, 1910, 1920, 1930, and 1940 was 400 million, 423 million, 472 million, 486 million, and 513 million, respectively. During the same period, Japan's population was 44.103 million, 49.518 million, 55.818 million, 64.203 million, and 72.967 million, respectively.[10] China's population was 7 to 9 times that of Japan. If the output of the aforesaid products is divided by different populations, the per capita value will be highly different. In other words, China's

*Table 8.5* Comparison of some industrial and mineral products as well as infrastructure between China and Japan

| Year | Coal (1,000 metric tons) | | Iron ore (1,000 metric tons) | | Pig iron (1,000 metric tons) | | Steel (1,000 metric tons) | |
|------|--------|--------|--------|--------|--------|--------|--------|--------|
| | *Japan* | *China* | *Japan* | *China* | *Japan* | *China* | *Japan* | *China* |
| 1900 | 7,429 | – | 25 | – | 30 | – | – | – |
| 1910 | 15,681 | – | 67 | – | 72 | – | 9 | – |
| 1920 | 29,245 | 21,320 | 180 | 1,336 | 530 | 259 | 811 | 68 |
| 1930 | 31,376 | 26,040 | 117 | 1,774 | 1,188 | 376 | 2,289 | 15 |
| 1940 | 56,312 | 44,334 | 496 | 6,813 | 3,658 | 1,106 | 6,856 | 534 |
| 1945 | 29,880 | 26,285 | 935 | 446 | 984 | 213 | 2,082 | 260 |

| Year | Number of knitting spindles (1,000 spindles) | | Generating capacity (million kWh) | | Length of railroad lines in service (km) | | Volume of mails sent (million pieces) | |
|------|--------|--------|--------|--------|--------|--------|--------|--------|
| | *Japan* | *China* | *Japan* | *China* | *Japan* | *China* | *Japan* | *China* |
| 1900 | 1,135 | – | – | – | – | – | – | – |
| 1910 | 2,012 | 834 | 621 | – | 8,661 | 8,601 | 1,512 | 359 |
| 1920 | 3,814 | 1,400 | 4,669 | 361 | 13,645 | 10,973 | 3,816 | 401 |
| 1930 | 7,045 | 3,829 | 15,773 | 1,546 | 21593 | 13,441 | 4,604 | 883 |
| 1940 | – | – | 34,566 | 3,331 | 25,126 | – | 5,027 | 1,005 |
| 1945 | – | – | 21,900 | 4,876 | 25,300 | – | – | – |

*Data source:* Mitchell, ed. (2002).

per capita output or share would be far lower than that of Japan, and this may better represent the gap between the two countries. However, the data on population show that Japan's population in this period grew faster than that of China. Japan had a growth rate of 1.3 percent, while China's growth rate exceeded 1 percent only from 1912 to 1920, was generally 0.5 to 0.6 percent in other years – about 0.56 percent before 1910, about 0.35 percent from 1921 to 1932, and 0.5 to 0.7 percent thereafter.[11]

Figure 8.3 shows the situation of some industrial and mineral products as well as infrastructure in modern Japan, from which the following three points can be observed. First, the growth was fast as a whole. Even if it is expressed here as logarithmic value, it almost rises in a linear way. However, there are some differences between sectors as well as between products. The growth rate is higher for some products, such as generating capacity and steel. Second, it basically maintained sustained growth in the observation period without a significant decline. Although the economy was in a stage of development, there is an economic cycle, and the economy will fluctuate in the process. Japan's economy fluctuated slightly, with obvious fluctuations only in the iron ore industry. Third, statistics were conducted for most products since the Meiji Restoration. In other words, there was production (or services), or these sectors developed since at least the late 19th century. A few products that are more complex or modern, such as steel, got off to a late start. Steel production began in the late 19th century with the establishment of Hachiban Ironworks (which commenced construction in 1897 and went into operation in 1901), the predecessor of Nippon Steel Company. Although Japan introduced the electric power system in the early Meiji period, it took a long time to build power grids and develop on a large scale.

Figure 8.4 shows the changes in the like products and infrastructure in modern China. China seemed to have corresponding products and services, and it also

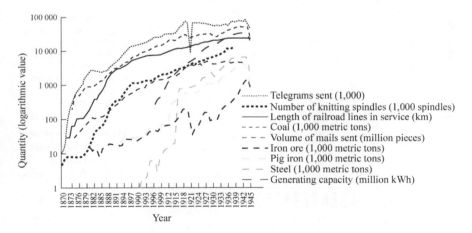

*Figure 8.3* Changes in some industrial and mineral products as well as infrastructure in modern Japan

*Data source:* Mitchell, ed. (2002).

## 182  Conditions and causes

achieved growth to a certain extent, but China was significantly different from Japan. First of all, China started significantly later than Japan with regard to the vast majority of products and services. This shows that China started later than Japan when it comes to industrialization or economic development. In the absence of these industries that symbolize modern economic activities, it is impossible to prove that the economy began to develop. Second, the growth rate is obviously low. Despite a growth trend (in logarithmic value), China did not have the same momentum of growth as Japan had, and the development of some products even saw a significant decline. Finally, there were large fluctuations in the process, with a serious decline for some products and services, such as steel, pig iron, mails, and iron ore. On the whole, China's economy seemed to be growing but was in fact struggling. Growth here implies starting from scratch. It is, after all, a good thing that some modern products of symbolic meaning could be produced, and it grew to a certain extent.

### 8.3  Development of education

#### 8.3.1  Schooling

Given the scarce information on education before 1949, it is not easy to gain a big picture of education at that time, and therefore it is only briefly introduced. Table

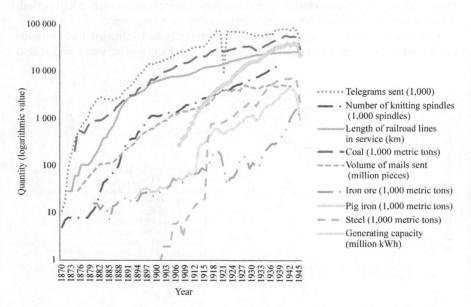

*Figure 8.4* Changes in some industrial and mineral products as well as infrastructure in modern China

*Data source: Mitchell, ed. (2002).*

*Natural resources and human resources*   183

8.6 shows the schooling and literacy level of China's rural population from 1929 to 1933. The population is divided into the slightly educated and the uneducated. Nationally, the proportions of men who were not educated and slightly educated are roughly the same, with a slightly higher percentage for uneducated people. Women, on the other hand, rarely received schooling. There is a huge gap between men and women. As a result, the illiteracy rate was high, close to 70 percent for men and close to 99 percent for women. Specifically, the proportion of men and women in northern China who received schooling was low, and the illiteracy rate was high, while more people in southern China received schooling, and the illiteracy rate was naturally lower. This shows that during this period, education in southern China was developed, while the northern region was relatively backward in this regard.

Table 8.7 shows the proportions of people who received schooling as reflected in the censuses in the first half of the 20th century. Illiterate people accounted for more than 68 percent, or about two-thirds of China's population were illiterate. The illiteracy rate was slightly lower for men, reaching 63.72 percent, while it was close to 90 percent for women. It is basically consistent with the previous figures. Ten percent of the literate attended old-style private schools, with a high proportion for men and a low proportion for women. The proportion of people who attended primary school was low, reaching only 7.6 percent; it was only 10 percent for men and less than 5 percent for women. Fewer people attended high school, accounting for less than 2 percent; it was less than 3 percent for men and less than 1 percent for women. The proportion of people who attended universities was only 0.38 percent; it was only 0.64 percent for men and 0.1 percent for women. As seen from these date, the educational level of Chinese people in the first half of the 20th century couldn't be worse. How could China develop the economy with such a state of human resources?

*Table 8.6* Schooling and literacy level of rural population in China from 1929 to 1933, Unit: %

| Region | Total population | Whether educated | | | Whether literate | | |
|---|---|---|---|---|---|---|---|
| | | Uneducated | Slightly uneducated | Unknown | Illiterate | Literate | Unknown |
| National (male) | 100.0 | 54.1 | 45.2 | 0.7 | 69.3 | 30.3 | 0.4 |
| National (female) | 100.0 | 97.1 | 2.2 | 0.1 | 98.7 | 1.2 | 0.1 |
| Northern China (male) | 100.0 | 57.7 | 41.7 | 0.6 | 72.9 | 26.6 | 0.5 |
| Northern China (female) | 100.0 | 98.0 | 1.9 | 0.1 | 99.1 | 0.8 | 0.1 |
| Southern China (male) | 100.0 | 50.2 | 49.1 | 0.7 | 65.2 | 34.6 | 0.2 |
| Southern China (female) | 100.0 | 97.3 | 2.6 | 0.1 | 98.3 | 1.6 | 0.1 |

*Data source:* Buck (1941), Table 10.

184    *Conditions and causes*

Table 8.8 shows the proportions of people who received various levels of schooling in some regions in 1947. Despite the incomplete data, we can roughly learn about the overview of educational level of the Chinese people in this period. In terms of the data on total figures, graduates of higher education accounted for 0.23 percent of the total population, senior high school graduates accounted for 0.58 percent, junior high school graduates accounted for 1.08 percent, higher primary school graduates accounted for 3.26 percent, and lower primary school graduates accounted for 4.86 percent, all of whom accounted for only 10.01 percent. Coupled with the students who did not finish studies (11.92 percent) and the graduates from old-style private schools (5.72 percent), they accounted for only 27.65 percent, while the remaining 72.35 percent of the population were uneducated.

There are obvious differences among regions. The proportion of illiteracy people in some areas was up to 80 percent, such as 85.47 percent in Hubei, 81.10 percent in northern Liaoning, and 81.26 percent in Jilin. The proportion was low in some areas, such as 34.51 percent in Nanjing, 37.50 percent in Hankou, 42.05 percent in Beiping, and 49.28 percent in Shanghai. It can be considered that such a difference was mainly due to urban versus rural areas. The illiteracy rate was low in cities but was high in other regions, including rural areas. It is noteworthy that it was 54.98 percent for Taiwan, which was about China's average as a whole. If we consider that the Taiwan region was more urbanized than the aforesaid areas in the mainland, it can be said that the education level in Taiwan was higher than that of the mainland. It is also worth considering that old-style private schools still played an important role and accounted for as high as more than 20 percent in some areas (Hankou), which was higher than the proportion of people who received modern education.

It can be seen from the preceding discussion that China's education was extremely backward before 1949. In a sense, it basically remained in the traditional

*Table 8.7* Proportions of people with various levels of education in the census in the first half of the 20th century, Unit: %

| Illiterate people | | | Literate people | | | | | | | | |
|---|---|---|---|---|---|---|---|---|---|---|---|
| | | | Old-style private schools | | | Elementary schools | | | High schools | | |
| Male | Female | Total | Male | Female | Total | Male | Female | Total | Male | Female | Total |
| 63.72 | 88.84 | 68.42 | 17.11 | 2.94 | 10.21 | 10.38 | 4.67 | 7.60 | 2.69 | 0.99 | 1.86 |

| Literate people | | | | | | | | | Unknown | | |
|---|---|---|---|---|---|---|---|---|---|---|---|
| University | | | Unknown | | | Total | | | | | |
| Male | Female | Total | Male | Female | Total | Male | Female | Total | Male | Female | Total |
| 0.64 | 0.10 | 0.38 | 0.48 | 0.17 | 0.33 | 31.30 | 8.87 | 23.15 | 0.15 | 0.05 | 0.10 |

*Data source: Statistical Yearbook of the Republic of China of 1948* and Statistics Bureau of the Comptroller Office of the Republic of China, Table 29.

Table 8.8 Proportion of the population with various education levels to the total population in some areas in 1947, Unit: %

| Region | Higher education | Secondary education | | Primary education | | Old-style private schools | Illiterate |
|---|---|---|---|---|---|---|---|
| | | Senior high school | Junior high school | Higher primary school | Lower primary school | | |
| Total | 0.23 (0.17) | 0.58 (0.43) | 1.08 (1.06) | 3.26 (1.95) | 4.86 (8.31) | 5.72 | 72.35 |
| Hubei | 0.08 (0.09) | 0.22 (0.24) | 0.48 (0.67) | 1.21 (1.70) | 2.05 (4.18) | 3.61 | 85.47 |
| Shanxi | 0.06 (0.01) | 0.21 (0.04) | 0.76 (0.13) | 2.60 (0.36) | 6.39 (13.99) | 2.5 | 72.95 |
| Fujian | 0.08 (0.05) | 0.32 (0.28) | 0.76 (0.95) | 1.70 (1.81) | 2.55 (6.45) | 11.12 | 73.92 |
| Taiwan | 0.31 (0.07) | 0.85 (0.29) | 1.09 (1.46) | 11.67 (3.37) | 9.46 (12.11) | 4.34 | 54.98 |
| Liaoning | 0.08 (0.08) | 0.28 (0.25) | 1.38 (1.31) | 5.38 (1.35) | 12.13 (7.64) | 5.31 | 63.82 |
| Northern Liaoning | 0.08 (0.04) | 0.28 (0.18) | 1.01 (0.69) | 2.75 (1.83) | 4.95 (4.71) | 2.39 | 81.10 |
| Jilin | 0.15 (0.08) | 0.40 (0.19) | 1.25 (0.65) | 1.76 (0.89) | 3.25 (4.52) | 5.60 | 81.26 |
| Nanjing | 2.36 (2.58) | 4.22 (3.86) | 5.72 (5.00) | 7.31 (6.93) | 8.38 (8.90) | 10.25 | 34.51 |
| Shanghai | 1.34 (0.80) | 2.33 (1.67) | 3.05 (4.02) | 4.65 (4.01) | 5.49 (13.42) | 9.93 | 49.28 |
| Beiping | 0.76 (0.91) | 3.06 (2.67) | 3.27 (3.05) | 8.08 (5.24) | 9.60 (8.99) | 12.31 | 42.05 |
| Qingdao | 0.48 (0.26) | 1.63 (1.15) | 2.82 (2.40) | 5.51 (4.52) | 8.10 (9.94) | 9.69 | 53.49 |
| Hankou | 0.59 (0.51) | 1.79 (2.13) | 3.12 (4.61) | 5.24 (7.35) | 6.48 (7.90) | 22.79 | 37.50 |

Note: Figures outside the parentheses refer to graduation, and figures inside parentheses refer to students who did not finish studies.

Data source: China Yearbook Press, Yearbook of China (1948), pp. 101–104.

## 186    Conditions and causes

era but did not enter the modern era. China's education was still in the stage in which education for individuals was the mainstream, and there was no modern public education. Many new-style schools were established during the Republic of China period, but they did not become popular, which was prominently closely related to economic development. Without economic development, individuals and households couldn't increase income, and the meager household income did not permit education expenses. From a social viewpoint, the government's fiscal revenue would not swell without economic development, and the possibility of developing education through public input was slight.

This can be compared through the relationship between Japan's modern economic development and education. In 1868 during the Meiji Restoration, about 43 percent of the Japanese people received some schooling (reading, writing, and using the abacus), and this figure was about 10 percent for women. These figures were higher than what China achieved around 1949. After the Meiji Restoration, the government placed a high value on national education, and in 1872, it promulgated the Schooling System and launched modern compulsory education. Although the compulsory education only covered lower primary schools at the time, this coverage gradually expanded as the economy developed and the educational level was enhanced. The enrollment rate for compulsory education was only 28.1 percent in 1873, rose to 81.5 percent in 1900, and reached 99.6 percent in 1940, which basically marked education for all.[12]

Other developed European and American countries launched compulsory education in almost the same time as Japan. Compulsory education was available in the United States (Massachusetts) in the 1850s, the United Kingdom in the 1870s, and France in the 1880s. These all came after the start of modern economic growth. However, Germany (Prussia) was the earliest to launch compulsory education. It achieved this in 1763, which preceded its modern economic growth. Germany's enrollment rate for compulsory education reached 98 percent in the 1860s, and Germany and Japan are highly similar in this regard. Japanese scholar Ryoshin Minami compared Japan's education with those of the United States and Britain in modern times and found that in 1870, the proportion of current students who underwent all stages of schooling (including university, high school, and primary school) to the population was 3.9 percent for Japan, 17.4 percent for the United States, and 5.5 percent for the United Kingdom. Japan lagged far behind the United States and slightly behind the United Kingdom in this regard. Japan reached the level of the United States around 1915, which was more than 40 years later, but Japan was on a par with the United Kingdom (15.5 percent in 1910). Later, in 1930, this proportion was 21.1 percent for Japan, 23.4 percent for the United States, and 13.63 percent for the United Kingdom. By 1940, Japan (24.0 percent) outperformed the United States (21.9 percent).[13]

### 8.3.2   Institutions and outcomes of education

The issue of education before 1949 deserves discussing. The preceding discussion only introduces the outcomes of education but not the situation of education itself, such as enrollment rates and the number of current students. A brief introduction

*Natural resources and human resources* 187

is made here. According to the data from the National Bureau of Statistics,[14] the highest numbers of current students at all levels before 1949 were as follows: 23.683 million for primary schools, 1.496 million for general secondary schools, 383,000 for secondary specialized schools, and 155,000 for institutions of higher learning. In 1949, the corresponding figures were 24.391 million, 1.039 million, 229,000, and 117,000, respectively. The number of current students at primary school exceeded the highest level before 1949, while the numbers of current students at other levels of education were slightly less than the highest levels before 1949. These stages of education did not return to the highest levels before 1949 until 1951, two years later.[15] It was a similar case for the number of graduates. Before 1949, the highest number reached 4.633 million for primary schools, 326,000 for general secondary schools, 73,000 for secondary specialized schools, and 25,000 for institutions of higher learning. In 1949, the corresponding figures were 2.387 million, 280,000, 72,000, and 21,000, respectively. Except for primary schools, these were close to the highest levels before 1949. The number of primary school graduates soon caught up (reaching 5.942 million in 1952), and the number of general secondary school graduates exceeded the highest level before 1949 in 1953 (454,000).

Education in modern China basically developed in the same way as other fields, which began in the second half of the 19th century, only that this development was conducted under the rule of the Qing government before the Xinhai Revolution. Therefore, it could only be regarded as exploration. The formal modern education system began to develop in the early years of the Republic of China period. After several improvements, the system established during the Republic of China period became dominant. The early system was built mainly in imitation of the Japanese system, and was later modelled upon European and American systems.

The number of current students, which shows the degree of educational development, increased year by year. The primary education was the earliest to develop, with the number of current students reaching 8.88 million in 1929 and 23.8137 million in 1946.[16] Given China's total population at the time, this is pretty good performance. In terms of secondary education, the number of current students increased from less than 100,000 in the first year of the Republic of China (1912) to 370,000 in 1930, and the number of graduates soared from 6,510 to 63,600 in the same period. Normal schools and vocational schools also developed rapidly, with the number of students increasing from 28,600 and 14,500 to 82,800 and 34,900, respectively.[17] According to statistics from other sources, the number of secondary education students stood at 188,700 in 1928 but reached 1,262,200 in 1945, which was fast progress. Of course, it also stagnated in some periods. It exceeded 400,000 in 1931, then remained at a level of more than 400,000 people for a long time, and there was no breakthrough until after 1939. The number of graduates was 75,000 in 1931 but reached 255,700 in 1945.[18]

The number of current students at normal schools soared from 87,900 in 1936 to 245,600 in 1946, and the number of graduates climbed from 24,200 to 47,800.[19] The number of students at vocational schools increased from 16,600 in 1928 to 137,000 in 1946. The number of students in specialized education increased from

## 188   *Conditions and causes*

7,406 in 1928 to 23,900 in 1947.[20] Compared to secondary education, higher education developed in a tortuous way, with only somewhat more than 40,000 current students in 1912 but fewer than 20,000 from 1916 to 1917, and then increasing to remain at a level of 44,000 in 1931.[21] The number of current students at the college level and above was 41,900 in 1936 but nearly doubled in 1946, reaching 83,500.[22] It can be seen that despite the Japanese Aggression, higher education developed rapidly.

Finally, overseas study is worthy of mentioning. China in modern times learned from the West, that is, it "went out". This is the same as the practice adopted after 1949, especially after the reform and opening up. It is also a standard model for backward countries to learn from advanced countries. As China was forced open by the West, two views were expressed in China: compete with the West and learn from the West. The introduction of the modern education system from the West as previously mentioned is one type of learning. Sending students overseas is another form. China began to send students overseas at the end of the 19th century, and this became a craze in a relatively short time. Importantly, in addition to learning state-of-the-art science and technology, these students also wanted to imitate Western systems. The practice of Chinese students studying in Japan is particularly noteworthy. Going to Japan for study basically began after the end of the First Sino-Japanese War and peaked around the Russo-Japanese War. Several thousand people went to Japan for study every year in the few years around 1905. It is an incredible phenomenon. Why did Chinese students go to a hostile country for study? Obviously, Chinese people at that time wondered why Japan, which had been inferior to China or the West, could defeat China or even Russia. Students studying in Japan included not only early revolutionaries such as Qiu Jin, Cai E, Song Jiaoren, Huang Xing, Chen Tianhua, and Liang Qichao but also those who later became communists such as Li Dazhao, Chen Duxiu, and Zhou Enlai, as well as many literary figures such as Lu Xun, Guo Moruo, and Yu Dafu and some Kuomintang members. They made significant contributions to the progress of China.

### 8.4   Changes in health

Before 1949, as we all know, China had a weak economy and corrupt officials, and people struggled to make both ends meet. At that time, many Chinese people were in poor health and had a short life. According to studies, the life expectancy of Chinese people in 1943 was only 30 years, 35 years from 1943 to 1948, and 40 years from 1948 to 1953.[23]

According to the research conducted by Chen Changheng (1934) and Chen Da et al. (1981),[24] although the infant mortality rate in China in the early 20th century varied greatly from region to region, it was basically between 110 and 285 per thousand, which is high. This can be confirmed not only by the prior discussions in this chapter but also by the statistics available at the time.[25] This proportion was about 150 per thousand or more in underdeveloped countries, such as Ceylon (now Sri Lanka), Malta, Egypt, India, the Philippines, and Romania. This was also high in some more developed countries, such as Mexico, Chile, Japan, Spain, Poland,

*Table 8.9* Total daily consumption of calories and protein by adult males as well as the proportion of calories supplied by various types of food from 1929 to 1933

| Geographic range | Number of regions | Number of male samples | Calories | Number of regions below the standard | Percentage of calories supplied by various types of food (%) | | | | |
|---|---|---|---|---|---|---|---|---|---|
| | | | | | Grain | Beans | Vegetable oils | Taro and potatoes | Animal |
| **Calories** | | | | | | | | | |
| National | 136 | 13,341 | 3,295 | 39 | 83.1 | 6.7 | 2.0 | 3.9 | 2.3 |
| Wheat-producing areas | 67 | 6,966 | 3,186 | 27 | 82.2 | 9.5 | 1.3 | 4.6 | 1.0 |
| Rice-producing areas | 69 | 6,375 | 3400 | 12 | 83.9 | 4.0 | 2.7 | 3.3 | 3.6 |
| **Protein** | | | | | | | | | |
| National | 136 | 13,341 | 100 | 12 | 76 | 9 | 7 | 2 | 4 |
| Wheat-producing areas | 67 | 6,966 | 108 | 14 | 73 | 11 | 10 | 2 | 2 |
| Rice-producing areas | 69 | 6,375 | 91 | 11 | 78 | 6 | 5 | 2 | 6 |

*Note:* The contributions made by various types of foods on the right side of the table are incomplete. It also includes fruits, sugars, and others. As the contribution made by these categories is small, it is omitted here. The original table also includes more a detailed regional distribution.

*Data source:* Buck (1941), Tables 8.4 and 8.7.

190    *Conditions and causes*

and Hungary. Some other countries were not very developed but had a relatively low infant mortality rate, such as Argentina and Greece. Of course, the countries that were clearly more developed, such as the Netherlands, Australia, Sweden, and Switzerland, had a very low infant mortality rate.

Next, we examine the caloric intake and nutritional status of the Chinese people. Table 8.9 shows the situation of adult males nationwide from 1929 to 1933. It is divided into the wheat-producing areas and rice-producing areas, or northern China and southern China. Overall, the caloric level was higher than 3,000, which was pretty good. Of course, some areas were below the standard, particularly wheat-producing areas. It was pretty good in rice-producing areas, indicating that rice-producing areas had relatively good nutritional supply. In terms of the types of food, cereal calories accounted for over 82 percent of the total calories, with little differences among regions. Protein accounted for more than 73 percent and was higher in rice-producing areas than in wheat-producing areas. Beans also accounted for a high proportion, and the proportion was higher in wheat-producing areas, which is, of course, closely associated with the growth environment of beans. The low proportion of animal protein indicates that the main source of nutrition for Chinese people consisted of plants rather than animals, which is also mirrored in the physique of Chinese people. Generally speaking, animal foods contain higher calories and nutrients than plant foods and are also more conducive to the development and growth of the body. The proportion of vegetable oils shown in the table is also low, indicating that Chinese people at that time did not enjoy good health, and it also confirmed the backward economy. It can be seen that, while the caloric intake was not low, Chinese people had a short life and a low health level due to a lack of balanced and sufficient nutrient supply, especially the little intake of foods rich in fat and other nutrients.

## 8.5   Conclusion

This chapter examined natural and human resources. Since China in this period did not start modern economic growth, the level and capacity to independently develop and utilize resources were limited. The private sector of the economy emerged in the Republic of China period, many fields introduced emerging industries and began machine production after the Industrial Revolution, and industry showed a certain momentum of development. However, China did not start modern economic growth for a host of reasons, except some signs of the emergence of this key link.

This also goes for human resources. The modern education system was gradually improved during the Republic of China period, and some high-level personnel with modern knowledge and skills were cultivated. However, in a big country with a population of more than 450 million, their number was insignificant, and their role was limited. This is also true of other areas of human resources, such as health. Without obvious economic development, people had poor health, and there was also a lack of trained physicians and medicines. The Chinese people were even called the "East Asian sick man" by Westerners.

## Notes

1 Natural resources include not only land, water, and minerals but also crops. Crops can be improved somewhat, including the introduction of new varieties and variety improvement.
2 The concept refers to the situation that some countries are rich in natural resources but are unable to make good use of them to develop their economies, thus becoming heavily dependent on resource exports.
3 The concept refers to the status of some low-income countries that export primary commodities (agricultural and mineral products) and import manufactured goods in the long term. This status is in line with the theory of comparative advantage. However, because the countries cannot make effective use of resources to develop the economy, the economy remains at a low level for a long time.
4 There are inaccuracies in the data on yield, such as mercury output. Guan Quan and Makino Fumio (1999) and Guan Quan (2018) provide more accurate estimates.
5 Data with a long time series for this period are only available for areas such as prices and national trade. There are no long-term continuous data for areas such as industry and agriculture.
6 Regarding details of mining production before 1949, see Guan Quan and Makino Fumio (1999) and Makino Fumio and Guan Quan (2007).
7 Regarding the development of mining in modern China, see Chang (1969), Guan Quan and Makino Fumio (1999), and Makino Fumio and Guan Quan (2007).
8 For the issue of industrial development in modern times in China and Japan, see Guan Quan (2018).
9 Regarding the data on international trade in modern Japan, there was Toyo Keizai (1935) in the early days and Shimano Takao (1980) in the long term. In addition, there are Yamazawa Ippei, Yamamoto Yuzo (1979), and Yukizawa Kenzo and Maeda Shozo (1978).
10 Maddison (2009).
11 For the issue of population, see Obuchi Hiroshi (1981), Obuchi Hiroshi and Morioka Hitoshi (1981).
12 Ryoshin Minami (1981).
13 Ryoshin Minami (1981).
14 National Bureau of Statistics (1959).
15 Ordinary secondary schools had 1.568 million students, secondary specialized schools had 383,000 students, and institutes of higher education had 153,000 students.
16 Wang Bingzhao (2013), p. 103.
17 Su Yunfeng (2007), pp. 132–135.
18 Wang Bingzhao (2013), p. 127.
19 Wang Bingzhao (2013), p. 149.
20 Wang Bingzhao (2013), pp. 164–165.
21 Su Yunfeng (2007), p. 141.
22 Dong Baoliang (2007), p. 159.
23 Hou Yangfang (2001), p. 439.
24 Chen Changheng (1934) Table 22; Chen Da (1981) pp. 145–147, 156–157.
25 Hou Yangfang (2001), p. 400.

# 9 Capital formation and technological progress

## 9.1 Introduction

This chapter examines capital formation and technological advancement, which are closely correlated. Usually, capital formation refers to investment, which is primarily production equipment. Therefore, production capacity is formed. It also includes infrastructure. Such production equipment contains technology. The more advanced the production equipment, the higher the technical level, hence higher productivity. Of course, there is another side to technology, namely "soft technology" or the skills accompanying the people. Production requires not only high-tech equipment but also highly skilled operators, as well as maintenance, design procedures, and R&D personnel. Although these human resources only cover education and health, the techniques and skills that people have mastered are partly the result of education and partly the result of practices.

China's capital formation went through a sticky patch in modern times. Before 1949, China was plagued by domestic strife and foreign aggression. Despite some progress in railways, highways, shipping, etc., China lay in tatters, and the people had no means to live, which was inconsistent with its image as a big country with a population of over 400 million and a long history. Investment in enterprises can be divided into three types before 1949: government-run enterprises, foreign-funded enterprises, and private enterprises. The first two types were dominant and had a large scale, newer technology, and abundant capital. In contrast, the private enterprises could only invest in some areas related to people's well-being, such as textiles, matchsticks, brewing, and food processing. Such a monopoly was a significant stumbling block to the progress and development of China's economy, with the direct result that China lagged behind other countries economically. Modern industries are the driver of industrialization and economic development. Monopolized by the government and foreign capital, the modern industrial sector found it impossible to develop. Modern industry requires lots of investment, technology, and personnel, which were not available for private enterprises. Coupled with restrictions and limited space for development, private enterprises had little room for development. It is not difficult to see why China lacked modern industry and technology in modern times.

Before 1949, China lagged far behind developed countries in terms of science and technology. As a result, China had a weaker economy, and the people had

DOI: 10.4324/9781003410386-12

*Capital formation and technological progress* 193

low living standards and were even bullied. China was one of the least developed countries. The famous Needham Question was obvious in China. As a result of backward technology, and poor economic development, China couldn't demonstrate its former glory in the world. After decades of hard work since 1949, China has made great strides, ranking among the world's best in terms of some general civilian technologies and even being comparable to developed countries in many high-end fields. China's economic development is largely underpinned by these achievements. China would not have today's achievements without the progress and application of science as well as technology. Although today's China is still inferior to the developed countries in some areas, it boasts the conditions and capabilities to catch up with them.

## 9.2  Capital equipment

The data on capital formation before 1949 are scarce, and we can only collect the data on the amount of investment by some government-run enterprises or foreign-funded enterprises. It is therefore difficult to get a big picture of China's capital formation. According to records, the total amount of investment made by China's national capital in industry and mining from 1872 to 1911 was 160 million yuan. There were a total of 521 factories and mines, including 89 million yuan for government-run factories and mines, 44 million yuan for 66 for government-run or government–business factories and mines, and 27 million yuan for 36 Chinese–foreign factories and mines. If these industrial sector and mining industries are divided by sector, it was a total of 41 million yuan for 72 mining factories, 758,000 yuan for three machinery factories, 41 million yuan for 193 textile mills, 18 million yuan for 100 food factories, and 59 million yuan for 153 other factories.[1] It can be seen that China's early industrialization was concentrated in the mining, textile, food, and other sectors, while the machinery industry lagged behind. Specifically, the mining and textile industries dominated in this period. The food and other industries began to emerge at the end of the 19th century. Machinery enterprises were established in only 1883, 1907, and another unknown year, which was an insignificant figure.

As the data on China's capital formation in this period are scarce, it is difficult to show the overall situation. Nevertheless, some scholars tried unique approaches. This chapter introduces the data on capital formation calculated by Thomas G. Rawski using the discrete mass index method. Thomas G. Rawski compiled the data on gross capital formation for some years in the period from 1903 to 1936. While these estimates are limited to the modern sector, they show the process of China's industrialization. According to his calculations, it was 81 million yuan for the whole country in 1903 (76 million yuan for the hinterland and 5 million yuan for the northeast region), 223 million yuan in 1910 (158 million yuan for the hinterland, and 65 million yuan for the northeast region), 476 million yuan in 1920 (352 million yuan for the hinterland and 124 million yuan for the northeast region), 848 million yuan in 1930 (613 million yuan for the hinterland and 235 million yuan for the northeast region), and 1.398 billion yuan in 1936 (873 million yuan for the hinterland and 525 million yuan for the northeast region).[2] Although the gross amount of capital formation fluctuated throughout the period, it rose rapidly as a whole, particularly after 1918 when World War I was over. It reached a considerable height in 1936, with a good momentum of growth. It is noteworthy that the northeast region developed from a very low level in the early days to a level that was more than half of that in the hinterland.

We then examine the results of investment, or the production capacity and infrastructure formed. Figure 9.1 shows the quantity of capital equipment (spindles, looms, and reeling machines) of Chinese cotton mills and silk reeling mills. It can be seen that the quantity of capital equipment increased overall despite some fluctuations and increased significantly after World War I. Except for the number of reeling machines in Shanghai, other equipment showed a trend of rapid increase, which also confirms the golden age of the Chinese bourgeoisie. These industries were light industries related to the people's livelihood, and were the pillar sectors of China's industry at that time. The investment in and development of these industries played a not insignificant role in China's industrialization.

Table 9.1 shows the estimates of China's capital stock in modern times.[3] Several observations can be made. The first is the amount of foreign capital and domestic capital. In 1894, foreign capital was equal to only 23 percent of domestic capital. Since then, foreign investment expanded, reaching about 62 percent from 1911 to 1914. Although it declined somewhat later, it was still considerable, approaching 50 percent in 1920. In 1936, it was divided into two parts: the northeast region and the rest of China. The proportion of foreign capital declined slightly to 46 percent. In particular, its proportion in the rest of China (except the northeast region)

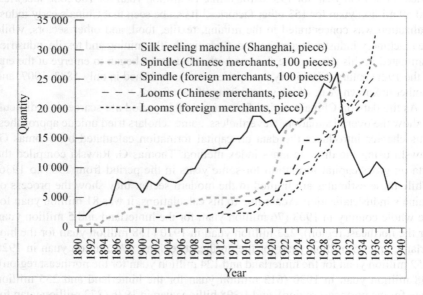

*Figure 9.1* Number of spindles, looms, and reeling machines

Data source: *History of Textile in Modern China* (1997) (volume 3), pp. 436–437, 450–451.

Capital formation and technological progress    195

decreased to 33 percent. However, it was a different case in the northeast region, with foreign capital equal to 138 percent of domestic capital. Japanese capital was dominant in the process. Great changes occurred from 1947 to 1948, when the War of Resistance against Japanese Aggression ended. Impacted by World War II,

*Table 9.1* Estimated capital in modern times

| Year/industry | Foreign capital | Domestic capital | | |
|---|---|---|---|---|
| | | Bureaucratic capital | National capital | Total |
| **1894 (whole country)** | | | | |
| Industrial sector | 2,791 | 3,063 | 1,891 | 4,954 |
| Transport | 2,615 | 1,694 | 101 | 1,795 |
| Business | 9,284 | – | 65,600 | 65,600 |
| Finance | 6,680 | – | 20,000 | 20,000 |
| Total | 21,370 | 4,757 | 87,592 | 92,349 |
| **1911–1914 (whole country)** | | | | |
| Industrial sector | 37,690 | 8,417 | 20,515 | 28,932 |
| Transport | 64,435 | 39,390 | 8,226 | 47,616 |
| Business | 67,968 | – | 166,200 | 166,200 |
| Finance | 14,515 | 4,489 | 52,000 | 56,489 |
| Total | 184,608 | 52,296 | 246,941 | 299,237 |
| **1920 (whole country)** | | | | |
| Industrial sector | 50,000 | 11,414 | 45,070 | 56,484 |
| Transport | 83,000 | 55,538 | 12,907 | 68,445 |
| Business | 87,000 | – | 230,000 | 230,000 |
| Finance | 19,000 | 23,253 | 102,700 | 125,953 |
| Total | 239,000 | 90,205 | 390,677 | 480,882 |
| **1936 [Rest of China (except the northeast region)]** | | | | |
| Industrial sector | 145,128 | 34,034 | 144,839 | 178,873 |
| Transport | 50,796 | 164,891 | 14,905 | 179,796 |
| Business | 119,295 | 3,000 | 378,000 | 381,000 |
| Finance | 183,456 | 563,700 | 210,000 | 773,700 |
| Others | 2,499 | – | – | – |
| Total | 501,174 | 765,625 | 747,744 | 1,513,369 |
| **1936 (northeast region)** | | | | |
| Industrial sector | 108,750 | 23,529 | 44,100 | 67,629 |
| Transport | 267,084 | 147,060 | 1,000 | 148,060 |
| Business | 18,932 | 23,529 | 42,000 | 65,529 |
| Finance | 10,235 | 24,118 | 4,430 | 28,548 |
| Others | 21,666 | – | – | – |
| Total | 426,667 | 218,236 | 91,530 | 309,766 |
| **1947–1948 (whole country)** | | | | |
| Industrial sector | 62,446 | 159,874 | 148,492 | 308,366 |
| Transport | 10,968 | 260,205 | 13,007 | 273,212 |
| Business | 15,348 | 3,000 | 364,000 | 367,000 |
| Finance | 22,888 | 344,000 | 20,290 | 364,290 |
| Total | 111,650 | 767,079 | 545,789 | 1,312,868 |

*Note:* The unit was 10,000 yuan for 1920 and before, and 10,000 legal tender in 1936 and afterward.

*Data source:* Xu Dixin and Wu Chengming (volume 2) (1990), p. 1043, (volume 3) (1993), pp. 746–761.

## 196  *Conditions and causes*

Western countries had no time to make investment in China. Besides, China was also in the process of the War of Liberation at the time. As a result, foreign capital had a small share, accounting for only 8.5 percent.

Second, domestic capital grew rapidly as a whole. Although the values of currencies around 1936 were different, we still can see the rapid growth. The reasons are twofold: First, the capital had originally been weak, and it then grew rapidly. It was a model of low starting point and fast growth. This is proved by the changes in the period from 1894 to 1911–1914. It more than doubled in less than two decades and increased by a further 60 percent by 1920. After 1936, particularly after the Japanese invasion of China in 1937, changes took place across the board. The gross capital in 1947–1948 was lower than that in 1936. It is often said that the economy after 1949 recovered to that in 1936. The same is true of Europe and Japan. Wars played havoc with the economies of many countries. The third is the difference between bureaucratic capital and national capital.[4] Before 1920, national capital had basically been dominant because it was, after all, ubiquitous in such a large country. After 1936, however, it changed. Bureaucratic capital surpassed national capital, and this remained until 1947–1948. This might be attributed to the development of financial capital and the construction of infrastructure. Finally, from the perspective of industry or capital distribution, private capital was concentrated in the commercial and financial industries in the early days, and it also saw rapid growth in the industrial sector later. Bureaucratic capital was first invested in infrastructure such as transport and gradually expanded to the financial and industrial sectors.

### 9.3  Infrastructure

The construction and ownership of infrastructure is examined next. We cannot talk of infrastructure without mentioning railways because railways were new technologies that emerged and became popular in the West in the 19th century. It was based on the power technology of steam engines and then on the subsequent electric power technology and internal combustion engine technology. It can be said that the popularization of railways in the 19th century and the early 20th century provided the basic support for the economic development of today's developed countries and also led to the growth of related areas, such as steel, coal, and timber. Thanks to the railway, coal and iron ore can be carried from mines to production bases, food and clothing can be transported from manufacturers to the consumer market, and people can move more conveniently and rapidly. At that time, China's railways lagged far behind those of developed countries as a result of backward technology, shortage of funds, and other political and economic factors. In a sense, the economic development of countries in modern times can be glimpsed from the situation of railway construction. Backward countries still lag behind in railway construction. Of course, it also hinges on other factors. Given abundant resources in some colonies, suzerains invested in railway construction there (such as India) in order to acquire handsome returns. A considerable length of railways in modern China was also built in this way, such as those in the northeast region.

Table 9.2 enumerates the length and construction speed of railways before 1949. It shows that China's railways began to be built in the late 19th century. It was built

*Capital formation and technological progress*  197

fast from scratch. In the early 20th century, China had railways with a length of some 10,000 km. This period can be said to be the first climax in China's railway construction. Thereafter, although the railway was being built in each period, little headway was made. It was still less than 25,000 km in length in 1948. Nevertheless, it is safe to say the railway provided irreplaceable support for the economic development at the time. China's highway construction got off to a late start, but progressed rapidly. Starting in the 1920s, railway construction saw rapid development during the Republic of China period, increasing from 29,000 km in 1927 to 111,000 km in 1936, up by 16 percent on average annually.[5]

Railway construction and operation requires not only the railway itself but also the means of operation, including locomotives as well as passenger and freight cars, and operating systems like signaling, monitoring, and management. Therefore, the railway industry is a gigantic system. Table 9.3 shows the number of railway cars owned as well as their carrying capacity and actual transport performance. It can

*Table 9.2* Railway construction, Unit: km

| Period | Nationwide length | Length of newly built railway in each period | Average length of newly built railway each year |
|---|---|---|---|
| 1876 | 15.00 | – | – |
| 1877–1894 | 364.27 | 364.27 | 20.24 |
| 1895–1911 | 9,618.10 | 9,253.83 | 644.34 |
| 1912–1927 | 13,040.48 | 3,422.38 | 213.89 |
| 1928–1931 | 14,238.86 | 1,198.38 | 299.60 |
| 1932–1937 | 21,036.14 | 6,797.28 | 1,132.88 |
| 1938–1948 | 24,945.52 | 3,909.38 | 355.39 |

*Data source:* Yan Zhongping et al. (1955), p. 180.

*Table 9.3* Number of railway cars owned, carrying capacity, and capacity of transport

| Year | Locomotive | | Passenger car | | | Freight car | | |
|---|---|---|---|---|---|---|---|---|
| | Quantity (piece) | Carrying capacity (metric ton) | Quantity (piece) | Carrying capacity (number of people) | Capacity of transport (10,000 person per km) | Quantity (piece) | Carrying capacity (metric ton) | Capacity of transport (10,000 metric tons per km) |
| 1907 | 413 | – | 685 | – | 1,020 | 5,937 | – | – |
| 1912 | 600 | – | 1,067 | 45,177 | 162,330 | 8,335 | 183,224 | 243,233 |
| 1915 | 629 | 5,619 | 1,280 | 61,174 | 99,264 | 10,652 | 243,070 | 225,077 |
| 1920 | 789 | 7,917 | 1,379 | 69,563 | 316,153 | 12,192 | 301,298 | 454,094 |
| 1925 | 1,131 | 11,966 | 1,803 | 101,101 | 376,112 | 16,718 | 452,272 | 411,132 |
| 1929 | 786 | 7,530 | 1,291 | 78,532 | 318,329 | 10,684 | 272,000 | 249,698 |
| 1935 | 1,243 | 13,535 | 2,047 | 108,602 | 434,885 | 15,482 | 443,667 | 648,880 |
| 1940 | 378 | – | 991 | – | 143,758 | 6,045 | – | 49,922 |
| 1947 | 1,954 | – | 2,715 | – | 851,798 | 26,164 | – | 273,556 |

*Data source:* Yan Zhongping et al. (1955), pp. 194–196, 207–208.

198  *Conditions and causes*

be seen that although the number of railway cars owned increased in the early 20th century, it increased slowly. The number in 1935 is almost triple that of 1907, indicating some progress in these nearly three decades. The carrying capacity witnessed a similar development process during this period, and the actual transport performance was about the same. It is a fact that the war in the period 1937–1947 led to a serious decline in railway. For example, almost all figures for 1940 returned to the level before 1912, or even lower than in 1907. It illustrates the enormous impact of the war on China's economy. War is more destructive to infrastructure than other areas because infrastructure is needed in a war, and destroying infrastructure is a tactical measure. Moreover, the construction of infrastructure takes time and also requires immense financial and material resources. Since a war significantly depletes financial resources, production in relevant fields will grind to a halt, making it impossible to repair railways, not to mention building new ones.

Table 9.4 shows the number and tonnage of ships. It shows a marked increase from 1910 to 1935, as well as a decline during the wars and subsequent recovery. In fact, the shipping industry in modern China advanced rapidly because waterway transport was highly important in China. The application of steamships and other modern technologies after modern times facilitated the rapid development of shipping. Of course, demand is also crucial. The transport industry needs market demand. As the economy develops, the demand for transport will increase. This is why infrastructure such as transport infrastructure is often invested and built in light of the level of economic development. The more economically developed the region, the greater the demand for infrastructure, and vice versa. In terms of tonnage, ships with a large tonnage accounted for a larger proportion, and its number also grew rapidly. Small and medium-tonnage ships also grew relatively rapidly. Ships of a small tonnage did not grow as fast as ships of a large and medium tonnage. Categories are, of course, determined by the tonnage. The number of ships is arranged by tonnage in the ascending order.

*Table 9.4* Classification of tonnage of ships in modern times

| Year | Total | | Above 1,000 metric tons | | 100–1,000 metric tons | | Less than 100 metric tons | |
|------|-------------------|------------|-------------------|------------|-------------------|------------|-------------------|------------|
| | Number of ships | Tonnage | Number of ships | Tonnage | Number of ships | Tonnage | Number of ships | Tonnage |
| 1910 | 317 | 100,974.62 | 34 | 80,388.81 | 44 | 16,145.52 | 239 | 4,440.29 |
| 1915 | 1,559 | 192,970.36 | 56 | 111,182.37 | 141 | 48,274.35 | 1362 | 33,513.64 |
| 1920 | 2,280 | 303,826.93 | 88 | 162,750.99 | 259 | 91,387.03 | 1933 | 49,688.91 |
| 1924 | 2,734 | 445,997.11 | 141 | 260,468.86 | 365 | 129,513.63 | 2228 | 56,014.62 |
| 1930 | 2,792 | 415,447.28 | 138 | 247,968.54 | 354 | 109,932.90 | 2300 | 52,545.84 |
| 1935 | 3,895 | 675,172.69 | 208 | 461,812.03 | 555 | 116,704.15 | 3,132 | 96,656.51 |
| 1940 | 507 | 58,912.00 | – | – | – | – | – | – |
| 1948 | 4032 | 109,2217.00 | – | – | – | – | – | – |

*Data source:* Yan Zhongping et al. (1955), pp. 228–229.

*Capital formation and technological progress* 199

## 9.4 Technological advances

It is difficult to study technological progress in modern China mainly for two reasons. First, the degree of economic development in modern times was limited. Despite some progress in certain fields, China did not start modern economic growth, many technologies did not become popular, and independent innovation was lacking. In contrast, Japan established the patent system in 1885 and approved 160,000 patents for inventions from 1885 to 1945. It also enacted the *Utility Model Act* in 1905, and granted 340,000 utility models between 1905 and 1945.[6] In China, the Beiyang government also promulgated regulations to reward inventions, but due to the war and limited overall progress, only a little more than 200 inventions were granted during the Republic of China period.[7] Second, as the continuous data on industrial and agricultural production are scarce, it is difficult to calculate related indicators such as the total factor productivity (TFP). The cases of a few industries is studied next.

### 9.4.1 Coal and iron industry

China's modern coal mining industry began to develop in the late 19th century. As foreign capital gradually entered China after the Opium War, coal became an indispensable energy source.[8] How to mine coal in China became a burning issue. After the 1860s, those in the Qing government who supported the Self-Strengthening Movement also ran a number of enterprises, which needed a wealth of coal as their energy source. The government could only rely on imports at the time. However, imports were expensive, and the supply was unstable. China's local manually operated coal kilns produced only a small quantity of coal, which was also of low quality. Manually operated coal kilns were mostly a sideline business run by agricultural workers, and coal was mined mainly for self-consumption. Any surplus was sold on the spot. Due to the backward roads (dirt roads) and means of transport (ox carts), long-distance transport was expensive, and its timeliness could not be guaranteed.

Under the manual mining method, coal was mined using pickaxes, transported on human backs, and lifted by means of winches. Water was manually drained, and mines depended on natural ventilation. This mode of production is not suitable for deep mining. If it is necessary to dig deep, draining water takes a lot of manpower, and it is inefficient and costly. Besides, carrying coal on workers' backs is also inefficient and is also a safety hazard. In terms of operation and management, most of the owners were landlords with small landholdings, small merchants, or farmers who raised funds to operate small coal kilns. It was difficult to scale up the operations due to limited funds. Most of the miners were local farmers who engaged in agricultural production and dug coal in the slack season. Because of technical and financial constraints, small coal kilns could only exploit coal exposed on the surface or in the shallow stratum, and the low-quality coal was not suitable for the modern large-scale machine industry. In view of these conditions, both government officials who supported the Self-Strengthening Movement and foreign forces had to solve the urgent problem of coal demand. In this period, Europe possessed mature modern coal mining technology and could achieve modern mechanized production. Europe had long ago used steam-engine-powered hoists, ventilators, drainage pumps, percussion drills, gadders, and disk cutters. Coupled with the generators and electric motors, coal mining entered an era of electrification, and production efficiency and safety were enhanced.

Figure 9.2 shows the changes in the proportions of mechanized coal and iron production from 1912 to 1937, which clearly shows a gradual upward trend. The proportion of mechanized coal mining rose from less than 60 percent in the early years of the Republic of China period to over 80 percent before the outbreak of the War of Resistance against Japanese Aggression. This can be said to be progress. Corresponding to the traditional mining method, "mechanized mining" refers to the use of mining machinery for excavation and transport, covering coal washing and screening. Under the traditional mining method, coal was excavated, transported, etc. manually, or large livestock was used for transport. This has been the most backbreaking, dangerous, inefficient work. Mechanization is one of the most important benefits of modern science and technology because it improves efficiency while reducing risks. After over 200 years of industrialization, the industrial sector in all developed countries and new industrialized countries have adopted the mechanized method. Of course, many underdeveloped countries still rely on manpower and animals in many production processes because they lack such technologies or the technologies are too costly.

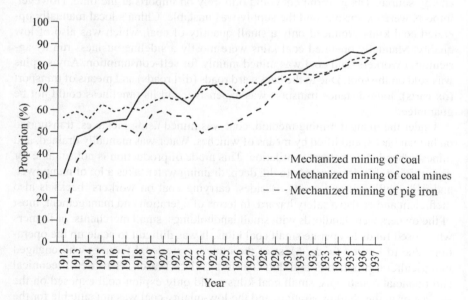

*Figure 9.2* Proportion of mechanized coal and iron production (1912–1937)
*Data source:* Yan Zhongping et al. (1955), p. 104.

*Capital formation and technological progress* 201

### 9.4.2 Textile industry

The late 19th century marked the budding stage of the modern textile industry. The Qing government and the people explored various approaches to develop this industry. Several well-known trailblazers in the textile industry emerged, who founded small silk reeling and production enterprises using improved Western machinery and the factory type. After China was defeated in the Sino-Japanese War, some enlightened people were motivated to save the country through industrial development. Most of them came from literati and officialdom in feudal China, who wielded their political power and social influence to seek government support, also raised private funds to open various modern enterprises at a time of drastic social changes in the late Qing Dynasty and the early Republic of China period. The textile industry became the focus of their investment for its low investment, abundant raw materials and labor, and broad market. Unlike the enterprises operated by government officials who supported the Self-Strengthening Movement, the textile enterprises founded by these industrialists kept growing, and their practices accumulated valuable experience for the development of the textile industry. In a sense, this process can be likened to the craze of going into business in the early days of reform and opening up in China. One is the period of change in the old era, and another is that in the new era. The common denominator of the two is the market.

As the textile industry developed, many experts with high academic performance emerged, who performed a key role in introducing, drawing on, and imitating Western technology and equipment. After the 1920s, they replaced foreign technicians in technical management, and some technical experts also participated in corporate decision making, becoming excellent entrepreneurs. They performed important technological transformation and inventions in light of national conditions. For example, Lei Binglin invented Lei-style long draft for spinning and dual-horn thread tubes for roving frames; Du Jinsheng developed made-made photographic weaving method; Feng Yunhe invented the chemical degumming method of ramie; Zhang Fangzuo et al. developed new-style agricultural spinning machines; Liu Chijun and Wang Ruiji developed the perfection-style spinning machines; Zou Chunzuo developed a three-step ironwood spinning machine; Mu Ouchu organized the development and promoted the July 7 spinning machine.[9]

In order to analyze the technological progress at the time from an economic viewpoint, the changes in the production technology of some enterprises are observed through the proportion of their investment. Figure 9.3 shows the number of workers and looms of the Yamei Silk Factory from 1920 to 1937, which represent labor input and capital investment, respectively. In theory, the result of the joint input by the two is the yield or output, expressed as isoquant curve, although it is not shown here. As the figure shows, the combination of the two shows a path of changes that tilt upward to the upper right in an almost linear line. It basically changed along this line from 1920 to around 1932. This has twofold meaning. First, the change to the upper right corner indicates that as labor input and capital investment increase, the output also increases. Since the figures given here are not proportional values, it is hard to say whether there were technological advances.

Usually, technological progress measured in this way indicates that there is more output under the conditions of the same input or that an increase in input leads to more output. While this situation stands for economies of scale, economies of scale per se imply technological advance or efficiency gains.

Another meaning is that changes in labor input and capital input are technically neutral. In other words, there is no significant change in the capital/labor ratio. If there is technological advance during this period, such progress is technically neutral. It is biased toward neither an increase in the labor input nor an increase in the capital input. Such technological progress is usually made in the short term because it is unlikely to accumulate huge capital in the short term. In the early days of economic development, there is somewhat of a tendency towards being labor-intensive, and such technological progress belongs to the labor-oriented type. Usually, because there is no additional input of capital equipment in the early stages of economic development, it is formed by using the labor force. As the economy develops, another type of technological progress, the capital-biased type, will emerge, because the labor force becomes increasingly (relatively) expensive and the capital increasingly (relatively) cheap, coupled with differences in the technical performance and productivity of capital equipment. This is shown somewhat in the years after 1933 in Figure 14.2: it moved toward capital-intensive.

It is also noteworthy that the length of the changing curve varies from year to year, which shows the different output caused by the input in each year. It can also be seen as the degree of technological progress. The length is longer for changes in 1925–1926, 1928–1929, 1929–1930, 1931–1932, and 1932–1933 than in other years, indicating more progress in these years than in other years. The changes in 1935–1936 were significant and also clearly shifted toward capital-intensive.

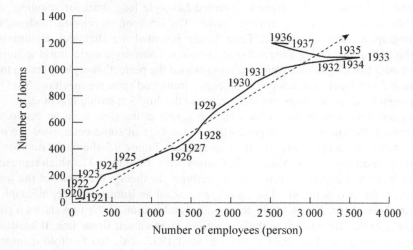

*Figure 9.3* Labor and capital input of the Yamei Silk Factory

Note: The numbers in the graph represent years.

Data source: *History of Textile in Modern China* (1997) (volume 3), p. 443.

*Capital formation and technological progress*   203

In addition, the changes in 1931–1933 clearly moved toward the labor-intensive direction. Of course, due to the short duration of such changes, it is hard to say whether a certain type of technological progress was made.

### 9.4.3   Flour industry

Similar to many other modern industries, the development of China's machine-made flour industry came as a result of the opening up. In 1863, British merchants set up the first machine-made flour mill in Shanghai. In 1878, the first machine-made flour mill funded by national capital appeared in Tianjin. New machine-made flour mills were established every year from the beginning of the 20th century. From 1896 to 1912, 90 new flour mills were set up nationwide, including 47 invested by national capital. Of course, foreign investment still had an advantage in terms of technology and scale. World War I brought opportunities to China's economy to some extent. From 1913 to 1921, 123 machine-made flour mills were established, of which 105 were funded by national capital, with a production capacity accounting for more than 80 percent. However, as Western European and Russian power exited, Japanese capital entered on a large scale. Foreign investment was involved in 18 of the 123 flour mills, including 15 flour mills with Japanese capital.[10]

After the end of World War I, foreign investors entered China on a larger scale. Coupled with the warlord dogfights in China, the flour industry declined, with only 85 factories newly built from 1922 to 1931, including 82 with national capital. After the outbreak of the September 18 Incident in 1931, the flour industry lost a large market and important production areas of raw materials, and the flour mills funded by national capital in the northeast region (accounting for 35.5 percent of the total number of factories in China) were also controlled by the Japanese puppet regime.[11] Of the 52 flour mills newly built nationwide from 1932 to 1936, 12 were foreign-funded mills, but their production capacity accounted for half of the total. Except for 11 mills, which were opened by Japanese investors or forcibly purchased from Chinese enterprises, only 26 new factories were established in the hinterland. During the War of Resistance against Japanese Aggression, the flour mills funded by national capital in the occupied areas met disasters of a magnitude unprecedented, and half of them were either placed under Japanese military control or forced to be operated by Japanese businessmen. Due to the sharp increase in the population of migrants and the demand for army provisions in the rear area, there appeared a short-term boom, with a total of 89 flour mills established, accounting for half of the total in the period. However, their scale was relatively small, with a production capacity accounting for only 23.4 percent of the total. From 1937 to 1945, 180 flour mills were newly built nationwide, including 23 in the northeast, 68 in the occupied area in the hinterland, and 89 in the rear area under Kuomintang rule. Of the 180 factories, 143 involved private capital, 14 involved bureaucratic capital, and 23 were foreign-funded and Sino-foreign joint ventures. 69 factories suspended production during the same period. After the victory of the War of Resistance against Japanese Aggression, the flour industry saw an unprecedented boom, with a large number of factories built. A total of 131 factories were

## 204　Conditions and causes

newly built from 1946 to 1949, which were primarily located in large cities, such as Wuhan, Shanghai, Tianjin, Chongqing, and Xi'an.[12]

Figure 9.4 shows the production function of the flour industry. The horizontal axis refers to the average number of factory workers, and the vertical axis refers to the average number of steel millstones of the factories. The two represent the labor input and capital input in production, respectively. The curve in the graph represents the theoretical output, meaning the amount of output and the tendency of the capital/labor ratio. Although the curve in the graph seems to be messy, it shows some significance. First, in theory, the curve should tilt toward the upper right corner, or the output should increase, as the input increases. Second, the directions of the curve show different meanings. If the curve moves to the right, it is biased toward labor-intensive. If it moves to the left, it is becoming increasingly capital-intensive.

The following can be roughly observed from the graph. First, except for the starting years in 1904–1905, when it moved to the right or labor-intensive, it basically moved to the left or capital-intensive. Second, two basic paths of change can be observed. One moved toward capital-intensive, and the other fluctuated up and down along the direction of two lines originating from the origin. The former refers to a shift from labor-intensive to capital-intensive, while the latter changed according to the constant capital/labor ratio. The result shows a change toward capital-intensive, but there were twists and turns in the middle. A reversal also occurred in the process – moving upward to the upper right before 1926 and then falling back toward the origin. In other words, the flour industry was significantly

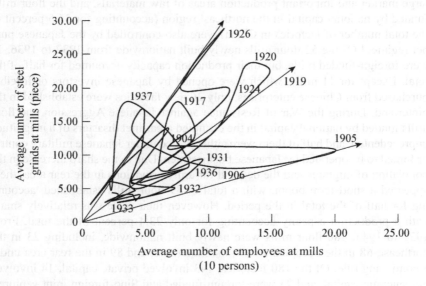

*Figure 9.4* Capital and labor input in the flour industry

Note: The unit for the number of workers on the horizontal axis is 10.

Data source: Institute of Economics Chinese Academy of Social Sciences, etc. (1966), pp. 32–35.

transformed around 1926. It changed from expansion to contraction, implying that fierce competition caused stagnation in the industry.

### 9.4.4 Machinery industry

Modern machinery technology has been introduced to China since the mid-19th century. In the early years, it was mainly introduced by bureaucratic capital. During the period of the Self-Strengthening Movement, military, shipbuilding, steel, and mine industries dominated, which all required the support of mechanical technology. It was inevitably accompanied by the construction of machinery repair factories of a certain size. As the industrial sector developed and technology became popular, private capital also began to be introduced, imitate existing technology, and gradually became the leading force. The development process of modern China's machinery industry can be divided into two periods: the introduction period and the pioneering period from the mid-19th century to 1912; and the formation period from 1912 to 1949. These two periods are characterized by the introduction and application of Western technology. Machines could be maintained and repaired locally, and some could be manufactured. Of course, it was imitation but not innovation. Nevertheless, from an economic viewpoint, this is still technological advance, whether through introduction or imitation, because it boosted productivity, strengthened China's technological level as a whole, and even led to a quantum leap.

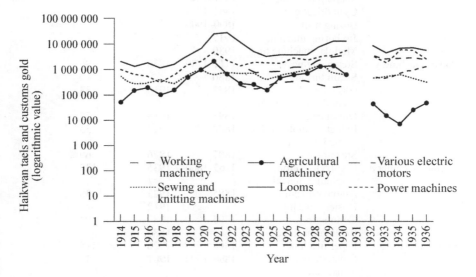

*Figure 9.5* Imports of various machinery and equipment nationwide

Note: Guanping taels from 1914 to 1931 and customs gold unit from 1932 to 1936.

Data source: Shanghai Municipal Administration for Industry and Commerce, Shanghai No. 1 Mechanical and Electrical Industry Bureau (1966).

## 206   *Conditions and causes*

Figure 9.5 shows the import of various machinery and equipment in China. The following two points can be observed. First, the changes shown are not obvious because of the logarithmic value, but there was some increase and an upward trend. Second, because the calculations are made in terms of money amounts, there are large differences for various types of machinery and equipment. However, it shows that the chief machinery and equipment, such as textile machinery, are prominent, which testifies to the demand of China's largest industry at that time. It was just due to the rapid development of this industry that more machinery and equipment were needed. As China could not manufacture these, they had to be imported.

Table 9.5 shows the years when various machinery and equipment began to be manufactured in foreign countries as well as the time of localization. Although the

*Table 9.5* Gaps between foreign products and domestic manufactured products

| Machine category | Name of machine | Start time abroad | Start time in Shanghai | Gap between domestic and foreign products |
|---|---|---|---|---|
| Working machinery | Lathe | 1797 | 1915 | 118 |
| | Planer | 1817 | 1925 | 108 |
| | Drill machine | 1817 | 1910 | 93 |
| | Milling machine | 1818 | 1918–1920 | 101 |
| | Universal milling machine | 1855 | 1930 | 75 |
| | Shaping machine | 1831–1840 | – | – |
| | Cylindrical grinder | 1864–1874 | – | – |
| | Boring mill | 1890–1900 | – | – |
| | Jig boring machine | 1917 | – | – |
| | Modular machine tool | 1930 | – | – |
| Power machinery | Steam engine | 1711–1780 | 1876 | 96 |
| | Steam turbine | 1880 | – | – |
| | Gas internal combustion engine | 1877 | 1910 | 33 |
| | Diesel engine | 1893 | 1918 | 25 |
| | Induction motor 1888 1923 35 years | 1888 | 1923 | 35 |
| | Steamboat | 1807 | 1876 | 69 |
| Textile machinery | Complete cotton spinning machine | 1765–1800 | 1935 | 135 |
| | Automatic loom | 1885 | 1923 | 38 |
| | Hosiery machine | – | 1912 | – |
| | Cotton gin | 1793 | 1887 | 94 |
| | Reeling machine | – | 1887–1890 | – |
| Light industry machinery | Paper machine | 1808 | 1926 | 118 |
| | Cigarette making machine | 1880–1890 | 1901 | 11 |
| | Printing press | – | 1900 | – |

*Note:* "–" means "not manufactured".

*Data source:* Shanghai Municipal Administration for Industry and Commerce, Shanghai No. 1 Mechanical and Electrical Industry Bureau (1966).

*Capital formation and technological progress* 207

data are not comprehensive and some equipment could not be produced domestically, some laws can be observed. The earlier the machinery and equipment were developed abroad, the later the time of localization. Equipment that was produced in foreign countries later was soon localized in China. This law was observed by the Japanese scholar Ryoshin Minami. He found that this law applied to power technology in the process of industrialization in Japan in modern times.[13] It shows a kind of late-mover advantage of latecomer countries in modern times. As industrialization advances, latecomer countries can imitate the technology of advanced countries. Because latecomer countries get off to a late start in industrialization, the equipment developed earlier in the West and the equipment developed later were exported to latecomer countries almost simultaneously. As latecomer countries industrialize, the imitated technology gradually matures. Although the equipment developed later may be more advanced and complex, the time taken for imitation can be shortened.

The table shows only the changes in some of China's industries and technology before 1949, and this is not direct evidence of technological progress. However, due to the constraints of data, it can only indirectly prove the following. First, China basically lacked its own innovative technologies in modern times but imported and purchased them from developed countries, including mechanical equipment and guidance service. It is an indirect manifestation of China's economic development and technological level in modern times. This is also the case for other developing countries. Second, although China was unable to manufacture and develop advanced technologies and equipment on its own, the technology introduced and products purchased could still promote an improvement in China's scientific and technological level and boost productivity and economic development. Third, by introducing and developing various industries to varying degrees, it laid a good foundation for subsequent industrialization and economic development. Some countries that are in a position and development stage like China are unable to achieve rapid economic development due to a lack of these technologies, such as most Southeast Asian, South Asian, West Asian, and African countries.

## 9.5 Conclusion

This chapter examined capital formation and technological advance, which are in large measure interconnected. Capital formation mainly refers to production equipment and infrastructure, which are underpinned by new technologies. Simply put, these are new products manufactured and new processes invented after the Industrial Revolution. These new technologies were mainly developed in Europe, and then diffused in other parts of the world. As a result of the influence of the Western powers in the mid-19th century, China and Japan were forced to open up to the outside world and join the world system. Then, given the different institutional progress and industrialization in the two countries, China lagged far behind Japan, as evidenced by this chapter through international comparison. However, China also made some strides. In addition to a few heavy industries and military industries,

## 208 *Conditions and causes*

some progress was also made in the light industry, laying a foundation for subsequent modern economic growth.

China had a weak economy and a system that lay in tatters before 1949 and was also invaded by foreign enemies. China made no real technological progress except for the introduction of some military technologies and civilian technologies. That is to say, China was basically stagnant technologically and could only fill some gaps by importing technology on a small scale. However, these technologies, which might be obsolete abroad, were new technologies for China that lagged far behind those of developed countries.

## Notes

1  Yan Zhongping et al. (1955), pp. 94–95.
2  Rawski (2009), p. 246.
3  For the method of estimation, see Xu Dixin and Wu Chengming (1990), Chapter 6.
4  National capital here refers to private capital other than government capital.
5  Rawski (2009), pp. 216–217.
6  For the system and role of patents in Japan, see Guan (2001) and Guan Quan (2003, 2018).
7  In 1912, the Ministry of Industry and Commerce of the Beiyang government issued the *Interim Regulations for Rewarding Handicrafts*, which were amended several times. However, this is simple regulation, not a patent law. For details, see Wang Jiafu and Xia Shuhua (1987).
8  According to statistics, from 1843 to 1875, there were 50 enterprises in modern times run by foreign investors in China. See Sun Yutang (1957) Volume I (1), p. 234.
9  See *History of Textile in Modern China* (volume 1).
10  When we discuss the industrial development in modern China, it is necessary to consider it together with Japan. For example, World War I mainly took place in Europe. Western European countries had no time for East Asian affairs, and this somewhat provided opportunities for development for both China and Japan. Some enterprises developed as a result. However, Chinese and Japanese companies competed with each other. Because Japan's economy developed earlier than China's, Japanese companies had the upper hand.
11  At that time, the flour industry in the northeast region was concentrated in Harbin.
12  These figures come from the Institute of Economics Chinese Academy of Social Sciences et al. (1966) and Shanghai Municipal Grain Bureau (1987).
13  See Minami (1987).

# 10 Role of government and finance

## 10.1 Introduction

Like many developing countries, China has made long-term exploration for institutional development, which can also be called a process of trial and error. Different from today's developed countries, China was a semicolonial and semifeudal society, indicating that it must start from scratch in all endeavors. Furthermore, modern China was disintegrated, and the people had no means to live, which aggravated the suffering and hardships. Some countries that were previously colonies only have the oral language without their own script and now still use English or other strong languages for communication due to the long-term rule of the big powers and colonizers, as well as due to their own history and culture and poor economic development. As a result, these countries and peoples lack self-esteem and self-confidence, so much so that it is difficult to concentrate national spirit and strength to develop the economy and achieve social progress. The institution building of these countries is either fully copied from (and sometimes imposed by) the developed Western countries or has retrograded to the traditional tribal state. The two cannot be integrated. For example, the upper classes of some developing countries were fostered by colonial-era suzerains. The upper classes living in a few prosperous cities speak foreign languages fluently, are well educated, and enjoy high positions and large incomes, whereas the vast majority of the populace live in traditional backward rural areas, lack enough food to eat, have no access to formal education, have no modern consciousness, and are accustomed to being ruled.[1]

The situation in China is slightly better. First, China has a long history and profound cultural traditions, which cannot be wholly negated by some aggressors, although some of China's traditions are not necessarily suited to modern society. Second, China did not become a colony of the Western powers. Moreover, China learned and integrated the modern (Western) spirit into the long-term struggle. Nevertheless, it must be acknowledged that many negative factors existed in China in modern times. First of all, the long-term feudal society resulted in practices that were contrary to modern ideas, such as resigning oneself to adversity, and there was a lack of the spirit of individuality and independence. Second, some people were at a loss when confronted with the powerful technological and military power of the Western powers and believed that they could not compete with the West. Two

DOI: 10.4324/9781003410386-13

## 210   *Conditions and causes*

extreme ideas also held in China at that time for various reasons: self-conceit and inferiority complex. How come China, a large country with a long history, lagged behind others in modern times? The Chinese people have long been puzzled by this problem. The Chinese went to great lengths to seek a path to rapid development and have also put in huge efforts and paid a price.

The fiscal and financial systems are also examined in this chapter. Fiscal policy serves the function of regulating income distribution and the macroeconomy. Fiscal policy has a longer history than many other economic activities because as long as there is a country, there is a government, and the government must have a fiscal system, including fiscal revenues and spending. Therefore, government funds must be used to regulate income distribution, such as taxing the rich more and the poor less, and using the tax collected from the rich to help the poor. The government operation itself needs money because it needs to employ public servants, make public spending, feed the armed forces, engage in diplomacy, provide education services, keep law and order, and have a certain amount of savings as a precaution. This is similar to a household. A household must have income and also make expenditures, and a portion of the income must be saved. Finance is mainly the result of Keynesian economics following the Great Depression of 1929. It means that it is necessary for the government to intervene appropriately in economic activities. The means of intervention are primarily fiscal and financial policies. When the economy is good, the government can reduce fiscal expenditures, indicating that the market may be overheated, and investment must be appropriately reduced. When the economic picture is bad, the government can support market activities by spending more, such as building public facilities to promote the production and distribution of various goods and also by creating jobs.

Financial policy has a similar effect. The government can regulate economic activity through the regulatory means of the central bank. When the economy improves, interest rates can be raised to check corporate loans in order to keep the economic performance stable. When the economy is bad, the central bank can lower interest rates, thus cutting the cost of corporate loans and stimulating economic activity. A common feature of the two is the use of funds and currency issues, unlike the activities of the real sector as discussed in other chapters, such as agriculture, industry, and service sectors. In terms of the use of funds, the funds belonging to the government are the fiscal responsibility of the government, including revenues and expenditures. Funds that belong to the market operate through financial institutions. There are both state-owned and private financial institutions. State-owned institutions are dominant in China, and this strengthens the link with the government.

## 10.2   Role of government

### *10.2.1   Early industries*

The situation of the industrial sector is discussed here. It should be said that the government played a role in industrial development in modern China. Especially before the Republic of China period, it was difficult for the people to invest in key industrial sectors due to a lack of funds, technology, and talents. Only the

Role of government and finance   211

government could engage in such activities. During the Meiji Restoration period, Japan adopted the same approach to tackle the same problem. However, given the bureaucratic style of the Qing government, the government mismanaged enterprises, and as a result, most enterprises had to be sold to the people. China and Japan faced the same problem in this regard.[2]

Table 10.1 shows the situation of factories set up by national capital during the period from the late Qing Dynasty to the Xinhai Revolution. In terms of quantity, the vast majority were enterprises operated by merchants (accounting for 80.4 percent of the total). There were few government-run or government–business joint enterprises, equivalent to only 15.8 percent and 12.7 percent, respectively. Sino-foreign joint ventures accounted for 8.6 percent of commercially operated enterprises and 6.9 percent of the total. Despite the small proportions, government-run enterprises or government–business joint ventures occupied an important position because these industries are important and large-scale. Moreover, government-run enterprises or government-business joint ventures had more capital than commercially operated factories by half. Sino-foreign joint venture factories also shared this characteristic. Moreover, many so-called businessmen in commercially operated factories were actually officials who went into business or invested in this capacity. Behind them was still the strong government.

The bureaucratic capital during the Beiyang government period mainly took over the Qing Dynasty's enterprises under the Self-Strengthening Movement but rarely established enterprises themselves. In terms of industry, most enterprises stagnated, except for Hanyeping Company and Jiangnan Shipyard, which developed somewhat. In terms of the military industry, they took over more than 10 machinery bureaus from the Qing government. Most of these did not develop normally due to the warlord dogfighting during this period. In the civilian industry, after the First Sino-Japanese War, a number of government-run or government–business joint enterprises were built, totaling more than 60. In terms of industry, there were electric power, papermaking, tobacco, matchsticks, and ceramics. There were also small factories, such as camphor factories, soap factories, rice mills, and printing factories. Although they were government-run, there was actually little bureaucratic capital. According to statistics, there were 29 factories in the civilian industry operated by bureaucratic capital during the Beiyang government period, with a total capital of 32 million yuan. They were small in scale. Except for public utilities, most of them were poorly managed, and some were even shut down. The same is true of the mining industry. Large mines were either merged by foreign capital or shut down.[3] Most of the government-run mines were small mines. During the Beiyang government period, over 20 new mines were established, mostly government–business joint enterprises. These were in a poor state of operations. According to statistics, there were 12 coal mines and 24 metal mines, with a total capital amount of 24 million yuan.[4]

### 10.2.2   Resource Committee

The relationship between the Resource Committee established during the Republic of China period and the state sector of the economy is discussed next. After

Table 10.1 Factories established by national capital in late Qing Dynasty

| Year | Total | | Commercially operated | | Government-run or government-business joint enterprises | | Sino-foreign joint ventures | |
|---|---|---|---|---|---|---|---|---|
| | Number of factories | Capital amount (10,000 yuan) | Number of factories | Capital amount (10,000 yuan) | Number of factories | Capital amount (10,000 yuan) | Number of factories | Capital amount (10,000 yuan) |
| 1872–1880 | 7 | 292.16 | 2 | 17.59 | 5 | 274.58 | – | |
| 1881–1890 | 38 | 1,254.3 | 28 | 171.5 | 9 | 1,019.86 | 1 | 62.94 |
| 1891–1900 | 111 | 3,487.54 | 92 | 1,933.56 | 13 | 765.39 | 6 | 788.6 |
| 1901–1911 | 340 | 10,185.25 | 277 | 6,042.84 | 39 | 2,317.84 | 24 | 1,824.58 |
| Date unknown | 25 | 746.22 | 20 | 689.76 | – | – | 5 | 56.46 |
| Total | 521 | 15,965.48 | 419 | 8,855.24 | 66 | 4,377.67 | 36 | 2,732.57 |

*Note:* The calculation results of individual capital amounts are different from those in the original text.

*Data source:* Yan Zhongping et al. (1955), p. 93.

*Role of government and finance* 213

the establishment of the Nationalist government in Nanjing in 1927, it gradually realized the importance of national capital in the economy. In 1928, the Ministry of Agriculture and Mining and the Ministry of Industry and Commerce were established. In 1930, the two were merged into the Ministry of Industry. In 1931, the National Economic Committee was established and tasked with planning and development. These institutions performed two main tasks. One was to selectively expand state-owned enterprises during the Beiyang government period. The other was to directly invest in and take over private enterprises and gradually strengthen national capital.

Significant events occurred in China and the world during this period. The Great Depression occurred, and Japan invaded and occupied Northeast China. In particular, the latter had a huge impact on the government at that time. On the one hand, the Nationalist government in Nanjing negotiated with Japan in the hope of curbing Japan's ambitions. On the other hand, it mobilized all forces to prepare for the War of Resistance against Japanese Aggression. In this context, the National Defense Design Committee was established in 1932 and was reorganized as the Resource Committee three years later. Although its affiliation changed several times, the name remained unchanged. Before 1937, there were 29 enterprises – primarily resource mines and modern factories – founded, co-operated, or managed by the Resource Committee.[5]

By 1937, 3,935 industrial and mining enterprises were registered with the Ministry of Industry under the Nationalist government in accordance with the Factory Law. Of these, 2,336 were distributed in Jiangsu, Shanghai, and Zhejiang in the middle and lower reaches of the Yangtze River, accounting for 56 percent of the total. Most of these belonged to the Resource Committee. After 1937, many enterprises began to move inland. In the early days of inland relocation, much equipment was relocated, which weighed 77,000 metric tons in 1938, 106,000 metric tons in 1939, and 116,400 metric tons in 1940.[6] During the War of Resistance against Japanese Aggression, the Nationalist government reshuffled its institutions and established the Ministry of Economy, to which the Resource Committee belonged. The Resource Committee had a broader scope of duties, including establishing and managing basic industries, developing and managing important mining enterprises, and establishing and developing the power business. The electric power industry was developed in the course of implementation. The generating capacity of power plants under its management increased from 1,533 kWh in 1937 to 17,301 kWh in 1941, and then to 70,136 kWh in 1945.[7] Coal output of coal mines under its management increased from 19,800 metric tons in 1937 to 517,500 metric tons in 1941, and then to 625,000 metric tons in 1945 (peaking at 760,000 metric tons in 1943). In the case of coke, it increased from 4,100 metric tons in 1938, to 39,700 metric tons in 1941, to 44,000 metric tons in 1945 (up from 70,000 metric tons in 1942).[8]

The Resource Committee was also responsible for the development of the petroleum industry. It established Yumen Oil Mine, took over Dushanzi Oil Mine in Xinjiang, and founded Sichuan Oil Mine. The petroleum products produced by its affiliated petroleum enterprises increased year by year. Gasoline output was merely 4,000 gallons in 1939 but increased to 1,896,000 gallons in 1942 and to

214    *Conditions and causes*

4,305,000 gallons in 1945. Kerosene output increased from 4,000 gallons in 1939 to 2,654,000 gallons in 1945. The diesel output increased from 7,000 gallons to 300,000 gallons. The natural gas output increased from 27,000 cubic meters in 1941 to 237,000 cubic meters in 1945.[9] Other important industries founded and administered by the Resource Committee include steel, machine manufacturing, etc. The iron ore output increased from 0.63 metric tons in 1937 to 47,700 metric tons in 1940, peaked at 80,700 metric tons in 1942, and decreased to 42,600 metric tons in 1945. Pig iron output increased from 2,500 metric tons in 1940 to 13,500 metric tons in 1942 and to 22,600 metric tons in 1945. Steel output increased from 116 metric tons in 1941 to 4,646 metric tons in 1943, to 7,603 metric tons in 1944, and to 10,200 metric tons in 1945.[10] In terms of machinery production, the horsepower of power engines increased from 706 hp in 1940 to 1,258 hp in 1943, and then as high as 2,205 hp in 1944. The number of tool machines increased from 122 in 1940 to 279 in 1943. The number of operating machines increased from 83 in 1940 to 259 in 1944.[11]

Table 10.2 shows the output of heavy industry products operated by the Resource Committee from 1938 to 1946 as well as their proportions of the total. The output of about half of the products accounted for almost 100 percent of the total, especially resource-based products such as gasoline, kerosene, diesel, and natural gas. Steel and iron sand also accounted for a high proportion. This shows the monopoly of the state departments over resources and the heavy industry and also reflects the special nature of the war system.

Moreover, other departments of the Nationalist government invested in or operated many enterprises. The construction of a munitions factory in the military industry system includes equipment of Hanyang Arsenal relocated to Chongqing, Gongxian Arsenal in Henan province relocated to Lanzhou in Gansu province, Guangdong Arsenal relocated to Binyang in Guangxi and Kunming in Yunnan province, in addition to the establishment of arsenals in the cities of Xi'an, Chengdu, and Liuzhou. Also, many industrial enterprises were under the management of the Ministry of Transport, including Central Auto Parts Manufacturing Plant, Liujiang Machine Factory, Quanzhou Machine Factory, Guilin Equipment Repair Factory, and Guilin Machine Factory. These enterprises employed a total number of 5,400 people in 1942.[12] In addition to the enterprises managed by the Resource Committee, the Ministry of Economy also had self-run enterprises and invested in enterprises operated by other institutions and local governments. From 1938 to 1945, these investments totaled 409 million yuan, including an investment of 320 million yuan in private enterprises. For example, Central Electrical Appliance Factory's number of employees rose from 487 in 1938 to 4,015 in 1944; its production output index (1939 = 100) was 27 in 1938, peaked at 351.7 in 1943, and was 297.5 in 1945. The turnover index rose from 29 in 1938, peaked at 365 in 1944, and was 328 in 1945.[13]

According to the research conducted by Zheng Youkui et al. from 1939 to 1945, the number of employees in the industries under the jurisdiction of the Resource Committee increased from 10,700 year by year, reaching 63,700 in 1945 and peaking at 69,700 (1943). Of these, the number of coal mine employees was the largest,

Table 10.2 Output of heavy industrial products operated by the Resource Committee

| Year | Coal (1,000 metric tons) | Electricity (100 million kWh) | Iron sand (10,000 metric tons) | Pig iron (1,000 metric tons) | Steel (1,000 metric tons) | Gasoline (10,000 gallons) | Kerosene (10,000 gallons) |
|---|---|---|---|---|---|---|---|
| 1938 | 504 (10.7) | 0.4 (5.5) | 3.5 (63.6) | 2.5 (5.5) | 0.1 (5.8) | 0.4 (100.0) | 0.4 (10.0) |
| 1939 | 192 (3.5) | 1.0 (10.5) | 4.2 (64.0) | 4.4 (7.0) | 1.5 (50.2) | 7.4 (100.0) | 3.2 (100.0) |
| 1940 | 306 (5.4) | 1.1 (9.9) | 2.7 (70.7) | 13.5 (14.0) | 4.7 (68.3) | 20.9 (100.0) | 11.3 (100.0) |
| 1941 | 517 (8.6) | 1.8 (13.8) | 5.5 (77.1) | 20.9 (29.8) | 7.6 (56.9) | 189.6 (100.0) | 59.7 (100.0) |
| 1942 | 746 (11.8) | 2.5 (18.0) | 5.1 (82.6) | 12.5 (31.2) | 10.2 (56.0) | 303.7 (100.0) | 55.9 (100.0) |
| 1943 | 758 (11.5) | 3.5 (24.0) | 3.5 ( ) | 22.6 (46.5) | 7.05 (48.0) | 404.8 (100.0) | 215.8 (100.0) |
| 1944 | 753 (13.7) | 5.2 (33.8) | 4.3 ( ) | 1.3 (4.3) | | 430.5 (100.0) | 165.4 (100.0) |
| 1945 | 625 (11.9) | 7.1 (35.9) | 1.5 ( ) | | | 505.8 (100.0) | 230.4 (100.0) |
| 1946 | 2197 (12.1) | 214.6 (59.2) | | | | | |

| Year | Diesel (10,000 gallons) | Natural gas (10,000 cubic meters) | Tungsten ore (1,000 metric tons) | Antimony (1,000 metric tons) | Tin (1,000 metric tons) | Mercury (metric ton) |
|---|---|---|---|---|---|---|
| 1938 | 0.7 (100.0) | 2.7 (100.0) | 12.6 (100.0) | 9.5 (100.0) | 1.8 (10.00) | 169 (100.00) |
| 1939 | 6.2 (100.0) | 23.3 (100.0) | 11.5 (100.0) | 12.0 (100.0) | 16.5 (100.0) | 91 (100.0) |
| 1940 | 14.1 (100.0) | 26.7 (100.0) | 9.5 (100.0) | 8.5 (100.0) | 7.0 (100.0) | 120 (100.0) |
| 1941 | 5.3 (100.0) | 27.3 (100.0) | 12.4 (100.0) | 8.0 (100.0) | 8.0 (100.0) | 163 (100.0) |
| 1942 | 2.9 (100.0) | 23.7 (100.0) | 11.9 (100.0) | 3.5 (100.0) | 3.8 (100.0) | 122 (100.0) |
| 1943 | 15.5 (100.0) | 6109.8 (100.0) | 8.7 (100.0) | 0.4 (100.0) | 5.1 (100.0) | 121 (100.0) |
| 1944 | 27.0 (100.0) | | 3.2 (100.0) | 0.2 (100.0) | 2.7 (100.0) | 63 (100.0) |
| 1945 | 38.1 (100.0) | | 2.3 (100.0) | 0.4 (100.0) | 2.0 (100.0) | 28 (100.0) |
| 1946 | | | | | | |

Note: The figures in parentheses refer to the proportion of the output by the Resource Committee in Kuomintang-ruled areas.

Data source: Yan Zhongping et al. (1955), pp. 157–158.

216   *Conditions and causes*

reaching 11,500 in 1940, 21,200 in 1941, 17,900 in 1942, 20,700 in 1943, 14,100 in 1977, and 16,100 in 1945. It accounted for about 25 percent of the total number of employees, peaking at 41 percent. This shows the labor-intensive nature of this industry. Although many coal mines during this period introduced much production equipment for mechanized mining, more workers were needed in general. It was followed by the number of steel workers, which was only 330 in 1939, increased to 11,200 in 1942, which basically remained the same since then, and then rose to 13,600 in 1945. It accounted for about 16 to 19 percent. The third is the metal industry, which had only 3,866 workers (1939) but peaked at 11,200, with an average of 6,000 to 8,000 people, accounting for 10 to 19 percent of the total. The fourth is the oil industry, which had only 4,158 workers in 1941 but 10,000 in 1944. The number mostly ranged from 7,000 to 9,000 people, accounting for 10 to 17 percent of the total. The fifth is the electrician industry, and the number of employees increased from 1,410 in 1939 to 7,153 in 1943. It was mostly between 4,000 and 7,000, accounting for less than 10 percent of the total. Other industries such as machinery, electricity, and chemicals were nearly the same, with the number of employees increasing from a few hundreds to 3,000–4,000.[14] In short, these industries played an irreplaceable role during the War of Resistance against Japanese Aggression. Even in capitalist countries, these important industries were directly managed by the government or even the military during a war.[15]

Table 10.3 shows the industrial production indexes in the rear area from 1938 to 1945. As the overall index shows, industrial production in this period grew rapidly (the index in 1945 was about 3 times that of 1938). This mainly took place in the period 1938–1942, after which it grew very slowly, as can be seen from the growth rates in the table. Specifically, there was still a large difference between public

*Table 10.3* Industrial production index in the rear area from 1938 to 1945

| Year | Total production index compiled by the Ministry of Economy | Production value index | | |
|---|---|---|---|---|
| | | *Total* | *Public enterprises* | *Private enterprises* |
| 1938 | 100.0 | 100.0 | 100.0 | 100.0 |
| 1939 | 130.6 | 116.1 | 129.1 | 112.6 |
| 1940 | 185.9 | 144.5 | 188.9 | 132.6 |
| 1941 | 243.0 | 191.7 | 325.2 | 155.9 |
| 1942 | 302.2 | 213.4 | 433.7 | 154.3 |
| 1943 | 375.6 | 204.2 | 477.6 | 130.7 |
| 1944 | 351.6 | 184.0 | 467.1 | 108.0 |
| 1945 | 316.8 | 166.5 | 405.6 | 102.4 |
| *Annual growth rate (%)* | | | | |
| 1938–1942 | 31.8 | 20.9 | 44.3 | 11.4 |
| 1942–1945 | 1.6 | −7.9 | −0.2 | −12.8 |
| 1938–1945 | 17.9 | 7.6 | 22.1 | 0.3 |

*Data source:* Xu Dixin and Wu Chengming (volume 3) (1993), p. 547.

*Role of government and finance* 217

enterprises and private enterprises. Public enterprises had a far higher growth rate than private enterprises. Public enterprises increased by about 3 times, while private enterprises remained almost stagnant. Of course, from 1938 to 1942, private enterprises also grew significantly but were stagnant as a whole or even retrograded for a time. Public enterprises were no exception. After 1942, both private and public enterprises showed a downward trend, although the two calculations were not exactly the same. As for the reasons for the decline of private enterprises, Xu Dixin, Wu Chengming, etc. believe that it was caused by hyperinflation, monopolies on material resources, and the appropriation of national capital. It can be said that it was caused by the national capital.[16]

## 10.3   Fiscal system and policies

This section mainly discusses the fiscal issue during the Republic of China period from 1912 to 1949 and only indirectly covers the fiscal system in some years in the late Qing Dynasty. The fiscal system for the Republic of China period can be discussed separately for two periods: the Beiyang government and the Nationalist government. The period of the Nationalist government can be subdivided into three periods: 1927–1936, 1937–1945, and 1946–1949. These periods have their respective characteristics, as well as common denominators. All of these periods suffered financial strain, difficulties in tax collection, and persistently high foreign debt. It can be inferred that China's fiscal situation remained dire from the late Qing Dynasty to 1949. Fundamentally, there are only two reasons. First, China as a whole was poor and weak, bullied by the great powers. It lost its autonomous right in some areas. Frequent wars and countless war indemnities in the period from the late Qing Dynasty to the Republic of China period aggravated the poor and backward country. Second, China remained in a traditional and backward state for a long time without starting modern economic growth. There were no modern industrial and service sectors, while the traditional small-scale peasant economy could hardly support rising tax pressure. However, the fiscal system in the Republic of China period also played a positive role. It is the prelude to the establishment of a modern fiscal system and also a kind of innovation under highly unfavorable circumstances. For example, reorganizing feudal land tax, implementing a new taxation system, striving for customs duty sovereignty, distinguishing the central and local government revenues and expenditures, creating procedures for fiscal budgets and final accounts, and creating a fiscal supervision system all accumulated experience for China to modernize its fiscal system.

Table 10.4 shows the fiscal situation during the Beiyang government period. The revenue minus government loans and borrowings was 334 million yuan in 1913, 432 million yuan in 1916, and 439 million yuan in 1919. If the budget revenue is subdivided, it mainly includes the feudal land tax for land and population as well as tribute rice, which account for 20 to 25 percent, and the excise tax which accounts for about 10 percent. The two together account for 30 to 35 percent. These two types of taxes, which exceeded 100 million yuan a year, were often withheld by local warlords rather than handed over to the central government.

## 218  Conditions and causes

*Table 10.4* Fiscal revenue and expenditure of the Beiyang government

*Revenue and expenditures*

| Year | Total expenditures | | Total revenue minus government loans and borrowings (million yuan) | Budget profit and loss | |
|---|---|---|---|---|---|
| | Amount (million yuan) | Index | | Amount (million yuan) | Proportion in total expenditure (%) |
| 1913 | 642.2 | – | 333.9 | −308.3 | 48.0 |
| 1914 | 357.0 | 100 | 357.4 | 0.4 | 0.1 |
| 1916 | 472.8 | 132 | 432.3 | −40.5 | 9.0 |
| 1919 | 495.8 | 138 | 439.5 | −56.3 | 11.0 |
| 1925 | 634.4 | 178 | 461.6 | −172.8 | 27.0 |

*Revenue budget as well as feudal land tax, and commodity tax*

| Year | Total revenue minus government loans and borrowings (million yuan) | Feudal land tax | | Commodity tax | |
|---|---|---|---|---|---|
| | | Amount (million yuan) | Proportion in the revenue (%) | Amount (million yuan) | Proportion in the revenue (%) |
| 1913 | 333.9 | 82.4 | 25 | 32.7 | 10 |
| 1914 | 357.4 | 79.2 | 22 | 34.2 | 10 |
| 1916 | 432.3 | 95.9 | 22 | 42.7 | 10 |
| 1919 | 439.5 | 90.5 | 21 | 39.3 | 9 |
| 1925 | 461.6 | 90.1 | 20 | 45.7 | 10 |

*Data source:* Yang Yinpu (1985), pp. 3–5.

Another key issue was the warlord dogfighting during the Beiyang government period. According to statistics, up to 179 wars erupted in the 11 years from 1912 to 1922, which seriously affected the government's fiscal expenditures and fiscal revenue. Due to frequent wars, there was neither stable economic growth nor an increase in tax revenues. From 1913 to 1925, military spending was 173 million yuan in 1913, 142 million yuan in 1914, 176 million yuan in 1916, 217 million yuan in 1919, and 298 million yuan in 1925, respectively. Its proportion in government expenditure increased from 27 to 47 percent. At the same time, the government had to make borrowings, with a loan fee of 99 million to 300 million yuan, which accounted for about 46 percent in the early stage but then fell to 26 percent later.[17]

As the government was in the red, the Beiyang government had no choice but to borrow heavily, particularly foreign debts. The total external loans taken out during the period (1912–1926) reached 991 million yuan, and it peaked at 332 million yuan in 1913 alone. Regarding the purposes of external loans, fiscal and financial expenditures accounted for 42 percent, ordnance and soldier's pay and provisions accounted for 31 percent, and principal and interest on external loans accounted

*Role of government and finance* 219

for 27 percent. In addition to external loans, the Beiyang government also took out internal loans. During this period, up to 28 kinds of public bonds were issued, with a value of 620 million yuan. Coupled with short-term treasury securities, lottery bonds, etc. (totaling 88 kinds, with a value of 100 million yuan), it totaled 723 million yuan.[18]

Since the Beiyang government often suffered fiscal deficit, the practice of taking out new loans to repay mature debts became a prominent feature. During this period, a total of 78 loans were taken out to repay mature debts. The cumulative debts reached 430 million silver dollars, accounting for 27.67 percent or nearly one-third of the debts during the Beiyang government period. It peaked at 83.48 percent (1922) and was above 20 percent in most years – reaching 66.28 percent in 1925 and 52.66 percent in 1924.[19]

Next, we discuss the situation of about 10 years from the establishment of the Nationalist government in 1927 to 1936. This period shows the following characteristics. First, the fiscal revenue and expenditure expanded, and the deficit increased. Second, the tax burden became heavier, and, in particular, tariffs, salt taxes, and the consolidated tax occupied an important position. Third, the number of public bonds issued increased. Fourth, military spending and debt costs accounted for a high proportion. Fifth, the currency system was reformed, and legal tender was issued. According to Yang Yinpu (1985), the actual fiscal expenditure was 151 million yuan in 1927, 714 million yuan in 1930, 769 million yuan in 1933, and 1.894 billion yuan in 1936. The actual revenue in these years was 77 million yuan, 498 million yuan, 622 million yuan, and 1.293 billion yuan, respectively. As a result, the government had a fiscal deficit, with a deficit of 74 million yuan, 317 million yuan, 147 million yuan, and 601 million yuan. This shows a highly serious fiscal problem.[20]

An important issue similar to that in previous periods is that military spending and debt costs remained high. Military spending accounted for 45.9 percent of actual expenditure for a long time, peaking at 87 percent in individual years (1927), but was low in 1934–1936. That is to say, society was relatively stable in these years. The debt fees changed, accounting for about 29 percent, which was not low. It was close to one-third for a long time. The two together accounted for 75 percent, which shows how the government's fiscal expenditure was used.[21]

In the period from the full outbreak of the War of Resistance against Japanese Aggression in 1937 to China's victory in 1945, huge military spending was required. Military spending inevitably caused massive waste. Moreover, the war played havoc with economic activities. As a result, production ground to a halt, and people lived in hardship. In this situation, it was difficult to increase taxes unless a mandatory method was adopted. Whether this approach would work was unknown. The data on the financial situation in this period are roughly as follows. The total expenditure was 2.091 billion yuan in 1937, 2.797 billion yuan in 1939, 10.003 billion yuan in 1941, 58.816 billion yuan in 1943, and 1,215.089 billion yuan in 1945. The actual revenue was 559 million yuan, 715 million yuan, 1.184 billion

220    *Conditions and causes*

yuan, 16.517 billion yuan, and 150.065 billion yuan, respectively. The fiscal deficit was 1.532 billion yuan, 2.082 billion yuan, 8.819 billion yuan, 42.299 billion yuan, and 1,065.024 billion yuan, respectively.[22] On the whole, total expenditures shot up as the war progressed, but revenues could not cover expenditures. As a result, the fiscal deficit increased sharply. Except for a slight decline in 1938, the fiscal deficit accounted for 71 to 89 percent of total expenditure every year. It shows that the government had a fiscal deficit during this period.

The fiscal revenue in this period was mainly obtained from tax revenue, but it was even insufficient. We studied the ratios of tax revenue to total revenue and actual revenue. Although the proportion of tax revenue to total revenue changed a lot, it was basically below 20 percent and even fell to about 5 percent in some years. However, the total revenue includes many bank advances and borrowings. Therefore, this is not the real picture. We must look at the proportion of taxes to actual revenue. This ratio differed greatly from what was just described. Except in 1940, it exceeded 50 percent, and even exceeded 80 percent in some years. This shows that the tax revenue in the fiscal revenue in this period was woefully inadequate.[23] Of course, this situation is easy to understand. Because of the full outbreak and persistence of the war, a vast swathe of territory was occupied, production stagnated, and factories were relocated or shut down. Even if there was production, the products were generally military supplies rather than civilian goods. Because the areas that the government could administer and control were limited, it was certainly difficult to increase taxes. Despite the fact that the government racked its brains over increasing taxes and that in fact taxes were increased significantly, it was still difficult to cover the widening deficit. Regarding revenue items, bank advances accounted for an average of over 80 percent, while revenue from other sources was small. On average, tax revenue accounted for less than 10 percent, borrowings less than 5 percent, and others less than 5 percent, indicating that the fiscal revenue during this period was basically covered by bank loans.[24]

The period from 1946 to 1949 is characterized by the Chinese Civil War. Despite the brief period of fewer than 4 years, the fiscal system was unsound or even crashed because of the state of war, as evidenced by the soaring prices in the later period. Due to the outbreak of the civil war, the fiscal situation of the Nationalist government further deteriorated. The fiscal deficit was dire due to the limited fiscal revenues, as confirmed by Table 10.5. Regardless of the estimation methods, the deficit accounted for over 60 percent of the annual expenditure or even over 75 percent in some years. In addition, based on the comparison of budget and actual expenditure, it can be seen that the budget was actually of little significance. For example, the budget in 1946 was 2,524.9 billion yuan under the legal tender system (which applies to all these data), and the actual expenditure was 7,196.9 billion yuan; the budget in 1947 was 9,370.4 billion yuan, and the actual expenditure was 40,910 billion yuan; in the first half of 1948, the budget was 96,276.6 billion yuan, and the actual expenditure was 340,000 billion yuan. The actual expenditure exceeded the budget by 1.8 times, 3.4 times, and 2.5 times, respectively.[25]

*Role of government and finance* 221

*Table 10.5* Actual fiscal revenue and expenditure from 1946 to 1948

| Year | Annual expenditure (100 million legal tender yuan) | Annual revenue (100 million legal tender yuan) | Deficit (100 million legal tender yuan) | Ratio of deficit to annual expenditure (%) |
|---|---|---|---|---|
| **Minister of Finance estimate** | | | | |
| 1946 | 55,672 | 12,791 | 42,881 | 77.0 |
| 1947 | 40,000 | 13,000 | 27,000 | 62.5 |
| 1948 (Jan.–Mar.) | 501,709 | 197,043 | 304,666 | 60.9 |
| **Estimate by the president of central bank** | | | | |
| 1946 | 75,748 | 2,870 | 46,978 | 62.1 |
| 1947 | 433,939 | 146,064 | 293,295 | 67.6 |
| 1948 Jan.-Jul. | 6,554,711 | 2,209,055 | 4,345,656 | 66.3 |
| **Estimates by newspapers and magazines** | | | | |
| 1946 | 71,969 | 21,519 | 50,450 | 70.2 |
| 1947 | 409,100 | 12,010 | 28,900 | 70.7 |
| 1948 (first half of the year) | 3,400,000 | 800,000 | 2,600,000 | 76.5 |

*Data source:* Yang Yinpu (1985), pp. 171–172.

## 10.4 Financial system and policies

### 10.4.1 Evolution of financial institutions

Financial institutions in modern China first emerged at the end of the 19th century. From 1897 when the first bank was established to 1911, 20 banks had been established, but most of them disappeared before the Republic of China period. The Beiyang government period was the period when the banking industry rose. From 1912 to 1927, as many as 313 banks were established, with an aggregate capital of over 200 million yuan. Banks were mostly established after World War I. In 1920, there were 103 banks with a total capital of 88.08 million yuan. In 1925, there were 158 banks with a total capital of 169 million yuan.[26] According to statistics, a total of 306 Chinese-funded commercial banks were established (with a capital of 176.713 million yuan) during the Beiyang government period, including 37 government-run banks (with a capital of 45.24 million yuan), 11 jointly run by government and business (with a capital of 12.093 million yuan), and 249 commercially run banks (with a capital of 117.78 million yuan). Commercially run banks accounted for 81.9 percent, and the capital amount accounted for 62.6 percent, indicating that commercially run banks had a large share, especially in terms of the number of banks. It also indicates the small scale of commercially run banks. Of course, changes also occurred during this period. There were many banks but low capital in some years, such as 1924. There were few banks but high capital in other

## 222 Conditions and causes

years, such as 1927.[27] In any case, this period saw the rise of China's banking industry. Despite significant changes, it mirrored major changes in the financial field. In the early days of economic development, the banking industry often expanded easily, but banks were often short-lived. It is a period without regular rules. In this sense, it is highly similar to the banking industry in Japan after the Meiji Restoration, when the Japanese banking industry was also in chaos at the time. After the elimination of banks that performed the worst, good banks survived.[28] According to statistics, 16 banks were established in 1928, 11 in 1929, 18 in 1930, 16 in 1931, 13 in 1932, 15 in 1933, 22 in 1934, 18 in 1935, 5 in 1936, and 3 in 1937, with 50 banks established in unknown years.[29] Although the two types of statistics do not correspond, we can see that the establishment of banks in China in the Republic of China period had two climaxes: one is in the 1917–1925 period, and the other is in the 1928–1935 period.

During the Beiyang government period, there were three Chinese-funded banks in southern China and 4 in northern China. This was of positive significance for the development of China's banking industry. The many small and medium-sized banks did not have the effect of economies of scale or the advantages to compete with foreign banks and old-style Chinese private banks. An appropriate scale and good reputation are the basis for the development of the banking industry. The emergence of these well performing banks is clearly of positive significance.

After the Nationalist government was established in Nanjing in 1927, China's economy changed in various respects, and the financial industry was no exception. First, the central bank was established shortly thereafter. Second, monopoly gradually deepened, and a "four lines and two bureaus" system was established. Finally, it was the unification of currency, or the issuance of legal tender. When the Nationalist government in Nanjing was established, it confronted a host of difficulties in the political, military, economic, and other fields. In terms of finance, in 1925, the annual revenue was 462 million yuan, the annual expenditure was 634 million yuan, and the deficit rate was 27 percent.[30] The currency system was huge and jumbled, and the financial industry was in a mess. The government nominally implemented the silver standard system, but in fact taels and silver dollars circulated simultaneously. The paper money in circulation included that issued by both domestic banks and foreign banks, as well as that issued by commercial banks and local banks. Separate currency regimes were even set up in Sichuan, Yunnan, Guangxi, Shanxi, the northeast region, and other regions.

The Central Bank was established in 1928 after a period of preparation. Since then, China's financial system gradually centered on the central bank, with the Bank of China and the Bank of Communications as the pillars. Coupled with the Farmer Bank of China and the Central Trust of China, established in 1935, and the reorganized Postal Savings and Remittance Bureau, China established a financial system with "four banks and two bureaus" by relying on government power. After several years of operation, the business volume of the central bank increased significantly. Its deposit balance increased from 91 million yuan in 1931 to 273 million yuan in 1934; the loan balance increased from 98 million yuan to 167 million yuan; and the value of banknote issued increased from 25 million yuan to 86 million yuan.[31] In

*Role of government and finance* 223

1936, it further developed, with deposits of 714 million yuan, loans of 478 million yuan, and issued banknotes of 340 million yuan.[32] As a result of the aforesaid institutional changes, the deposit balance of 164 banks nationwide in 1936 was 4.551 billion yuan. Of this, the central bank, the Bank of China, the Bank of Communications, and the Farmer Bank of China had a total deposit balance of 2.676 billion yuan, the 7 banks including "top three in southern China" and "top four in northern China" had a total deposit balance of 818 million yuan, and the other 153 commercial banks and provincial banks had a total deposit balance of 1.057 billion yuan, which accounted for 58.8 percent, 18 percent, and 23.2 percent, respectively. All commercial banks had a total deposit balance of 1.875 billion yuan, and the ratio of all commercial banks to the four state-owned banks was 41.2:58.8, which narrowed to less than 1:10 after the War of Resistance against Japanese Aggression.[33]

For the currency reform, the silver standard system in 1935 was abandoned in favor of a legal tender system based on the exchange standard. In other words, legal tender was issued, and paper currency policy was implemented. This reform had a huge impact, notably as evidenced by the abandonment of the centuries-old silver dollars in favor of paper currency. People had to adapt to this practice. It brought a host of problems in the process of implementation. Any currency reform meets with complex problems, but this reform was successful. Due to the low ratio, the shares in circulation increased, monetary tightening was reversed, and the finance industry stabilized. The year 1936 saw the best performance of China's economy during the Republic of China period. After the outbreak of the War of Resistance against Japanese Aggression, China's economy was dealt an unprecedented blow, with disrupted industrial and agricultural production and large-scale relocation of factories to the hinterland. Half of the market was occupied by the Japanese army. We see a pattern of the Kuomintang-ruled areas and the occupied areas and the financial system lying in tatters. Nevertheless, inspired by the nationwide efforts to fight the Japanese aggressors, the financial industry formed a united front force featuring the four state-owned banks and ensured the normal operation of finance.

Table 10.6 shows the deposits and loans of the state-owned banks, commercial banks, and provincial banks during the period 1937–1945.[34] There was a significant increase in both deposits and loans, particularly after 1941. Despite the tendency toward inflation after 1942, deposits and loans generally increased. In particular, the proportion of the state-owned banks increased considerably, and this can be regarded as the formation of an absolute monopoly. At the same time, the status of commercial banks and provincial banks declined. This is understandable if the war is taken into account, but it resulted in monopoly and inefficiency in peacetime.

Figure 10.1 shows the changes in the actual number of new-style banks and Shanghai old-style Chinese private banks in the early 20th century. Old-style Chinese private banks maintained a good momentum of development despite both new establishments and shutdowns, but the changes are very obvious.[35] With 1912 and 1941 as the dividing lines, there were three stages, or two major fluctuations. In the early 10 years in the early 20th century, there was a pattern of up and down. After 1912, there was an upward trend until around 1925. It began to decline thereafter

## 224  Conditions and causes

*Table 10.6* Deposits and loans of banks of various types from 1937 to 1945

| Year | Deposit/loan (100 million legal tender) | State-owned bank Balance (100 million legal tender) | Proportion (%) | Commercial banks and provincial banks Balance (100 million legal tender) | Proportion (%) |
|---|---|---|---|---|---|
| **Deposits** | | | | | |
| 1937 | 33.09 | 21.91 | 66.3 | 11.15 | 33.7 |
| 1939 | 60.59 | 46.26 | 76.3 | 14.33 | 23.7 |
| 1941 | 138.15 | 109.32 | 79.1 | 28.33 | 20.9 |
| 1943 | 357.45 | 310.89 | 87.0 | 46.56 | 13.0 |
| 1945 | 5379.12 | 5271.72 | 98.0 | 107.40 | 2.0 |
| **Loans** | | | | | |
| 1937 | 22.20 | 14.71 | 66.3 | 7.49 | 33.7 |
| 1939 | 35.92 | 25.78 | 71.8 | 10.14 | 28.2 |
| 1941 | 51.24 | 30.95 | 60.4 | 20.29 | 39.6 |
| 1943 | 210.90 | 159.50 | 75.6 | 51.40 | 24.4 |
| 1945 | 1,673.43 | 1,511.42 | 90.3 | 162.01 | 9.7 |

*Data source:* Hong Jiaguan (2008), pp. 411, 419.

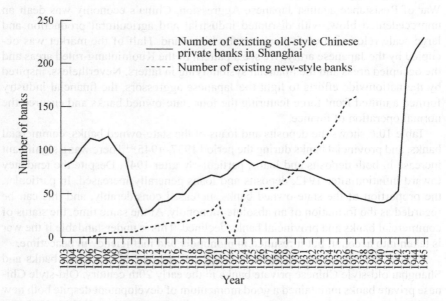

*Figure 10.1* Changes in the actual number of new-style banks and Shanghai old-style Chinese private banks

*Data source:* Xu Dixin and Wu Chengming (volume 2) (1990), p. 698; Sun Jianhua (2008) pp. 465–466, 599.

*Role of government and finance* 225

but began to rise explosively after 1941. It can be said that the changes after 1912 were largely caused by the development of modern banks. While old-style Chinese private banks did not see an obvious decline and even saw expansion in some years, which show diversity in China's economic development in this period, they were at a disadvantage amid competition. On the one hand, modern large enterprises and large capital needed the support of modern banks. On the other hand, traditional SMEs and local economies needed the assistance of traditional financial industry. The two resulted in a pattern of China's financial industry, which also reflected the trend of a dual structure in the economy during this period.

Regarding the banks, except for an obvious decline in 1922–1923, the number of banks basically rose all the way. It started from scratch and then enjoyed a momentum of great development. In terms of the actual number, banks outdid old-style Chinese private banks around 1930. Thereafter, new-style banks expanded tremendously, while old-style Chinese private banks began to go downhill. If we consider that banks have more capital and more advanced means of operation, this trend of development and decline is easier to understand.

### 10.4.2  Money supply and demand

Table 10.7 shows China's amount of currency in circulation in the first half of the 20th century, including the quantity of various currencies, as well as the total figures. Since China implemented the silver standard system before 1936, silver coins accounted for a large proportion, far more than other types of currency. It was followed by copper coins, especially in the early days. Copper coins also accounted for a high proportion, but as paper money was issued and circulated on a large scale, copper coins began to be taken out of circulation, and the aggregate quantity also decreased. The paper money that replaced copper coins rose fast, replacing copper coins as the second largest currency type from 1930 onward and accounting for about half of silver coins in 1936.

*Table 10.7* Money in circulation, Unit: million yuan

| Year | Total | Silver coins | Copper coins | Paper money | | | | |
|------|-------|--------------|--------------|-------------------|----------------|--------------------------|------------------------------------------|----------------------------------|
| | | | | Domestic banks | Foreign banks | Government-owned banks | Pseudo-Manchukuo's central bank | Banks in areas occupied by Japan |
| 1901 | 2,042.3 | 1,600.7 | 425.0 | 8.9 | 7.7 | – | – | – |
| 1910 | 1,933.6 | 1,517.2 | 375.8 | 24.9 | 15.8 | – | – | – |
| 1920 | 2,062.8 | 1,651.8 | 321.1 | 52.2 | 37.7 | – | – | – |
| 1930 | 2,701.7 | 2,162.9 | 266.4 | 206.5 | 66.0 | – | – | – |
| 1936 | 2947.7 | 1,737.8 | 233.6 | 790.7 | 85.9 | – | 99.7 | – |
| 1937 | 3,094.5 | – | – | – | – | 1,639.0 | 313.6 | 13.0 |
| 1940 | 12,683.7 | – | – | – | – | 7,935.0 | 3,940.7 | 808.0 |
| 1945 | 7,700,100.0 | – | – | – | – | 1,031,900.0 | 3,834,766.0 | 2,833,434.0 |
| 1948 | 663,694,600.0 | – | – | – | – | 663,694,600.0 | – | – |

*Data source:* Ryoshin Minami and Makino Fumio (2014), p. 386.

## 226  Conditions and causes

Quantitatively, the amount of silver coins in circulation did not increase much but increased only somewhat in one period, mainly from the late 1920s to early 1930s. As a result, the total amount of money in circulation in China did not increase much for a long time. There was virtually no increase from 1901 to 1920 and a gradual increase thereafter. This proves in a way that China's economic development during this period was slow. It began to pick up speed in the late 1920s. During the Nationalist Government in Nanjing period, it grew obviously, as mainly reflected in the growth of paper money. After 1937, inflation occurred due to the full outbreak of the War of Resistance against Japanese Aggression, and this inflation became increasingly rampant. After the end of the War in 1945, it further deteriorated. Hyperinflation occurred in 1948. It is noteworthy that after Japan's invasion of China, the amount of money in circulation ballooned, accounting for more than half of China's total and even in excess of 85 percent from 1944 to 1945.

Figure 10.2 shows the structure or the respective proportions of the various types of currency in circulation during the Republic of China period. Before 1936, the currency consisted of silver coins, copper coins, and paper money, and paper money was issued by both domestic banks and foreign banks. Due to the silver standard implemented in China before 1936, silver coins occupied the largest share, accounting for about 80 percent for a long time. It was followed by copper coins, but its proportion fell from 20 to less than 10 percent. The proportion of paper money rose from less than 1 to about 30 percent, demonstrating the vitality of

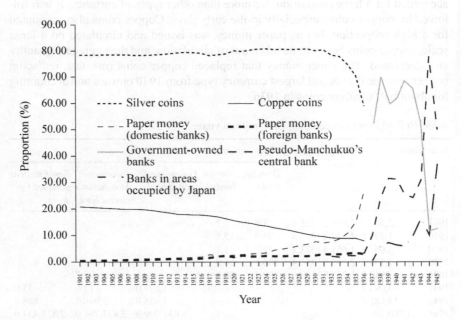

*Figure 10.2* Proportion of various types of currency in circulation

*Data source:* Ryoshin Minami and Makino Fumio (2014), p. 386.

*Role of government and finance*  227

paper money and its modern nature. Regarding the paper money issued, domestic banks had a slightly larger share than foreign banks during the Beiyang government period, and the share of domestic banks further expanded during the Nanjing Nationalist Government period.

After 1937, it changed significantly. The meaning of this change is threefold. The first is the currency reform conducted by the central government, which decided to implement a legal tender system in 1935. The system went into effect in 1937. The second is that the central government began to monopolize the financial industry, which is also manifested in the proportion of government-owned banks. The proportion of government banks plunged from 1944 to 1945, but as Japanese forces withdrew from China after the end of the War of Resistance against Japanese Aggression in 1945, the proportion of government banks reached 100 percent. The third is the drastic changes caused by Japan's invasion of China. Before the end of the War, the puppet Manchukuo's Bank and banks in Japanese-occupied areas together accounted for up to 85 percent, showing its special nature during the period of the War.

## 10.5   Conclusion

This chapter examined China's institutional building, the relationship between the government and the market, and the country's fiscal and financial systems. Generally, modern China had a tough job in institutional building. Given the national conditions of a fragmented country, there was basically no likelihood of independent economic development. However, the power of the government has always been strong. The government has largely a dominant position, as evidenced by economic development and industrial development. The Resource Committee of the Nanjing Nationalist government occupied an important position in many spheres and also played a key role during the War of Resistance against Japanese Aggression.

Regarding fiscal and financial issues, this chapter reviewed the fiscal and financial issues during the Republic of China period. Shortage of fiscal and financial resources was the shared problem. Fiscal revenue were woefully inadequate due to unfavorable economic development, insufficient tax revenues, and social unrest. If we consider the various indemnities and debts that the great powers imposed on China, China's fiscal resources were overstretched. Due to the frequent wars, military spending had to be raised. Wars also play havoc with production and people's livelihoods, aggravating the fiscal shortage in this period. This was also true of financial resources. Due to the powerful foreign forces and domestic chaos before 1949, traditional financial institutions and market-oriented operations coexisted with modern financial institutions, and old-style Chinese private banks and exchange shops coexisted with banks and stock markets, with each performing different roles. As the economy developed, the modern financial industry developed fast and gradually become the mainstream, and a trend of concentration was formed. Several major financial institutions monopolized a sizeable market.

## 228 *Conditions and causes*

### Notes

1 Many African countries as well as Asian countries such as the Philippines and India have this characteristic.
2 For the situation of Japan, see Kobayashi Masaaki (1977).
3 Xu Dixin and Wu Chengming (1990), p. 791.
4 Xu Dixin and Wu Chengming (1990), p. 800.
5 For example, Central Iron and Steel Mill, Central Radio Works, Central Electrical Equipment Factory, Central Machinery Plant, Xiangjiang Power Plant, Central Electric Ceramics Manufacturing Plant, Copper Works, Xiangtan Coal Mine Company, Tianhe Coal Mine, Gaokeng Coal Mine, Yanchang Oil Mine, Yiluo Coal Mine, Anqing Power Plant. See Xue Yi (2005), pp. 169–170.
6 Xue Yi (2005), p. 201.
7 Xue Yi (2005), p. 228.
8 Xue Yi (2005), p. 258.
9 Xue Yi (2005), p. 273.
10 Xue Yi (2005), p. 277.
11 Xue Yi (2005), p. 279.
12 Xu Dixin and Wu Chengming (1993), p. 508.
13 Zheng Youkui et al. (1991), p. 60.
14 Zheng Youkui et al. (1991), p. 112.
15 During the war, the Japanese military sent people to directly supervise and manage the production of key materials.
16 Xu Dixin and Wu Chengming (1993), pp. 548–552.
17 Yang Yinpu (1985), p. 13.
18 Yang Yinpu (1985), p. 15.
19 Jiao Jianhua (2013), p. 364.
20 Yang Yinpu (1985), p. 43.
21 Yang Yinpu (1985), p. 70.
22 Yang Yinpu (1985), p. 102.
23 Yang Yinpu (1985), p. 116.
24 Jiao Jianhua (2013), pp. 780–781.
25 Yang Yinpu (1985), p. 170.
26 Du Xuncheng (2002), p. 1. Moreover, for the name and capital scale of the banks established in this period, see Sun Jianhua (2008), pp. 242–243.
27 Du Xuncheng (2002), pp. 137–138.
28 Regarding changes in Japan's early financial industry, see Ryoshin Minami (1981).
29 Zhu Yingui (2012), pp. 58–59.
30 Yang Yinpu (1985), p. 3.
31 Hong Jiaguan (2008), p. 62.
32 Hong Jiaguan (2008), p. 64.
33 Hong Jiaguan (2008), p. 96.
34 Only odd-numbered years are shown here.
35 Regarding the changes in old-style Chinese private banks during the Republic of China period, see Zhu Yingui (2012).

# 11 International trade and foreign capital

## 11.1 Introduction

As previously mentioned, international trade and the introduction of foreign capital in modern China were achieved in the context of unfavorable conditions in two areas for China. First, China came under great pressure from foreign powers and carried out international trade and introduced foreign capital in the context of no autonomy in some areas. This is, of course, unfair. Second, China was in a state without modern economic growth. In international trade, there was only vertical division of labor but no horizontal division. In other words, China could only export primary products such as mineral products and agricultural products and import industrial manufactured products. This situation belongs to a "comparative advantage trap". Foreign capital entered China against its will. Of course, there is no denying that China benefited somewhat from international trade and the introduction of foreign capital, such as acquiring some technologies and accumulating experience.

Countries all over the world have a long history of international trade. Exchange and trade were carried out in the early days of living and production for humanity, but it took place mostly between tribes or areas rather than between countries. China was an early country to carry out international trade, as evidenced, for example, by the famous Silk Road. Moreover, China also had booming maritime trade. In addition to tribute trade with neighboring countries, China was also engaged in various economic and trade exchanges and even opened up the Maritime Silk Road. However, China enforced a self-isolation policy for a long time, and its exchanges with foreign countries were limited, making it hard for the Chinese people to learn about the world and for foreigners to learn about China. There is a lack of reliable data on China's early trade, and it is impossible to study the state of international trade and economic development. It is only in modern times, when China was forced open by foreign powers, that trade statistics became available for use.

This chapter also examines foreign investment in China. As we all know, the investment of foreign capital in China in modern times was partly coercive due to the powerful military, political, economic, and scientific and technological strength of the foreign powers. Foreign capital investment in China in modern times can be roughly divided into two stages. The first stage is the "indirect" investment

DOI: 10.4324/9781003410386-14

230  Conditions and causes

spearheaded by the United Kingdom, mainly under unequal treaties with various clauses for resource exploitation. For example, they invested in the concession area and opened mines. The second stage refers to the forcible implementation by Japan in the form of aggression, and this can be called the "direct type". For example, Japan occupied the northeast region. In any case, it was an act of seizing and plundering China's resources – shades of colony. Such predatory investment further widened the gap between China and the rest of the world.

## 11.2  International trade

Figure 11.1 shows China's foreign trade performance from 1864 to 1936. It shows that calculations based on either the current price or the constant price indicate an upward trend, despite fluctuations in the process (such as during World War I). The largest decline occurred in 1929–1931. On the one hand, it stemmed from the worldwide economic crisis that occurred in 1929. On the other hand, it was caused by the September 18 Incident launched by Japan in Northeast China. However, changes in the trade value denominated in the U.S. dollar tell a somewhat different story. It showed a downward trend at least to some extent after peaking in 1918, and this trend became aggravated after 1929.

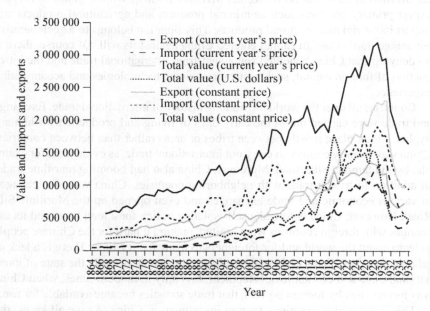

Figure 11.1  China's foreign trade in modern times

Note: The current price at the time was 1,000 haikwan taels, and the constant price was 1,000 yuan for 1936.

Data source: Zheng Youkui (1984), Appendix II; Liu Foding et al. (1999), pp. 292–294.

*International trade and foreign capital* 231

Figure 11.2 shows the various indexes of China's foreign trade as well as terms of trade over the same period. It can be seen that the various indexes changed consistently and that only the dollar-denominated indexes show an unusual situation, which is consistent with the graph in the figure. The total terms of trade and the net terms of trade are shown here. The former refers to the comparison of all imports and exports, and the latter refers to the volume of barter trade. From the perspective of trend, the total terms of trade first rose and then fell, with a turning point around 1908. The net terms of trade before 1908 were higher than the 100 in 1913 and then remained basically below 100. This shows the unfavorable situation of China's foreign trade. In other words, it needed to export more in order to import the same amount of goods.

Table 11.1 shows the import and export of goods by the means of production and the means of consumption in modern China. In terms of imports, the proportion of means of production rose from 8 to over 50 percent, and the proportion of means of consumption decreased from over 90 percent to less than half. This shows to some extent that China began to embrace industrialization. Regarding the means of production, the proportion of machines and large tools was small, increasing from less than 1 to about 8 percent. The proportion of building supplies and equipment rose from 8 to more than 40 percent. This indicates that China had a low level of industrialization and generally relied on imported building materials

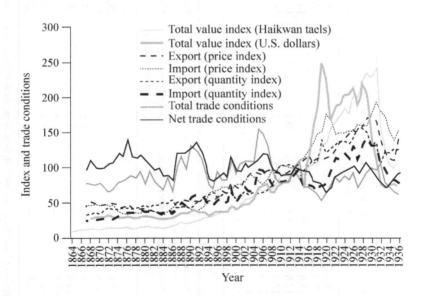

*Figure 11.2* Various indexes of China's foreign trade as well as terms of trade in modern times

*Note:* 100 in 1913.

*Data source:* Zheng Youkui (1984), Appendix II; Kong Min (1988), pp. 375–376.

*Table 11.1* Proportion of imports and exports of various goods in modern China, Unit: %

**Import**

| Year | Total | Means of production | | | | Means of consumption | | |
|---|---|---|---|---|---|---|---|---|
| | | Total | Machines and large tools | Raw materials | Building supplies and equipment | Total | Raw materials for consumer goods | Direct means of consumption |
| 1873 | 100 | 8.1 | – | – | 8.1 | 91.9 | 8.5 | 83.4 |
| 1893 | 100 | 8.4 | 0.6 | – | 7.8 | 91.6 | 13.0 | 78.6 |
| 1903 | 100 | 15.0 | 0.7 | – | 14.3 | 85.0 | 22.3 | 62.7 |
| 1910 | 100 | 17.6 | 1.5 | 0.1 | 16.0 | 82.4 | 17.0 | 65.4 |
| 1920 | 100 | 28.5 | 3.2 | 0.2 | 25.1 | 71.5 | 16.9 | 54.6 |
| 1930 | 100 | 26.9 | 3.7 | 1.9 | 21.3 | 73.1 | 17.3 | 55.8 |
| 1936 | 100 | 44.4 | 6.1 | 2.7 | 35.6 | 55.5 | 13.0 | 42.5 |
| 1947 | 100 | 52.8 | 8.2 | 2.4 | 42.2 | 47.2 | 15.0 | 22.2 |

**Export**

| Year | Total | Raw materials | | | Semifinished products | | Finished products | |
|---|---|---|---|---|---|---|---|---|
| | | Agricultural products | Mineral products (manual mining) | Mineral products (mechanized mining) | Manual | Mechanized | Manual | Mechanized |
| 1873 | 100 | 2.6 | – | – | 37.4 | – | 58.3 | 1.7 |
| 1893 | 100 | 15.6 | – | – | 28.4 | 0.1 | 53.4 | 2.5 |
| 1903 | 100 | 26.8 | 0.2 | 0.2 | 17.2 | 14.7 | 32.9 | 8.0 |
| 1910 | 100 | 39.1 | 0.2 | 0.5 | 13.1 | 11.9 | 28.3 | 6.8 |
| 1920 | 100 | 36.4 | 0.9 | 2.8 | 8.2 | 12.3 | 31.2 | 8.3 |
| 1930 | 100 | 45.1 | 1.2 | 3.4 | 3.5 | 12.2 | 27.1 | 7.4 |
| 1936 | 100 | 44.1 | 2.6 | 1.6 | 6.7 | 5.6 | 32.4 | 7.1 |
| 1947 | 100 | 30.6 | 4.4 | – | 2.0 | 10.5 | 33.0 | 19.5 |

*Note:* Building supplies and equipment include vehicles, ships, small tools, apparatus, semifinished products, raw materials, etc. Agricultural products include agriculture, forestry, animal husbandry, and fishery products.

*Data source:* Yan Zhongping et al. (1955), pp. 72–73.

*International trade and foreign capital*   233

and equipment. In terms of means of consumption, it was originally direct means, or finished products. Raw materials for means of consumption are equivalent to semifinished products, such as cloth. Raw materials for means of consumption increased from 8 to about 15 percent, while direct consumer goods fell from over 80 to about 20 percent.

Exports are divided into raw materials, semifinished goods, and finished products. In the late 19th century, the exports of primary commodities were few and even negligible. Semifinished and finished goods were dominant. In particular, finished goods accounted for 58 percent, although the so-called finished goods at this time were handmade products like handicrafts. In the 20th century, the proportion of both types of products for export declined, while the proportion of agricultural products in primary products gradually increased. The proportion of agricultural exports peaked at 45 percent, indicating that China's exports during this period were mainly primary products but that finished goods still occupied a share. Further observation shows that since the 20th century, the proportion of machine-made semifinished products and finished products gradually increased. In particular, the proportion of machine-made semifinished products exceeded that of handmade products, indicating that China gradually realized machine processing and manufacturing by importing mechanical equipment, and industrialization advanced.

Table 11.2 shows the structure of trade under another classification method during the Republic of China period. Products are classified according to the United Nations Standards and can be directly compared with those in other countries during other periods. Quantitatively, exports featured nonfood raw materials (other than fossil fuels), primarily mineral products, or natural resources. It is followed by food, primarily agricultural products such as grain. Coming third are industrial products, which include textiles, food processing, some light industries, tea, etc. It includes few mechanical products. This situation reflects the trade structure and status of China at that time: China exported primary products and imported industrial products. This pattern did not change much throughout the Republic of China period.

Unlike exports, imports featured industrial products, which accounted for about 45 percent in the early days, and then declined but remained above 20 percent. This shows the low level of industrial production in China at that time, which needed to supplement its industrial production through imports. It was followed by food, which remained at 20 percent for a long time. China also imported a great deal of food while exporting food, and its imports were no less than exports. It shows that China had inadequate output such as grain. On the other hand, it was the result of division of labor in terms of variety and processing degree. China exported grain and various nonstaple foods and imported processed manufactured products such as canned food and biscuits. Other significant imports include mineral fuels and lubricants, but the imports of chemicals, as well as machinery, transport machinery, etc., in the later period increased, indicating a higher level of industrialization in China.

*Table 11.2* Trade structure during the Republic of China period, Unit: %

| Year | Food | Beverage and cigarettes | Non-food raw materials (except mineral fuels) | Fossil fuels, lubricating oil | Animal and plant fat | Chemical products | Industrial products | Mechanical and transport machinery | Others | Special commodities |
|---|---|---|---|---|---|---|---|---|---|---|
| **Export** | | | | | | | | | | |
| 1913 | 26.46 | 1.04 | 46.89 | 1.65 | 4.07 | 2.46 | 15.29 | 0.01 | 2.04 | 0.09 |
| 1918 | 19.85 | 1.51 | 45.08 | 1.91 | 9.73 | 2.23 | 17.02 | 0.01 | 2.41 | 0.21 |
| 1923 | 23.18 | 2.80 | 45.78 | 2.78 | 5.95 | 1.61 | 14.20 | 0.04 | 3.16 | 0.50 |
| 1928 | 22.42 | 2.64 | 49.95 | 2.87 | 4.30 | 1.40 | 14.32 | 0.04 | 1.93 | 0.12 |
| 1933 | 20.07 | 0.60 | 38.62 | 4.93 | 4.79 | 1.40 | 24.83 | 0.08 | 2.98 | 0.01 |
| 1938 | 19.15 | 0.47 | 43.37 | 4.03 | 4.53 | 2.31 | 14.16 | 0.30 | 2.32 | 0.03 |
| 1943 | 1.20 | 0.31 | 42.78 | 21.85 | 10.67 | 2.11 | 5.54 | 5.03 | 2.61 | 0.05 |
| **Import** | | | | | | | | | | |
| 1913 | 18.15 | 3.67 | 3.62 | 6.73 | 0.35 | 12.64 | 46.44 | 2.26 | 8.11 | 1.66 |
| 1918 | 21.21 | 5.29 | 4.80 | 8.05 | 0.17 | 3.24 | 44.74 | 2.98 | 6.38 | 3.15 |
| 1923 | 24.4822 | 5.28 | 9.35 | 8.94 | 0.17 | 5.56 | 34.94 | 4.71 | 5.71 | 0.86 |
| 1928 | 1.95 | 5.98 | 9.25 | 8.89 | 0.32 | 6.08 | 35.78 | 4.51 | 5.90 | 1.34 |
| 1933 | 23.57 | 2.46 | 10.56 | 9.17 | 0.62 | 5.19 | 26.19 | 7.24 | 4.56 | 2.06 |
| 1938 | 12.86 | 1.79 | 3.91 | 4.04 | 0.51 | 4.86 | 30.33 | 2.87 | 7.15 | 0.16 |
| 1943 | 30.38 | 2.01 | 4.87 | 1.65 | 1.25 | 15.96 | 23.45 | 10.61 | 9.35 | 0.46 |

*Note:* The total is 100, which is not shown here.

*Data source:* Ryoshin Minami, Makino Fumio (2014), p. 448.

*International trade and foreign capital*   235

## 11.3   Foreign capital

### 11.3.1   Coal mining

The government and foreign capital had been involved in the development of China's coal mining industry in modern times from the outset.[1] Moreover, the government and foreign capital were dominant in this industry, while private capital had little power and influence. This is in line with the characteristics of this industry and, to a greater extent, with China's national circumstances at that time. First, the importance of this industry is self-evident. In terms of economic interests, it is a lucrative industry, and no government will remain indifferent because the original price or cost of a resource industry is far smaller than those in other manufacturing industries or is even zero. If it is the government's property, the cost includes only the worker wages and the equipment investment. If it is private property, private owners only need to pay certain taxes or management fees to the government, and the remaining costs are only the worker wages and equipment investment. In this case, it was no wonder that foreign capital was involved. Second, the national conditions are that, after the Opium War, China gradually lost sovereignty in some areas, and foreign forces infiltrated into China by fair means or foul. The profitable industry of coal mines was, of course, coveted by them. Foreign capital was powerful during the development of China's coal mining industry in modern times, especially in the early days. Third, the coal mining industry needs huge funds as well as corresponding technology. Since modern mining technology was imported from Europe, foreign investors held unique advantages.

China gradually lost its autonomy over mining after the First Sino-Japanese War. Germany proposed leasing Jiaozhou Bay from the Qing government for its service in the return of Liaodong Peninsula to China. Later, Germany simply sent troops to occupy Jiaozhou Bay. In 1898, Germany forced the Qing government to sign the Sino-German *Jiao'ao Lease Treaty*, which stipulated that Germany would build two railways and have the right to exploit minerals in areas within 15,000 m from the line. The UK followed suit. The British Peking Syndicate Limited signed an agreement with the Shanxi Bureau of Commerce and obtained mining rights for local areas. Not to be outdone, Russia signed the *Contract for Jointly Establishing Eastern Railway Company* and the *Renewal Contract* with the Qing government in 1896 and 1898 to seize the right to exploit coal mines within 15,000 m from the railway line. In 1901 and 1902, it signed relevant contracts with the local governments of Liaoning, Jilin, and Heilongjiang provinces in the same way. Under the excuse of its service in the return of Liaodong Peninsula to China, France also obtained the mining rights over six coal and iron mines in Sichuan, Chongqing, etc. in 1899 and, together with Belgium, obtained mining rights in the areas along the Beijing–Hankou Railway in 1900. Since the First Sino-Japanese War, Japan plotted to exploit China's mining industry. Especially after the Russo-Japanese War in 1905, Japan invaded and occupied the coal mines in Fushun and Yantai and inherited Russia's mining rights in China. During World War I, Japan seized mining rights for the areas along the Jiaoji Railway in Shandong when the European

## 236 *Conditions and causes*

powers were involved in the war, becoming the country with the most extensive mining rights in China. During the same period, countries such as Italy and Belgium were also involved in Chinese coal mines.

After the First Sino-Japanese War, the great powers obtained extensive mining rights and made investments in China, virtually monopolizing China's coal mining industry. From 1895 to 1936, foreign investors opened 32 coal mines in China, accounting for half to one-third of China's total output. During the same period, national capital also set up dozens of new-type coal mines. By 1936, there were 61 modern coal mines with an annual output of over 50,000 metric tons in China, including 8 with an annual output of over 60,000 metric tons (Kailuan, Fushun, Zhongxing, Zhongfu, Luda, Jingxing, Benxi and Xi'an). This year, the raw coal output nationwide was 39 million metric tons, including 29.6 million metric tons for new-type coal mines.[2] Foreign investors obtained mining rights in China mainly through the following channels. First, obtain the right to build roads, and then the right to exploit mines along the railway line. Second, negotiate with the Chinese government to obtain mining rights in a province or part of the region. Third, designate a specific area and obtain special approval from the government. Fourth, negotiate and conclude contracts with private owners, and then obtain government approval. The modes of operation include wholly owned mines and joint ventures.

Table 11.3 shows the output of foreign-invested coal mines from 1913 to 1942 and their proportions. First, in terms of proportion, foreign capital accounted for half or more than half of the total before 1936. It occupied absolute dominance in 1942, which was caused by Japan's all-out invasion of China. Before the all-out invasion, foreign investors had tried every means to acquire as much benefit as possible, but it was not so serious. Second, even before 1936, Japan was most powerful in China and even surpassed Britain in terms of foreign capital, and its power gradually increased. However, Japan was so greedy and ambitious that it lunched an all-out invasion of China. Third, on the whole, the proportion of direct investment was comparable to that of participation in investment. The United Kingdom generally participated in making investment, while Japan increasingly made direct investment. Germany made a little investment, mainly by participating in investment.

Figure 11.3 shows the changes in the proportion of foreign capital in China's coal mining industry from 1912 to 1937, including total mining and mechanized mining. Total mining includes traditional mining. It clearly shows that foreign capital accounted for about half in terms of total mining, with a slight upward trend. It peaked at more than 60 percent. Foreign capital accounted for a higher proportion in mechanized mining, but it showed a gradual downward trend, falling from more than 90 to less than 70 percent. This shows that the proportion of national capital in mechanized mining was on the rise, which is also a kind of progress. Nevertheless, the high proportion of foreign capital in China still shows its tremendous impact and distinct advantages.

### 11.3.2 *Other industries*

Given the national situation before 1949, the current fair introduction of foreign investment was nonexistent or at least was not prevailing. It was more of a predatory

*Table 11.3* Output and proportion of foreign-invested coal mines from 1913 to 1942, Unit: 10,000 metric tons (%)

| Country | Way of investment | 1913 | 1919 | 1926 | 1936 | 1942 |
|---|---|---|---|---|---|---|
| Total for the whole country | | 1,287.98 (100.0) | 2,014.68 (100.0) | 2,304.00 (100.0) | 3,990.30 (100.0) | 6,595.21 (100.0) |
| Total foreign capital | Total | 713.66 (55.4) | 969.18 (48.1) | 1,224.21 (53.1) | 2,221.84 (55.7) | 5,961.40 (90.4) |
| | Direct investment | 286.51 (22.2) | 405.68 (20.1) | 640.66 (27.8) | 1,458.39 (35.3) | 5,920.84 (89.8) |
| | Participating in investment | 427.15 (33.2) | 563.50 (28.0) | 583.55 (25.3) | 813.46 (20.4) | 40.57 (0.6) |
| Japan | Total | 319.00 (24.7) | 501.45 (24.9) | 804.23 (34.9) | 1,478.57 (37.1) | 5,825.00 (88.3) |
| | Direct investment | 163.90 (12.7) | 356.20 (17.7) | 628.99 (27.3) | 1,408.39 (35.3) | 5,825.00 (88.3) |
| | Participating in investment | 155.16 (12.0) | 145.25 (7.2) | 175.24 (7.6) | 70.19 (1.8) | – |
| UK | Total | 248.88 (19.3) | 430.75 (21.4) | 386 (16.7) | 6,550.05 (16.4) | 40.57 (0.6) |
| | Direct investment | 41.18 (3.3) | 49.47 (2.5) | 11.67 (0.5) | – | – |
| | Participating in investment | 206.70 (16.0) | 381.28 (18.9) | 374.37 (16.2) | 6,550.05 (16.4) | 40.57 (0.6) |
| Germany | Total | 93.45 (7.3) | – | 33.94 (1.5) | 88.22 (2.2) | 95.83 (1.5) |
| | Direct investment | 63.60 (4.9) | – | – | – | – |
| | Participating in investment | 29.85 (2.3) | – | 33.94 (1.5) | 88.22 (2.2) | 95.83 (1.5) |

*Note:* There were also data for Russia and Belgium, but due to the small investment and a short time frame, they are not listed here. The figures for earlier years add up to less than 100.

*Data source:* Compilation Group of the *History of Coal Mines in Modern China* (1990), pp. 247–248.

238  *Conditions and causes*

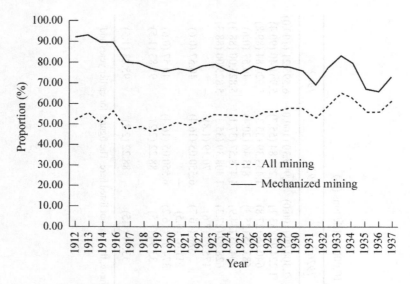

*Figure 11.3* Proportion of foreign investment in coal mining
Data source: Yan Zhongping et al. (1955), pp. 123–124.

nature caused by power politics. In other words, it was a deal concluded through some kind of political and even military threat. This is the essence of China's semi-colonial nature. While foreign investors still needed to hire Chinese workers for the exploitation of resources and ancillary production, it is conceivable that the wages of Chinese workers were meager. Moreover, according to the technical and management level at that time, the Chinese workers had abominable working conditions, and casualties often occurred.

Table 14.4 shows the proportion of foreign capital in pig iron and iron ore production from 1900 to 1937. It accounted for as high as 100 percent or complete monopoly in the early stage. In terms of pig iron production, foreign capital accounted for as high as 97.6 percent, even in 1937, mostly in the form of participation in investment or shares for foreign capital. In terms of iron ore, foreign capital in the early days was mainly loans, participation in investment gradually became dominant, and then military occupation ensued. It should be noted that Japan occupied Gongzhuling Iron Mine in Anshan, an important iron ore production base in China at that time, before 1937.

Table 11.5 shows the proportions of spindles, wire bars, and looms in Chinese and foreign cotton mills in China. From 1897 to 1936, the number of spindles at Chinese cotton mills maintained a stable proportion, accounting for over 50 percent at the end of the 19th century and close to 70 percent in the early 20th century. In 1947, as a result of the withdrawal of foreign forces, the proportion of Chinese cotton mills increased significantly, almost accounting for 100 percent. In another sense, the proportion of foreign-funded cotton mills was consistently 40 percent and fell to about 30 percent only in the early 20th century, which is also a high

*International trade and foreign capital*  239

*Table 11.4* Monopoly power of foreign capital in iron ore and pig iron production in modern China, Unit: %

| Year | Pig iron | | | Iron ore | | | |
|---|---|---|---|---|---|---|---|
| | Proportion in total output | Participation in investment | Loans | Proportion in total output | Military occupation | Participation in investment | Loans |
| 1900 | 100.0 | – | 100.0 | – | – | – | – |
| 1910 | 100.0 | – | 100.0 | 100.0 | – | – | 100.0 |
| 1920 | 100.0 | 48.3 | 51.7 | 100.0 | – | 26.9 | 73.1 |
| 1930 | 99.3 | 99.3 | – | 99.7 | – | 46.9 | 52.8 |
| 1937 | 97.6 | 97.6 | – | 99.7 | 73.5 | 4.4 | 21.8 |

*Data source:* Yan Zhongping et al. (1955), p. 127–129.

*Table 11.5* Comparison of spindles, wire bars, and looms in Chinese and foreign cotton mills, Unit: %

| Year | Spindles | | Wire bars | | Looms | |
|---|---|---|---|---|---|---|
| | China | Foreign countries | China | Foreign countries | China | Foreign countries |
| 1897 | 59.3 | 40.7 | – | – | 100.0 | 0.0 |
| 1900 | 67.7 | 32.3 | – | – | 100.0 | 0.0 |
| 1910 | 69.7 | 30.3 | – | – | 100.0 | 0.0 |
| 1920 | 58.1 | 41.9 | – | – | 51.0 | 49.0 |
| 1925 | 55.9 | 44.1 | 41.3 | 58.7 | 53.8 | 46.2 |
| 1930 | 57.2 | 42.8 | 23.2 | 76.8 | 49.5 | 50.5 |
| 1936 | 53.8 | 46.2 | 32.6 | 67.4 | 43.6 | 56.4 |
| 1947 | 99.0 | 1.0 | 100.0 | 0.0 | 100.0 | 0.0 |

*Data source:* Yan Zhongping et al. (1955), p. 136.

proportion of foreign investment for a sovereign country. The data on wire bars and looms are incomplete. The proportion of foreign capital was about 50 percent for looms and over 60 percent for wire bars, higher than that of spindles. The advantages of foreign capital are obvious.

Table 11.6 shows the situation foreign investment by country in 1936, 1940 and 1948. It is divided into two categories: direct investment and borrowings. The three years are representative. The year 1936 represents the highest level before the outbreak of the War of Resistance against Japanese Aggression. In 1940, the War of Resistance against Japanese Aggression was in the stage of strategic stalemate, and foreign capital increased significantly. In 1948, the War of Resistance against Japanese Aggression was already over, and foreign investment was greatly reduced. In terms of the aggregate, 1940 saw an increase of almost 72 percent over 1936, and the figure in 1948 was lower than that in 1936 and less than half of that in 1940. In terms of categories, direct investment was the mainstream, far more than borrowings. From the perspective of country, Japan accounted for about half of the

240   *Conditions and causes*

*Table 11.6* Foreign investment in China during wartime

|  | 1936 | 1940 | 1948 |
|---|---|---|---|
| Total | 3,941.4 | 6,762.0 | 3,197.3 |
| Direct investment | 3,127.3 | 5,540.8 | 1,487.0 |
| Borrowings | 814.1 | 1,221.2 | 1,710.3 |
| Japan | 1,818.3 | 4,451.6 | − |
| Direct investment | 1,560.1 | 4,121.0 | − |
| Northeast China | 1,288.6 | 3,036.4 | − |
| The rest of China (except Northeast China) | 271.5 | 1,084.6 | − |
| Borrowings | 258.2 | 330.6 | − |
| United States | 1,328.2 | 3,82.9 | 1,410.1 |
| Direct investment | 1,263.8 | 250.0 | 385.0 |
| Borrowings | 64.4 | 132.9 | 1,025.1 |
| UK | 1,020.8 | 940.3 | 1,115.4 |
| Direct investment | 870.7 | 765.4 | 715.5 |
| Borrowings | 150.1 | 174.9 | 399.9 |
| France | 276.3 | 257.5 | 297.2 |
| Direct investment | 185.4 | 176.4 | 226.1 |
| Borrowings | 90.9 | 81.1 | 71.1 |
| Germany | 136.4 | 137.0 | − |
| Direct investment | 47.0 | 44.0 | − |
| Borrowings | 89.4 | 93.0 | − |
| Soviet Union | 26.1 | 276.1 | − |
| Direct investment | 26.1 | 26.1 | − |
| Borrowings | − | 250.0 | − |
| Other countries | 335.3 | 316.6 | 374.6 |
| Direct investment | 174.2 | 157.9 | 160.4 |
| Borrowings | 161.1 | 158.7 | 214.2 |

*Note:* The unit is million U.S. dollars, and the currency value is that of 1936. In the figure for 1940, the year for Japan is 1945.

*Data source:* Xu Dixin and Wu Chengming (volume 3) (1993), p. 600.

total in 1936 and for 66 percent in 1940, which shows the advantage of Japanese power in the 1930s and 1940s. Japanese investment was also characterized by its concentration in Northeast China, which is highly related to its earliest infiltration, occupation, and rule in Northeast China. In 1936, both the United States and the United Kingdom made a large amount of investment, but in 1940, the United States reduced its investment significantly, while the United Kingdom still maintained a high level. It shows the historic nature of British interests in China. In 1948, Japan withdrew, while the United States and Britain increased investment, especially the United States. On the one hand, this reflected the growing strength of the United States. On the other hand, it showed the increased willingness of the United States to intervene in China. The total amount of investment made by other countries was relatively small compared to the aforesaid three countries. It shows that after the 1930s, China's foreign investment mainly came from Japan, the United States, and the United Kingdom.

## 11.4 Conclusion

This chapter discussed China's international trade and foreign capital. International trade offers the following revelations. First, both the theory of economics and the practical experience of China's economy have proved that a country's economic development is related to the external environment. Self-isolation in any shape or form harms the development of the local economy and also impedes the progress of society because, although economic and trade ties are on the surface trade in goods and services as well as investment and financial activities, they are essentially a type of people-to-people communication. People diffuse their knowledge and technologies as well as experience and lessons while conducting economic and trade exchanges. No one is born wise, and no country can acquire state-of-the-art technology and knowledge without interacting with other countries. Total self-isolation will lead people nowhere, as China learned the hard way. Second, China's opening up is a tortuous process, and therefore China's economic development has been accompanied by ups and downs. Opening up and international trade can spur economic development, which in turn facilitates international trade. The two complement each other in a virtuous circle. As China was forced to open up while lagging behind other countries in modern times, it had been in a passive situation and mired in the "comparative advantage trap" in international trade. Third, whether there is unimpeded international trade depends on the success of domestic industrialization. If industrialization is successful, international trade can grow smoothly. If industrialization is unsuccessful, or if only simple industrial products can be produced, international trade is limited to exporting primary products and importing manufactured goods. To bring about domestic industrialization, it also needs good international economic and trade relations. The two reinforce each other. China has done an excellent job in this regard, at least after the reform.

Regarding foreign capital, foreign capital entered China before 1949 as a result of China's national conditions, but it was not normal investment. Instead, it was to a great extent forced and unequal for China. Foreign capital entered China on a large scale by means of great power and privilege. It prioritized the exploitation of natural resources for the sake of export. Such a situation is no different from colonialism. Although foreign capital objectively brought some benefits to China in the form of technology introduction and job creation, and China learned advantaged knowledge and skills, Chinese people did not have the initiative on the whole, and China had more losses than gains.

### Notes

1 For the development of the coal mining industry in modern China and its relationship with foreign investment, see the Compilation Group of *History of Textile in Modern China* (1990).
2 The Compilation Group of *History of Textile in Modern China* (1990), p. 61.

# Part IV
# Comparison and revelation

# 12 Summary and outlook

## 12.1 Introduction

As the final chapter of the book, we sum up the lessons learned through the comparison between China and Japan, and study the factors and facilitating conditions that affect economic development. As two East Asian countries, China and Japan had been relatively close in the premodern era, but there was an obvious divergence since modern times. Japan was ahead of China in embracing industrialization and modernization and was the first non-European or American country to achieve economic development. China failed to move with the times but fell further behind in modern times. It was only after 1949 that China showed willingness and endeavored to catch up with the advanced countries, but China still lagged behind Japan because Japan made faster progress during this period. It was only after the reform and opening up that China realized rapid economic growth and narrowed the gap with Japan, even though China's per capita GDP is still only a quarter of Japan's.

One of the principal reasons that China and Japan began to diverge since the mid-19th century was institutions. Japan launched a momentous adjustment as of the Meiji Restoration in 1868 and soon embraced parliamentary democracy, although the *mikado* remained as the head of state. The "Civilization and Enlightenment", "Enrich the Nation; Strengthen the Army", and "Encourage Industry", the three slogans put forward during the Meiji period, became symbols of the times. Japan indeed worked toward these goals and achieved tremendous success. Coincidentally, the Meiji period (1868–1911) was followed by the Taisho period (1912–1925), and this coincided with China's Xinhai Revolution (1911) and the founding of the Republic of China (1912).

We believe that China's modern history should begin with the Republic of China period because the imperial rule was overthrown and China embraced the republican system during this period. In the 70 years or so from the Opium War to the Xinhai Revolution, Western Europe breathed fresh air into China, and some reforms were implemented. But the imperial rule remained largely unchanged, and it was impossible to achieve real modern economic growth. According to our observation, China's private sector of the economy gradually emerged in the early days of the Republic of China and thrived. Many emerging industries were also introduced and became popular since this period. The Self-Strengthening Movement

DOI: 10.4324/9781003410386-16

## 246  *Comparison and revelation*

in the late 19th century could only be a quick fix to maintain the imperial rule, and there was no real economic development. In this sense, the gap of 43 years between the Meiji Restoration and the Xinhai Revolution meant the difference in economic development between China and Japan. This gap has always existed and has even widened in some years. There is still a gap of about 40 to 50 years between China and Japan.

### 12.2  The gap between China and Japan

In a sense, China and Japan, two countries in East Asia, are highly special. This special nature is actually rare in the world. To begin with, they are close neighbors, and their exchanges go back a long way. There are lingering relations in many areas. On the other hand, they are enemies, and the relationship is chaotic in many respects. Second, the two countries have always been competing in East Asia, resulting in misconception and distrust. Finally, although there are several competing neighboring powers in Europe, none of their relations are as complex and subtle as China–Japan relations.[1] For example, India and Pakistan in South Asia were separated only after World War II. Such relations do not exist in Southeast Asia, Central and Western Asia, Africa, the Oceania, and even North America.

Therefore, it is necessary to carefully study the bilateral relations from all perspectives such as history, culture, politics, economy, and diplomacy, hoping to discover the perspectives to promote bilateral relations. Brief discussions are conducted in light of reality by summarizing the overall difference between the two countries in modern industrial development. We briefly compare the overall gap in economic development or the gap in per capita GDP between China and Japan. Table 12.1 shows the per capita GDP of China and Japan from 1820 to 1950 as well as the ratio. Before modern times (1820), Japan was almost on a par with China. After modern times, Japan left China behind. The ratio of the per capita GDP between Japan and China rose from 1.12 times in 1820 to 2.17 times in 1900, to 3.61 times in 1929, and to 4.36 times in 1938. China's per capita GDP moved horizontally for a long time and even declined, from 600 international dollars in 1820 to 545 international dollars in 1900, and then moved horizontally for a long time and even fell to 439 international dollars in 1950. During the same period, Japan's per capita GDP rose from 669 international dollars in 1820 to 1,180 international dollars in

*Table 12.1* Changes in per capita GDP in China and Japan

|  | 1820 | 1870 | 1890 | 1900 | 1913 | 1929 | 1938 | 1950 |
|---|---|---|---|---|---|---|---|---|
| China | 600 | 530 | 540 | 545 | 552 | 562 | 562 | 439 |
| Japan | 669 | 737 | 1,012 | 1,180 | 1,387 | 2,026 | 2,449 | 1,921 |
| Japan/China | 1.12 | 1.39 | 1.88 | 2.17 | 2.52 | 3.61 | 4.36 | 4.38 |

*Note:* The data in the table are the international dollars in 1990, which is a fixed currency unit calculated based on multilateral purchasing power parity.

*Data source:* Maddison (2009), pp. 178–180.

Summary and outlook 247

1900, to 2,026 international dollars in 1929, and to 2,449 international dollars in 1938. It can be seen that the gap in economic development between China and Japan widened over 100 years or so in modern times. Japan started modern economic growth, while China lagged far behind.

The gap between China and Japan also existed in terms of talents, capital, technology, management, product quality, social competence, etc. These issues will be mentioned in subsequent discussions. A simple collation is performed here using the theory of economics. The process and degree of differences in industrial development between China and Japan in modern times can be explained using the production possibility curve and Rybczynski theorem.[2]

Figures 12.1(a) and (b) show such a situation. Figure 12.1(a) on the left shows the pattern and model of industrial development in modern Japan, while Figure 12.1(b) on the right shows the situation in China. Through comparison, it can be seen that Japan has two more production possibility curves than China, indicating a higher level of development. Supposing that both countries were traditional agrarian states at the beginning of the modern times (and this is the case), the figure shows that the traditional industry has a comparative advantage, the output was significant, many resources were invested, and the production possibility curve is biased toward the horizontal axis. The production possibility area here is $I$. Both countries began to develop industry from point $A$, because industrialization is the core content of modern economic growth or economic development. Owing to resource limitations, such as abundant labor but a lack of capital, it is only possible by prioritizing the development of light industries in the early stages of industrialization, including food, textiles, etc. Most countries went this way, such as the United Kingdom, because it means the rational distribution of resources. However, there are exceptions. For example, China in the planned economy period after 1949 and many other socialist countries adopted a policy of operating the industrialization of heavy industry that overstretched local resources. These ended in failure. Despite some results, it is not the best choice. This strategy of industrialization of light industries caused the production possibility curve to move outward, and the direction of movement is biased toward the horizontal axis. Economic development was

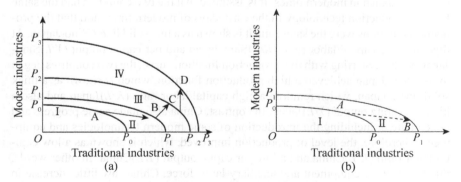

Figure 12.1 (a) Pattern of industrial development in modern Japan. (b) Pattern of industrial development in modern China

## 248  *Comparison and revelation*

achieved somewhat, and at least certain industries were introduced, as shown in the figure as the new area II for production possibility. Mechanized production methods were imported. Although productivity and efficiency are not necessarily high, introduction itself is progress. At least, China seemed to have achieved this in this regard.[3] The gap emerged when Japan moved from the production possibility area I to the production possibility area II and then to the production possibility areas III and IV, but China did not achieve this. The difference between area III and area II is that area III means not only outward expansion but also moderate change in the direction. In other words, it grew somewhat toward the vertical axis. Although it registered certain growth in the early stage, it was not significant. This can be seen from the direction of the arrow in the figure. The movement from area I to area II is horizontal or even toward the lower right, while the movement from area II to area III is toward the upper right or has the overtones of balanced expansion. It is of great significance because the vertical axis represents capital-intensive industries or modern industries. Such transformation or movement reflects the essence of industrialization. Although Japan had not yet completely achieved the industrialization of heavy industries in modern times (before World War II), it achieved this goal to a certain extent as a result of this transformation. In contrast, China did not achieve the movement from area II to area III and expansion. It just remained at area II, or it was even incomplete. If the movement from area II to area III is significant, it explains the gap between China and Japan. If China did not even reach area II, the gap is even larger. Area IV is more important. Although area IV is drawn for Japan here, we are not sure whether it actually realized this. It only symbolically indicates such a possibility. If area IV was realized, Japan was ahead of China by two stages. If not, it was only one stage ahead of China. However, we think that Japan reached area IV because China had no modern economic growth or economic take-off at all in modern times. We call it "failed economic take-off". If this judgment stands to reason, it is entirely possible that Japan was ahead of China by two regions.

In order to further learn about this gap between China and Japan, the production function principle is used for analysis. Figure 12.2 shows the development status of China and Japan in modern times. It is assumed that the two countries had the same level of production technology in the early days of modern times and that the production functions were the same, and it is shown as a fine solid line $F$Sino-Japan. At this time, the capital/labor ratio $(K/L)$Sino-Japan and per capita output $(Y/L)$Sino-Japan are low. Starting with this production function curve, the two countries began to develop. Japan achieved a high production function, which is shown as a thick solid line $F$Japan, which required a high capital/labor ratio $(K/L)$Japan and also a high per capita output $(Y/L)$Japan. In contrast, China also made some progress and development, including the introduction of some modern technologies and equipment. Therefore, the level of production improved, which is shown as a low capital/labor ratio $(K/L)$China and a low per capita output $(Y/L)$China. In other words, due to a lack of equipment and ancillary labor force, China saw little increase in per capita output. The increase in equipment and the growth of ancillary labor force in Japan contributed to the growth of per capita output. Correspondingly, the

Summary and outlook 249

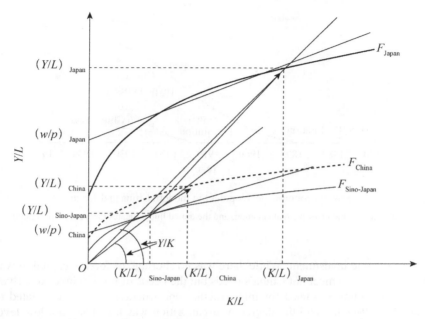

*Figure 12.2* Production function of development in China and Japan in modern times

productivity of capital ($Y/K$) is also different, which was higher in Japan than in China because the quantity of equipment and the performance directly affect the output. In other words, the value created by capital is different. This is important in the process of economic development because it largely symbolizes technological progress and also stands for production efficiency. If there is much capital input but little output, it means waste and inefficiency. If there is little capital input but high output, it means that capital is efficiently used. Further, the wage rates in China and Japan were also different. Japan's wage rate rose significantly as the economy grew, while China's wage rate rose slightly.[4]

Figure 12.3 shows the economic development in modern China and Japan. Japan began to see modern economic growth in the mid-1880s and was on track for normal development after about 20 years of economic take-off.[5] Although it was not comparable to the rapid growth after World War II, Japan's economic growth rate was the highest even among the developed countries before the war. In contrast, China saw a certain momentum of development since the beginning of the Republic of China period. China somewhat met the conditions for economic take-off after more than 20 years of development, but this take-off was unsuccessful due to a host of internal and external factors.

Internal factors include inadequate investment. Despite some investment at the time, including investment in modern and traditional industries, the overall investment was insufficient. This can be seen from domestic savings, which were scarce in the context of economic development at that time and could not meet the needs

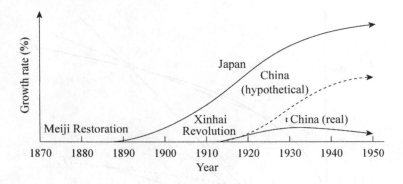

*Figure 12.3* Patterns of economic development in modern China and Japan

*Note:* The solid line indicates the real situation, and the dotted line indicates theoretical speculation.

of considerable investment. While there was no shortage of foreign capital, it was obviously used to meet not China's needs but the needs of foreign investors. Even if foreign capital was used for infrastructure construction, it was not related to people's well-being, and the degree of urbanization was low. Due to a low level of economic development and a shortage of tax revenue, the government suffered fiscal shortages and had no funds for investment.[6]

External factors are clear. On the one hand, since the mid-19th century, the Western powers regarded China as "a lucrative country". In addition to waging wars to make China their respective colonies, they plundered China's resources by all means. As a result, China had no energy to develop its economy independently. Most importantly, Japan's invasion unsettled China's normal economic order and put China's development trajectory off course. Were it not for Japan's full-scale invasion of China, China could have started modern economic growth in the 1930s or 1940s, as shown by the dotted line in Figure 12.3. Japan's aggression dealt a severe blow to China's economy on all fronts. China had no choice but to serve in the war (wartime economy) without adequate preparation. Coupled with the damage inflicted by the war, this attempt at economic development failed. We call it "failed economic take-off" (shown as the solid line in Figure 12.3), and the time of China's economic development was delayed.[7]

## 12.3 Experience in economic development and lessons learned

The factors influencing economic development are summarized here in conjunction with the content of this book, with reference to the theory of economic development. Some of these factors are natural, and some are human-made. All or some factors apply to the various countries. Compared with Japan in modern times or compared to the years after 1949 or even 1978, China lacked some factors and was therefore unable to achieve economic development. Figure 12.4 shows the factors influencing economic development or the conditions that facilitate it. They

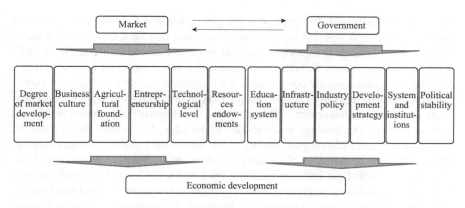

*Figure 12.4* Factors influencing economic development

are divided into two categories: the market and the government. The two influence each other, with each containing 6 factors. Some factors are somewhat connected while others are not.

The first is the degree of development of the market or whether there is a national market. Some countries were in a tribal state and self-sufficient and lacked a unified national market (such as some African countries), which goes against economic development, particularly industrial development. As we know, industrial development requires agglomeration or urbanization, as well as abundant labor force, which are transferred from rural areas. In the absence of a unified national market, each tribe exists independently of others. Influenced by religion and culture, people find it difficult to leave the tribe and become citizens and industrial workers. Second, a lack of a unified market also means underdeveloped business culture, which plays an important role in information transmission. Merchants carry commodities from one region to another, so that local people have access to products unavailable locally. Merchants also diffuse cultures and messages, exposing people to the outside world. Moreover, merchants are business savvy, well travelled, well informed, and more interested in new things, and they can therefore become a key force in industrialization. In addition, merchants are usually richer than ordinary farmers and urban dwellers. In the early days of industrialization, many businesspeople invest in industry, either independently or in cooperation with others. Of course, business culture alone is not enough. A certain agricultural foundation is also needed. The degree of agricultural development largely determines the success or failure of industrialization in the early stages because agriculture contributes to industrialization in many ways, including the use of surplus agricultural funds for industrial construction, the transfer of surplus agriculture labor to industry, and foreign exchange earnings from agricultural exports for purchase of industrial equipment. Agriculture provides food for industrial workers and urban dwellers, provides raw materials for the industry, and also serves as a market for industrial products.[8] As some countries (such as African countries) are agriculturally underdeveloped and are in a primitive tribal state, it is difficult to achieve industrialization. It is

## 252 *Comparison and revelation*

universally recognized that entrepreneurs play a leading role in industrialization and economic development and are the most important factor. J. A. Schumpeter defines entrepreneurs as a group of innovative people who are different from ordinary business operators. Schumpeter's innovation refers to "creative destruction", which means smashing the conventions and introducing new technologies. In comparison, ordinary operators simply pursue maximum profits and are unable to promote economic development.[9] Of course, the development of industry requires a certain degree of technology and ancillary knowledge. In the early days, there are mostly traditional technologies, mainly in the handicraft industry. Industrialization necessitates the introduction of modern industries, or mechanized production. Usually, it starts with light industry (such as food and textiles) and gradually moves toward heavy industry (such as metallurgy, chemical engineering, and machinery). This depends on a country's resource endowment. The technology used and industries developed vary according to the national circumstances of each country. Some countries are vast in size and sparsely populated. Some are populous countries with a small territory. Some are landlocked countries that find it hard to engage in international trade. Other countries poor in resources cannot develop their own industries and must depend on international trade.

These market factors are more favorable for China than for other developing countries. First of all, China has a farming culture and commercial civilization that have lasted thousands of years. Even in traditional society without modern means of transport, the market in rural areas was highly developed, not to mention the role of merchant culture. There are famous merchant groups in many parts of China, who travelled widely and promoted the formation of a unified national market as well as the transmission of information. Instead of operating in local small areas, these merchant groups engage in wide-ranging activities, and some participate in international trade. China is a great agricultural country with millennial agricultural civilization. Farmers were the mainstay before industrialization, and agricultural production technologies have been developed. Some regions are known for their abundance of products. Entrepreneurship came into play somewhat during the Republic of China period. A wealth of small and medium-sized enterprises were established nationwide, especially in coastal areas. Many people distinguished themselves in the silk reeling, textile, papermaking, matchstick, flour, machinery, chemical engineering, and other industries, and the first group of entrepreneurs who emerged have contributed significantly to the formation and development of industry during the Republic of China period.[10] Regarding the level of technology, modern industrial technologies were introduced as early as the late 19th century, but these were mainly limited to the military industry and a small number of heavy industries. During the Republic of China period, light industry technologies began to be introduced and were mastered by the Chinese people. After Japan invaded and occupied Northeast China, many enterprises, mainly in heavy industry, were established, which made important contributions to industrial development after the founding of the People's Republic of China.

The market factor just discussed cannot solely bring about economic development. In many cases, government assistance or promotion is needed because

*Summary and outlook*  253

the market foundation in most countries is volatile, and there is a lack of a unified market, business culture, and entrepreneurship, not to mention technology. Most of today's developed countries are European countries. The residents of North America and Australia are mainly the descendants of Europeans. Europe possesses the aforesaid market characteristics, such as business culture, entrepreneurship, and technology. Japan, which is the first developed country in East Asia, possessed more of these conditions compared with other backward regions and countries. Nevertheless, the role of the government in its economic development is clear.[11] In other words, the majority of countries in the world lack the conditions to rely solely on market forces to achieve economic development. In most cases, the government is involved and sometimes dominant, as evidenced by the Four Asian Tigers and China. Of course, the role of the government has been controversial. It is difficult to generalize what the government should and should not do. It depends on the national conditions of a given country.

Regarding the role of the government, the first is to build a modern education system to cultivate the personnel necessary for economic development. The government must be involved in the early development of both primary education and higher education. As the economy develops, the private sector will also be involved in education and contribute to increasing access to education. The second is the construction of infrastructure, including roads, railways, aviation, electric power, communications, as well as the supply of tap water and gas in cities. These industries usually have a natural monopoly that require a wealth of capital and are beyond the means of private capital. At the same time, as private capital pursues private benefits, it is difficult for them to guarantee services of a public nature. Of course, alongside economic development and social progress, these areas may also become the private sector. In this case, there is a good environment in terms of both law and supervision, and it may be better operated by the private sector. The third is industrial policy, which is highly controversial. Japan is the birthplace of industrial policy. In order to catch up with European and American countries after World War II, Japan implemented a legion of industrial policies, including foreign exchange control, support for certain industries, and the combination of industry, government, and universities. In addition to industrial policy, the government has the more important job of formulating development strategies. Compared to industrial policy, the development strategy is of greater significance and has a longer effect. There are generally two types of development strategies: inward-looking development and outward-looking development. The former makes use of existing domestic resources to the greatest extent, while the latter focuses on the use of external resources. The two have their respective strengths, as well as different focuses and effects. However, due to the national conditions of each country and the nature of government, appropriate or inappropriate strategies may be formulated.

System and institutions can also be important. This is a complicated issue: whether it is government-led or market-led. In other words, it is worthwhile to study how the government is positioned, how it performs its role, and what economic activities it participates in. These should hinge on the national conditions and stages of development of each country. In general, the government should be

254    *Comparison and revelation*

responsible for secondary allocation, maintaining public order and the public sector, regulating the behavior of the market in accordance with laws and regulations, and appropriately regulating the economic cycle through macroeconomic policies. Other activities should be left to the market and entrepreneurs. Finally, political stability is an important issue that is difficult to explain. If a country is to develop its economy, there must be, first and foremost, a stable political scene. A chaotic political situation, frequent coup d'états, or scrambling for power is obviously detrimental to economic development. The governments of many developing countries do not adopt a Western-style approach to democracy. Instead, there is one-party rule or a few leaders have the final say. This system is often referred to as "authoritarianism". In our view, if the goal of the government or ruling party is to develop the economy and bring benefits to the people, it can be called an authoritarian government. If it grabs the power just to maintain rule, spares no effort to stifle the opposition, and indulge in corruption, it can be called an autocratic regime or an autocratic system.

The relationship between the market and the government as well as the factors related to both have been previously studied. In fact, other factors are not included in the aforesaid framework. For example, the population issue is not specifically discussed. Moderate population growth is one of the necessary conditions for economic growth and development. Since it does not belong to the market or the government, it is not included in the graph. According to theories of economics and population, as well as the development experience of various countries, population growth must be moderate. Too slow a population growth does not meet the demand for labor in industrial and urban development. Too fast a population growth is prone to cause negative effects. For example, massive unemployment will impose a burden on society and the government. In addition, there should be social, cultural, geographical, and other factors, such as religion and values concept, whether it is collectivism or individualism, and whether it is a landlocked country or a coastal country. These factors are constant and cannot be changed in a short time. Therefore, they are discussed as a social basis. However, some factors indeed affect the economic development. For example, too strict a religious belief is detrimental to economic development, and the geographical environment of tropical countries is not conducive to industrialization.[12]

## 12.4  Conclusion

Here, the situation in modern China is judged based on the factors and conditions that affect economic development as just discussed. Regarding the market, China has a good foundation, as mentioned earlier. As a basic necessity for economic development, the market factor is usually relatively constant. As far as modern China is concerned, the problem mainly lies with the government. Since China entered the modern period (Republic of China) later than Japan, the role of the government also came into play later than in Japan. Moreover, the government of the Republic of China was inferior to the government of Japan in the Meiji period. The Beiyang government (Beijing government) basically exercised warlord rule and lacked

*Summary and outlook* 255

innovation and the ability to govern the country. Coupled with warlord dogfighting and frequent government changes, it was hard to formulate sound development strategies and policies. Even the subsequent Nanjing government (the Nationalist government) was also inferior to the government of Japan in the Meiji period. It lacked long-term strategies and was overburdened with the issues of complex domestic and international relations. There are objective and subjective reasons. Objectively, the government of the Republic of China inherited a messy situation caused by the Western powers since the late 19th century. Coupled with the fact that China had been a poor and weak country for a long time, it was difficult to reverse the situation in a short time. The subjective reason is that the government failed to unite the forces in the country to form a synergy and formulate strategies and policies for economic development.

As the incompetent government could not play its due role or its role was limited, the market mechanism could not work properly. Due to a lack of financial resources, infrastructure was inadequate, which impeded the flow of people, materials, and information and prevented the people from broadening their horizons. In the absence of rapidly developing industry, the level of urbanization was low, and the surplus agricultural labor could not go to the cities. As a result, agricultural productivity was not freed, and the small-scale peasant economy could not be improved. Due to a low level of industrial development and the few entrepreneurs, there was a lack of market opportunities. Similarly, since industrial development was incomplete and the level of technology was low, China could not meet the needs of the international market and could not compete with Japan. It was often at the mercy of others. Of course, as the economy was underdeveloped, there was no investment in education, which affected the cultivation of talents and impeded economic development. This led to a vicious circle. A government that was incompetent and did nothing restricted the role of the market, which affected the development of the economy.

**Notes**

1  Regarding Sino-Japanese relations, see Guan Quan (2013).
2  Rybczynski theorem was put forward by the British-Polish economist Tadeusz Rybczynski. It means that if the commodity prices remain constant, an increase in the endowment of one factor will lead to an increase in the output of a product that intensively uses this factor, while the output of another product declines. For details, see standard international economics textbooks such as Dominick Salvatore (2015), Appleyard and Field (2003).
3  We believe that the introduction of technology is also a kind of technological progress for backward countries. See Guan Quan (2003).
4  For content similar to this book, see David N. Weil (2011), p. 149.
5  For a study of the initiation of modern economic growth in Japan, see Okawa Kazushi and Rosovsky (1973) and Ryoshin Minami (1981).
6  As there is no continuous data on China's GDP in modern times, it is difficult to calculate the investment rate even if there are some investment data, such as Ryoshin Minami and Makino Fumio (2014).
7  The view that China's economy grew somewhat during the Republic of China period is not true. See Rawski (2009).

## 256 *Comparison and revelation*

8 For the role of agriculture in the early days of industrialization, see Guan Quan (2014, 2018).
9 For Schumpeter's innovations, see Schumpeter (1990). Guan Quan (2014, 2018) made added some supplement.
10 For the development of China's industry and entrepreneurship during the Republic of China period, see Guan Quan (2018).
11 For the development of the Japanese economy, see Ryoshin Minami (1981).
12 For the content of this section, see Guan Quan (2014, 2018).

# References

## Chinese literature

Cao Chengke. "Mining and Metallurgical Engineering in China in the Last Thirty Years". *Chinese Engineering in China in the Last Thirty Years (Part I)*. Taipei: Taiwan Chinese Literature Company, 1946

Chen Changheng. *Almanac of China's Economy*. Beijing: Ministry of Industry of the Republic of China, Commercial Press, 1934

Chen Da. *Population of Modern China*. Tianjin: Tianjin People's Publishing House, 1981

China Continuation Committee. *The Christian Occupation of China*. Beijing: China Social Sciences Press, 1987

Ding Changqing and Ci Hongfei. *The Road to Agricultural Modernization in China: Agricultural Structure, Commodity Economy and Rural Market in Modern China*. Beijing: The Commercial Press, 2000

Dong Baoliang. *History of Higher Education in Modern and Contemporary China*. Wuhan: Huazhong University of Science and Technology Press, 2007

Du Xuncheng. *National Capitalism and the Government of Old China*. Shanghai: Shanghai Academy of Social Sciences Press, 1991

Du Xuncheng. *A General History of Finance in China: Volume 3: The Beiyang Government Period*. Beijing: China Financial Publishing House, 2002

Editorial Board of *History of Textile in Modern China*. *History of Textile in Modern China* (volumes I and II). Beijing: China Textile Publishing House, 1997

Fang Xianting. *China's Cotton Textile Industry*. Shanghai: The Commercial Press, 1934

Guan Quan. "Industrial Production in China in the 1910s: Evaluation and Estimate of Agricultural and Commercial Statistics Table". *China Review of Political Economy*, Vol. 4, 2011

Guan Quan. "China Must Overtake Japan Before Its Rise". *Academic Frontiers*, Vol. 22, 2013

Guan Quan. *Development Economics: China's Economic Development*. Beijing: Tsinghua University Press, 2014

Guan Quan. "Mining Production in the Republic of China Period". *Research on the History of Industry and Technology*, No. 2, 2017

Guan Quan. *Industrial Development in Modern China: A Comparison with Japan*. Beijing: China Renmin University Press, 2018

Guan Quan. *China's Economic Development: Centennial Course*. Beijing: China Renmin University Press, 2019

Guan Yongqiang. *Income Distribution in Modern China: A Quantitative Study*. Beijing: People's Publishing House, 2012

## 258 References

Guo Qin. *Industrial History of Hunan in Modern and Contemporary Times*. Changsha: Hunan People's Publishing House, 2013

Hong Jiaguan. *A General History of China's Finance: Volume 4: The Nationalist Government Period*. Beijing: China Financial Publishing House, 2008

Hou Yangfang. *History of China's Population: Volume 6*. Shanghai: Fudan University Press, 2001

Hu Rongquan. *China's Coal Mines*. Shanghai: The Commercial Press, 1935

Jia Xiuyan and Lu Manping. *History of Prices in the Republic of China*. Beijing: China Price Publishing House, 1992

Jiang Tao. *History of China's Population in Modern Times: Hangzhou*. Hangzhou: Zhejiang People's Publishing House, 1993

Jiao Jianhua. *Fiscal History of the Republic of China* (volumes 1 and 2). Changsha: Hunan People's Publishing House, 2013

Li Bozhong. *Theory, Method, Development, Trend: A New Study of China's Economic History* (revised edition). Hangzhou: Zhejiang University Press, 2013

Liu Foding, editor-in-chief. *History of Modern China's Economic Development*. Beijing: Higher Education Press, 1999

Liu Foding, Wang Yuru, and Yu Jianwei. *Economic Development of Modern China*. Jinan: Shandong People's Publishing House, 1997

Qiao Qiming. *Social Economics of Rural China*. Shanghai: The Commercial Press, 1945

Shanghai Municipal Administration for Industry and Commerce and Shanghai First Mechanical and Electrical Industry Bureau. *Shanghai National Machinery Industry*. Shanghai: Zhonghua Book, 1966

Shanghai Municipal Grain Bureau, Shanghai Municipal Administration for Industry and Commerce, and Institute of Economics of Shanghai Academy of Social Sciences. *History of the Flour Industry in Modern China*. Shanghai: Zhonghua Book, 1987

Sheng Bangyue. *China's Modern Agriculture in Buck's Vision*. Beijing: Social Sciences Academic Press, 2008

Su Yunfeng. *The Budding and Growth of New Education in China: 1860–1928*. Beijing: Peking University Press, 2007

Sun Guoda. *The Migration of National Industry: The Hinterland Migration of Private Factories in the Period of the War of Resistance against Japanese Aggression*. Beijing: China Literature and History Publishing House, 1991

Sun Jianhua. *Financial Development and Institutional Change in Modern China: 1840–1945*. Beijing: China Financial & Economic Publishing House, 2008

Wang Bingzhao, et al. *A General History of Education in China: Republic of China: III*. Beijing: Beijing Normal University Press, 2013

Wang Jiafu and Xia Shuhua. *Patent Law of China*. Beijing: Qunzhong Publishing House, 1987

Wang Yunwu, editor-in-chief. *Statistical Analysis of Degree of Urban Industrialization in China*. Shanghai: The Commercial Press, 1934

Wang Yuru. *Research on the Price Structure of Modern China*. Xi'an: Shaanxi People's Publishing House, 1997

Writing Group of History of Coal Mines in Modern China. *History of Coal Mines in Modern China*. Beijing: Coal Industry Press, 1990

Wu Baosan, et al. *China's National Income (1933)*. Shanghai: Zhonghua Book, 1947

Wu Chengluo. *General Annals of Industry in Modern China (Part 1)*. Shanghai: The Commercial Press, 1929

Wu Chengming. "An Investigation of Agricultural Productivity in Modern China". *Researches in Chinese Economic History*, No. 2, 1989

## References    259

Xie Xueshi and Zhang Keliang. *History of Anshan Iron and Steel: 1909–1948*. Beijing: Metallurgical Industry Press, 1984

Xu Dixin and Wu Chengming. *History of Capitalist Development in China: Volume 2*. Beijing: People's Publishing House, 1990

Xu Dixin and Wu Chengming. *History of Capitalist Development in China: Volume 3*. Beijing: People's Publishing House, 1993

Xue Yi. *A Study on the Resource Committee of National Government*. Beijing: Social Sciences Academic Press, 2005

Yang Dajin. *Industrial History of Modern China (Shang Xia)*. Shanghai: The Commercial Press, 1940

Yang Yinpu. *Financial History of the Republic of China*. Beijing: China Financial & Economic Publishing House, 1985

Yang Zihui, editor-in-chief. *Research on Demographic Data in All Dynasties in China*. Beijing: Reform Press, 1996

Yuan Shuyi and Dong Conglin. *The Transformation of Small-scale Peasant Economy in Modern China*. Beijing: People's Publishing House, 2001

Zhang Shouguang. *The Great Change: Enterprises in the Rear Area in the Period of War of Resistance against Japanese Aggression*. Nanjing: Jiangsu People's Publishing House, 2008

Zhang Shouguang. *Research on Industry in the Rear Area in the Period of War of Resistance against Japanese Aggression*. Chongqing: Chongqing Publishing House, 2012

Zhao Wenlin and Xie Shujun. *History of China's Population*. Beijing: People's Publishing House, 1988

Zheng Youkui. *China's International Trade and Industrial Development: 1840–1948*. Shanghai: Shanghai Academy of Social Sciences Press, 1984

Zheng Youkui. *Research on China's Foreign Relations in Modern Times*. Shanghai: Shanghai Academy of Social Sciences Press

Zheng Youkui. *Resource Committee of Old China: Historical Facts and Evaluation*. Shanghai: Shanghai Academy of Social Sciences Press, 1991

Zhu Yinggui. *Modern China: A Study of Finance and Securities*. Shanghai: Shanghai People's Publishing House, 2012

## Translated literature

[U.S.] Appleyard Dennis R. and Alfred J. Field. *International Economics* (4th edition). Translated by Gong Min, et al. Beijing: China Machine Press, 2003

[France] Bergere Marie-Claire. *The Golden Age of the Chinese Bourgeoisie: 1911–1937*. Translated by Zhang Fuqiang and Xu Shifen. Shanghai: Shanghai People's Publishing House, 1994

[U.S.] Buck. Translated by Zhang Lyuluan. *Series of Classic Oversea Studies on Modern Chinese Culture*. Shanghai: The Commercial Press, 1936

[U.S.] Buck, editor-in-chief. *Land Use in China*. Chengdu: Chengdu Chengcheng Publishing House, 1941

[U.S.] Kennedy Paul. Translated by Chen Jingbiao et al. *The Rise and Fall of the Great Powers*. Beijing: International Culture Publishing Company, 2006

[U.S.] Kindleberger Charles P. Translated by Gao Zugui. *World Economic Primacy: 1500–1990*. Beijing: The Commercial Press, 2003

[U.S.] Kuznets Simon. *Modern Economic Growth*. Translated by Dai Rui and Yi Cheng. Beijing: Beijing University of Economics Press, 1989

[U.S.] Kuznets Simon. *Economic Growth of Nations: Total Output and Production Structure*. Translated by Chang Xun, et al. Beijing: The Commercial Press, 1999

260    *References*

[UK] Maddison Angus. *The World Economy: Historical Statistics*. Translated by Wu Xiaoying, et al. Beijing: Peking University Press, 2003

[UK] Maddison Angus. *Chinese Economic Performance in the Long Run: 960–2030* (2nd edition). Translated by Wu Xiaoying, et al. Shanghai: Shanghai People's Publishing House, 2008

[U.S.] Perkins Dwight H. *The Development of Agriculture in China: 1368–1968*. Translated by Song Haiwen, et al. Shanghai: Shanghai Translation Publishing House, 1984

[U.S.] Rawski Thomas G. *Economic Growth in Prewar China*. Translated by Tang Qiaotian, et al. Hangzhou: Zhejiang University Press, 2009

[U.S.] Salvatore Dominick. *International Economics* (11th edition). Beijing: Tsinghua University Press, 2015

[U.S.] Schumpeter Joseph. *The Theory of Economic Development*. Beijing: The Commercial Press, 1990

[U.S.] Schumpeter Joseph. *Capitalism, Socialism and Democracy*. Beijing: The Commercial Press, 1999

[Japan] Tokihiko Mori. *A Study on the History of China's Cotton Textile Industry*. Translated by Yuan Guangquan. Beijing: Social Sciences Academic Press, 2010

[U.S.] Weil David N. *Economic Growth*. Translated by Wang Jinfeng, et al. Beijing: China Renmin University Press, 2011

## English literature

Chang John K. *Industrial Development in Pre-Communist China: A Quantitative Analysis*. Chicago: Aldine, 1969

Guan Quan. "Technological Innovation and the Patent System in Prewar Japan". *Hitotsubashi Journal of Commerce and Management*, Vol. 36, No. 1, 2001

Kubo Toru, Quan Guan, and Fumio Makino. "Industrial Output Estimates in Republican China". *Discussion Paper No. D99–14*, Institute of Economic Research Hitotsubashi University, 2000

Liu Ta-chung and K. C. Yeh. *The Economy of the Chinese Mainland: National Income and Economic Development, 1933–1959*. Princeton, NJ: Princeton University Press, 1965

Minami R. *Power Revolution in the Industrialization of Japan: 1885–1940*. Tokyo: Kinokuniya, 1987

Perkins Dwight H. *Agricultural Development in China: 1368–1968*. Chicago: Aldine Publishing Company, 1969

Perkins Dwight H. "Growth and Changing Structure of China's Twentieth-Century Economy". In *China's Modern Economy in Historical Perspective*, edited by Dwight H. Perkins, 115–165. Palo Alto: Stanford University Press, 1975

Yeh K.C. "China's National Income, 1931–1936". In *Modern Chinese Economic History*, edited by Chi-ming Hou and Tzong-shian Yu, 95–128. Taipei: Institute of Economics, Academia Sinica, 1979

## Japanese literature

Guan Quan. "Locality of Power Revolution: Estimation and Analysis". *Economy and Economics*, No. 84, 1997

Guan Quan. *Innovation of Modern Japan: Patents and Economic Development*. Tokyo: Fukosha, 2003

References 261

Guan Quan. "Industrial Production of Manshukoku: Estimation Based on 'Statistical Table of Factory'". *Tokyo Keizai University Journal: Economics*, Vol. 245, 2005

Guan Quan and Makino Fumio. "Estimation of Mining Production Value of China: 1912–1949". *Discussion Paper No. D99–7*, Hitotsubashi University, 1999

Kazushi Okawa, Rosowsk. *Japan's Economic Growth: Trend Acceleration in the 20th Century*. Tokyo: Toyo Keizai Inc., 1973

Kiyokawa Yukihiko. *Japan's Economic Development and Technology Prevalence*. Tokyo: Toyo Keizai Inc., 1995

Kiyokawa Yukihiko. *Modern Filature Technology and Asia: A Comparative Technology History of Technology Introduction*. Nagoya: Nagoya University Press, 2009

Kobayashi Masaaki. *Japan's Industrialization and Privatization Policies: Government and Enterprises*. Tokyo: Toyo Keizai Inc., 1977

Komiya Ryutaro. *Economy of Modern China*. Tokyo: Tokyo University Press, 1989

Makino Fumio and Guan Quan. "Prewar Mining Production Development in China". *Tokyo Gakugei University Memoirs: Humanities and Social Sciences*, Vol. 58, 2007

Obuchi Hiroshi and Morioka Hitosh. *Economic Demography*. Tokyo: Shinhyoron, 1981

Ryoshin Minami. *Power Revolution and Technology Progress: Prewar Manufacturing Industry Analysis*. Tokyo: Toyo Keizai Inc., 1976

Ryoshin Minami. *Japan's Economic Development*. Tokyo: Toyo Keizai Inc., 1981

Ryoshin Minami. *Japan's Economic Development* (3rd edition). Tokyo: Toyo Keizai Inc., 2002

Ryoshin Minami and Makino Fumio. *Asian Long-Term Economic Statistics (3) China*. Tokyo: Toyo Keizai Inc., 2014

Ryoshin Minami and Kiyokawa Yukihiko, eds. *Japan's Industrialization and Technology Development*. Tokyo: Toyo Keizai Inc., 1987

# References

Chinese Academy of Sciences and Central Administration for Industry and Commerce. *Statistics on Machine-made Flour Industry in Old China*. Beijing: Zhonghua Book, 1966

Department of Comprehensive Statistics of National Economy of the National Bureau of Statistics. *Statistical Data for 50 Years after the Founding the People's Republic of China*. Beijing: China Statistics Press, 1999

Division of Fixed Assets Investment Statistics, National Bureau of Statistics. *China's Fixed Assets Investment Statistics: 1950–1985*. Beijing: China Statistics Press, 1987

Division of Statistics, Ministry of Economic Affairs. "Statistics of Important Industrial and Mineral Products in the Rear: 1941–1942". *Economic Statistics Journals*, No. 1, 1943

Eastern Asia Research Institute. "World Mineral Statistics: 1925–1940". *Eastern Asia Statistics Series*, Vol. 4, 1942

Kong Min, editor-in-chief. *Compilation of Data on Nankai Economic Index*. Beijing: China Social Sciences Press, 1988

Liu Dajun. *China Industrial Survey Report* (volume I, II and III). Reference materials of the Resource Committee of the Military Commission, No. 20, 1937

[UK] Maddison Angus. *The World Economy: Historical Statistics*. Translated by Wu Xiaoying, et al. Beijing: Peking University Press, 2009

The Ministry of Industry and Commerce. "General Report on the Survey and Statistics of Workers' Life and Industrial Production in China". Beijing: 1930

[UK] Mitchell B.R. *International Historical Statistics: Asia, Africa and Oceania 1750–1993* (3rd edition). Translated by He Liping. Beijing: Economic Science Press, 2002

## 262    References

National Bureau of Statistics. *The Great Decade*. Beijing: People's Publishing House, 1959

National Economic Survey Committee of the Ministry of Economy. "Summary of the Preliminary Report on the Survey of Major Urban Industries in China". Nanjing: 1948

Shimano Takao. *Annual Statistical Table of the Quantity of the Goods Produced, Imported and Exported*. Tokyo: Yukoshoin, 1980

Shou Leying, Editor-in-Chief. *Industrial and Commercial Figures in Modern China (Vol. 3-4)*. China Literature and History Publishing House, 2006

Shou Uni-president. *Annals of Industrial and Commercial Figures in Modern China (Vol. 1-2)*. China Literature and History Publishing House, 1996

Statistical Bureau of the Comptroller's Office of the Republic of China. *Statistical Yearbook of the Republic of China*. Nanjing: China Cultural Undertaking Company, 1948

Sun Yutang, ed. *Materials on Industrial History in Modern China* (volume 1 and 2). Beijing: Science Press, 1957

Tan Xihong and Wu Zongfen, eds. *Summary of the Preliminary Report on the Survey of Major Urban Industries in China*. Nanjing: National Economic Survey Committee of the Ministry of Economy, 1948

Toyo Keizai Inc. *Japan Trade Inspection*. Tokyo: Toyo Keizai Inc., 1935

Xu Daofu, ed. *Statistics of Agricultural Production and Trade in Modern China*. Shanghai: Shanghai People's Publishing House, 1983

Yamazawa Ippei and Yamamoto Yuzo. *Trade and Balance of Payments (Long-term Economic Statistics, Vol. 14)*. Tokyo: Toyo Keizai Inc, 1979

Yan Zhongping et al. *Selected Statistics of China's Economic History in Modern Times*. Beijing: Science Press, 1955

Yukizawa Kenzo and Maeda Shozo. *Long-Term Statistics of the Trade of Japan*. Kyoto: Dohosha, 1978

Zhang Youyi, ed. *Data on Agricultural History in Modern China: 1927–1937* (volume 3). Beijing: Sanlian Bookstore, 1957

Zhao Yunsheng. *The Biography of the Great Capital of China (All Ten volumes)*. Times Literary Publishing House, 1994

Zhonghua Yearbook Press. Nanjing: *China Yearbook*, 1948

# Index

Note: Page numbers in *italic* indicate a figure and page numbers in **bold** indicate a table on the corresponding page.

agriculture 23–24, 43–44; 1910s 26–31, **28–30**; 1930s–1940s 31–43, **31–33**, *34*, **35–37**, **39–41**, *42–43*; overview 24–25, **25–26**; and regional development 151–153

capital, foreign 229, 241; coal mining 235–236; other industries 236–240, **237**, *238*, **239–240**
capital equipment 193–196, *194*, **195**
capital formation 192–198, 207–208
changes: agriculture 23–44; consumer prices 137, 138–141, *138–140*, 148–149; demographic 121–125, **122**, *125*; health 188–190, **189**; industrial structure 10–18, **11–14**, **16–17**; living standards 137, 141–145, **143**, *144*, 148–149
cities: industrial development 90–98, **92**, *93*, **94**, **97**
coal industry: and government 101–104, *101*, **104**; technological advances 199–200, *200*
coal mining: and foreign capital 235–236
consumer prices 137, 138–141, *138–140*, 148–149

demand *see* supply and demand
demographic changes 121–125, **122**, *125*
development of industry 46, 86–87, 89–90, 114–116; 1910s 47–52, **47–48**, **50**, *51*; 1930s hinterland 52–59, **53–55**, **57**, *59*; 1930s Northeast 59–76, **61–64**, *65–66*, **67–69**, *70*, **71**, *72–75*; 1940s North 76–81, **77–78**, *79–81*; 1940s in the rear 81–86,

**82**, **84**, *86*; cities 90–98, **92**, *93*, **94**, **97**; coal 101–104, *101*, **104**; flour 104–107, *106*; mining 99–101; textile 107–114, *109*

economic development 3–4, 18–19; background 5–8, **7**; changes in industrial structure 10–18, **11–14**, **16–17**; economic growth rate 8–9; experience and lessons learned 250–254, *251*; *see also* development of industry
economic growth rate 8–9
education 182–188, *182*, **183–185**
emergence of entrepreneurs 110–113
enterprises: and entrepreneurship 108–110
entrepreneurship: and textile industry 107–114, *109*
equipment, capital 193–196, *194*, **195**
evaluation: of entrepreneurs 113–114
experience in economic development 250–254, *251*
exploitation: resources 174–178

finance 210, 222–223
financial institutions 221–225
financial system and policies 221–227, **224–225**, *224*, **226**
fiscal system and policies 217–221, **218**, **221**
flour industry: and the market 104–107, *106*; technological advances 203–205, *204*
foreign capital 229–230, 241; coal mining 235–236; other industries 236–240, **237**, *238*, **239–240**

264 *Index*

government 210–211; and coal industry 101–104, *101*, **104**; financial system and policies 221–227, **224**, *224*, **225**, *226*; fiscal system and policies 217–220; Resource Committee 211–217

health, changes in 188–190, **189**
hinterland: agriculture 31–43, **31–33**, *34*, **35–36**, **39–41**, *42–43*; industry 52–59, **53–55**, **57**, *59*
human resources 173–174; changes in health 188–190, **189**; development of education 182–188, *182*, **183–185**; utilization of 174–182, **174–176**, *178*, **179–180**, *181*

imbalance 150, 167–169, **168**; 1910s 155–157; 1930s 157–166; agriculture 151–154, **152–153**; industrial sector 155–167, **156**, **158**, *160–161*, *165*; population 151; service sector 154–155, **154**; War of Resistance against Japanese Aggression 166–167
income distribution 145–148, **148**
industrial sector: regional development 155–167, **156**, **158**, *160–161*, *165*
industrial structure: changes in 10–18, **11–14**, **16–17**
industry 46, 86–87, 89–90, 114–116; 1910s 47–52, **47–48**, **50**, *51*; 1930s hinterland 52–59, **53–55**, **57**, *59*; 1930s Northeast 59–76, **61–64**, *65–66*, **67–69**, *70*, **71**, *72–75*; 1940s North 76–81, **77–78**, *79–81*; 1940s in the rear 81–86, **82**, **84**, *86*cities 90–98, **92**, *93*, **94**, **97**; coal 101–104, *101*, **104**; flour 104–107, *106*; and government 210–211; mining 99–101; textile 107–114, *109*; *see also specific industries*
infrastructure 196–198, **197–198**
institutions: financial 221–225; and outcomes of education 186–188
international comparison: resources 179–182
international trade 229–234, *230–231*, **232**, **234**, 241
iron industry: technological advances 199–200, *200*

Japan: gap between China and 246–250, **246**, *247*, *249–250*

labor force 119–121, **128–129**, **131**, 134–135; demographic changes

121–125, **122**, *125*; labor mobility 129–132; labor supply 125–129; urbanization 132–133, **133**
lessons learned 250–254, *251*
living standards 137–138, 141–145, **143**, *144*, 148; and income distribution 145–147

machinery industry: technological advances 205–207, *205*, **206**
market, the: and flour industry 104–107, *106*
mining industry: development of 99–101
mobility, labor 129–132
money supply and demand 225–227, **225**, *226*

natural resources 173–174; changes in health 188–190, **189**; development of education 182–188, *182*, **183–185**; utilization of 174–182, **174–176**, *178*, **179–180**, *181*
North China: industry 76–81, **77–78**, *79–81*
Northeast China: agriculture 37–43, **37**, **39–41**, *42–43*; industry 59–76, **61–64**, *65–66*, **67–69**, *70*, **71**, *72–75*

outcomes of education 186–188

policies, financial 221–227, **224–225**, *224*, *226*
policies, fiscal 217–221, **218**, **221**
population 119–121, 134–135; demographic structure 124–125; demographic transition 123–124; increase 121–122; labor mobility 129–132; labor supply 125–129; and regional development 151; urbanization 132–134
prices *see* consumer prices
problems: entrepreneurship 107–108
progress *see* technological progress

rear area 81–86, **82**, **84**, *86*; War of Resistance against Japanese Aggression 166–167
regional development 150, 167–169, **168**; 1910s 155–157; 1930s 157–166; agriculture 151–154, **152–153**; industrial sector 155–167, **156**, **158**, *160–161*, *165*; population 151; service sector 154–155, **154**; War of Resistance against Japanese Aggression 166–167
Resource Committee 211–217

*Index* 265

resources: utilization of 174–182, **174–176**, *178*, **179–180**, *181*; *see also* human resources; natural resources

schooling 182–186
service sector: and regional development 154–155, **154**
supply, labor 125–129
supply and demand: money 225–227, **225**, *226*
system, financial 221–227, **224–225**, *224*, *226*
system, fiscal 217–221, **218**, **221**

technological progress 192–193, 207–208; capital equipment 193–196, *194*, **195**; coal and iron industry 199–200, *200*; flour industry 203–205, *204*; infrastructure 196–198, **197–198**; machinery industry 205–207, *205*, **206**; textile industry 201–203, *202*
textile industry: and entrepreneurship 107–114, *109*; technological advances 201–203, *202*
trade *see* international trade

urbanization 120–121, 124, 132–135; labor mobility 129
utilization of resources 174–182, **174–176**, *178*, **179–180**, *181*

War of Resistance against Japanese Aggression 166–167